Pg 69 - effect
today

// felt

72 - effect of Scopes = Cons. realize
their beliefs no longer functioned
as the law of the land - would
need to organize to articulate
and defend their positions

203 - distrustful of entire
edu. establishment - don't
feel they need specific
examples for grievances

in general - dispute about purpose
of education
prog - challenge beliefs, think for self
cons = transmit received knowledge,
values - patriotism, religion, capitalism
3 Rs

The Other
School Reformers

The Other School Reformers

Conservative Activism in American Education

Adam Laats

Harvard University Press

Cambridge, Massachusetts, and London, England   2015

First printing

Library of Congress Cataloging-in-Publication Data

Laats, Adam.
　The other school reformers : conservative activism in American
education / Adam Laats.
　　pages cm
　Includes bibliographical references and index.
　ISBN 978-0-674-41671-0 (alk. paper)
　1.　Education—Political aspects—United States.　2.　Conservatism—
United States.　3.　Educational change—United States.　I.　Title.
　LC89.L33 2015
　379—dc23　　　　　　　　　　　　　　　　　2014012890

For Sandra with love, gratitude, and admiration

Contents

The Other
School Reformers

Introduction

critical thinking

I didn't think of myself as ignorant. Or naïve. But a veteran teacher would have probably expected the phone call that took me by surprise.

A parent called to accuse our English department of warping the values of her teenage son. Our crime? Teaching Rudolfo Anaya's novel _Bless Me, Ultima._ The book, this parent charged, taught that Catholicism was a ruse, a fake, a scam. She did not want our school to undermine the Catholic faith of her family.

I had never thought of the novel that way. To me, it seemed like a compelling coming-of-age story, one in which the young protagonist wrestles with age-old questions of faith and identity. To be sure, the traditional _curandera_ theology of the young hero's grandmother often comes across as more legitimate than that of his hellfire Catholic priest. But I did not think that a parent would ever take offense. This was the late 1990s, not the 1950s. School, I assumed at the time, should always encourage young people to think critically about the big questions, even if that questioning led to difficult conclusions.

For my younger self, the encounter forced me to confront my own progressive stereotypes. Everyone agreed, I had naively assumed, that schools should train each new generation to critique and question all received wisdom. Anyone who dissented from this vision of proper schooling, I assumed, would be from an eccentric fringe, a collection of kooks who did not understand modern education. But this outraged mother revealed herself to be the opposite. She was strident, to be sure, but she was also enormously educated, articulate, caring, and even a little bashful. She had firm beliefs about proper education, but her gentle demeanor made me recognize how profoundly blinkered my outlook had been.

Conservative ed. activism

In many ways, this book has its roots in that episode. This mother's protest against the reading material in her son's school echoed the sorts of outrage voiced by conservative activists across the twentieth century. School, conservatives have insisted, is not meant to undermine faith, but to bolster it. Teachers, conservative activists have argued, make a mistake when they try to cram skepticism down the throats of trusting children. This book asks basic questions about this sort of conservative school reform: How often have conservative activists intervened in American education? With what goals? And with how much influence? Looking into the historical record, could we find a recognizable tradition of this sort of educational activism?

Time and again, as the following chapters demonstrate, commentators have found themselves surprised by the realities of conservative educational activism. In one famous instance, when the obstreperous journalist H. L. Mencken headed off to Dayton, Tennessee, to observe the hurly-burly of the Scopes "monkey" trial in 1925, he had expected to find a depressing stuck-in-the-mud southern hinterland, a collection of ramshackle hovels presided over by closed-minded fundamentalist patriarchs. Instead, as he told his readers in the *Baltimore Sun,* "The town . . . greatly surprised me. I expected to find a squalid Southern village, with darkies snoozing on the horse-blocks, pigs rooting under the houses and the inhabitants full of hookworm and malaria. What I found was a country town full of charm and even beauty."[1] In 1950 Pasadena, to cite another example, journalist David Hulburd remembered his surprise at meeting conservative leader Louise Padelford. This was not the witch-hunting McCarthy clone he had expected. Rather, Padelford, Ivy League educated with a PhD in romance languages, had "clear blue eyes that look out at the world with wide-open frankness; her ear is keen, her wit quick, and her smile enchanting."[2] Like these surprised journalists, I had been caught off-guard by the ways my conservative antagonist had confounded my stereotypes about conservatism and education. As I began the research for this book, I wondered how much I would be surprised by the historical realities of the conservatives I studied. Too often, journalists and scholars have allowed their presumptions to congeal into inherited wisdom. Did those stereotypes match the historical record?

To be sure, conservative activists have also seemed dedicated, at times, to confirming stereotypes. In ways that might make conservative intellectuals and apologists squirm, the conservatives we'll meet in these pages often seem like nothing more than scattered voices of protest, a paranoid fringe. In the late 1930s, for instance, one New Jersey

American Legion post threatened to uphold American democracy and freedom of speech by breaking leftist skulls with baseball bats and iron rods.[3] Or in the mid-1970s, one conservative school activist later remembered, his all-white church had sent the women and children to hide in the basement when rumors spread about African Americans coming to town. The menfolk, meanwhile, armed themselves and stood on high alert.[4]

Such extralegal violence and rock-ribbed adherence to obsolete values seem to confirm the worst stereotypes of conservatism in America, just as other conservative activists confound those stereotypes. In order to know anything about conservative traditions in education, then, we need to look beyond anecdotes. Instead of treating conservatives as Punch-and-Judy heroes or villains, this book examines the historical record to make sense of the goals and strategies of conservative activists in specific historic contexts. Instead of viewing this history of conservative educational activism as either a heroic rearguard action or a vague force opposing the forward sweep of culture, this book attempts to understand both the change and the continuity of conservative activism in education.

This book argues that a powerful tradition of educational conservatism has had a decisive role in shaping schools and culture. Educational conservatives have insisted, in short, on two central ideas. First, schools matter. Conservatives, like their progressive foes, have rarely questioned the notion that the schools of today generate the society of tomorrow. Second, because schools matter, their content and structure must be guarded ferociously. Ideas that challenge inherited wisdom must not be crammed down the throats of young, trusting students. And teachers must not abdicate their roles as intellectual and moral authorities. Educational conservatism, in other words, has been the long and vibrant tradition of defending tradition itself in America's schools. Without understanding this tradition, we will never truly understand either American conservatism or American education.

Education scholars have long noticed the persistent power of educational conservatism. Near the end of his remarkably influential career in American education and thought, John Dewey concluded glumly that "repressive and reactionary forces . . . increasing in strength" had managed to maintain "the fundamental authoritarianism of the old education."[5] Years later, historian Michael Katz asserted that public education had always been "conservative, racist, and bureaucratic."[6] Arthur Zilversmit, in his study of the successes and failures of progressive education, agreed that most Americans held a "strange, emotional attachment to traditional schooling patterns."[7] More recently, Michael Apple has argued that conservatives have mounted "a powerful, yet odd, combination of forces" that has won the central battle to define cultural and educational "common sense."[8]

In spite of this notice, scholars have had little success in understanding educational conservatism. Who were these "reactionary forces" of tradition, this "powerful, yet odd, combination"? What motivated them? How did they imagine their role in American education and culture?

In order to organize the enormous complexity of American educational conservatism, this book will focus on four specific episodes ranging from the 1920s to the 1970s. Together, these four controversies arguably constituted the most famous and most studied school battles in twentieth-century America. Each controversy attracted overwhelming national and international attention. Most important, each controversy forced conservatives to articulate their visions of proper education. If we want to understand the tradition of conservative activism, there is no better place to start than by studying these episodes in detail.

 First, in 1925, a long-simmering public debate over the teaching of evolution came to an explosive boil in the hamlet of Dayton, Tennessee. As we'll examine in Chapter 2, an amiable young teacher, John Scopes, agreed to serve as the protagonist in a test of Tennessee's new anti-evolution law. When celebrity Bible-defender William Jennings Bryan offered to assist the prosecution, the test case became an international media circus. Soon, equally famous skeptic Clarence Darrow agreed to defend Scopes. The ensuing trial did not settle the matter of evolution education by any means, but the context and controversy raised central questions posed by 1920s-era conservatives about the proper form and content of schooling.

Next, as we'll see in Chapter 3, conservative activists in organizations such as the American Legion and National Association of Manufacturers had long harbored suspicions about the left-leaning tendencies of school textbooks. In 1939, those suspicions found a specific target: a series of social-studies textbooks by Harold Rugg. Conservative leaders such as the American Legion's Homer Chaillaux accused Rugg's books of pushing students toward a skeptical anti-capitalist vision of America's past. Rugg's sinister books, conservatives charged, replaced America's healthy traditions with a subversive pessimism.

A decade later, conservatives in Pasadena, California, rallied against their new superintendent. As Chapter 4 describes, Willard Goslin had been brought to town as the very best leader the affluent school district could find. Soon, however, his vision of good schools clashed with the thinking of conservatives in Pasadena and around the nation. Goslin proposed to abolish report cards, raise taxes, and rezone the district. He hoped to integrate teachers, parents, school workers, and community members in school decision making. To conservative leaders such as Louise Padelford, such changes smacked of the wrong-headed impulses she and her conservative allies pilloried as the typical excesses of "progressive education."

The last controversy on which this book will focus, in Chapter 5, took place in Charleston, West Virginia, and surrounding Kanawha County. In a now-familiar pattern, conservative activists such as school board member Alice Moore grew alarmed at the moral turpitude and pedagogical malfeasance packed into a new set of language arts textbooks. Why must textbooks encourage racial animosity by including the voices of violent African American criminals, conservatives asked. Why must they denigrate religion? Why must they teach children that patriotism is only for suckers? In this case, conservative outrage led to a long and violent school boycott.

The fights in each of these chapters took on the tone and texture of their specific time and place. A detailed look will show us the ways these visions have clashed and changed over the course of the decades. Only by examining each in detail can we hope to overcome long-held stereotypes and glib assumptions about the nature of conservative educational activism. By doing so, we can avoid the trap of imposing a convenient definition upon conservatism. Instead, we can observe the arguments and ideas presented by conservatives themselves. These four school battles could have happened anywhere. They raised issues of perennial interest to conservatives everywhere: evolution, science, traditional education, progressive education, the Bible, patriotism, communism, sex, youth, delinquency, and the nature of American culture, to name a few.

Also important, each of these well-known controversies enlisted conservative engagement, even leadership, from around the nation. Though each had its roots in a specific local issue, each controversy did more than just articulate local concerns. In each case, a quarrel that began in a small-town drugstore, or a district school board meeting, or a local newspaper, soon attracted participation from conservatives nationwide. As a result, these battles can tell us about more than just local variations in conservatism. They can tell us about more than just the goings-on in certain conservative corners of the nation. Each can serve as a vantage point from which to study educational conservatism in its era.

If given the power, historians might have asked for different timing. It would be nice to have a more even spread of dates and places. And of course historians can quibble endlessly about which episodes should be included or left out. But the benefits of focusing on these four particular episodes far outweigh the potential problems. Any other approach threatens to introduce a procrustean bed of definition. This look at the four most famous educational confrontations of the twentieth century allows conservatives to define and speak for themselves, instead of stretching or shrinking them to fit historians' or pundits' expectations of "real" conservatism.

Of course, by looking at these four controversies, many important conservative voices and episodes will get short shrift. This book must not be viewed, then, as an encyclopedic treatment of twentieth-century educational conservatism. Rather, this approach gives us a unique perspective on one important tradition among educational activists. Like the activist mother who complained about my reading list, conservatives have battled time and again to preserve a certain vision of proper schooling. As the next chapter will argue, this perennial activism can best be understood as a vital tradition of "educational conservatism." To be sure, many influential conservatives did not take leading roles in this tradition. As a result, many important figures and groups show up only in passing, if at all. Readers will not find much about Robert Taft, for instance, or conservatives in the Catholic Church. Intellectuals such as William F. Buckley or Russell Kirk who often claim pride of place in other histories of American conservatism barely figure in this tradition.

In spite of these caveats, this close study of four defining controversies is the best approach to understanding the history and meanings of American educational conservatism. My hope is that future teachers and scholars will understand the import of this powerful tradition of educational conservatism. Perhaps future new teachers will have a better sense than I did of the conservative world they will be entering.

CHAPTER ONE

What Does Jesus Have to Do with Phonics?

Understanding Educational Conservatism

I'm certainly not the first to wonder about the impact of conservative ideas and activism in American education. Given generations of earnest and even brilliant attempts at wholesale progressive reform, historians have asked, why does the basic footprint of schooling remain so stubbornly conservative?[1] Yet even the most perspicacious scholars offer unsatisfying explanations of the sticky traditionalism of American education. For example, at the tail end of the twentieth century, historians David Tyack and Larry Cuban argued that traditional schooling practices had not generally been sustained by "conscious conservatism." Rather, conservative education policies had been maintained by "unexamined institutional habits and widespread cultural beliefs."[2]

This explanation underestimates the leading role played by what this book calls the "other school reformers"—conservative activists just as earnest as progressive educators, just as dedicated to shaping schools to fit their vision of proper education and culture. These activists were not vague trends; they were not amorphous tendencies. They were, instead, specific people making specific claims about specific educational programs. Separated by decades, working for different causes, these activists did not simply rely on "unexamined institutional habits" or "widespread cultural beliefs" to accomplish their goals. Quite the opposite. Conservatives worked hard to examine and articulate their prescriptions for proper schooling in their specific times and places.

Indeed, so much conservative school activism has been directed toward the specific, limited goals of unique controversies that we must ask a difficult question: Is there any value in discussing these conservatives as a group, as a coherent tradition? In other words, is there any reason to talk about "educational conservatism"? Or have conservatives throughout the twentieth century simply reacted to immediate concerns, simply cobbled together policy prescriptions that had little meaningful connection to one another?

I believe the chapters that follow demonstrate the existence and the importance of a recognizable tradition, a puzzlingly underexplored impulse best called "educational conservatism." Though there have been significant changes among educational conservatives, there are powerful threads that connect the sorts of conservative ideas and activism we saw in 1925 with those on display in 1939, 1951, and 1975.

A Slippery Task

Before we can make sense of these connections in the tradition of educational conservatism, we must attempt to define conservatism as a whole. In all of these discussions, labels get complicated very quickly. Key terms such as "conservative," "progressive," and "traditional" quickly pile up in contradictory ways. As with the emotion-laden labels "democracy" and "freedom," school activists, like other political activists, have bandied these terms about as weapons.[3] For instance, should schools be "modern" and "democratic"? Should they "indoctrinate" or "subvert" students? As the chapters to come will illustrate, the use of these terms must be understood as political acts. Pasting a "conservative," "traditional," "liberal," or "progressive" label on any given educational policy or reform often tells us more about the person doing the labeling than about the policy itself.

Given the difficulty of labeling, historians often get nervous about offering a definition of conservatism. After all, conservatism has always included a shifting conglomeration of ideas and meanings. Definitions tend to be too broad, too narrow, or too partisan to be of real use. For some, conservatism has meant a defense of limited government. For others, a traditional Protestant public sphere, an ordered society, or freer markets. In different decades and different circumstances, conservatism has meant opposition to the New Deal, opposition to loosening family structures, opposition to desegregation, to modernism in theology or socialism in politics. As historian Kim Phillips-Fein has argued recently, the perspective with which historians have viewed conservatism has resulted in a grab bag of different definitions and timelines.[4]

In many cases, educational issues became the heart and soul of conservative public activism. Yet the centrality of such issues to the development of American conservatism has not been adequately recognized by historians. This absence is doubly puzzling since the study of conservatism has become something of a growth industry among historians in the past twenty years. The field has expanded beyond a narrow exploration of the political roots of Ronald Reagan's 1980 victory to include a sense of the longer history of conservatism and the many varieties of theological, economic, cultural, and political activism that have contributed to the conservative impulse. Yet in spite of all this scholarly activity, conservatives' preoccupation with education and schooling has not received the attention it deserves from historians.[5]

A few examples will illustrate the conundrum. Recently, Kim Phillips-Fein offered an insightful catalog of recent historical work about American conservatism.[6] As Phillips-Fein pointed out, historians have learned a great deal about American conservatism in the past twenty years.[7] Each new perspective, Phillips-Fein argued, has enriched our understanding of the meanings and timing of conservatism. In passing, she noticed the centrality to conservatives of public schools,[8] higher education,[9] and intellectual institutions.[10] Yet even given the explosion of interest in the many varieties of conservatism, Phillips-Fein could not find examples of historians who explored the reasons why conservatives remained so interested in educational issues.

Similarly, in their widely read history of conservatism in the 1970s, Bruce Schulman and Julian Zelizer included chapters on religion, business, foreign affairs, and family life, but nothing on schooling or education policy.[11] Of course, books can only have so many chapters, and editors cannot include chapters that no author has written. In this case, however, such a chapter would have added great depth. The educational conservatism at play in the Kanawha County controversy of 1974–75—the subject of Chapter 5—had a decisive impact on key ideas of race and racism, and a long-term impact on the formation of important conservative institutions such as the Heritage Foundation.

Even historians who purport to examine the themes of conservatism in American education tend to tell the story of conservatism as an odd duck, a quirky academic tantrum rather than part of a coherent conservative tradition. For instance, Herbert Kliebard's widely read *Struggle for the American Curriculum, 1893–1958* (1987) promised to tell the story of the battle between "different interest groups competing for dominance over the curriculum."[12] Kliebard framed this struggle as the fight between a certain sort of "humanist" conservative against three versions of progressive reformers: "developmentalists," "social efficiency educators," and "social meliorists."[13] Kliebard's "humanists" included such prominent academics as William Torrey Harris in the 1890s,[14] Michael Demiashkevich in the 1930s,[15] and Arthur Bestor in the 1950s.[16] These thinkers hoped, in Kliebard's words, to save "as best they could their revered traditions and values in the face of rapid change."[17] However, Kliebard's humanists did not mount the sorts of coordinated, self-consciously conservative campaigns we'll see in this volume from the 1920s through the 1970s and beyond.[18] Kliebard's humanists did not hope to use traditional teaching to make American society more traditional; they only hoped to maintain academic achievement as the true purpose of schooling.

If we hope to understand the history of conservatism we must include a more thorough study of the ways conservatives in different decades and in different contexts have approached issues of education and schooling. After all, however we define conservatism, we see that its central tenets are always intimately, inseparably bound up with complicated notions of learning and schooling.

By including educational conservatism in the study of American conservatism as a whole, we can also gain a new perspective on the timing of that conservatism. As part of their lively debates about the boundaries of American conservatism, historians have argued for different timelines for conservatism's career. Depending on historians' primary interests, stories of American conservatism have been told in strikingly different ways.

In the field of intellectual history, for example, George Nash's 1976 argument about the timing of conservatism has proven remarkably influential.[19] Nash argued that the modern conservative intellectual movement only came together after 1945. Before that time, Nash insisted, there were only "scattered voices of protest" among conservative intellectuals.[20]

From the perspective of political history, on the other hand, a different view of conservatism emerged. As historian Donald Critchlow has argued, from a political perspective conservatism transformed itself from a group of "kooks" in the mid-1950s to a group firmly in control of American politics by the end of the twentieth century.[21] Other historians have echoed this notion that conservatism evolved from a group of political outsiders in the 1950s to the ultimate insiders with the election of Ronald Reagan.[22]

Then again, when historians have defined conservatism primarily as a fight against big government, different timelines and different lead actors have emerged. David Farber began his history of modern conservatism with the 1938 election of Senator Robert Taft of Ohio. Taft made his career as a fervent opponent of the New Deal and all it represented.[23] This "progenitor of modern conservatism," Farber argued,[24] defined the movement simply as opposition to "liberalism."[25]

Some historians have argued that the histories of twentieth-century conservatism must begin in the 1920s. Allan Lichtman insisted that the modern conservative movement began in the aftermath of World War I.[26] Leonard Moore asserted that "the 1920s were . . . the first years of the modern Right."[27] Kim Nielsen sought to demonstrate that in the 1920s, "conservative women, though few, were well organized, vocal, and ideologically sophisticated."[28] Yet as Leo Ribuffo has noted, "early, mainline conservatism languishes in the academic doldrums."[29]

Perhaps the difficulties of connecting 1920s-era conservatism with that of later generations come from the real and important transformations that revolutionized the meanings of conservatism in the 1920s and 1930s. As we'll see in the coming pages, leading educational conservatives in the 1920s called loudly for an increased role for the federal government in local schooling. They assumed that their vision of non-sectarian Protestant religiosity must form the backbone of public education. And they spent very little time arguing that they were not racist. Among later generations of conservatives, all of those positions underwent radical changes.

But such changes do not mean that the conservatism that emerged along with the New Deal or after World War II is best described as something entirely new. As this volume will demonstrate, educational conservatives repeated and revived themes and goals from the 1920s through the 1970s, time and again. Leading conservative organizations—groups such as the American Legion and the Daughters of the American Revolution—continued to reform schools in conservative directions from one generation to the next. By making room for this tradition of educational activism in our study of conservatism, we can see that conservatives themselves often experienced no difficulties connecting the generations from the 1920s onward.

In addition, incorporating the themes and tradition of educational conservatism into our study of the history of American conservatism as a whole can offer a new perspective on the ways conservative activists brought together a variety of issues into a coherent, recognizably conservative ideology. Too often, as Jennifer Burns has argued, historians and other scholars seize glibly upon George Nash's 1976 typology of conservatism.[30] Nash argued that three strains of conservative thought came together after World War II to form the modern conservative intellectual movement. Libertarianism, anti-communism, and Burkean traditionalism made up a powerful "fusionist" conservatism. This sense of conservatism as an alliance, a conscious coming-together of disparate strands of conservatism, fits well with the intellectual movement described by Nash. After all, leading thinkers such as Frank Meyer made a powerful case for this definition.[31]

Outside of the elite intellectual circles on which Nash focused, however, the notion of a conscious alliance of distinct conservative visions grates awkwardly and misleadingly against historical experience. Most of the conservative activists in the fight for better schooling did not separate out their reasons for doing so. That is, "patriotic" school reformers did not decide to make tactical common cause with "religious" conservatives, enrolling the help of "free-market" leaders as they went. Rather, activists tended to blend together conservative themes more seamlessly and organically. Of course, some leaders had different emphases and primary goals. As we'll see throughout this book, the American Legion focused on what could be called "patriotic" reforms. The National Association of Manufacturers defended its vision of big-business capitalism. And religious leaders throughout the twentieth century saw the main goal of school reform as protecting the faith of the innocent schoolchildren.

But to a remarkable extent, school activists did not distinguish between those demands. Throughout the twentieth century, conservatives insisted that school reform could increase both patriotism and public religion. School reform could convince Americans to support both freer markets and freer citizens; school reform could create both better manners and better readers. These policies were not presented as separate goals, but rather parts of a unified whole. Conservatism, for most educational activists, was not a deliberate fusion of disparate strands of ideology but rather variegated fruit from the same tangled vine.

This does not mean that there is one simple correct definition for educational conservatism. Indeed, this book is devoted to a detailed examination of the many different meanings of conservatism in twentieth-century American education. The goals, ideas, and strategies of conservative activists differed in different times, in different situations, and on different issues. By focusing tightly on four prominent controversies, this book hopes to avoid imposing a simplistic definition. Rather, this book allows the conservatives involved to explain their own purposes and their own ideas about proper schooling and proper society. After all, educational conservatism, like any other sort of conservatism, looks different when articulated by different people—professional writers and activists or parents, teachers, and school board members caught up in an unexpected school controversy. It looked different in 1925 than it did in 1940, 1950, or 1975, and it looked different in Tennessee, Pennsylvania, California, and West Virginia.

Nevertheless, just as with the broader conservative impulse, it is not enough to simply shrug our shoulders and conclude that we can say nothing about the unifying themes of educational conservatism. As historian John Lewis Gaddis has argued about the nature of historical thinking, simply because we cannot be absolutely certain of historical facts does not imply that facts themselves do not exist.[32]

If, then, there is a theme that loosely backs the historic expressions of educational conservatism, what is it? To be useful, this theme must not be understood as a simple definition, or as an essence, or as a litmus test to true conservatism, but rather as a broadly shared understanding that has spanned the generations and varieties of conservative activists and thinkers. It must reach beyond nostalgic griping about walking to school ten miles barefoot, uphill both ways. It must mean more than a simple preference for narrowly understood school traditions. After all, such notions can be shared by all sorts of people, whether or not they share a broader, recognizably conservative outlook.

Educational conservatives, I suggest, have agreed with progressives in their firm belief that schooling can save or destroy society. But they have disagreed sharply in the contours of that belief. To be done right, conservatives have believed, schooling must pass along a set of traditional values and ideas about patriotism, religion, culture, and economics. If done wrong, schooling can warp and pervert the new generation, damning America to decay and helplessness. Educational conservatism has been the tradition of defending tradition itself. Schools, conservatives have insisted for generations, must maintain tradition, not undermine it.

Just as educational progressives dreamed that establishing anti-authoritarian classrooms could foster a new blossoming of authentic American democracy, so conservatives yearned to keep or create schools that trained each new generation to uphold traditions in politics, religion, and culture. It is worth repeating that educational conservatism in America's twentieth century has taken on many different shapes and addressed a wide range of issues. Conservatives have wanted many different things out of schools and schooling. Some of the traditional values on which conservatives insisted have changed as American culture has changed. More than that, some of the fundamental ideas of conservative activists concerning race, religion, and the proper role of the state and of educational experts have changed dramatically. But one thing that drove conservative activists to become school reformers has been a deeply held notion that proper schooling—and only proper schooling—will make a proper society. For conservative activists and thinkers just as much as for progressives, schools held transformational potential. If students learned that they were just a type of clever ape, students would act like animals. If students learned that they deserved to have their needs met, they would become grasping, self-centered monsters. If students learned that they must put the interests of the group before the interests of liberty, they would become blank-eyed collectivists. If students learned that authority—even duly constituted—represented a danger, they would become wild-eyed nihilists.

If, on the other hand, students learned that goodness and right remained real and powerful truths, they would become upright citizens. If students learned that American traditions represented humanity's best hope for freedom and justice, they would become thoughtful patriots. If students—whether in 1925, 1940, 1950, or 1975—learned that they were the heirs of thousands of years of embattled civilization, they would become truly educated.

For educational conservatives, no matter how much they differed in their specific issues and interests, these ideas remained central and immensely powerful. What went on in schools and classrooms mattered. The very survival of the nation often hinged on two related educational elements: both the ideas that were taught and the method by which those ideas were taught. Dangerous ideas must be kept out. Wholesome ideas must be kept in. And schools must not lose sight of the way those ideas must be transmitted. Young people must not be forced by a wrongheaded impulse toward "progressivism" simply to wander around in an intellectual meadow. Schooling, for conservatives, must consist of a systematic and deliberate transmission of the right ideas into young people. The future of the nation depended on it, whether conservatives viewed this future from 1925 or 1975.

A Moving Target

But in addition to the durable themes and tenacious institutions of educational conservatism, there have also been dramatic changes among different generations of educational conservatives. The argument in this book that educational conservatism represents a coherent and important cultural and political tradition must not be taken to imply that educational conservatism has always remained a single set of beliefs or policy prescriptions. The thinking of educational conservatives on key themes such as race and religion and on important issues such as evolution has changed dramatically over the years. So has the conservative consensus on the proper role of "experts" or of the federal government.

In the 1920s, for example, white conservatives generally did not insist that their policies were race-neutral. They usually took the desirability of white dominance for granted. As historian Jeffrey Moran has demonstrated, issues of evolution, fundamentalism, and education in the 1920s raised just as much controversy among African Americans as among whites. Yet conservative whites felt little need or desire to explain the racial implications of their activism. In the 1920s, white conservatives did not reach across the color line to their religious brothers and sisters.[33]

By the 1950s, white conservatives had developed a more complicated attitude toward race. As a group, white conservatives after World War II paid more explicit attention to the specifically "conservative" meanings of racial issues than did the previous generation. In the face of widespread protests by racial liberals, conservatives usually insisted that their conservative attitudes did not represent racism. Even among conservative groups that promoted racial segregation, leading voices argued that the true educational dangers were communist subversion and progressive pedagogy.[34] In some cases, even brutal white supremacist regimes cloaked their educational campaigns in rhetoric of racial paternalism. For instance, white segregationists in Mississippi established a committee to maintain segregated schools "to preserve and promote the best interests of both races."[35]

Outside of the massively resisting South, as Chapters 4 and 5 explore, conservatives also insisted that their positions did not include knee-jerk racism. In 1950s Pasadena, for instance, conservatives argued that their anti-zoning position did not imply anti-African American segregationism. And in 1970s West Virginia, conservative school reformers believed that their opposition to some African American writers did not imply old-fashioned racism. In both cases, white conservatives publicly brandished the support of a few African American allies. Unlike white conservatives in the 1920s, those of later generations worked hard to prove that their educational activism was not racist, some more credibly than others.

Similarly dramatic changes in conservative attitudes took place concerning the controversial topic of religion in public schools. In the

1920s, conservative Protestants fought for Protestant domination of public schools. Conservatives assembled a potent political coalition to promote a raft of religious curricula, including mandatory Bible readings and teacher-led prayers. Most famously, conservatives opposed evolution in public schools with remarkable success. In all these campaigns, conservatives sought—and often achieved—legal recognition for the dominance of public schools by a non-sectarian Protestant religiosity.[36]

In the second half of the twentieth century, in contrast, conservatives who wanted more religion in public schools found themselves fighting for much narrower aims. For instance, in many cases, conservatives hoped only to have prayer allowed, not mandated. A broad array of Americans, including many conservatives, expressed dismay at the Supreme Court's decision in 1962's *Engel v. Vitale*. In that case, the court ruled that public schools must not require students to recite a state-composed non-denominational prayer.[37] Former president Herbert Hoover protested that such a move represented the end of public education. The Roman Catholic hierarchy agreed that public schools must at least include this sort of inoffensive, ecumenical religiosity.[38] In marked distinction to 1920s campaigns to mandate Protestant religiosity, by the 1960s conservatives from Protestant, Catholic, and even secular backgrounds hoped only to include broadly religious practices.

Dramatic changes in educational conservatism can also be seen in the key issue of creationism and evolution. As historian Ronald Numbers has pointed out, the policy demands of creationists changed dramatically across the twentieth century. In the 1920s, William Jennings Bryan and his allies fought to ban evolution from public schools. By the end of the twentieth century, leading creationist Duane Gish claimed the mantle of Bryan's arch-foe, Clarence Darrow. Gish proclaimed, "Clarence Darrow thundered that it was bigotry to teach only one theory of origins."[39] As Numbers demonstrated, it was not Darrow, but fellow Scopes defense attorney Dudley Field Malone who had thundered this in 1925. But the point was clear: Instead of keeping evolution out, by the end of the century creationists hoped only to get creationism in. Creationists and evolution supporters had neatly swapped positions between 1925 and 1995.[40]

Perhaps more powerfully, the thinking of conservatives has changed about the proper role of the federal government. In the 1920s, as we will see in Chapter 2, leading conservative activist Hiram Evans pushed hard for a well-funded federal department of education. By the 1940s, conservative pamphleteers such as Allen Zoll denounced federal intrusion into local school affairs. As the Pasadena story in Chapter 4 illustrates, such anti-federal animus among conservatives often served as a litmus test for conservative orthodoxy. Hostility toward increased centralization and increased federalization of educational policy remained powerful throughout the twentieth century and into the twenty-first.

This dramatic shift from trust to hostility toward the federal government illustrates a more profound change among educational conservatives. In the 1920s—at least in the early 1920s—conservatives often assumed they represented the mainstream in educational and intellectual life, as well as in politics. From the 1930s into the 1970s and beyond, conservatives have tended to view the educational and intellectual establishment with profound skepticism.

For it was not only the federal government that later conservatives distrusted. In the field of education, conservatives often developed a virulent antipathy toward a perceived hostile elite—a gaggle of self-important, self-identified "experts"—that had insidiously seized control over elite colleges and intellectual institutions. In many cases, conservatives personified this danger in the increasing influence of philosopher John Dewey.[41] As intellectual historian Andrew Jewett argued recently, Dewey came to be a "universally recognized symbol" of changing ideas about culture and education, the incarnation of a successful campaign to transform American culture by transforming American universities.[42]

Of course, many conservatives in the 1920s already worried about the state of higher education. In 1923, for example, anti-evolution firebrand T. T. Martin lamented, "we sent our young men to the great German universities, and, when they came back, saturated with Evolution, we made them Presidents and head-professors of our colleges and great universities."[43] Yet throughout the 1920s leading conservatives still made it a point to engage in debate with college presidents, hoping to reclaim such schools for conservative ideals.[44]

After the 1920s, most conservatives assumed that elite colleges had long been lost to a host of pernicious ideas and intellectual fads. By 1938, for example, Daniel Doherty of the American Legion attacked the "intellectual hypocrisy and its complement, intellectual smugness" of the elite Teachers College progressives who hoped to take America's schools in socialist directions.[45] Commenting on the Pasadena controversy, Pasadena PTA member Mary Allen agreed. At some time in perhaps the "late twenties and early thirties," Allen charged in 1955, American education as a whole had been taken over by "some of Dewey's followers prepared to use the schools to introduce a new social order."[46] In the Kanawha County fight of 1974 and 1975, conservative activist Elmer Fike was not surprised to hear of Kanawha County's woefully progressive textbooks, since he believed that the "radicals" had taken control of educational publishing long before.[47]

To be sure, this distrust of the educational establishment has jostled along in tension with conservative dreams of renewed influence and prestige among educational elites. In the 1930s, as we will see in Chapter 3, the American Legion's Daniel Doherty eagerly accepted an invitation to speak at Columbia University, the very same university he accused of hypocrisy and smugness. Doherty hoped he could re-establish conservative ideals as the guiding lights in elite schools. And in the 1970s, as this book explores in Chapter 5, conservative intellectuals hurried to intervene in a school controversy in West Virginia. Part of their ultimate mission was to establish in the Heritage Foundation an intellectual institution able to stake out conservative ground among the skewed leftist world of Washington DC think tanks.

Yet despite these important tensions, it is fair to say that, by and large, educational conservatives ever since the bruising experience of the Scopes trial in 1925 have taken the role of usurped outsider, pushed unfairly out of the centers of educational influence by effete and impudent snobs. The theme of the aggrieved outsider echoes loudly across the different controversies examined in these chapters. From the 1930s through the 1970s, from New Jersey to California, conservative activists have lamented the overweening influence of puffed-up educational experts.

In important ways, then, educational conservatism has changed as the traditions to be defended have changed. On central issues of race and religion, positions among conservatives changed dramatically across the decades. The traditions defended by conservatives have shifted as American culture has shifted. By the end of the twentieth century, for instance, leading conservatives did not defend America's tradition of white supremacy. Rather, they defended America's tradition of fairness toward all races. And conservatism has seen a significant shift in the way conservatives view themselves in relation to both an educational establishment and the federal government. In the 1920s, some conservative leaders believed centralization could promote conservative practice and thinking in America's schools. After the experience of the Scopes trial and the advent of the New Deal, however, conservatives viewed with alarm the significant and purportedly growing influence of left-leaning educational experts.

In all these important ways, conservatism has seen dramatic transformations across the decades of the twentieth century. Is it fair, then, to suggest that there has been a coherent tradition among educational conservatives? Is it fair to argue that there is even such a recognizable thing as "educational conservatism"?

Educational Conservatism

As the chapters to come will demonstrate in detail, the continuities among conservative activists have outweighed the significant changes. Conservatives in decade after decade have repeated themes, ideas, and stories. In most cases, this has not been a conscious decision, but rather an intuitive participation in a potent cultural and intellectual tradition. For example, conservative school reformers from every generation have argued that classroom practices have a decisive influence on broader cultural and political trends. If teachers and students fail to respect traditional forms of learning, American society is threatened with disintegration. To thwart this danger, conservatives believe teachers must deliver traditional knowledge and values directly to their charges.

In 1923, for example, Anne Minor offered a passionate call for greater classroom traditionalism. At the time, Minor served as president general of the National Society of the Daughters of the American Revolution. In that role, she directed national policy and hoped to inspire members from around the country with her speeches at annual Continental Congresses. In her 1923 address, Minor warned her audience that they must all closely inspect their local teachers. Only teachers with "high character, high ideas, and *unimpeachable loyalty to America*" must be allowed.[48] Even the most "brilliant mind," Minor intoned, did not a good teacher make, if that teacher did not teach "truth and integrity, orderliness and obedience, loyalty and love of country."[49]

Unfortunately, Minor warned, thousands of teachers felt no such loyalty. They had been trained in colleges to view teaching as a chance to undermine the certainties of their students' native patriotism. "*We want no teachers*," Minor insisted, "*who say there are two sides to every question.*"[50] When it came to patriotism, there was only one side, the American side. This was no mere classroom issue, Minor believed. If children did not receive training in traditional patriotic values in school, the future of the nation was in peril. "*Guard well your schools*," Minor told the assembly, "*lest the life of the nation be poisoned at its source.*"[51]

Decades later, on the other side of the continent, conservative activist and parent "S.R." articulated a similar vision of the importance of proper classroom practice. Writing from Pasadena, California, S.R. warned in early 1950 that classroom methods dictated America's future. Worried that too many of Pasadena's public school children spent their class time in pleasant "Progressive" activities such as painting or listening absently to music, S.R. insisted that schools must return to drilling students in reading, writing, and arithmetic, the "foundation of education, the three R's."[52] Not only that, but education must remain primarily focused on passing along the wisdom of the ages to each new generation. "Children have the right," S.R. insisted, "to learn by being taught all and more than their parents and grandparents learned—one step ahead instead of backward, through each generation."[53] More was at stake than just student learning. If too few students received a decent education in basic skills, they would become easy political prey for a class of "propaganda leaders" who planned to move the country in leftist directions.[54]

A generation later, prominent conservative education critics Norma and Mel Gabler made similar arguments from their base in Longview, Texas. What went on in America's classrooms mattered, the Gablers wrote in their 1986 book *What Are They Teaching Our Children?* Teachers in modern schools took an unacceptable hands-off approach to student morality. "Humanistic educators," the Gablers argued, insisted that students must be allowed to decide moral questions for themselves.[55] Such misguided teachers did not recognize the central truth of proper education. They did not pass along "the experience gained from thousands of years of Western civilization."[56] Instead, "modern"[57] teachers engaged in the moral equivalent of putting their students in flimsy boats in dangerous and choppy seas. Though the teachers themselves knew of the rocks and shoals, they did not guide their students through to safety. Instead, teachers forced their students to choose their own values and ideas.[58]

This style of teaching did more than guarantee an ignorant and morally monstrous new generation. Nearly every social problem of the modern age, the Gablers wrote, from youth crime to drug use, from premarital sex to suicide could be traced back to the kinds of teaching that went on in America's classrooms.[59] As did Anne Minor in 1923, or S.R. in 1950, or the many activists who articulated similar themes across the twentieth century, the Gablers cared deeply about changing cultural and political norms. All these educational conservatives connected negative changes in culture, politics, and society to daily pedagogical decisions in classrooms, to monthly policy decisions in local school board meetings, and to countless discussions between parents and children in homes nationwide. Time and time again, as the chapters to come demonstrate, conservative activists consistently linked classroom practice to social and cultural reform. If schools could do a better job at preserving traditional forms and content, conservatives argued, society itself had a chance to remain healthily conservative.

At times, conservatives in different generations unconsciously echoed one another almost verbatim. For instance, in the 1920s and in every decade since, conservative pundits have repeated a similar story. Though the specific content and circumstances have varied across the decades, conservatives from every period have expressed shock and outrage at the educational materials their sons and daughters have brought home from school.

In 1922, for example, William Jennings Bryan warned that even among rich and powerful families, schools had the ability to undermine traditional home values. One of Bryan's acquaintances, a US congressman, told Bryan that his daughter had returned from college only to inform him that "nobody believed in the Bible stories now." Nor was this an isolated case, Bryan argued. Other congressmen and prominent clergy had shared similar stories. Children had gone off to school only to return with a set of values and ideas abhorrent to their parents.[60]

The start of the campaign against the Rugg textbooks claimed a similar origin. American Legion stalwart Augustin Rudd had moved from the trenches of World War I to a comfortable life as a cinema manager on Long Island, New York. As the story was told and retold for decades, Rudd's idyllic home life received a nasty shock in 1938 when he noticed a disturbing trend in his daughters' school textbooks.[61] As Rudd's wartime superior officer explained, Rudd found "to his utter astonishment" that his daughters were learning to doubt the superiority of the American system of republican government and capitalistic economics."[62] Rudd's shock and outrage led him to campaign against the use of left-leaning textbooks in social-studies classes nationwide.

Years later, a commentator noted a similar pattern in the public schools of Pasadena, California. As Frances B. Lucas explained in the pages of the *Daughters of the American Revolution Magazine* in late 1951, many parents had become "alarmed because their children became unruly." Though these young people had always been respectful and polite, "suddenly they were persistent in their own ideas, disobedient, and resented parental discipline." When the concerned parents investigated these dramatic changes in their children's behavior, they quickly found what they considered to be the source. Parents in Pasadena concluded that "'progressive' pamphlets" used in the district's schools had taught children the value of sass and immorality. One pamphlet bore the ominous title "How to Re-Educate Your Parents." Though progressive educators might have celebrated the students' determination to question established traditions and encouraged the youths' ability to express skepticism at arbitrary authority, the Pasadena parents were not amused. The teacher who had allegedly used the re-education pamphlet quickly found herself out of a job.[63]

The Gablers told a similar story. As they looked back from the vantage point of the mid-1970s, Mel and Norma Gabler remembered that their educational activism had begun in 1961 when their teenage son asked them to look at his school textbooks. At first, as told by sympathetic biographer James Hefley, the Gablers refused to believe their local public school needed any outside supervision. After all, Mel Gabler was president of the local Parent-Teacher Association. At the time, as Hefley put it, the Gabler family had worked its way to being

> the cream of self-reliant Middle America. They lived by the old landmarks, took child-rearing seriously, supported community institutions, sang "God Bless America" with a lump in their throats, and believed that the American system of limited and divided governmental power was the best under the sun.[64]

Finally, however, Mel consented to look at the books. What he saw, Hefley wrote, "set Mel on fire."[65] As the Gablers told the story a decade later, what Mel read in those books opened his eyes. At that point, they wrote in 1986, they "also began to grasp progressive education's grand scheme to change America."[66] Young Jim Gabler's textbooks did not mention that American government was founded by men who ardently believed in separation of powers and a strictly limited central government. The textbooks instead trumpeted "the benevolence of Washington D.C., and the building of world brotherhood through the United Nations."[67] The Gablers could not stand the thought of their children indoctrinated by such incorrect and misleading ideas. They worried that such books might influence their children to disrespect American patriotic traditions and work instead for an insidious international socialism. By the 1980s, the Gablers claimed they could rattle off hundreds of similar stories, as parents from around the country shared their stories of horrors brought home from school.[68]

In every iteration, the story has remained remarkably consistent. In 1922, as in 1951, as in 1986, conservative activists told of their outrage at the materials and ideas their children brought home from school. The examples repeated here barely scratch the surface of this ubiquitous tradition among conservative activists. It was not only that these textbooks were insipid or boring, though some activists said they were. For conservative activists, it was the ideological tendency of those school materials that inspired them to take action. Reading such noxious tripe, children soon mocked the Bible or the Constitution, sneered at parental authority, or promoted a socialist world brotherhood. Of course, these stories were not just statements, but strategies. Conservative activists may certainly have had the experiences they described. But the oft-repeated and well-worn stories served as more than just personal glimpses. Each speaker from each generation hoped to shock his or her listeners into a sense of emergency, a sense of outrage.

In these stories as well as in their rhetoric throughout their educational campaigns, activists have agreed—even in very different times and very different situations—that classroom practices must remain traditional. Children must go to school to imbibe the wisdom of the ages, not to question authority and doubt the value of tradition. In addition, even in very different circumstances, conservative school reformers have unconsciously echoed the theme that pernicious classroom materials or classroom practices had shocked them into aggressive public activism. Such connections across the decades help make the case for a coherent tradition of educational conservatism.

Most important, this book's chapters demonstrate the institutional continuity among educational conservatives. Organizations such as the American Legion and Daughters of the American Revolution (DAR) maintained an explicit focus on fixing schools to fix America. This central focus on education guided both groups from the 1920s through the rest of the century.[69] As we'll see in Chapters 3 and 4, neither of these groups can fairly be dismissed as fringe voices. The DAR, for instance, regularly received the flattering attention of politicians from across the political spectrum, including Calvin Coolidge,[70] Herbert Hoover,[71] Franklin Delano Roosevelt,[72] and J. Edgar Hoover,[73] among others. The American Legion worked closely with both the Federal Bureau of Investigation and leading politicians.[74]

Leaders of the DAR insisted as early as 1928 that the proper name for their sort of educational activism was "conservative."[75] And the DAR's staunchly conservative leadership inspired other educational activists across the country and across the decades, from Pasadena in 1950[76] to Longview, Texas, in 1962.[77] Similarly, the American Legion's educational activism only makes sense when seen as a concerted effort across the decades. As Chapter 3 describes, Legion outrage over school textbooks in the 1940s must be understood as part and parcel of its educational activism stretching back into the 1920s. Whether fighting against the influence of communists and subversives in schools, leading good-citizenship programs, or publishing and censoring school text-books, the DAR and the Legion maintained a powerful presence in America's schools. This explicitly conservative activism connected leaders and members across the generations in a self-aware network of school reformers.

Conservative Schools

Whether ignoring racial injustice or denying racism, fighting for Protestant hegemony or Christian inclusion, seeking more power for the federal government or less, conservatives articulated common themes and echoed common ideas. In every decade, conservatives argued for the need to respect traditional classroom practices. They fought for traditions of patriotism, public religion, and American exceptionalism. In spite of important changes in conservative positions on important school issues, educational conservatism has a demonstrable tradition from the 1920s through the rest of the century and beyond. Some elements of that tradition have changed as culture and politics changed, but it is misleading to examine each new conservative educational campaign as entirely new and unrelated to the longer conservative tradition.

This conservative tradition has been enormously, decisively influential in American education. But that does not mean that the tradition itself has worked as some sort of disembodied force, an impersonal reality against which progressive reformers have flailed. In other words, educational conservatism has not been the product mainly of "unexamined institutional habits and widespread cultural beliefs."[78] Rather, educational conservatism has been the product of decades of activism by specific men and women—the "other school reformers" depicted in these pages. Certainly, those activists appealed to unexamined habits and widespread beliefs, just as progressive school reformers did. But unless we come to grips with the fact that educational conservatism is an activity, not just a palpable but incorporeal presence, we will continue to misunderstand and mischaracterize the nature of American education.

been an ongoing activism

CHAPTER TWO

Monkeys, Morality, and Modern America

Conservative Educational Activism in the Scopes Era

No one at the trial that day went home disappointed. As the world-famous antagonists squared off on the outdoor platform, trading gibes and taunts, the crowd laughed, shouted, and applauded. They had come to see a big show, and they got one.

There had been some doubts in their minds that this much-ballyhooed "Trial of the Century" would live up to its name. So far, the audience had heard a few terrific speeches, but they had also sat through hour after hour of technical discourse on the nature of science and religion. They had endured long hot days of monotonous recited statements. Judge John T. Raulston had moved the trial outside, to mitigate the July heat and to relieve some of the pressure on the overloaded courtroom floors. Workers had built a wooden platform adjoining the courthouse, under the shade of Dayton's cottonwood trees. Under those trees on this seventh day of the trial, they witnessed a once-in-a-lifetime confrontation that made little legal sense, but a world of dramatic sense.[1]

Clarence Darrow, the 1920s embodiment of skepticism and modern doubt, planned to interrogate William Jennings Bryan, the personification of traditional Presbyterian public religion. Darrow appeared for the defense, Bryan for the prosecution. In a regular court case, there would be no reason for defense lawyers to go head-to-head with prosecutors on the witness stand. But this was no ordinary case. Beyond the carnival streets of Dayton, Tennessee, the rest of the nation and the world also watched this trial with bated breath. One sociologist at the time guessed that the newspaper output from the trial would have

Clarence Darrow (standing with hands in galluses) confronts William Jennings Bryan on the witness stand. (Courtesy Smithsonian Institution Archives, image SIA2007–0124)

filled almost a million pages.[2] Film crews appeared as well, as did what the *Chicago Tribune* called the world's first radio broadcast of the event.[3]

Darrow questioned prosecution attorney Bryan about his understanding of religion, history, and society. Did Bryan really believe that Jonah had lived inside a big fish for three days? Did Bryan not know that if Joshua had made the earth stand still, it would quickly have "been converted to a molten mass of matter"?[4]

Bryan gave as good as he got. If it was difficult for Darrow to believe in miracles, the problem lay not with the miracles, but with the man.[5] The audience craned their necks to get better views. They did not want to miss a word of this interchange between America's most famous skeptic and its leading defender of the faith.

What did the audience think of this showdown? Although the opinion of that crowd in 1925 is mostly lost to historians, some evidence is clear from the transcript. The crowd liked to cheer. They liked to laugh. And they did not seem to favor one side over another. In this confrontation, they laughed just as readily at Darrow's barbs as at Bryan's. Despite the accusation of a famous visiting reporter that the local crowd was made only of "yokels,"[6] "the lower orders,"[7] and "ignorant

. . . dishonest . . . cowardly . . . ignoble . . . immortal vermin,"[8] the East Tennesseans who crowded into Dayton to see the trial did not reflexively reject the defense's big-city ways. They had proved it on the fifth day of the trial, when attorney Dudley Field Malone had rebuked Bryan and demanded of the prosecution, "Keep your Bible . . . in the world of theology where it belongs and do not try to tell an intelligent world . . . that these books . . . can be put into a course of science."[9] On that day, Malone had pleaded with the court and the assembled audience, "For God's sake let the children have their minds kept open."[10] At the end of Malone's speech, the audience exploded in applause. They hooted their approval. They stomped and shouted; one policeman slammed a table so hard with his nightstick the table split. When a colleague rushed over to help restore order, the policeman shouted, "I'm not trying to restore order. Hell, I'm cheering."[11] The audience at this dramatic trial liked to hear both sides. They cheered for the defense as readily as they cheered for the prosecution. They cherished the Bible, but they also cherished America's tradition of dissent. Some may have been "yokels," but they were more like the rest of America than the rest of America might have liked to admit.

this idea of debate

In order to make some sense of why this trial seemed like such a big deal to America in 1925, we need to make sense of what the audience felt that day in July. If we can understand what Darrow and Bryan meant to their American audiences, we can get a better understanding of what this clash meant to people at the time. This was more to them than a contest of wits between two noted rhetoricians; this became a living symbol of the culture wars that raged throughout the 1920s. The trial offered conservatives a chance to prove their case: the best education was traditional education.

The Skeptic and the Defender

By the time of their showdown in the Scopes trial of 1925, Darrow and Bryan had taken on iconic, archetypical status in American culture. They represented two opposing visions of what made America great, despite the fact that both men claimed to represent the great American underdog and both were leading members of the Democratic Party.[12] That fact was conveniently forgotten in the years preceding the Scopes trial, as Americans associated each man with starkly opposed visions of American culture.

Perhaps the incident that lay heaviest in most people's minds when they thought of Clarence Darrow was his role in the trial of Nathan

Leopold and Richard Loeb. This 1924 trial captured the attention of the public every bit as much as the Scopes trial would the following summer. The story had all the elements of compelling melodrama. Two rich young men had imbibed new ideas from their readings of Nietzsche and evolutionist Ernst Haeckel. They decided to kill a third boy to see if they could get away with it.

They couldn't. But they could still shock and terrify Americans who concluded that such amorality must represent a new trend in American youth culture. During their high-profile trial, reporters titillated readers by noting that the two seemed "unconcerned" by their actions. Instead, they looked every inch the "nattily attired sons of millionaires, displaying their education and their intelligence . . . not at all bothered by the fact that they were suspected of murder."[13] Even after they pled guilty, during a court session in which the "tragic" mother of the victim sobbed out her story, reporters noted the two defendants laughed together at being called "cold-blooded killers." Loeb told reporters that day that he considered such epithets "funny."[14]

When he agreed to act as counsel for these two, Darrow knew he risked taking on their unpopularity. For Darrow, it was an opportunity to fight the will of the mob. It was a chance to stand up for America's best values, including the idea that every accused person deserves the best legal defense. In the words of an imaginative early biographer, Darrow knew this case would "once again bring down on his head the wrath of the mob, the hatred and vituperation of the pack."[15] Darrow had always pictured himself as the voice of the voiceless, bold enough to stand up for those who had no one to stand up for them. He had started his career, after all, as the defender of socialist leader Eugene Debs in 1894.[16] Between the Debs case and that of Leopold and Loeb, Darrow built a reputation as America's top trial lawyer and one of its best-known defenders of the underdog.

Darrow avoided some obvious traps in the Leopold and Loeb trial. For instance, he declined to cross-examine the victim's sobbing mother. But Darrow also had to deny in court that this was such a momentous killing, at a time when every headline screamed the opposite. "Bad enough," Darrow called the murder, "of course, but everybody who has had any experience with the criminal class knows it is utterly absurd for this to be branded, as it has been repeatedly, as the greatest, most horrible and atrocious killing that ever happened."[17] That kind of attitude solidified Darrow's reputation as the archetype, the epitome of the intellectual maverick. Of course, he won plenty of support in this role, but for those who fretted that traditional values were breaking down, the man who sought to stand in the public limelight frankly athwart the current of social norms and shout, "Stop," came to represent everything that had gone wrong in American culture.

In order to save his clients from the death penalty, Darrow argued that the boys were not entirely responsible for their own actions. Their education, training, and upbringing made them into the people that they were, Darrow argued. The court, Darrow hoped, could at least show them the small mercy of a life sentence.[18] Darrow's legal opponent called that argument nothing short of "anarchistic."[19] Anyone who believed in ultimate morals, in social norms and values rooted in a transcendent foundation of right and wrong, Darrow's critics jeered, could not accept his convoluted legal argument. As one disgusted observer wrote, Darrow "demonstrates that nobody in this world is responsible for any of his actions. Since I am the helpless victim of a mechanistic universe . . . the blame falls not on me but on my ancestors and society."[20] For the audience in Dayton, Tennessee, as for the rest of America, Darrow embodied this kind of modern thinking. Not all of them liked it.

Darrow embodied the skeptic in other ways as well. In Prohibition-era America, Darrow publicly and loudly fought for repeal. He called Prohibition supporters "killjoys" and admitted he liked to take a drink now and again. Nor did Darrow pose as a man of religion. "I don't mind telling you," he told a crowd in the months leading up to the Scopes trial, "I'm not crazy about church. I don't mind their going to heaven their way, but I don't want them to tell me not to go to hell my way."[21] And even as Darrow prepared to defend John Scopes, he volunteered his legal services to another high-profile case, one in which children of atheists had been compelled to take part in religious services in their public schools.[22] A drinker, a religious skeptic, a defender of murderers and socialists—to conservatives, Darrow became the 1920s symbol of the perils of life in Modern America. As the Scopes trial garnered more and more public attention, Darrow's participation pushed it from a narrow constitutional test case to a full-blown epic battle between the forces of good and evil.

Of course, each side assumed it was the good and the other was the evil. No less than Clarence Darrow embodied the stereotype of the modern scoffer; William Jennings Bryan symbolized the forces of down-home tradition. Just as Darrow came to Dayton after a long career as the famous "Attorney for the Damned,"[23] so Bryan had worked for decades in the public eye as the steadfast "Great Commoner." In the 1920s, Bryan built a large readership for his weekly Bible columns. By 1923 he claimed to be reaching ten to twelve million people each week with his conservative, Bible-based theological reflections.[24]

Bryan's earliest political fame had come in the 1890s, with his impassioned "Cross of Gold" speech at the Democratic National Convention of 1896. The speech and Bryan's wily politicking made him the symbol of the Populist crusade of that decade. Bryan's style and strategy made him the embodiment of insurgent farmers and miners hoping to snatch more than the scraps from the laden tables of Gilded Age America.[25]

As his career developed, Bryan cultivated an image as the voice of steadfast morality in public life. After running unsuccessfully for president as the nominee of the Democratic Party three times, Bryan accepted a post as secretary of state under Woodrow Wilson. Bryan showcased his temperance beliefs and his staunch anti-militarism in some dramatic and very public positions. At state dinners and luncheons, Bryan refused to serve alcoholic drinks, delivering ceremonial toasts instead with pure water. Such stunts earned him the scorn of those who felt embarrassed by his provincialism. They winced at the idea that Bryan's rigid Puritanical morals would represent the entire United States in the eyes of the world. But such theatrics played well with ardent supporters of temperance.[26]

Similarly, Bryan's dramatic resignation from his post registered his Christian distaste for Wilson's policy vis-à-vis wartime Germany. Bryan had hoped to avoid embroilment in the Great War. He hoped the United States could serve as a model and an interlocutor for a more peaceful solution to international disputes. When German submarines sank the *Lusitania,* a cruise ship with 128 Americans on board, Wilson responded sternly. Bryan urged Wilson to remain neutral. As Wilson showed a stronger and stronger antipathy to the German cause, Bryan resigned.[27]

Bryan brought his decades as the symbol of the hard-working, faithful, Christian, traditional American to Dayton. By 1925, he had also come to personify the anti-evolution movement. He used the language he had polished in his long career to condemn the secret scheming of "oligarchs" who hoped to shatter students' faith by cramming evolution theory down their throats.[28] Opposed to this small, aggressive group of self-appointed experts, Bryan claimed, ranged the "ninety per cent of the people who are still Defenders of the Faith."[29] Bryan planned to represent their traditional beliefs, come what may.

The Showdown

As Darrow grilled Bryan in the scorching heat of Monday, July 20, 1925, the audience drank in every word. When one or the other scored a rhetorical point, the audience responded with laughter, applause, and shouts. Of course, the relatively small crowd gathered to watch this interrogation cannot fairly be assumed to be representative of American society as a whole. The things they applauded do not necessarily tell us anything about the sentiments of the entire nation. By looking at a couple of the laugh lines in this tense exchange we cannot make conclusions about the state of America's mind as a whole, but we can get some idea of the two perceived positions in this 1920s battle over the nature of public education and American culture.

Early on in the examination, Darrow pressed Bryan to explain his views on the origins of the Bible. If it was divinely inspired, what did that mean? Why should readers in 1925 assume that the words written lo those many centuries ago still explained the basic truths of the origins of life on earth? Bryan delivered a line that sent the audience into loud and long laughter. "I believe," Bryan explained, the Bible "was inspired by the Almighty, and He may have used language that could be understood at that time. . . . Instead of using language that could not be understood until Darrow was born."[30]

The audience loved it. Bryan's comment captured the resentment many conservatives felt during the 1920s. Darrow represented a clutch of ideas, including evolution, a dismissal of patriotic feeling, contempt for Bible-based theology, and hostility to traditional family structure. Not surprisingly, many conservatives viewed folks like Darrow with suspicion and resentment. These conservatives often felt as if the heady wine of progress had blinded Darrow and other progressives to the dangers of too-rapid change and to the emptiness of the promises of modern life. Why was it so funny to the Dayton audience that the Bible would have been understandable to people before Darrow? Again, we can't really know for sure, but it is likely because they resented the assumption of Darrow and people like him that their progressive ideas represented the only truth, that older understandings of truth and value should be cast indiscriminately into the dustbin to make room for bold new thinking. Conservatives resented the notion that only new ideas were worthwhile, that schools ought to be inculcating students with notions fundamentally different from the ones their parents grew up with. Worst of all, sneerers like Darrow wrapped their insouciance in an insufferable attitude of self-righteousness. As with all jokes, the audience at Dayton did not need such a long explanation of why they found Bryan's gibe funny. It was funny because it included some sense of all these ideas, wrapped up in a single, potent one-liner.

The laughs that day were not all at Darrow's expense. As the interrogation went on, Darrow pressed Bryan to give his estimation of the Bible's supposed date for the worldwide flood survived by Noah. Bryan sensed the danger. If he gave a specific date, he could open himself up to detailed questions about different interpretations of the exact date. Instead, Bryan had to admit he did not know the answers to a series of questions posed by Darrow.

"What do you think?" Darrow pressed him.

"I do not think about things I don't think about," Bryan responded, hoping to get a laugh. But Darrow beat him to the punch.

"Do you think about things you do think about?" Darrow asked.

"Well, sometimes," Bryan answered sheepishly. The audience laughed again, this time at Bryan.[31] Just as Bryan had managed to zero in on the resentment that people felt toward the smug superiority of skeptics like Darrow, Darrow was able to zing Bryan by highlighting the chink in conservatives' armor. If progressives came off as too quick to abandon traditional ideas and classrooms, so conservatives could seem unaware of the ideas on offer by modern scholarship. Bryan was vulnerable to the charge that he did not think. So the wider conservative movement lay open to the charge that it wanted to cripple schools by forcing out any new idea, no matter how valuable. When it came to education, conservatives in the 1920s and for the rest of the twentieth century had to answer accusations of willful ignorance, of a stubborn unwillingness to contend with important ideas. As Bryan hemmed and hawed about whether he thought about things, so conservatives had to work extra hard to prove that they were not simply the party of heads-in-the-sand obscurantism.

The reason the unfolding events at the Scopes trial fascinated so many Americans was because the trial promised to bring these two contending visions of American education and culture together in one Tennessee town, each side represented by its best-known champion. Although the audience in Dayton cannot simply be used as a stand-in for the entirety of American opinion, they did share many of the ideas of 1925 America as a whole. Some were nervous about the aggressive secularism and arrogance of skeptics such as Darrow. Others were scornful of the willful ignorance of conservatives such as Bryan. They hoped the confrontation between the two would settle these questions once and for all. After all, the question of evolution and the nature of public education had dominated the nation's headlines for several years before the Scopes trial.

Anti-Evolution in State Legislatures

If we are to understand the many meanings of the Scopes trial to 1920s-era America, we need to delve briefly into the history of struggle over the teaching of evolution. One of the first public outbreaks of the controversy came in Kentucky in 1922. That year, the state legislature seriously considered the nation's first anti-evolution bill. Less famous names than Darrow and Bryan gave the nation a preview of the arguments from the Scopes trial. For instance, one of the staunchest opponents of Kentucky's bill, University of Kentucky president Frank McVey, argued that such a bill would shut the state off "from all contact with the modern world" since "all the natural sciences" were based on evolution.[32]

Nonsense, argued state senator Harry F. Greene. Although the Kentucky bill would have banned much more than just evolution, Greene told his colleagues, "If he [McVey] is not teaching evolution what is he hollering for? If the university is not teaching evolution this bill does not hit it."[33] Greene's claim was not quite true. The Kentucky bill would have actually banned a much wider array of ideas. It would have installed traditional Protestant religiosity as the guideline for ideas acceptable at all of Kentucky's schools, from elementary to university. In spite of Greene's narrow focus on the idea of evolution, the bill under consideration would have banned "Darwinism, Atheism, Agnosticism, or the Theory of Evolution."[34] What's more, a state senate amendment would have prohibited any public library in the state from owning any materials "containing such teaching that will directly or indirectly attack or assail or seek to undermine or weaken or destroy the religious beliefs and convictions of the children of Kentucky."[35] That meant more than just evolution. It would have given conservatives extraordinary power to ban books that they thought implied a criticism of evangelical Protestantism. After all, the number of books that could fairly be accused of undermining or weakening religious faith, even indirectly, was shockingly vast.

As at the Scopes trial a few years later, the question in Kentucky was about the nature of public education. Conservatives wanted schools to protect the Protestant faith of their pupils. They insisted that one leading function of public education was precisely to transmit that faith from the older generation to the younger. And in 1922, those arguments carried a great deal of political weight. The Kentucky bill failed by only one vote, and that swing vote had only come about as part of a backroom compromise. In return for cooperation in defeating the school bill, bill opponents assured conservatives that evolution would be eliminated from all public schools.[36]

In the early 1920s, such arguments about evolution and the proper nature of public education roiled state legislatures nationwide. Soon after Kentucky's debate, state legislators in South Carolina considered and narrowly defeated a similar bill.[37] In 1923, such debates rocked state capitols in Georgia, Texas, West Virginia, Alabama, Iowa, and Tennessee.[38] Anti-evolution activists had more luck elsewhere. In Florida, legislators approved a resolution against any sort of teaching that could challenge traditional Protestant faith.[39] Ku Klux Klan support pushed through an anti-evolution free textbook law in Oklahoma.[40] Indeed, no story of conservative educational activism in the 1920s would be complete without a look into the leading role played by the Klan's sheeted vigilantes, something we will explore later in this chapter.

The next year, 1924, the State Board of Education in California officially warned teachers to limit the time they spent teaching evolution.[41] Similarly, the North Carolina Board of Education banned a biology book that they thought strayed too far from Genesis.[42] As had become traditional, national politicians used their control over teaching in Washington DC to make political hay. In 1924, the US Congress passed an amendment that prohibited teachers in the Capital from teaching anything that might lead to "disrespect of the Holy Bible."[43] In 1925, several more bills came before state legislatures. Most were defeated: West Virginia, North Carolina, Georgia, Florida, and Texas.[44] But that was not the end of the battle, even in those states. In Texas, for example, the governor ordered textbook publishers to remove evolution from Texas editions.[45] Finally, in 1925 the anti-evolution movement scored its biggest success when Tennessee passed the Butler Act in 1925. The law was stronger than the resolution in Florida, the textbook bill in Oklahoma, or the teaching law in Washington DC. But like those laws, the Tennessee anti-evolution law passed on March 23, 1925, insisted that no teaching would be allowed to challenge students' belief in the Genesis version of the creation story.[46]

The Best Laid Plans . . .

Americans who feared the heavy hand of Protestant religion in public school classrooms watched these legal developments with a wary eye. The leaders of the American Civil Liberties Union (ACLU) saw a chance to defeat these laws in court. In May 1925, the ACLU published an advertisement in the *Chattanooga Times,* offering to pay the legal costs of any Tennessee teacher willing to serve as a test case against the new law.[47] At the time, it was a novel strategy for the young organization. The founders of the ACLU during World War I had envisioned their organization as more of a direct-action group. Instead of lawsuits, early ACLU activism consisted of walking picket lines and pressuring officials to oppose restrictive laws.[48] With their offer to Tennessee teachers, ACLU leaders tried out a new strategy, one that would become their trademark approach to civil liberties for decades to come.

In contrast to some of the myths told of the origin of the Scopes trial, at the time and for years to come, young John Scopes was not arrested as he valiantly tried to enlighten a class of sullen, hostile hillbillies. He was not led in handcuffs out of the school as he protested in vain. Rather, the trial came about as part of a publicity stunt staged by earnest town boosters in the hamlet of Dayton, Tennessee. Responding to the ACLU's offer, a group of prominent Dayton citizens met around the tables at Robinson's Drug Store in downtown Dayton. They discussed the possibilities that an ACLU-funded test case could bring some needed publicity to their town. An easygoing young schoolteacher agreed to serve as the main character in what seemed like a fairly harmless charade.[49] None of this small group of Daytonians could have imagined that their simple plan would soon become the symbol of the educational culture wars that rocked 1920s America.

To be fair to those Dayton plotters, when they agreed to accept the ACLU's offer, no one predicted the attention the trial would attract. Leaders of the ACLU hoped for a simple test case. They wanted a quick conviction that they could then appeal to higher courts to demonstrate the unconstitutionality of Tennessee's anti-evolution law. They hoped such a test case could put an end to the campaign for anti-evolution laws in state legislatures nationwide.[50]

But they and the rest of America were about to experience some of the possibilities of America's developing culture of celebrity.[51] The trial soon took on a public life of its own. Boosted by the news that Darrow and Bryan had volunteered to represent the two sides, reporters and activists promoted the idea that this "monkey" trial would soon settle the vexing question of evolution education and all its concomitant controversies. What was the role of science in schools? Of religion? What was the nature of humanity? The origin of life on earth? What values did America want to pass on to its children in its public schools?

It is deeply ironic, then, that in the end the trial did not legally confront even the simplest questions about evolution. It was not because the defense did not want to. On the contrary, the defense brought a string of experts to Dayton. Theologians promised to explain that evolution did not threaten Christian belief. Scientists planned to demonstrate that evolution was far from "just a theory."[52] They would show that evolution made up one of the central building blocks of modern scientific thinking. As one opponent of Kentucky's 1922 anti-evolution bill had lamented, without evolution, there "would be little left for [schools] to teach."[53]

William Jennings Bryan originally hoped just as fervently that the trial would offer a chance to array the best anti-evolution experts against the best the defense could muster. Bryan felt confident "that our side was prepared to hold its own against their committee of scientists."[54] Bryan believed until the last minute that the trial would offer him a chance to demonstrate the unscientific nature of evolution. He hoped to bring such a chorus of anti-evolution expertise to Dayton that the public would be convinced to end its flirtation with evolution. He told one confidant, "I am expecting a tremendous reaction as a result of the information which will go out from Dayton."[55]

Other conservatives shared Bryan's optimism. Writing from a fundamentalist convention in Seattle, Texas leader J. Frank Norris guaranteed that he could assemble a crack team of "real scientists" who "could meet any hoax or fraud that might be made by the defence."[56] If anyone could do it, Norris could. He had jumped into the anti-evolution crusade with all his energy and dedication. His uncompromising tone and folksy style had made him a favorite among Texas conservatives, but his hot temper also made him a few enemies. In 1926, Norris would help fuel the stereotype of fundamentalism as a violent, irrational hysteria when he shot a man dead in Norris's own office.[57]

In the aftermath of that fatal shooting, Norris protested that he was only defending himself from a violent assault. But he knew that many of his enemies liked to assume the worst. Similarly, in the months leading up to the Scopes trial, Norris knew that his scientific beliefs went against those of many scientists. But, like Bryan and most other anti-evolutionists in the 1920s, Norris assumed that those scientists had lost their way.

Conservatives like Norris felt that a clutch of over-reaching scientists—those who embraced evolution—had been deluded by a previous intellectual commitment to the philosophy of materialism. Such scientists, conservatives believed, had mistakenly ruled out supernatural intervention in the origins of life. Evangelical magazines such as

Chicago's *Moody Bible Institute Monthly* and Minneapolis's *Christian Fundamentals in School and Church* ran articles about the most "Modern Scientific Discoveries."[58] Such discoveries, conservative readers found out, would soon prove that evolution was a hoax, easily disproved by "recent discoveries in geology."[59] Bryan himself received personal assurances from the most famous anti-evolution scientist of the 1920s, George McCready Price, that those fools who still clung to evolution were "out of date,—behind the times,—and don't know it."[60] Until the trial itself, Bryan looked forward to the prospect of debunking the unscientific pretensions of such self-satisfied fools. He planned to assemble an array of leading scientists that would convince the world as ardently as they had convinced Bryan.

What's in a Name?

One of the most severe shocks of the Scopes trial was to come from the fact that this panel of anti-evolution experts never materialized. Thoughtful evolution opponents had to wonder why anti-evolution scientists—the ones they had been reading about for years—did not appear to trounce the unscientific theory of evolution. The Scopes trial, as the most public symbol of the ways American culture had changed in the past fifty years, forced conservatives to confront the disturbing fact that they no longer dominated the most influential centers of American intellectual life. As we'll see in the chapters to come, future generations of conservative educational activists no longer assumed that they could put together a crack team of experts who would sweep away muddled progressive opposition. Later conservatives, indeed, often shared a virulent suspicion of mainstream educational or intellectual experts, assuming that any such expert must be steeped in foul notions such as evolution, socialism, or theological modernism. Not that conservatives in any generation ceded the mantle of true science or true intellectual expertise to their opponents, but after the Scopes trial conservatives in every generation had to recognize an inconvenient truth. Conservative ideas about science, religion, and culture no longer ruled unquestioned in institutions such as universities and churches. Conservative activists in later decades no longer shared the easy confidence that their intellectual allies could simply expose and humiliate the baseless presumptions of evolutionists, socialists, and their ilk. These epochal changes were not caused by the Scopes trial, of course, but for those involved, the trial itself served to dramatize these transformations in America's traditions of authority.

[handwritten margin note: Skeptism of experts]

At the time, the shock waves from the Scopes trial seemed to hit hardest among those 1920s conservatives who had identified with the nascent fundamentalist movement. The trial's confounding challenge to conservative truths forced many conservatives to re-examine their relationship to a complicated fundamentalist movement. To be fair, the term "fundamentalism" has been impossible to define rigidly since its inception in the early 1920s. As one Baptist editor moaned in 1923, "The Fundamentalist controversy almost makes one despair of the churches. Millions of people have been confused by this controversy."[61] It was easy to be confused. The term was used in two distinct senses, but usually those using it did not specify which meaning they intended. For some, the term meant primarily one side of a denominational struggle that raged throughout the decade. For others, "fundamentalism" was used as a catch-all term for any kind of religious, cultural, political, or intellectual traditionalism. But those who participated in the denominational struggles also often took part in the wider campaign for traditionalism. And those who participated in the broader cultural fundamentalism often sympathized with the denominational traditionalists. It was certainly easy for people to be confused about the meaning of fundamentalism.

William Bell Riley wanted to clear up any confusion. He was one of the leaders of the denominational struggles that were called the fundamentalist-modernist controversy. By the 1920s, a significant and influential number of Protestants, especially within the Northern Presbyterian denomination and Northern Baptist Convention, had accepted the tenets of theological modernism. Modernists were often sympathetic toward "higher criticism," an inquiring attitude toward the authorship of the Bible and the life of the historical Jesus. One historian has defined theological modernism as "the conscious, intended adaptation of religious ideas to modern culture . . . the idea that God is immanent in human cultural development and revealed through it . . . [and] a belief that human society is moving toward realization . . . of the Kingdom of God."[62] In brief, theological modernism insisted that religion must not ossify, flattened into obsolescence between the dusty pages of unread scripture. Rather, it must be a vital part of a culture and society that was transforming at breakneck speed.

Riley, like other fundamentalists, had long worried that such ideas undermined Protestant orthodoxy. He worried that modernists placed too much intellectual weight on the affairs and interests of humans, instead of laying all human experience before the will and power of God. Worst of all, fundamentalists in the 1920s could no longer hide from the fact that theological modernism had become almost irresistibly influential in American intellectual culture. Leading schools such as the University of Chicago Divinity School had become hubs for modernist theology. Two leaders of the school—Dean Shailer Mathews and Professor Shirley Jackson Case—won acclaim as forceful expositors of the new ideas. In 1919, in *The Revelation of John,* Case analyzed the Book of Revelation as a political allegory about the declining Roman Empire, with meanings mostly relevant to the time the book was written. In 1924, Mathews published *The Faith of Modernism,* an impassioned defense of theological modernism.[63]

Riley hoped to rally the orthodox to a defense of doctrinal fundamentals. His background and personality made him a formidable culture warrior. Raised in Kentucky, he took over his pastorate in Minneapolis in 1897.[64] His talent for organization and flair for preaching helped his First Baptist Church to grow by leaps and bounds. Riley was involved in everything, from condemnations of dancing and card-playing to attacks on excessive wealth among his congregants.[65]

His work at First Baptist and as a traveling evangelist convinced Riley of the dangers of theological modernism. The ambitious Riley likely also sniffed a path to national and international fame, the chance to become a figure of great historical importance. He hoped to lead a crusade to restore the church to its theological roots. By the end of his life in 1947, it may have been that thwarted ambition that led him to explain the disappointing career of fundamentalism as a result of the scheming wiles of "Jewish Communists."[66]

Such bitterness, however, lay decades in the future for Riley. In 1919, he founded the World's Christian Fundamentals Association (WCFA). He hoped this group could be an umbrella organization for all those who clung to orthodox Protestantism. He offered a nine-point creed to define his movement. All true believers, Riley insisted, must acknowledge that the Bible was inerrant. It was not, as modernists asserted, a mere collection of ancient writings to be considered as part of Christian tradition. Rather, it was the Word of God, to be honored above all other sources of knowledge. Christians must also recognize the Trinity, the divine nature of Jesus, the nature of original sin, Christ's substitutionary atonement, Christ's resurrection, the impending return of Christ to earth, a second birth in faith, and a real, physical heaven and hell.[67]

To Riley, this creed defined the most important aspect of fundamentalism. He mocked "funny Fundamentalists" who claimed the title but did not agree with his creed.[68] He insisted that the "true Fundamentalist" was only one who held to the WCFA creed.[69] For Riley, and for other leaders of the denominational struggle, the essence of fundamentalism lay not in the wider cultural campaign against the perils of modernity, but in this struggle for control over the nature of Protestant belief.

Recent historians have agreed that this denominational struggle defined fundamentalism. George Marsden, for instance, has defined fundamentalism as "militantly anti-modernist Protestant evangelicalism."[70] While this definition fits with Riley's brand of denominational brawling, the definition unfairly limits fundamentalism to one of its many meanings. It is not flexible enough to include the wide spectrum of conservatives who gathered around the new label. To cite one example, in a 1925 survey at the University of Michigan, almost twenty percent of Catholic students identified themselves as fundamentalists.[71] Anti-fundamentalist activist Maynard Shipley agreed that many Catholics were of a "Fundamentalist persuasion."[72] If we impose a definition limited only to a certain sort of Protestant activist, we won't be able to make sense of these conservative Catholics who considered themselves part of a broader fundamentalist impulse.

An earlier generation of historians assumed that "fundamentalism" in the 1920s could refer to virtually any sort of conservatism. They often conflated the anti-evolution drive with the fundamentalist movement. They included the Ku Klux Klan as "fundamentalist," although the Klan did not express much interest in the denominational struggles that animated Riley and his allies. William Leuchtenburg, for instance, in his influential 1920s history, *Perils of Prosperity* (1958), described all of the vibrant conservative activism of the 1920s as an effusion of "political fundamentalism."[73]

This was not just a blind spot of 1950s historians. Writers and activists in the 1920s often did the same. In the 1920s, no popular writer led the charge against fundamentalism more energetically than the famous journalist H. L. Mencken. Mencken spared no effort in his attempt to discredit the movement. He consistently lumped together all conservative educational activists as fundamentalists. For example, although Bryan carefully avoided calling himself a fundamentalist and many of the residents of Dayton did not consider themselves fundamentalists, Mencken pointedly ignored such niceties. From his perch at the *Baltimore Sun*, Mencken labeled the entire population of Dayton as "fundamentalist" and he pilloried Bryan as "the fundamentalist pope."[74] Less famous writers in the 1920s sometimes gave fundamentalism similar meanings. One writer in 1926 assumed that fundamentalism meant nothing more than a sort of generic psychological tendency, a desire to "drag man back from to-day's dawn to yesterday's candle-light."[75]

Conservatives also sometimes used the term as a synonym for a generic conservatism. One sympathizer defined a fundamentalist as nothing more than a person who "accepts without questioning [the] great ultimates" of life, death, religion, and politics.[76] To this writer, fundamentalism meant a laudable adherence to time-tested notions, in opposition to the modern tendency to chase after every passing intellectual fad. Some conservatives labeled themselves fundamentalists, but they did not necessarily agree on what that label meant. In North Carolina, for instance, just after the Scopes trial, a network of evolution opponents organized a statewide group to oppose evolution education in the Tarheel State. At first, they called themselves the Committee of One Hundred, representing all one hundred North Carolina counties. They soon changed their name to the North Carolina Bible League. The group proudly identified itself as a collection of "snorting fundamentalists." What they meant by the term included ideas such as local power, traditional Protestant domination of public schooling, and unrelenting, unapologetic patriotism. Beyond that, they could not agree on much else.[77] Eventually, the Bible League divided between "straight-laced" fundamentalists and "liberal" ones. Leaders of the liberal faction thought their movement should welcome any conservatives who wanted more Protestant religiosity in public schools. Their "straight-laced" opponents insisted that their group should only include those who fought for both more religious schools and more orthodox theology.[78]

As with any political or cultural label, the term became both a rallying cry and an insult, depending upon who was using it. J. Frank Norris insisted that all "true" fundamentalists were part of a "happy, beautiful fellowship."[79] To be a fundamentalist meant to share a set of notions about the proper meanings of religion and culture. In the wake of the Scopes trial, however, conservative US representative Thomas L. Blanton of Texas complained that "the newspapers make fun of us and call us 'fundamentalists' whenever we want to inquire into what the children are being taught."[80] Critics such as Mencken and Darrow had succeeded in convincing a significant number of Americans that to be a fundamentalist meant simply to be isolated and ignorant. It meant those who stood in the way of progress. As one wag put it, the term must have derived from the Latin: "*Fundo*, or 'I make solid'; *Mente*, 'in the head.'"[81]

Although at least one leading fundamentalist argued that those concerned with denominational orthodoxy ought not to have gotten mixed up in the wider anti-evolution movement,[82] most of those who considered themselves fundamentalists—whatever they meant by that term—thought that the issue of evolution was both a symptom and a symbol of everything that had gone wrong with American culture. They considered it their duty to fight against the teaching of such a pernicious notion in public schools, from kindergarten through university. Why? What was so dangerous about evolution?

Don't Make a Monkey out of Me

Just as fundamentalism meant different things to different people in the 1920s, so too did evolution. To opponents, it represented at the same time a scientific theory, a path to atheism, a wedge for communism, and a stand-in for every other pernicious idea of modern American life. To its supporters, it symbolized a progressive age of scientific discovery, liberation from centuries of superstition, and a profound positive change in the ways humans understood their role in the universe. Just as with fundamentalism, few of the people who fought for or against evolution education at the Scopes trial and throughout the 1920s clearly defined what they meant by "evolution." As a result, people tended to talk past one another. Darrow argued that science ought not be limited. Bryan agreed. But they meant very different things.

To Bryan and many other evolution opponents, evolution was bad science. One danger it represented was a wholesale abandonment of real science in favor of a dubious new approach to knowledge. Bryan was determined not to give up the title of science to those who supported evolution. To that end, he joined the emphatically pro-evolution American Association for the Advancement of Science. Bryan insisted that the advancement of science did not need to be linked to the advancement of evolutionary theory.[83] Until the end, Bryan presented himself as the real defender of science. He called those who argued in favor of evolution mere "pseudo-scientists."[84] As he repeated in endless stump speeches, Bryan did not oppose the teaching of real science. "We do not ask," Bryan insisted, "for the exclusion of any scientific truth, but we do protest against an atheist teacher being allowed to blow his guesses in the face of the student."[85] As he often did, Bryan articulated here some of the shared notions of anti-evolution activists in the 1920s. Most insisted that they did not oppose true science. However, they objected to the inclusion of untested, unverified ideas about evolution in that category.

Bryan's claims to scientific status enraged mainstream scientists. One of Bryan's leading opponents in these years was the well-known Princeton biologist Edwin Conklin. Conklin disagreed with Bryan's understanding of the nature of science. It was Bryan, Conklin accused, who was a "non-scientific person." Bryan's mistaken activism in Kentucky hoped foolishly to "repeal a law of nature with a law of Kentucky."[86]

Conklin had mainstream science on his side. A few years before the Scopes trial, Conklin had argued what science had come to mean. It did not mean the kind of by-the-book classification that Bryan demanded. Indeed, science had come to represent the very antithesis of Bryan's efforts. "The *spirit* of science," Conklin argued,

> is freedom to seek and to find truth, freedom to hold and to teach any view for which there is rational evidence, recognition that natural knowledge is incomplete and subject to revision, and that there is no legitimate compulsion in science except the compulsion of evidence.
>
> The *method* of science is to proceed from observations to tentative explanations which are then tested by further observations and experiments, thus reaching general observations or theories. Scientific theories are not mere guesses but are based upon careful, detailed observations. . . .
>
> The *aim* of real science, as well as of true religion, is to know the truth, confident that even unwelcome truth is better than cherished error, that the welfare of the human race depends upon the extension and diffusion of knowledge among men, and that truth alone can make us free.[87]

All of these aspects of science, according to Conklin, were brought together in the theory of evolution. To exclude it from schools meant giving up on science, indeed giving up on truth itself, in order to appease a few loudmouths like Bryan. It meant caving in to Bryan's "medieval theology."[88]

Not true, Bryan argued. Conklin and other modern scientists had missed the boat. True science did not mean setting off in unknown directions in hopes of digging up an unsuspected truth. Instead, science meant "classified knowledge," the organizing and sorting of verified facts according to a proven authority.[89] The ultimate authority, according to Bryan and other scientific conservatives, remained the Scriptures. Ideas and facts that seemed to conflict with that proven authority must be rejected. Modern scientists like Conklin, Bryan believed, made the mistake of reversing the order. Instead of beginning with the truth and rejecting notions that wandered outside it, they began with random facts and mutilated the truth in order to fit.

Beyond arguments about the unscientific nature of evolution, conservatives at the Scopes trial and throughout the 1920s insisted that evolution education would lead to a breakdown in social morality. With evolution taught in schools, conservative activists insisted, children would learn that they were nothing more than clever apes. Is it any wonder, they asked, that people soon acted like animals? Fundamentalist preacher and school founder Bob Jones Sr. told audiences across the country that 1920s trends in education, including evolution, had led directly to the current "lawlessness in this country."[90] At the time, Jones could not have known that the college he founded in 1926 would become in fifty years the nation's leading hub for Christian school publishing, nor that his son and grandson would continue his legacy of strict fundamentalist education. But still he worried in the 1920s that without such educational havens, young people would fall with dizzying speed for the seductive "Perils of America."[91] Texas fundamentalist leader J. Frank Norris agreed. As the Texas state legislature considered an anti-evolution school bill in 1923, Norris assured them that they must act in order to save the social order. If they did not, Norris warned, if they "let atheistic evolution have its way . . . how long will it be until the recent incident in Russia is repeated in the United States, where professors met in the streets of Moscow and burned God in effigy!"[92] Bryan also grimly predicted that "all the virtues that rest upon the religious ties between God and man" would soon collapse as a result of widespread atheism if such teaching did not stop.[93]

In the eyes of fundamentalist Protestants, even worse than such social upheaval was the eternal cost to be paid. Evolution, they argued, led to sin and loss of faith. In short, one correspondent from South Carolina noted, "Evolution is the spiritual path that leads to Sodom." Sin and damnation resulted from any denial of the basic truths of Christian faith. Evolution, in this fundamentalist's understanding, was merely one particularly underhanded way to encourage students to deny those truths, in the guise of scientific theory.[94] Bob Jones told a story that dramatized this danger. In one of Jones's most popular 1920s sermons, he told of a good fundamentalist family that had sent their daughter to

> a certain college. At the end of nine months she came home with her faith shattered. She laughed at God and the old time religion. She broke the hearts of her father and mother. They wept over her. They prayed over her. It availed nothing. At last they chided her. She rushed upstairs, stood in front of a mirror, took a gun and blew out her brains.[95]

Was this cost worth the benefit? Was it worth being caught up on the latest trends in mainstream science if it led to such heartbreak and sin? Fundamentalists like Jones hoped to prove to their audiences that it was not.

Anti-evolution evangelist T. T. Martin explained how this devilish process could work. To Martin, "Ramming poison down the throats of our children is nothing compared with damning their souls with the teaching of Evolution."[96] Such vitriolic attacks gained the self-described "Blue Mountain Evangelist" much more public notice than the rest of his preaching.[97] For Martin, the Scopes trial was the highlight of his public fame. From his prominent bookstand on the streets of Dayton he peddled his book *Hell and the High Schools* and kept audiences rapt with his warnings about the dangers of evolution.[98] For those who wondered why evolution was such a pernicious idea, Martin described the path a student might take.

First, he or she would read in school a book like Harold W. Fairbanks's *Home Geography for Primary Grades*. In this classroom text, Fairbanks described the evolutionary history of sea mammals such as seals and whales. According to Fairbanks, "Their grandfathers lived upon the land ever so long ago. . . . They used to go into the water for food and at last they spent the most of their time there. Their bodies and legs became changed so that they could swim or paddle through the water."[99] According to Martin, young Christians reading this simple evolutionary tale would soon conclude that the Genesis story of creation could not also be true. In that story, God created humans and animals in roughly their present state. As a result, in Martin's telling, students must soon conclude, "Listen to those lies in the Bible!" If, as Martin asserted, Jesus vouched for the veracity of the Scriptures, then He must also become suspect in children's minds. Soon, inexorably, such teaching would turn a young child to atheism and, according to Martin, "That child's faith in the Saviour is gone forever, and her soul is doomed for Hell; and with your taxes, you paid to have it done." Public schools, in this logic, must prevent atheism; banning evolution was merely the single most obvious place to begin.[100]

Who Shall Control?

When conservative activists in the 1920s mobilized to fight against the teaching of evolution, they often had a much more ambitious goal than simply banning one idea. In fact, many leading conservatives agreed that evolution could in fact be taught in schools, if it were done as just an idea, not as scientific truth. Most agreed with William Jennings Bryan that the real danger came only when evolution was taught as a fact, rather than as just one idea among many.[101] Alfred Fairhurst, a fundamentalist educator, hoped that "both sides" of the issue could be taught in colleges.[102] But only in colleges. Younger students ought to be protected from the atheistic implications of evolution, Fairhurst argued. In higher education, he asserted, evolution "ought to be taught *honestly* and fully to the select few who have the ability to comprehend it in all its bearings."[103] Even the most ardent anti-evolutionists could agree that evolution might be included in schools, if it was done right. T. T. Martin, for instance, suggested a new series of textbooks, "graded books, from primary to university," each of which could present "fairly and honestly both sides of the Evolution issue."[104]

The veteran Bible teacher and school administrator James M. Gray of the Moody Bible Institute agreed that young people needed to be exposed to the idea of evolution. Gray argued that the problem with evolution was that it was usually taught as a fact and it was taught to very young students. Those approaches were dangerous, Gray maintained. It did not follow, however, that evolution had to be utterly excluded from schools. Just as young people needed to learn about the dangers of poison and guns, so they should be taught about evolution.[105]

But conservatives insisted that evolution as taught in 1920s schools was usually used as a wedge idea to weaken the Christian faith of young students. Many conservatives would have agreed with Bryan when he claimed, "Atheists, Agnostics, and Higher Critics begin with Evolution: they build on that."[106] The simple reason to oppose the teaching of evolution, Bryan insisted, was to keep "the religion of the school children protected."[107] From his Minneapolis headquarters, William Bell Riley called the "Evolutionary Controversy" nothing less than an all-out "war" that would not let up until public schools no longer harbored "teachers and textbooks that scorn Christian faith."[108] One Indianapolis women's group described their fundamentalist school campaign as a fight for more than just banning the idea of evolution. This group saw their anti-evolution goal as "the preservation of the public schools of America, the Bible and the faith of our fore-parents." Like other fundamentalists, these Hoosier women agreed that evolution was both part of this wide-ranging campaign and a symbol of everything it fought against.[109]

The wording of state, local, and federal anti-evolution laws reflected this much broader goal. Anti-evolution activists did not only

traditional moral values + patriotism [handwritten annotation]

want to remove one idea from schools, they hoped to guarantee that public schools reinforced traditional Protestantism, traditional patriotism, and traditional social mores. Just as the Kentucky senate had tried to ban any book that even indirectly challenged the Protestant faith of Kentucky's public school students in 1922, so other lawmakers hoped to ensure that no idea that might weaken faith could sneak into public schools.[110] In North Carolina, for instance, the Mecklenberg County Board of Education banned "anything that brings into question . . . the inspiration of the Bible."[111] This meant much more than just banning evolution. This meant ensuring the dominance of Protestant religion in all aspects of Mecklenberg County's schools. This meant maintaining schools as places where young people absorbed the wisdom of the past, not places where children learned to question received ideas. Despite this much wider claim, all of the people involved called these kinds of measures "anti-evolution."

Similarly, when the US Congress banned "disrespect of the Holy Bible" among Washington DC teachers, it attracted notice as an anti-evolution measure, although it included much more. For one thing, the law granted the Bible a superior status; it recognized the traditional reverence for the Bible as America's Holy Book. In addition, the rule also insisted that teachers refrain from any implication that the United States did not have the best form of government in the world. Such legislation combined anti-evolution agitation with a much wider militancy in favor of a certain vision of traditional American values.[112] *[handwritten annotation: American military?]*

Other state bills made similar demands. The language of a North Carolina bill from 1927 would have prohibited any notions that could "contradict the fundamental truth of the Holy Bible."[113] Another state bill that same year, from West Virginia, proposed to ban "all nefarious matter" from public schools.[114] In Florida, lawmakers considered a bill that banned "any theory that denies the existence of God, that denies the divine creation of man, or that teaches atheism or infidelity, or that contains vulgar, obscene, or indecent matter."[115]

The many meanings of evolution and anti-evolution in the 1920s made for confusing public debate. Conservatives wanted to protect their vision of schooling from the inroads of a host of novel intellectual trends. Evolution came to function as both a symbol of all those trends and one of the controversial ideas. As much as anything else, these complicated meanings led to much of the attention paid to the Scopes trial. For many Americans at the time, the trial would not just settle the narrow issue of whether a teacher could teach evolutionary theory. At stake was the much more fundamental question of what kind of culture American schools would inculcate in their pupils. Indeed, for many conservatives, at stake was the very definition of education itself as a process of transmitting knowledge and morals from one generation to the next. The anti-evolution activism of many conservatives in the 1920s represented a powerful articulation of the common theme of educational conservatism across the entire twentieth century. Conservatives fought in every decade and in every context for schooling that would heal and reform society by keeping pernicious ideas out and wholesome ideas in. By teaching students subversive ideas—ideas many 1920s conservatives embodied in a vaguely defined notion they called "evolution"—schools would lead America to disaster. But by blocking such ideas, conservatives hoped to save society by saving schools.

The White Elephant in the Room

Looking back on the trial that made him an instant celebrity, a much older John Scopes remembered that so many showmen and hucksters descended on Dayton, "Ringling Brothers or Barnum and Bailey would have been pressed hard to produce more acts and sideshows and freaks than Dayton had."[116] It must have been quite a scene. As with any crowd, the presence of so many reporters and spectators drew the attention of all those who hoped to capitalize on the attention. One white supremacist rolled in from Georgia "in a bungalow on wheels, wearing an opera hat, an alpaca coat, and an ancient pair of trousers similar to those worn by policemen." He had hoped to promote his theories of evolution and African inferiority, but not many Daytonians were interested.[117]

Indeed, questions about race and racism took a very different shape among 1920s conservatives than they did in later decades. In the years just before and after the Scopes trial, white conservatives showed very little interest in reaching across the color line. Most white activists seemed not to notice racial issues at all in their culture-war campaigns. In this sense, the educational conservatives of the 1920s differed markedly from later generations of American conservatives. As we'll see in chapters to come, white conservatives in the 1950s and 1970s worked hard to deflect accusations of racism. They often loudly showcased their allegiance with black conservatives as evidence.

In the 1920s, in contrast, as historian Jeffrey Moran has argued, white conservatives ignored the powerful fundamentalist and conservative impulses of majorities of African Americans. As Moran put it, "moral conservatism appealed to the majority of black leaders and ministers who ranged themselves in opposition to the same cultural changes that engaged their white counterparts." Nevertheless, Moran pointed out, "all of the major fundamentalist organizations remained lily-white during the 1920s."[118]

The thunderous silence on issues of race at the Dayton trial may seem puzzling at first. After all, Clarence Darrow had established himself for decades as a fervent anti-racist. In a speech in 1901, for example, he declared his goal of "perfect equality" between white and black in America.[119] He blasted the injustices of racial segregation and skewered the illogic of white supremacists who claimed to be superior to African Americans, yet demonstrated their moral inferiority at every turn. Just as he had built his career on defending the downtrodden and outcast, Darrow established early on his commitment to deflating the most sacred cows of American racial ideology.[120]

Yet Darrow did not accuse Bryan of anti-black racism. Why not? We have seen that neither Darrow nor Bryan spared any rhetorical effort in their confrontation. Bryan had to defend himself against accusations of ignorance and fanaticism. He had to defend himself against charges of obscurantism and stupidity. But Bryan never had to prove that his conservative attitudes toward religion and schooling did not make him a racist. The uncomfortable historical truth is that Bryan's ambivalence on issues of racial justice put him squarely in the mainstream of white American thought in the 1920s.[121]

The savvy Darrow likely understood that mainstream opinion among white intellectuals as a whole reflected a depressingly complacent white supremacy. Even some of those who raged most forcefully against Bryan and the anti-evolution campaign agreed that white America deserved its spot atop a justified racial hierarchy. Henry Fairfield Osborn, for example, the prominent mainstream scientist and president of the American Museum of Natural History, mercilessly attacked Bryan's anti-evolution ideas.[122] But Osborn also endorsed the staunch white supremacist notions of Madison Grant.[123] Indeed, among white mainstream scientists—the very experts who insisted on including more evolutionary theory in the nation's public schools—ideas of "scientific racism" remained influential throughout the 1920s.[124]

The point here is not that white conservatives in the 1920s were less racist than non-conservatives. Like non-conservatives, white conservatives in the 1920s did not agree entirely on the proper morality of racial issues. Rather, the important idea to note is that 1920s white conservatives felt no need to defend themselves against charges of anti-black racism. Such racism often found enthusiastic supporters among white activists of every political stripe. White racism in the 1920s found adherents among conservatives as well as progressives, among anti-evolution activists as well as among evolutionary scientists.

In addition to Darrow's reluctance to raise the issue, in spite of his own unabashedly egalitarian racial position, this complicated racial thinking among white conservatives in the 1920s can be seen in the debates among conservative evangelical Protestants over the propriety of supporting the resurgent Ku Klux Klan. As we'll see, the 1920s Klan interested itself deeply in issues of schooling and education reform. And as much as any group at the time or later, the Klan symbolized white supremacist ideology. Indeed, in the 1920s, the Klan stood for an even more narrowly defined white Protestant Americanism. Yet this virulently racist conservatism did not automatically earn the Klan the censure of conservative intellectuals. As coming chapters explore, this experience stands in stark contrast to that of later generations, when conservative activists worked long and hard to differentiate themselves from both the charge of racism in general and the tarnished alliance of the Klan in particular.

In the 1920s, conservatives of good will could respectfully disagree about supporting the hugely powerful Ku Klux Klan. William Jennings Bryan disavowed the group.[125] So did the influential Bible teacher James M. Gray of the Moody Bible Institute. Gray endorsed some of the stated goals of the Klan, such as increasing the role of the Bible and prayer in American public life. But he asked in 1923, "why cannot such a mission be carried out without secrecy, without increasing race and religious animosity, and without going about the country in disguise?"[126] Texas fundamentalist J. Frank Norris, on the other hand, eagerly endorsed the hooded order. In 1922, for instance, Norris defended his local Klan as "some of the most honorable citizens of Fort Worth."[127]

White conservatives did not agree on the issue, nor did they agree on issues of race and racism. In the 1920s, such disagreements did not force a split among the ranks of conservative activists and intellectuals. Unlike the experience of later generations of conservatives, activists and school reformers in the 1920s could simply muddle along, deeply ambivalent about questions of race and racial morality.

When the white supremacist from Georgia toured the crowded streets of Dayton, he expected to attract crowds of conservative-minded folks eager to trumpet the supremacy of the white race. He was disappointed. The huge crowds did not seem interested in mouthing racist platitudes. But Daytonians and the swarms of visitors did not hasten to disavow the Georgian's explicit racism, either. Most white locals did not seem to care about the issue. In Dayton, Tennessee, as in much of the nation, questions of race and racism went largely unasked among whites. Such questions did not form a dividing line between "conservative" and "progressive" as they would in later decades. White conservatives in the 1920s felt no need to defend themselves against charges of anti-black racism. Other issues interested white citizens in Dayton and around the nation. Many white Daytonians saw the event not as a test of racial justice, but rather simply as a way to increase business.[128] Local white merchants eagerly worked the simian angle. One butcher shop proudly advertised, "We handle all kinds of meat except monkey." A drug store proclaimed, "Don't monkey around when you come to Dayton but call us."[129]

The trial itself could not compete with the carnival outside. There was some novelty interest in the big-city defense attorneys. Besides Darrow, the ACLU brought in two other high-profile New York City lawyers, Dudley Field Malone and Arthur Garfield Hays. In order to avoid some of the inevitable charges of outsider invasion, the defense also recruited John Randolph Neal, a former University of Tennessee law professor well known for both his sharp intellect and sloppy attire.[130] And although Bryan stole the show for the prosecution, most of the real work was done by a team of attorneys that included Tom Stewart, the local attorney general, and Ben McKenzie, Stewart's predecessor. The prosecution also included the Hicks brothers, Herbert and Sue.[131] Finally, the team included local attorney Wallace Haggard and two second-generation prosecutors, Gordon McKenzie, Ben's son, and William Jennings Bryan Jr.[132]

The trial opened on Friday, July 10, 1925. The furious momentum of America's culture war over evolution bogged down immediately in the legalistic process of selecting a jury. The prosecution was satisfied with the jury pool, but Darrow asked each man—and they were all men—a series of questions about his knowledge of evolution and his relationship to Dayton and Scopes. Darrow guessed that every member of the jury pool desperately wanted a front-row seat for the big event, so he did not allow them to make vague statements about their neutrality. One minister, for instance, tried to worm his way out of admitting he had ever preached about evolution. Under pressure from Darrow, he admitted to general applause that he had preached "against it, of course!"[133] Darrow could only reject three jurors from the pool and he used one of his rejections on this fellow. Most of the questioning was repetitious. The audience heard their neighbors attest to their home addresses and occupations. They heard each man attest to his vague

knowledge of the events in the case. Even the allure of the famous lawyers and the presence of so many out-of-town reporters could not make
this plodding courtroom procedure exciting.[134] Wary, perhaps, of wan-
ing public interest, editors worked to spice up the coverage. The *New
York Times,* for example, proclaimed in a front page headline: "Jury
Includes Ten . . . One Is Unable to Read."[135]

On Monday morning, Judge Raulston quickly informed those
selected jurors that they would be excused from the courtroom.[136]
Before they could hear the evidence, the judge himself had to consider the defense's challenge to the constitutionality of the case. Neal
and Hays each argued against the law itself. Hays suggested that the
anti-evolution bill was as ridiculous as a hypothetical law "prohibiting
the teaching of the heliocentric theory."[137] Hays argued that such laws
were not reasonable or necessary. Therefore, they exceeded the authority of the state.[138]

But the drama of that Monday came when the famous Darrow rose
to lay out his case. As had his colleagues, he insisted that the case be
thrown out since the law itself was unconstitutional. According to Darrow, the law unfairly established biblical Christianity as the religion
of Tennessee. If it were allowed to stand, then any of the "bigotry and
ignorance" of the "sixteenth century . . . no matter how foolish, wicked,
ambiguous, or ancient" could return to Tennessee's schools.[139] Darrow
went on for hours, and then some. When he finally concluded, the audience in the courtroom and around the nation exploded with applause.
Even prosecutor Ben McKenzie agreed that the speech was the best he
had ever heard.[140]

The next day, Darrow hoped to press forward with that momentum.
At the opening of the session, before the jury entered, he objected to
the opening of the court with a prayer. Judge Raulston admitted that he
sometimes omitted the prayer, but felt that the large crowd and the for-
mality of these proceedings required one. Darrow, Malone, and Hays
grumbled at the heavy-handed use of conservative Protestant ministers
to create an "atmosphere of hostility" to their cause.[141] They asked that
other religious leaders besides those of the "fundamentalists" be allowed
to offer opening prayers.[142] In the end, Judge Raulston demonstrated
either a lack of understanding of the dilemma or a callous disregard for
the objections of theological liberals when he agreed to let the Pastors'
Association select the person to deliver each prayer.[143] In his report on
the day's proceedings for his Baltimore readers, Mencken scoffed at the
judge's scheme. The Dayton Pastors' Association, Mencken insisted,
consisted of only ministers who were "fundamentalists . . . powerfully

orthodox."[144] In his later reports, Mencken made no mention of the fact that the Pastors' Association ended up surprising everyone with their balanced approach; they alternated between conservative and liberal religious men to lead each day's prayers.[145]

It was not the only time Mencken would glibly assume too much about the conservatives at the trial. He repeatedly referred to them as "Ku Klux theologians" peddling "Ku Klux influence."[146] In reality, most of the conservative activists who supported Tennessee's anti-evolution law did not join the hugely popular Ku Klux Klan.[147] But Mencken was not simply spinning stories. The Tennessee Klan had offered very public support for the state's anti-evolution law, including a "Klan night" for a Billy Sunday revival meeting as the state legislature considered the bill.[148]

Burning Crosses and Red Schoolhouses

In order to understand the swirl of cultural issues at stake in the Scopes trial, we must examine the extent of such Klan activism, not only in Tennessee, but around the country.[149] In the 1920s, the Klan mattered. It burst onto the national scene just as controversies over the nature of education were heating up. In some cases, it was the Klan that led anti-evolution campaigns. In Oklahoma, for example, the state Klan pushed through a 1923 textbook bill.[150] The Oklahoma law provided free textbooks to all the state's students but it mandated that it would only pay for books that did not include evolution.[151]

And just like other conservatives in the 1920s, the Ku Klux Klan did not limit its educational activism to the fight against evolution. It also led the campaign to mandate the reading of the King James Bible in public schools. In Ohio, for instance, the 1925 Buchanan Bible Bill was seen as a test of the "political power of the Ku Klux Klan." The Ohio Klan threatened the governor with "political oblivion" after he vetoed the bill.[152]

In the 1920s, the Klan was a very different organization from later incarnations of the group that appeared in the 1950s and beyond. Most Klan activism in those later decades centered on white supremacy and racial violence. The Klan in that later era became famous for church bombings and terrorist enforcement of racial segregation, especially in the South. The Klan in the 1920s also embraced white supremacy wholeheartedly. In the South, it acted just as violently as and even more aggressively than later Klans against African American political and educational empowerment. But those unfamiliar with the history of the

1920s Klan are often surprised at the relative openness of the 1920s organization. Unlike later Klans, in the 1920s the group marched openly and often happily throughout the nation's capital and cities nationwide. Their parades seem almost quaint to later generations. Instead of dynamite or burning crosses, many Klan floats in the 1920s featured a "Little Red Schoolhouse."[153] In Trumbull, Ohio, a Klan parade marched to the theme of "One Flag, One School, One Bible."[154]

Also unlike later Klans, the 1920s organization was a mass movement. State and national leaders did not reveal their membership lists, but somewhere between three and six million native-born Protestant white men joined in the early 1920s.[155] More than 500,000 women joined the women's auxiliary.[156] It was even rumored that President Warren Harding joined the group in a secret White House ceremony.[157] The 1920s Klan had its greatest strength not just in the South, but nationwide, especially in Indiana, Colorado, and Oregon.[158]

This booming organization presented ambitious leaders with a powerful and lucrative possibility. Anyone who could keep the sprawling group together could assert an enormous impact on American politics and culture. Plus, each new member represented a ten-dollar initiation fee, most of which went to national headquarters. Add in exclusive contracts for robes, hoods, and endless ceremonial trinkets, and control of the Klan "empire" in the 1920s was too sweet a plum to remain long in the hands of its founder, William Simmons. In late 1922, a coup by his top aides replaced Simmons with the energetic Dallas dentist Hiram Wesley Evans.[159]

Evans knew he needed to consolidate this unwieldy organization. It was growing so fast it threatened to break into a shattered funhouse mirror of factions and local groups. The shrewd new Imperial Wizard reckoned that education had become such a central issue to conservatives in the 1920s that it could unite his loose organization into a controllable whole. It seems that Evans hoped to unite his followers by giving them a goal on which they could all agree: fixing America by fixing its schools. In doing so, Evans plugged his Invisible Empire into the long tradition of educational conservatism. As we'll see in following chapters, whatever their differences of ideology, religion, or strategy, conservative activists have agreed wholeheartedly that the place to heal America is in school.

This does not mean that Evans's school reform plans simply prefigured those of later conservatives. Far from it. For those familiar with the antipathy of later conservatives to the federal government, Evans's strategy may seem shocking. Unlike the conservative activists we'll meet in later chapters, Evans proposed a massive increase in federal power. To do so, Evans threw his support behind the ambitious Smith-Towner Bill.[160] If enacted, the bill would introduce a new cabinet-level Department of Education with a hefty hundred-million-dollar budget. That money would fund better teacher training and pay. It would expand basic literacy education to all. And perhaps most important, from Evans's perspective, it would pay for an aggressive new Americanization campaign in America's public schools.[161]

In the ugly rhetoric of the Klan, Evans promised one audience in Michigan that this new federal department would help the Klan to "take every child in all America and put him in the public school of America. . . . We will build a homogenous people, we will grind out Americans like meat out of a grinder."[162] He told a gathering of state leaders that this must become the central mission of the Klan. Evans insisted, "The greatest duty of America today is to build up its educational system. . . . You must see that some sentiment is created for education. . . . Any lesser program would be unworthy of a Holy Cause so far blessed with the support of Almighty God."[163]

Evans was not much of a consistent intellectual theorist, but he was no fool. He knew that Klan members nationwide had already made education one of their central recruiting tools. Education reform could adapt itself to local conditions and ideologies while still uniting the Klan nationwide. In different regions, the Klan had different specific educational programs. In Alabama, for instance, the Klan engaged in a double-headed educational campaign to improve public education for white children and weaken it for African Americans. Alabama Klan members used every political gambit—including both legal campaigning and extralegal terrorism—to limit funding for black schools, while increasing pay for teachers at white rural schools. In at least one case, the Birmingham Klan helped fund public education for whites. In 1925 the city schools had a budget shortfall. Without Klan fundraisers, white schools would have had to cut five days from their academic years. Thanks to Klan mobilization, white schools stayed open. Since civil rights remained tied to basic literacy, the Alabama Klan focused its effort on making sure public education reinforced a strict racial hierarchy.[164]

In Indiana, where the Klan came to control every level of state and local government, the organization implemented an educational program that combined better funding for white schools with elimination of Catholic teachers and principals. As sociologist Kathleen Blee has documented, women's Klan groups used gender-specific strategies to

intimidation of teachers

undermine the respectability of Catholic teachers. Women activists assembled "poison squads" who used the power of gossip to render life unbearable for targets. Evidence suggests that some Catholic teachers gave in to the pressure and left the profession. In other cases, as in one Muncie episode, Catholic teachers had enough local prestige that they could successfully resist such whispering campaigns.[165]

As historian Leonard Moore has demonstrated, Klansmen in Indiana also conducted campaigns against Catholic teachers and administrators. In Indianapolis, for instance, the Catholic president of the school board, Charles W. Barry, became the subject of Klan harassment. Local Klan leaders claimed that Barry had been ordered by the sinister Catholic hierarchy to make public schools worse. If public schools suffered, the Klan charged, Catholic schools would become more popular. More and more innocent Indianapolis children would become subject to the sinister influence of Catholic doctrine. In response, the Indianapolis Klavern managed to put its own ticket of school commissioners in office.[166]

In the state legislature, too, Indiana Klansmen exerted their control in favor of anti-Catholic school policies. One bill would have forbidden the wearing of religious garb for teachers, hoping to reduce the numbers of Catholic nuns in public school teaching positions. Another bill mandated daily Bible readings in all public schools. Plus, the state legislature tried to pass a bill forbidding any graduates of Catholic schools to teach in public schools.[167]

The Klan-dominated state legislature also pushed in March 1923 for increased public school funding. The new money would have paid for increased teacher pay and the construction of several new school buildings. Part of the goal of this burst of school construction was to allow for more complete racial segregation. One of the new schools, Crispus Attucks High School, would serve African Americans in a more thoroughly segregated facility.[168]

The Indiana Klan dreamed big. In addition to public school changes, the Hoosier Klan hoped to open its own university. Valparaiso University almost came under the control of the group in 1923. The Klan's goal, according to their newspaper, was to make the school into a "poor man's Harvard." Due to funding disagreements between the state and national leadership, however, the university plan fell through at the last minute.[169]

Another way the Klan's regional efforts differed is illustrated in Oregon. In Oregon, the Klan took the lead in a state law that banned all private education. Though the law never had a practical effect on schooling, the Klan claimed a symbolic victory when Oregon voters passed it on November 7, 1922. The law would, in effect, have made private schooling illegal. At the time, Oregonians understood that the goal of the law was to reduce the influence of Catholic education. In the end, the law did not change schooling, since the US Supreme Court ruled it unconstitutional in 1925. In spite of that fact, the law sent a chilling message to Catholics nationwide. Oregon's ambition was not unique. Legislatures in at least eight other states—Alabama, Oklahoma, Washington, Michigan, Indiana, Texas, California, and Arkansas—considered similar bills.[170]

anti catholic ed.

Just as ominous for Catholics, the school law passed by a significant 12,000-vote margin. Clearly, public opinion about Catholic education tipped Klanward in Oregon.[171] Klan members themselves claimed credit for what they called "our school bill." In the weeks before the election, after all, Klan activists had passed out propaganda in favor of the bill. They traveled from house to house distributing leaflets and pamphlets. It was tiring, Klansmen remembered, but it worked.[172]

Just as in Indiana and nationwide, saving the schools became a central preoccupation for the Klan in Oregon. Among the literature they distributed before the 1922 election was an anti-sectarian screed, *The Old Cedar School*. In this pamphlet, written awkwardly in the dialect voice of an "Old Pioneer," author George Estes spelled out the dangers of non-public schooling. If every group—from the Methodists to the Catholics—insisted on its own schools, the Republic would surely fail. Right-minded citizens must join the Klan in defending common education for all in public education. In case readers missed the point, a cartoon ran along the bottom of each page depicting a traditional Klan rider hastening—alas, too late!—to the rescue of the common public school.[173]

In Oregon and nationwide, Klan activists promoted universal public education as a solution to such sectarian infighting. By imposing a uniform white Protestant nationalism in public schools, Klan members hoped to symbolize that hoped-for unity. The most common symbols of that effort were Klan-donated flags and Bibles. In Indiana, at least, this symbolic donation often became nearly ubiquitous. Sociologist Kathleen Blee noted that "nearly every" Women's Klan in that state did so.[174] For Klan activists in the 1920s, Bibles and flags represented proper symbolic markers for wholesome public education.

unity under white Protestantism

For many Klan members in the 1920s, the fight against evolution symbolized all these educational efforts. Evolution represented the modern world run amok. To Klan members, evolution demonstrated

Robed and hooded Klansmen present an American flag to an Ohio school, 1928. (Courtesy Center for Archival Collections, Bowling Green State University)

the way so-called experts could insist on changes in education that did not adequately respect the traditions that had made America great. The Scopes trial gave them a chance to pit their best leaders against the worst the other side could offer. It would allow conservatives, including Klan members, to engage with every notion that had wormed its way into schools in the past generation. It allowed them to cheer on as Bryan gamely sought to stop this process dead in its tracks.

No Experts Needed

In Dayton, though, the gathering crowd of assembled experts took on a decidedly pro-evolution look. On Wednesday, July 15, the prosecution made its strategy clear. Since it could not come up with any of the experts it had promised, the prosecution team instead switched to a narrow indictment of Scopes's actions. He had broken Tennessee law by teaching evolution. Case closed.

The prosecution's new strategy was an act of desperation. Bryan had lobbied all of his many contacts in the vain hope of assembling a team of unbeatable scientific experts. He pleaded with George McCready Price, the leading fundamentalist scientist of his generation, to tear apart the scientific foundations of evolution at the trial. But either through accident or arrangement, Price was out of the country at the time. Price told Bryan he could not return for the trial. To be honest, Price told Bryan, he did not hold out much hope for any beneficial result from the hubbub in Tennessee.[175]

Bryan asked the Catholic anti-evolution pundit Alfred McCann to serve. McCann, in spite of his Catholicism, had become a favorite of the Protestant anti-evolution movement with his compelling book *God— Or Gorilla*. Not only did McCann decline the invitation, McCann told Bryan privately that he did not like the idea of the trial. To McCann, it smacked too much of mob hysteria. He suggested Bryan simply allow the people to teach evolution. McCann insisted that the flawed theory would soon doom itself.[176]

There may have been more to McCann's refusal. Catholics in the 1920s had a complicated relationship to conservative school reform. Even those who opposed evolution education could not forget the recent criminalization of Catholic education in Oregon and Klan-led attacks on Catholic teachers in Indiana and across the nation. Though Bryan distanced himself from the Klan, conservative Catholics like McCann still kept away from Bryan. The Klan, after all, had combined anti-evolution and anti-Catholicism in a potent ideological blend.

The tricky issue of Catholicism and conservatism would not get resolved any time soon. Conservative Protestants, including some of those who fought most ardently for conservative school reform in the 1920s, shot down the presidential ambitions of Catholic candidate Al Smith in 1928.[177] Due to Oregon's school law, and the many other bills like it, suspicion of their Protestant fellow conservatives lingered among conservative Catholics.

Due in part to this angry reputation of fundamentalism in the 1920s, most anti-evolution experts, like McCann, refused Bryan's requests for expert assistance. The only anti-evolutionist scientist willing to come to Dayton was Howard Kelly. Kelly's credentials were indeed impressive. He was a respected professor of gynecology at Johns Hopkins University. He had also become a prominent opponent of evolution theory.[178] Best of all, from Bryan's perspective, he was willing to testify against evolution in Dayton. However, Kelly admitted that other species may indeed have evolved. He only held that humans could not have done so. In the end, Bryan decided that such testimony might confuse more than clarify their case.[179]

Instead, the prosecution presented just a handful of witnesses on Wednesday. They included the school superintendent, two high school students, and drugstore owner Frank Robinson. Robinson testified simply that Scopes had admitted that any teacher who used George Hunter's *Civic Biology* would of necessity be teaching evolution. After less than an hour, the prosecution rested.[180]

The defense had bigger plans. They hoped to prove both that evolution did not challenge the faith of Christian students and that it was a necessary part of a modern education. To do so, they assembled a bevy of theologians and scientists as expert witnesses. Once again, however, the jury was to miss out on the testimony. When the defense called its first expert witness, zoologist Maynard Metcalf, the prosecution asked the judge to excuse the jury. Attorney Stewart argued that they should not hear this testimony about the nature of evolution until the judge had decided whether or not such testimony was admissible.[181]

For the benefit of the judge, then, as well as for the assembled journalists and gawkers, Metcalf laid out mainstream scientific thinking on the subject of evolution. As had other prominent scientists since the anti-evolution campaign started, Metcalf insisted, "The fact of evolution is a thing that is perfectly and absolutely clear."[182] There was no doubt among the scientific community that species had evolved from one another. At the time, however, scientists had not reached a consensus about the exact method of that evolution. As Darrow told the assembled court the next day, the defense hoped to demonstrate by such expert testimony that "men of science and learning . . . show first what evolution is, and . . . any interpretation of the Bible that intelligent men could possibly make is not in conflict with any story of creation."[183]

The prosecution did not agree. They argued that the judge must not allow such expert testimony. It was irrelevant, they insisted, to the simple charge that Scopes had broken the law. Yet Bryan still managed to work in an hour-long speech about the dangers of teaching evolution. For the court, Bryan defined the issue at hand as simply a matter of whether a small "minority" could be allowed to "teach that the Bible is not true and make the parents of these children pay the expenses of the teacher to tell their children what these people believe is false and dangerous."[184]

As Bryan described it, this question of control remained at the heart of the case. Should taxpayers be forced to finance a public education that fundamentally contradicted their most cherished beliefs? Bryan said no. He articulated the view of many evolution opponents when he described the difference at issue. As Bryan put it, "The Christian believes man came from above, but the evolutionist believes he must have come from below."[185]

The result of teaching evolutionary theory, Bryan insisted, could be seen in the recent argument of none other than Clarence Darrow. In his defense of Leopold and Loeb, Darrow had argued that the two young murderers ought to be granted some minor clemency for their diabolical murder. If they got such ideas in their heads, Darrow had argued, they only got them because of their education, of their reading of such philosophers as Nietzsche. And now, Bryan concluded, Darrow and other evolutionists fought to make sure that every student in America would be drilled in the evolutionary theory that gave birth to Nietzsche's materialistic philosophy.[186]

No experts were needed, Bryan insisted. It did not take an expert to understand this simple case. The members of the jury, Bryan insisted, were "more experts on what the Bible is than any Bible expert who does not subscribe to the true spiritual influences . . . of what our Bible says."[187] Experts would only confuse the issue and distract from a simple case.

Future conservative educational activists would echo Bryan's sentiments for generations, as we'll see in coming chapters. Bryan did not insist that true science was at fault. He did not argue that true intellectuals had gone wrong, or that universities as they ought to be were somehow suspect. But Bryan's Scopes trial strategy resolved a tension among educational conservatives from earlier years. As did other leaders such as Hiram Evans, an earlier Bryan had earnestly believed that experts with mainstream credentials would surely demolish the intellectual pretensions of evolution. Casting about for such conservative expertise and finding none available, Bryan strategically turned to an accusation that a warped core of intellectual pretenders had unjustly seized control of universities and some Protestant denominations. Expertise itself was not disregarded by educational conservatives of Bryan's day or later decades—conservatives did not deserve the accusation of a narrow "anti-intellectualism"—but the deluded false expertise of what Bryan called a usurping band of "oligarchs" would ever after be suspect among conservative educational activists.[188]

At the trial itself, Judge Raulston agreed with Bryan. On Friday, July 17, he ruled that the defense's expert testimony would not be allowed. The defense and their supporters threw up their hands. If they could not present such testimony, they had no more hope for the trial. Mencken concluded that "the main battle is over."[189] He had watched Bryan's fulminations with disgust. Mencken claimed to have been "genuinely staggered" by the ideas Bryan spewed in his early court statements.[190] Mencken could not believe that any educated person could hold such beliefs about the nature of humanity. It seemed just as obvious to Mencken that humans had evolved from other forms of life as it did to Bryan that such notions were impossible.

Mencken was not alone in his bitterness. Darrow allowed himself to scoff at Raulston's bias in the case, earning a citation for contempt of court. Come Monday afternoon, Darrow apologized and Raulston dismissed the citation. That Monday, Darrow also sprung his surprise witness, William Jennings Bryan himself. But before Bryan could take the stand for the interrogation that turned the end of the trial into its unexpected climax, Darrow objected to a large "Read Your Bible" sign near the jury box. The defense did not want it to prejudice the jury.[191]

America's Book in America's Schools

Just as Mencken insisted that he could not believe any educated American in the year 1925 could deny that humans belonged in a wider class of mammals, so members of the prosecution could not believe anyone could possibly object to the Bible. In the words of second-generation prosecution attorney J. G. McKenzie, when the time comes that people could no longer safely be encouraged to read their Bibles, then it would be "time for us to tear up all of the Bibles, throw them in the fire and let the country go to hell."[192]

McKenzie articulated a very common belief in the 1920s. Though religious minority groups continued to oppose the use of the Protestant Bible as part of public life, large majorities of Americans in the 1920s agreed that the Bible was a non-sectarian book. It belonged, they thought, in its traditional role as a mainstay of government and education. In order to give this belief the force of law, conservatives in the 1920s pushed for laws mandating the reading of Bibles in public schools. In fact, although Bryan claimed in his Scopes trial testimony that students should not be forced to learn evolution since they were not forced to learn the Bible, Tennessee had passed a law in 1915 requiring every student to hear the Bible read as part of his or her school day.[193] Many of the conservative educational activists who insisted on the removal of evolution from the nation's schools insisted just as ardently that Bibles must remain a central part of those schools. In order to understand the full range of conservative school policy in the Scopes era, we need to understand why the Bible represented such an educational panacea to so many Americans in the 1920s.

The push for such laws generally did not attract the same attention as the anti-evolution campaign. There was no big Scopes trial at which the issue of Bible reading in public schools took over every front page. It simply did not seem as controversial to most Americans in the 1920s. Perhaps for that reason, the campaign to mandate the reading of the Bible in every public school enjoyed remarkable success. Eleven states passed laws that mandated Bible reading as part of every school day.[194] Many other states considered such laws. Just as with evolution laws, local school districts tended to take action when states did not. Big cities such as New York, Baltimore, and Washington DC all passed mandatory-reading rules in the 1920s. One interested observer at the time guessed that about half of American cities of 100,000 or more passed such rules. Even more small towns did so.[195]

By the end of the 1920s, such Bible rules had often become irresistibly popular. For example, the school board of Atlanta fought bitterly over the question of evolution in Atlanta's schools. They eventually ejected a conservative board member who had become an unmanageable gadfly on the issue.[196] Board members insisted that they would never submit to conservative or fundamentalist control of their city's schools. But this did not mean that the board considered Bibles improper for public education. In 1929, for instance, one board member hastened to explain his vote against a new Bible textbook. That member, W. C. Couch, had voted against the new textbook. But he had only voted that way, he explained, because the textbook claimed to explain the Bible. He thought the Bible could explain itself. "I have never been opposed," Couch clarified, "to reading the Bible in the schools, to teaching it in the schools nor to buying the Bible for the schools."[197]

Fundamentalist Protestants zealously supported such laws. For fundamentalists, the Bible was more than just a healthy dose of morality. Many conservative evangelical Protestants assumed that the Bible had a supernatural power to convert souls to Christianity. The Gospel, in their opinion, could instantly and permanently convert those who glanced through its pages. One missionary called the Gospel of John "the most unique, the most startling, the most compelling, and most unearthly message that has ever commanded God's attention."[198] If students in schools could be convinced to read from the Bible, such evangelicals believed, they would be saved.

One book missionary told a tale of such literary power, one that repeated this common trope among conservative evangelicals. "A man was given a tract by the roadside," the missionary described, and "simply glancing at it, and coming to a hedge, he stuck the tract into the hedge; but it was too late; his eyes had caught a few words of the tract which led to his conversion."[199] Not surprisingly, those who held such a high estimation of the power of holy print worked long and hard to make sure every young reader would encounter such words. Book missionaries at the Moody Bible Institute of Chicago did more than just support mandatory reading laws. They shipped millions of Gospels and religious tracts to schools around the country.[200]

But even conservatives who did not believe in the supernatural power of the Bible to convert still agreed that it ought to be a part of school. The campaign to include the reading of the Bible in public schools, usually without any comment by the teacher and allowing for parents to exempt their children from the activity, carried almost irresistible momentum throughout the decade. Advocates claimed that reading from the Bible formed an essential component to the formation of morals in young people. From the White House, President Calvin Coolidge encouraged the campaign. "The foundations of our society," Coolidge wrote, "and our Government rest so much on the teachings of the Bible that it would be difficult to support them if faith in these teachings should cease to be practically universal in our country."[201]

Religious educator Luther Weigle of Yale Divinity School agreed. He argued, "the ignoring of religion by the schools of America endangers the perpetuity of those moral and religious institutions which are most characteristic of American life." Instead of a proper education, based on religious morality, American education, in Weigle's opinion, had become filled with "pseudo-scientific materialism and pagan ethics . . . sex fiction and shoddy verse . . . indecent shows and raucous jazz." Weigle warned that the increasing absence of Bible reading in public schools was the cause of the "pagan lustfulness of a world that is drifting away from God and good."[202]

Weigle was no fundamentalist. One student of Weigle's career has called him an "evangelical liberal," espousing a theology that set him apart from "the modernists to the left and the fundamentalists to the right."[203] Nevertheless, like President Coolidge and large majorities of Americans nationwide, Weigle saw his push for more Bible reading in schools as a matter of simple common sense. The Bible, in this view, was the foundation of morality. It spelled out a moral life, even for those who did not embrace the fundamentalist view that it was an inerrant book.

Another theological moderate, W. S. Fleming, campaigned for school Bible laws because society needed such laws to fight off the decline to both sin and savagery. Fleming was a former Chicago pastor who worked full time as the "field force" for the National Reform Association. He pointed out that most prisons provided Bibles for all inmates. To Fleming, that process seemed backward. It would do more

[handwritten margin note: Morality can 4 be rep. from ed.]

good, he insisted, to get those Bibles in students' hands before they ended up in prisons. Ohio's governor had recently vetoed a mandatory Bible school law. If Ohio had passed their bill, Fleming argued, "as her neighbor, Pennsylvania, did, with the same result, more than half of her present 9,310 convicts would now be law-abiding citizens."[204]

The Bible had a strong symbolic power. It represented for many Americans the essence of morality. As such, it could not be separated from education. Just as the younger McKenzie at the Scopes trial insisted that America would "go to hell" without its Bibles, so many Americans throughout the 1920s believed that the Bible must be a part of any proper education. If education meant the transmission of ideas across generations, then the Bible—as a sort of textbook of morality—must remain a central part of that education. By advocating for the mandatory reading of the Bible in public schools, activists in the 1920s tied themselves to the long tradition of educational conservatism. As we will see time and again in chapters to come, conservatives fervently believed that the content of schooling could determine the path of American politics and culture. In the 1920s, many activists insisted that the Bible embodied all that was right and proper for educational content. By making sure that young people heard the Word, conservatives assumed that schools would fulfill their roles as transmission stations of traditional morality. Students who listened to the Bible in school would grow into adults who understood basic issues of right and wrong. Such adults could keep American society on the right path.

[handwritten margin note: + good for country]

"Bumping Off the Defendant"

Nevertheless, the judge agreed to have the "Read Your Bible" sign removed.[205] It did not go far. Someone put the sign back up in clear view of the courthouse, along the side of the extra latrines that had been built to accommodate the crowds. But not many people on that last Monday of the trial likely looked in that direction. The conflict on the stage attached to the side of the courthouse was too engaging.

The crowd swelled into the thousands to hear Darrow and Bryan go head-to-head in Darrow's surprise questioning of Bryan. The outcome did not matter much to the legal aspect of the trial. As Mencken and other observers had realized, once Judge Raulston ruled out expert testimony it was only a matter of nine minutes for the jury to convict John Scopes.[206]

Darrow's interrogation of Bryan fascinated the town and the nation nevertheless. Regardless of what happened to Scopes, audiences across the country read and listened avidly to this contest between America's most famous skeptic and its most famous Bible teacher. Audiences listened to hear each champion articulate his vision of culture and schooling. Both men acknowledged that this case—and their clash on that outdoor stage—was about much more than the fate of one young teacher. As Bryan put it, the real question was "Who Shall Control" America's public schools. Would they be safe in the hands of conservative parents, folks who wanted their children to learn about science and culture, language and math, but all in an environment that encouraged their continuing faith in God and Country? Or would their schooling undermine their most basic notions of right and wrong? Would students be taught that they were nothing more than advanced animals scrabbling about on an insignificant rock on the edge of a cruel and haphazard universe? Or would young people learn that they had been created by a loving God as part of His inscrutable plan? Would children be taught eternal truths? Or would they be taught instead to question those truths?[207]

Darrow agreed on the stakes. As he grilled Bryan, Darrow declared, "We have the purpose of preventing bigots and ignoramuses from controlling the education of the United States."[208] For Darrow, allowing one sect to assert religious control over public schools meant a reversion to medieval obscurantism. Bryan and his cronies, in Darrow's opinion, sought nothing less than the imposition of a new Inquisition. They wanted to ban any notion they did not understand, and they did not understand much. Bryan and Darrow did not agree on many ideas that day, but they agreed that the stakes were nothing less than control over the nature of American education.

They were right. The Scopes trial brought into sharp relief America's cultural divide. In order to agree on what to teach in American schools, Americans had to agree on basic questions of the nature of life and the function of education. In the 1920s and ever since, those questions have evaded any satisfying answer. The attention paid to the Scopes trial brought together the leading exponents of two very different visions of schooling and allowed them to spar verbally in the courtroom. It promised to bring clear perspective into what had become murky water, water muddied by competing ideas about what schools should be doing.

The tumultuous goings-on in Dayton prodded the sharp-tongued H. L. Mencken to articulate his vision of what education meant. To Mencken education meant a process of disabusing children of cant and superstition. Education, in Mencken's view, meant teaching students to question their received notions, to examine every belief and every claim and reject those that did not adequately make their cases. Mencken's unbounded contempt for Bryan sprang from Mencken's belief that Bryan pandered only to ignorance. Bryan, Mencken accused, feared education, "for wherever it spreads his trade begins to fall off, and wherever it flourishes he is only a poor clown."[209]

Mencken's notion of the nature and purpose of education energized much of the opposition to conservative educational activism in the 1920s. The Scopes trial itself forced those who agreed with Mencken to articulate their ideas about the nature of education. Why did they want children to learn about evolution? Why did they believe that students could receive a good education even if they did not study from the Bible or salute the American flag? In the halls of the US Congress, Fiorello LaGuardia sought to make these ideas plain. LaGuardia, at the time representing his East Harlem district, insisted that students must be allowed to explore every idea, including evolution. When his Texas colleague Thomas Blanton introduced a measure that would forbid the teaching of evolution in Washington DC schools, LaGuardia pounced. He feared any motion that would encourage more "hysteria" about the nature of America's schools. There was only one way to ensure that students would be "safe in schools," in LaGuardia's opinion, and that is if they were "learning to think." Like Mencken and a host of Americans in the 1920s, LaGuardia believed the nature of education to be a fundamental questioning of received notions of right and wrong. In spite of the recent "wave of intolerance," LaGuardia insisted that schools must be allowed to encourage such authentic education.[210]

Conservatives such as William Jennings Bryan, the denominational fundamentalists, and the activists in the Ku Klux Klan all saw education as a fundamentally different thing. For conservatives, education should mean the training of young people in basic cultural notions. Students should be taught what was right and what was wrong. Students should be trained to behave morally. They should also learn how to read, write, and cipher. For such conservatives, evolution symbolized the willful abandonment of such ideas. Freethinking meant a loss, a willy-nilly abandonment of tested values. Young people were particularly susceptible to such dangerous notions. They did not yet understand the value of values; they had not yet incorporated the habits of moral Americans.

There was nothing new about such dangers, from the conservatives' perspective, but education had always existed precisely to inoculate young people against the allure of such seductive theories. By studying corrosive ideas like evolution and atheism, young people were

very much like early ed

→ conservatives → no free thinking

walking along a cultural cliff edge, heedless of the danger. Worst of all, in the 1920s students were positively egged on by commentators such as Mencken or irresponsibly complacent liberals like LaGuardia.

The Scopes trial forced both sides to articulate these complicated ideas about the nature of schooling and culture. It also demonstrated how widely the gap yawned between the two sides. Even observers at the trial walked away with very different ideas of what they had just seen. Just a few days after the trial, Bryan died peacefully in his sleep at age sixty-five.[211] The way commentators remembered his performance in the last big public controversy of his long career showed the divide between the two sides.

J. Frank Norris, the Texas Baptist fundamentalist, proclaimed that Bryan's testimony had been the "Greatest Victory of his Career." Bryan, Norris told his readers, had been able to outwit the scheming Darrow and help the Bible win the day.[212] T. C. Horton, a prominent West Coast fundamentalist leader at the Bible Institute of Los Angeles, agreed that Bryan had dismayed Darrow in his masterful testimony. Every witness, Horton insisted, had seen Bryan as nothing less than "a real man, face set like a flint, eyes lighted with a radiant glow, standing four square upon his feet, with Bible in hand, ready to fight for it, ready to die for it, for he had tested it, proved it, believed with all his heart that it was worth defending to the death."[213] Conservatives did more than just praise Bryan. After his untimely death, they contributed their time and resources to what William Bell Riley called a "memorial . . . a . . . Fundamentalist University, erected in [Bryan's] memory and destined to wear his name while time should last."[214]

Other observers saw something very different. One reporter from New York City noted that Bryan's testimony had been an unmitigated failure, an embarrassment for all those who might share Bryan's belief. As Darrow grilled him, this reporter concluded, "there was no pity for his [Bryan's] admissions of ignorance of things boys and girls learn in high school, his floundering confessions that he knew practically nothing of geology, biology, philology, little of comparative religion, and little even of ancient history."[215] Mencken was even harsher. Bryan's display, Mencken concluded, proved that Bryan had become nothing but a "walking malignancy."[216] Bryan's testimony in the face of Darrow's sensible questions was "frenzied and preposterous, and after that pathetic."[217] Bryan, in Mencken's opinion, had proven himself to be "feeble and often downright idiotic."[218]

When observers insist on such different visions of what they have just seen, clearly the matter at hand has not been settled. Indeed, one of the most perspicacious comments about the ultimate impact of the trial came from New York correspondent Russell Owen. After spending his days in Dayton watching the drama unfold, Owen concluded, "Each side withdrew at the end of the struggle satisfied that it had unmasked the absurd pretensions of the other."[219]

Activists on each side claimed victory. And both sides had justification. For their part, conservative school campaigns claimed long-lasting success. The controversy of the Scopes trial intimidated three influential groups susceptible to public opinion: politicians, textbook publishers, and classroom teachers. After the Scopes trial, two more states passed anti-evolution legislation—Mississippi in 1926 and Arkansas in 1928. Even when conservatives could not pass legislation, they managed to pressure state boards of education in at least California, North Carolina, Texas, and Louisiana to prohibit evolutionary material from their state textbook orders.[220] Harder to trace is the number of local school boards and school administrators who similarly opted to avoid controversy by banning the controversial teaching of evolution.

Even when district administrators and classroom teachers wanted to teach evolution, it became harder to find teaching materials that would help them do so. Publishers have long been famous for their political timidity. Once they discovered the potential market loss that could follow the inclusion of evolutionary material, publishers rushed to edit out such references. For instance, the new 1926 edition of George Hunter's *Civic Biology*—the textbook at issue in the Scopes trial—watered down its language. Editors eliminated the word "evolution" from much of the book.[221] Much of the content remained essentially the same, but the words made it much less clear to students, parents, teachers, and politicians alike that students were learning about evolution. For instance, one paragraph heading in the 1914 edition about the "Evolution of Man" became in 1926 the "Development of Man."[222]

Other publishers made similar changes. Henry Holt and Company changed Truman Moon's widely used *Biology for Beginners*. One edition, specially edited for "Texas" education, cut out three chapters about the "Descent of Man" entirely.[223] Students in other states could still read those chapters, but even their editions included significant changes. As with other textbooks, editors made changes to deflect potential criticism without fundamentally changing the books. They watered down language and downplayed the notion of evolution as a basic building block of scientific understanding. For instance, Moon's 1921 preface declared that biology was "based on the fundamental idea of evolution."[224] In 1926 editors changed this line to the "fundamental idea of development."[225]

The influence of the conservative campaign against evolution education in the 1920s lasted for decades. Textbook publishers in the 1930s, 40s, and 50s often continued to decrease the amount of explicit evolutionary content in their schoolbooks. They worried that nervous school boards at the state or local level would simply choose their competition if they included too much talk about it.[226]

Of course, even if publishers remained too timid to publish frankly evolutionary books, teachers could still teach evolution. Evidence suggests that many did. But many more read the lessons of the Scopes trial as a warning. Though John Scopes himself had little to lose by serving as a genial test case, most other teachers could not afford to risk their jobs. One survey of biology teachers in 1942 indicated the depth of this intimidation. The authors surveyed thousands of teachers nationwide and concluded that teachers taught evolution in "notably less than half" of American high schools.[227] Even those teachers who taught evolution often watered it down "beyond recognition" by pairing it with the teaching of divine creation, or by teaching that evolution did not include the origins of humanity.[228]

Just as interesting as the numbers of teachers who did not teach evolution were the reasons they gave in explanation. About eight percent incorrectly believed that their state had banned evolution education. The intense campaigns by conservatives in the 1920s may have passed anti-evolution laws in only five states and the District of Columbia, but in the popular mind they had passed many more.[229]

The survey gave teachers a chance to describe their specific reasons for avoiding evolution. Some cited instructions from their local boards of education or building principals. Others said that evolution violated their personal beliefs. One teacher from North Carolina suggested that evolution education was a "taboo subject to most people." A California teacher added, "Controversial subjects are dynamite to teachers."[230]

No matter what zoologists like Maynard Metcalf said in his Scopes trial testimony, evolution was not part of science for most American students. In their school campaigns surrounding the Scopes trial, conservatives managed to score a lasting success in pushing evolution beyond the boundaries of an education that remained largely traditional for most American students. Those traditions extended beyond the science curriculum. Most students in American schools continued to pray and read the Bible long after the fierce 1920s controversies. A survey by the National Education Association in 1949 found that Bible

[handwritten: religion still very much in schools in 60s]

reading remained standard in the public schools of at least thirty-seven states. Twelve states required it; the rest allowed it with or without legal permission.[231] By 1960, that picture had not changed much. A survey in that year found roughly forty-two percent of school districts tolerated or required Bible reading. Fifty percent reported a daily prayer.[232]

Long into the twentieth century, the aftermath of 1920s conservative school activism dominated American schooling. But such victories came at significant cost. To a greater extent than in the past, conservative activists after the Scopes trial had to contend with a new image as ignorant and unlettered. At the tail end of the trial, for instance, Bryan issued a public statement complaining of Darrow's unjust accusations of ignorance. Bryan reviewed his many academic degrees, both earned and honorary. As the US secretary of state, Bryan sniffed, he had met with "kings, emperors, and prominent public men." None of those luminaries had considered him "an ignoramus," the way Darrow had. Bryan insisted that it was not because his allies "lack intelligence that they oppose evolution." Bryan hoped, quixotically it turned out, to maintain an image of conservative school reform as urbane, pluralistic, and educated. But he complained that his enemies never gave him a chance.[233]

Bryan's lament may have been true enough. But it could not undo the damage Darrow's attack had inflicted. The conservative side in the Scopes trial emerged tarred with a lasting image as witch hunters, marshaling the forces of superstition and ignorance to keep real science out of America's schools. William Bell Riley struggled to overcome such accusations. As he fought in favor of Minnesota's 1927 anti-evolution bill, he tried to portray the battle as more than a fight between "experts on the one hand, and, as someone has said, 'organized ignorance,' on the other." Riley tried to appear confident as he insisted, "This is not a debate between the educated and the uneducated."[234]

Riley acknowledged that conservatives had been accused of believing in "'a flat earth' . . . 'an immovable world' . . . [or] 'a canopy of roof overhead.'"[235] But in the aftermath of the Scopes trial, many Americans believed that such antiquated notions did indeed make up conservative beliefs. In spite of the arguments of Riley, Bryan, and other conservatives, their movement was forced to grapple with charges that they represented only an irrational commitment to outdated traditions. After the school controversies of the 1920s, conservatives tended to assume more quickly that self-appointed experts would use their influence to undermine and subvert conservative ideas about education and schooling.

The tension of the Scopes trial, of Darrow and Bryan on that outdoor platform, symbolized and summarized much of this ultimate result. Bryan thundered that he meant to defend the rights of parents to control what teachers taught. He insisted that the function of a school was to teach children the three Rs without challenging their religious beliefs. Bryan concluded that "the hand that writes the pay check rules the school."[236] The crowd agreed.

Darrow relentlessly drilled down into the logic behind Bryan's beliefs. Did he not know the basic facts of science? Did he not understand the simplest concepts of anthropology, astronomy, physics? If not, how could he claim to be an advocate for education? Education, to Darrow, meant precisely the challenging of tired superstitions. It meant teaching students to question received wisdom, discarding the false and embracing the true. The audience agreed with Darrow, too.

In spite of the melodramatic setting of this epochal conflict, there was no real resolution. Everybody went home convinced his side had won. But that does not mean there was no result. Conservatives realized that their beliefs no longer functioned as the law of the land. They realized that they would need to organize to articulate and defend their notions of proper schooling. They realized that trends toward secularization and increasing pluralism could not be dismissed as mere New York fads. In order to save students, conservatives recognized that they would need to remain ever vigilant for threats to proper education.

CHAPTER THREE

Pulling the Rugg Out

Textbooks and the American Way

There was no judge, no jury. But the meeting of the Progressive Education Association on February 22, 1941, had the tense feeling of a public trial nonetheless. Nearly 1,000 people crammed themselves into the ballroom of the Benjamin Franklin Hotel in Philadelphia to witness the first face-to-face confrontation of a long-running school controversy. As the crowd had in Dayton years before, the audience in Philadelphia hooted, jeered, cheered, and shouted throughout the tumultuous debate.[1]

On the stage, articulating the aspirations of beleaguered progressive educators nationwide, Professor Harold Rugg made his case for progressive education, democracy, and his once-popular social-studies textbooks. Rugg pulled no punches. He had grown weary of defending his books, and this was his chance to take the initiative. The books, Rugg insisted, were part of the "modern movement in education." This movement was America's only hope, its only chance to teach the new generations the skills and knowledge they needed to "make democracy really work."[2]

By this point, the gloves were off. For the last few years, a coalition of conservative groups and activists had forced Rugg's books out of thousands of American schools. A loose and shifting array of patriotic organizations such as the American Legion and Daughters of the American Revolution, business groups such as the National Association of Manufacturers and the Advertising Federation of America, and conservative journalists such as Bertie Forbes and George Sokolsky had run Rugg ragged. They had accused Rugg of sedition and subversion. They had attacked not only Rugg's books, but Rugg himself. At this

Philadelphia meeting, Rugg relished his chance to confront some of his foes in person. Rugg did not hold back. Men such as Alfred Falk and Mervin Hart did not deserve to influence educational policy, Rugg told the audience. Such men, Rugg charged, must be treated as enemies of America, enemies of true democracy. "These men," Rugg blasted, "are not friendly enemies; they are enemies, enemies of our children."[3]

On that Philadelphia stage, Rugg's conservative opponents counterattacked. As president of the Advertising Federation of America, Alfred Falk had long complained that Rugg's books trashed the American way of life. Falk had been drawn into the controversy years earlier by his concern about Rugg's attack on advertising as propaganda.[4] He had cooperated closely with allies in the American Legion to have Rugg's books removed from as many American schools as possible.[5] At this Philadelphia confrontation, Falk accused Rugg of deliberately departing from the American tradition of education. The books, Falk accused, represented the first large-scale effort at leftist indoctrination favored by Rugg and other misguided left-wing academics. Not only did the books "represent a backward step in the progress of educational technique," Falk charged, but even worse, Rugg's books were "not truthful." They gave America's innocent schoolchildren a false and misleading picture of America's society and economy.[6]

The other conservative activist on stage agreed heartily. Merwin K. Hart, president of the New York State Economic Council, an anti-tax group, insisted that Rugg's attack on private enterprise was an attack on America. More fundamentally, Hart told the Philadelphia crowd, Rugg's "socialistic viewpoint" represented a misguided and pernicious attempt to thwart "human nature" itself.[7]

As had conservative educational activists in the 1920s, these leaders of the anti-Rugg campaign worried that Rugg's textbooks would warp young minds and pervert America's future. As would educational conservatives for decades to come, the conservatives on stage at this Philadelphia meeting assumed that school mattered, that textbooks mattered. If a self-appointed expert such as Harold Rugg tried to spew his socialist bile into America's schools, conservatives assumed, right-thinking Americans had an urgent duty to stop him. This was not a matter for polite and measured policy discussions. This was an emergency.

The confrontation in Philadelphia took place at the climax of years of conservative efforts to remove Rugg's books from America's schools. Not only Rugg's books, but a variety of textbooks came under fire for promoting socialism or anti-American principles. On the morning

What is American?

of the Philadelphia meeting, for instance, a *New York Times* headline announced that the National Association of Manufacturers had published a list critical of hundreds of textbooks. Too many books, the NAM study asserted, maintained an "un-American tone."[8]

Of all these purportedly subversive books, Rugg's drew the most ferocious criticism. And the attacks took their toll. By the time of the Philadelphia meeting, sales of Rugg's titles had dropped precipitously. During the 1930s, the books sold millions of copies.[9] One salesman recalled that the Rugg books used to sell themselves. Every school district, every teacher, it seemed, wanted to have these cutting-edge books.[10] When conservative activists began their accusations, the demand dried up. According to Rugg himself, his books had sold 177,000 volumes in 1939 and 152,000 in 1940. By 1941, that number had dropped to 40,000.[11] Between 1939 and 1941, school districts across the nation banned the books or at least debated the issue. From Binghamton, New York,[12] to Delta, Colorado;[13] from East Cleveland, Ohio,[14] to Cedar Rapids, Iowa;[15] from San Francisco[16] to Mt. Kisco, New York,[17] cities and towns pulled Rugg books from their school shelves.

The precise number of districts that did so is impossible to pin down. Indeed, some historians have argued that the anti-Rugg campaign was more smoke than fire.[18] In some cases, hype clearly played a role. For instance, one headline in the *New York Times* screamed, "Rugg's Books Barred from More Schools."[19] A few months later, the same paper ran a small item on page twenty-one, reporting that Georgia's State Board of Education had investigated the Rugg books and found them salutary and effective.[20] Such endorsements never attracted the same public notice as the flashy headlines about books banned, books burned.

But even with over-inflated expectations about the impact of the anti-Rugg campaign, the controversy had undeniably important and long-reaching effects. The books that had once been in the hands of up to half of America's middle school students, according to one estimate, soon became hard to find.[21] Part of this decline was surely due to the unremarkable life cycle of every textbook. After a number of years, most textbooks become outdated unless revised and updated.

But the more significant lesson to draw from the campaign against Professor Rugg's books was this: the anti-Rugg movement demonstrated successful conservative opposition to certain ideas about the purpose of schooling in America. Rugg and others had hoped to use schools to "reconstruct" American society in more collective directions. Conservatives, by campaigning against Rugg books, demonstrated the

Rugg → collective society

profound and powerful opposition in America to any such attempt. Even when the anti-Rugg campaign did not succeed, conservative activism demonstrated that significant numbers of Americans wanted schools to maintain and even celebrate the cultural, economic, and political status quo.

Back to the Beginning

The angry meeting in Philadelphia came after years of controversy over the Rugg textbooks. Though there had been scattered complaints about Rugg's books as far back as 1924,[22] the controversy only began in earnest at a school board meeting in Garden City, Long Island, on January 22, 1938. That night, retired army major Augustin Rudd addressed his local school board on the topic of the Rugg books. As had conservative activists before and after him, Major Rudd told the board that he had been alerted to the dangers of local textbooks when he had browsed through the books his children brought home.[23] At that winter meeting, Rudd insisted that Rugg's textbooks posed an immediate danger to American schools and schoolchildren. The ideas they contained, as the indefatigable Rudd told anyone who would listen, disparaged America's history, economy, and politics. The books contained what Rudd called "'weasel words'" meant to plant doubt and skepticism in the minds of young people.[24]

The Garden City school board agreed to investigate. But Rudd did not wait for them to act. Rudd was no stranger to combat, having served as a cavalry officer in World War I. When the Second World War broke out, Major Rudd would return to active service, eventually receiving a promotion to colonel.[25] Rudd engaged the textbook issue as he might have engaged the German army. After speaking to his local school board, Rudd marshaled every ally he could find. An active member of the American Legion, Rudd contacted the national leadership to enlist them in the anti-Rugg cause.[26]

Rudd also led the local chapter of a smaller patriotic organization, the National Defenders. At another Garden City school board meeting in July 1938, Rudd described his tireless activism in the months since the January meeting. He had met with the school superintendent. He had met with the social-studies department chairman at the high school. He had returned to the school board meeting to warn of the dangers of the Rugg textbook series. And he had taken his message to every news outlet he could find. The National Defenders encouraged all its members to mimic Rudd's activism. Prodded by Rudd's campaign, a reporter from the *New York Herald Tribune* contacted Professor Rugg to inquire. Rugg told the newspaper reporter curtly that there was no story; there was no controversy. "And there won't be any," Rugg predicted, "unless you make one."[27]

Professor Rugg and His Books

Rugg might have been too optimistic about the possibility of avoiding a controversy. But once the fight began, he offered an illuminating analysis of its roots. As Rugg wrote in 1941, "The nub of the attacks upon me is, in short, my social and educational philosophy."[28] The textbooks themselves had become a fixture in many American public schools. The controversy centered on a fourteen-volume series, six books for the high school level and eight books for grades three through eight.[29] The books themselves were not the issue, Rugg insisted. Rather, Rugg believed conservatives mobilized to block the progressive philosophy that Rugg embodied. On this point, Rugg was entirely correct. The controversy more closely concerned Rugg himself and what he represented than the specific content of his textbook series. Conservatives protested against more than just the textbooks; they protested against Rugg's intentions with these books. They accused Professor Rugg of hoping to convince America's young people that society and government needed drastic reform. Most conservatives, in contrast, wanted children to learn about America's past as a storehouse of glories. Rugg, conservatives charged, wanted schools to teach each new generation that society required radical transformation, while conservatives wanted schools to teach each new generation to treasure the wisdom of the past.

For many conservatives, any textbook from a leftist author would have been equally suspect. It was enough for many that red-hunter Elizabeth Dilling had listed Rugg as "pro-soviet" in her popular 1935 expose of American communism.[30] Many conservatives did not need additional proof. They did not need to examine specific texts closely by such an author to conclude that any of his works would be dangerous for America's schoolchildren.

Even those conservative activists who did look more closely at Rugg's career found ample confirmation of their suspicions. Rugg, after all, had consistently emphasized his desire to change society by reforming the schools. He had begun his wildly successful textbook series as a collection of classroom pamphlets from his work at the Lincoln School.[31] Since the early 1920s, in his pamphlets and other publications, Rugg had advocated ways to change society by changing *the act of questioning*

classroom practice. Schools, Rugg had written, must train students to be skeptical of received authority. It was the job of a conscientious social-studies teacher, Rugg taught, to teach students to question all received wisdom and come to their own conclusions. In Rugg's earlier work, he had encouraged teachers to abandon traditional methods of teaching. Teachers must not attempt to impose facts directly on students. Instead, Rugg wanted teachers to ask repeatedly, "What do *you* think?"[32] For Rugg, this was more than just a classroom method. It trained students in the form of democracy required by modern America.

Other textbooks, Rugg believed, taught students the opposite. In 1933, Rugg bemoaned the tendency of contemporary teaching. Most schools drilled students in the baleful "gospel of success," Rugg charged. Schools indoctrinated young people with the moral benefits of "free competition, laissez-faire, and the exploitation of your neighbor for your own profit." Instead of teaching young people how to become active participants in modern democratic America, such teaching turned children into "potential racketeers."[33]

But Rugg did not despair. Peter Carbone, the closest student of Rugg's social and educational thinking, concluded that Rugg's sometimes-muddled ideology often approached the utopic.[34] Carbone has argued that Rugg believed proper education could lead to a true democratic paradise. In the world of improved schooling, America could achieve what Rugg called "the highest order of social good . . . social purity . . . true social cooperation."[35]

Rugg was not alone in his progressive dreams. During the 1920s and 1930s, Rugg worked with a group of scholars who hoped that wholesale school reform could reconstruct American society in egalitarian directions. Based mostly at Teachers College, Columbia University, this group of self-described "Frontier Thinkers" wanted to make schools the progressive edge of a radically reforming society. As historian Lawrence Cremin has noted, during the 1930s this group of scholars became one of the most dynamic and influential voices for shaking up the educational status quo.[36] The group's most prominent members included Rugg, George Counts, William Heard Kilpatrick, and R. Bruce Raup. In 1934, the discussion group launched its influential journal, *Social Frontier*, with Counts as editor.[37]

During the tumultuous days of the mid-1930s, as the Great Depression ravaged the economy and radical social change seemed a real possibility, *Social Frontier* opened its pages to radicals on both the left and right. In one 1935 issue, Communist Party chairman Earl Browder contributed a somewhat jumbled article. Browder insisted that school reform alone could not solve society's problems. Yet he hoped that progressive teachers could use schools as their "special sector of a common battle-front" in the fight against capitalist hegemony.[38]

Scholars such as Rugg and his Teachers College colleagues often explicitly disavowed Browder's communist line.[39] Nevertheless, for many conservative activists, the willingness of the Teachers College group to publish communist rants proved their suspect ideological roots. Rugg and the others—whether they called themselves "Frontier Thinkers" or "social reconstructionists"—danced too close to the communist flame, in the opinion of many conservative critics.

As would every generation of educational conservative, Rugg's conservative opponents did not disagree with Rugg on one point. School reform, all agreed, held the key to social change. Conservatives agreed that Rugg could change society by changing the textbooks. But the way Rugg wrote them, conservatives believed, the books would change society in dismal and dangerous ways. As one woman complained at a public meeting about Rugg's textbooks, "Righteousness, good government, good homes and God—God most of all—Christ is on trial today. . . . You can't take the youth of our land and give them this awful stuff and have them come out safe and sound for God and righteousness. Are our homes falling down? Where are the altars in the homes?"[40]

Other conservatives seconded the notion that Rugg's textbooks could change the way young people understood their society. One critic argued that young people reading Rugg's books would soon be

> convinced that our 'capitalistic system' is the fault of selfish fellows like Benjamin Franklin and Thomas Jefferson who wanted to save their property; that the poor man wasn't given proper consideration, that in Russia the youth are engaged in creating a beautiful, new democratic order, that modern business is for the benefit of the profit-makers, that advertising is an economic waste, that morality is a relative value, and that family life will soon be radically changed by state control.[41]

Such conservative opponents of Rugg's books did not need to be shown specific passages in which Rugg advocated such measures. The fact that a left-leaning academic—a professor from New York City who had advocated using schools to radically change American society—had produced them was often proof enough.

Rugg hoped to use his textbooks to move society in his direction, toward greater central planning and more rational control by true experts. Conservatives, on the other hand, hoped to use schools precisely to thwart this "reconstruction"—to use the same power of schools to pass along traditional values of religion, patriotism, and economics. For many conservatives, the specific content of the Rugg textbooks simply proved an already obvious point. Authors such as Rugg set out to hurt American society. Any textbook written by such a fellow must be speedily removed from the reach of innocent young minds.

The Real Threat: Teachers College, Columbia University

As we've seen in Chapter 2, conservative activists had long looked askance at the claims of self-described educational "experts." In elite colleges and universities, such dubious experts seemed to have taken over. Many religious conservatives might have agreed with the warning of Texas conservative J. Frank Norris, even if they might not have used Norris's colorful language. Norris claimed in 1921 that too many college students only heard "the forty-second echo of some beer-guzzling German Professor of Rationalism."[42] In the 1920s, conservatives had worried that so-called academic "experts" could not be trusted to protect the faith of gullible and romantic young minds. But leaders in the 1920s continued to claim, at times, the alliance of the nation's educational experts. Hiram Evans, for instance, hoped that more federal influence on local schools would mean a deepening of America's conservative values. Giving centralizing experts more control of public schooling, Evans believed, would allow those schools to implement a more thoroughgoing Americanization program. And William Jennings Bryan assumed—before the Scopes trial, at least—that a significant proportion of scholars still gave intellectual priority to traditional faith and culture. He believed that only a handful of misguided pseudo-scientists would insist on the centrality of evolution. These conservative leaders from the 1920s worried about the status of most experts while hoping—sometimes hoping against hope—that enough experts still remained true to traditional ways of thinking.

In the 1930s, the conservative activists involved in the Rugg controversy continued their fraught relationship with America's array of experts. As in the 1920s, conservatives furiously debated the moral status of the colleges and universities that most experts called home. Some conservatives condemned America's entire system of higher education as compromised and subverted. Higher education as a whole seemed, to many conservatives, beyond saving. Experts peering out from the heights of ivory towers called for red revolutions and social reconstructions, conservatives feared. Other conservative activists discriminated more carefully. Higher education as a whole might not be the problem, some argued, but rather only those few self-appointed experts who unfairly dominated intellectual life with a skewed leftist vision. Either way, conservatives did not disavow the value of education or expertise as a whole. With some exceptions, they did not become the anti-intellectuals they have been accused of becoming.[43] Rather, conservative activists lamented the usurpation of elite intellectual status by a cadre of leftist academics. Conservatives usually continued to value educational credentials and expert status, even as they warned that most educational experts laid false claim to that title.

This anxiety about expertise often emerged in conservative rhetoric as nervousness about the state of American higher education. Among the patriotic activists of the American Legion, for instance, questions about the reliability of America's colleges and universities surfaced time and time again throughout the 1930s. In 1935, New York congressman and American Legion founder Hamilton Fish denounced the socialism and communism that had corrupted leading schools such as Columbia, New York University, City College of New York, the University of Chicago, Wisconsin, Penn, and North Carolina. Such schools, Fish charged, had become "honeycombed with Socialists, near Communists and Communists."[44] A less prominent Legionnaire voiced a similar complaint in 1935. "[C]olleges all over the land," Legionnaire Phil Conley warned, had begun teaching "the overthrow of our government . . . through subterfuge and through destroying faith and confidence in our democratic institutions."[45]

Among these devious elite schools, many conservatives felt, the worst of all was the institutional home of Harold Rugg and his Frontier-Thinking cronies, Teachers College, Columbia. By the late 1930s, tension between the American Legion and Teachers College had long been simmering. Since its inception in 1919 as an organization for World War I veterans, the Legion had prided itself on its educational activism.[46] In the 1930s, that educational leadership role came under stinging attack from prominent Teachers College voices. In 1935, Harold Rugg himself publicly accused the American Legion of a "devilish program against the American way of teaching."[47]

A few years later, Teachers College Press published a punishing denunciation of Legion educational activism, in the form of William Gellerman's *The American Legion as Educator* (1938). Gellerman, a Legion member himself and an instructor at Northwestern University, blasted the Legion as "one of the most powerful pressure groups in American society today."[48] The influence of the Legion, Gellerman charged, never worked for the public good, but only for self-interest. The educational policies of the Legion in particular represented "an expression of entrenched business and military interests which attempt to hide their true purposes under democratic guise."[49] Legion control, Gellerman accused, was strongest and most destructive in the field of education. Legion educational activism supported a cruel status quo by maintaining an obsolete system of education. The Legion vision of schooling, according to Gellerman, included little more than endless drilling with patriotic and religious pablum. Any dissenting opinions in American schools struggled to survive against the merciless and relentless onslaught of Legion control.[50]

Though the inflammatory book had been written and approved as a Teachers College doctoral dissertation, the leaders of Teachers College distanced themselves from Gellerman's work. Nevertheless, the leaders of the American Legion took quick offense.[51] National Commander Daniel Doherty leaped to seize the initiative. Gellerman's work came as no surprise, Doherty charged. Nor should it be paid any attention, since it reflected the warped and stunted intellectual status of American higher education. "Many of our institutions of higher learning," Doherty accused, "are hotbeds of Communism."[52]

Nevertheless, when Dean William F. Russell invited Doherty to speak to a summer session at Teachers College, Doherty quickly accepted. Even with all the bad blood between them, Doherty harbored private dreams that the bulk of the students still respected conservative American values. Only a small faction of leaders such as Harold Rugg, Doherty hoped at first, had seized control of the university and pushed it in subversive directions. Most of the teachers, Doherty optimistically declared in a private letter to a confidant, likely represented "strong allies" of the Legion. Doherty planned to use his speech to denounce the subversive tendencies he saw represented by the likes of Gellerman.[53]

Doherty soon learned to his chagrin that the Teachers College crowd could not be won over so easily to Legion principles. Doherty encountered a hostile silence when he denounced Gellerman. Nor did anyone applaud Doherty's call to support Legion educational activism. Worst of all was the reaction when Doherty asked,

> Why not rid this institution of such baleful influences? The name of Columbia is besmirched from time to time when preachments containing un-American doctrines emanate from those who identify themselves with this institution. It is time that Columbia, through the action of its trustees or other authorized body, differentiated between educators and propagandists. Do you like having it called 'the big red university'?[54]

Doherty did not get the reaction he had hoped for. The Teachers College crowd hissed and booed. Quick on his feet, Doherty shot back, "If it were not for the freedom and democracy in this country, I would not have the freedom to say these things, and you would not have the right to hiss."[55]

In spite of Doherty's defense of an open society, the American Legion had not hesitated to conduct a covert investigation of Gellerman. Before his speech in New York, Doherty directed the Legion's publicity director Edward McGrail to dig up Gellerman's incriminating leftist connections.[56] One earnest Legion investigator had sought out any information that might be used to discredit Gellerman, whom the investigator referred to as a "communist . . . skunk."[57]

Doherty had hoped that Gellerman represented an unpopular minority, even at Teachers College. However, bruised by the hostile reception he had endured, Doherty moved to a strategy of attacking Teachers College as a whole. Doherty argued in the aftermath of his New York speech that the problem ranged beyond Teachers College. Many other institutions of higher education had by 1938 committed themselves to "attacking the existing order and [to] disparagement of old and substantial values."[58] Such subversive strategies, Doherty concluded, threatened American democracy. Radicals such as Gellerman and his Teachers College cronies exploited young people with "emotionalized" doctrines and disgusting, unscrupulous anti-American propaganda.[59]

Within the American Legion, Doherty was not alone in his condemnation of Teachers College as a whole. Homer Chaillaux, in 1939 the energetic leader of the Legion's National Americanism Commission, refused even to sit on the same stage as Frontier Thinker George Counts.[60] Chaillaux's correspondence reveals his deep and abiding distrust of everything associated with Teachers College. In late 1939, Chaillaux collaborated with advertising executive Alfred Falk on ways the two organizations could work together. Both hoped that the combined resources of the Legion and the Advertising Federation of America could break Teachers College's grip on American education. Falk warned Chaillaux about the "well-defined group of left-wingers and educators" at Teachers College. All of these intellectuals, Falk wrote, had been "collaborating for a number of years on this huge project of reconstructing our society."[61] Falk worried that Teachers College had become the "well-spring and incubator of much of this [subversive] activity."[62] Chaillaux promised Falk that some Legion "friends" had achieved positions "on the inside at Columbia University."[63] With his well-placed spies, Chaillaux promised, the Legion could help. Chaillaux hoped to use his inside men to discredit Rugg and Counts personally. Chaillaux predicted that his undercover efforts would soon make both professors "sufficiently unpopular to reduce their present drawing power."[64]

For public consumption, the Legion published articles that charged Teachers College and the Frontier Thinkers with egregious subversion. To cite just one widely read example, in an article in the September 1940 issue of the *American Legion Magazine,* activist O. K. Armstrong called the *Social Frontier* journal one of the "mouthpieces of this Fifth Column attacking Americanism in the schools."[65] George Counts, Armstrong charged, taught teachers to seize power. Rugg was no better. Armstrong quoted Rugg's 1933 *Great Technology* to prove that Rugg and his social reconstructionist comrades intended to do more than just improve American education. Rugg, Armstrong quoted, wanted to collectivize American society. Rugg, Armstrong insisted, demanded that schools be used to promote a "new conception of government."[66]

Not all Legion leaders agreed. For instance, even the ferociously anti-red assistant director of the Legion's National Americanism Commission, R. Worth Shumaker, wrote in 1941 that Teachers College remained a "great institution." It was only the "Frontier Thinkers" such as Rugg and his colleague George Counts who had sullied Columbia's name.[67]

But such voices of moderation exerted little influence. Beyond the wide reach of the American Legion, other conservative activists and writers agreed that Teachers College had become the headquarters of educational subversion. One Seattle armchair pundit warned that the "John Dewey Groups" at Columbia University had taken the lead in subversion. Such thinkers, she warned, had long promoted "schemes to overthrow our American system of government."[68]

Journalist and publisher Bertie Forbes, soon to take a leading role in the anti-Rugg campaign himself, agreed that Teachers College was the epicenter of the 1930s educational catastrophe. By the late 1930s, Forbes charged, many colleges had become tainted by left-wing professors. In Forbes's opinion, Columbia University was "generally regarded as infested by similar faculty members." Forbes, for one, looked forward to an official purge of such "radical professors."[69]

After initiating the anti-Rugg campaign in 1938, cinema manager Augustin Rudd remained involved. By 1941, he had helped found the Guardians of American Education in New York. Along with advertising executive Alfred Falk and American Legion activist Hamilton

Hicks, Rudd concluded by 1941 that the root of America's education problem was Teachers College. The Guardians analyzed Rugg's
Teachers College syllabi and found them shockingly subversive. One
of Rugg's classes in Educational Foundations, the Guardians charged,
indoctrinated students in a dangerous left-wing philosophy. The class
taught a "denial of certain natural and inalienable rights of man."[70] Just
as Rugg did in his textbooks, the Guardians accused, Rugg trained
future teachers to embrace a thoroughly anti-American viewpoint. The
Guardians claimed Rugg's course syllabus pushed students to "admit
the far too rottenness" in American politics and culture.[71] Teachers College taught this philosophy to future teachers, the Guardians
warned. Those teachers then spread out across the nation and forced
this anti-American thinking down the throats of thousands of unsus-
pecting young schoolchildren.

teacher training

As the Guardians warned in a broadside pamphlet, the Rugg books
were only "a small part of a well-organized plan to wrest from us our
publicly supported institutions of learning and use them to proselyte
for this 'new social order.'" The problem, the Guardians believed,
was broader than Rugg. At root, such educational subversion could be
traced to "a large group of educators, stemming originally from Teachers College, Columbia University."[72]

Rugg himself noticed the overwhelming influence many conservatives attributed to the Teachers College label. In his memoir about the
controversy, Rugg paraphrased comments he heard time and again. "I
haven't read the books," Rugg quoted many conservatives as saying,
"but—he's from Columbia, and that's enough."[73]

The deep and abiding suspicion of Teachers College among conservative educational activists lasted beyond the time of the Rugg textbook
controversy itself. In 1943, by which time Rugg's books had largely disappeared from American classrooms, one angry Legionnaire wrote to
American Legion headquarters in Indianapolis to warn the Legion of
the ideological threat posed by Teachers College. In his long letter, this
legionnaire from North Cohocton, New York, called Thomas H. Briggs
of Teachers College just another of the "socialist fanatics of Teachers
College." Such fanatics, the legionnaire warned, had been very successful in infiltrating the institutions of American education, especially
including the National Association of Secondary School Principals.
Briggs and his comrades hoped to use public schools to foment violent
revolution, the legionnaire concluded.[74]

Even into the 1950s, the image of Teachers College as the center
of a web of sinister subversive progressives remained powerful, if often

unexamined, among conservatives. For example, in his blockbuster 1955 polemic in favor of phonics instruction, Rudolph Flesch accused Teachers College of orchestrating a long-range scheme to keep phonics out of the hands of needy children.[75] Similarly, when activist Mary Allen analyzed the 1950 controversy that engulfed the schools of Pasadena, California—a controversy we'll examine in the next chapter—Allen blamed the "Frontier Thinkers." It was this group of "Dewey's followers," Allen charged, who had destroyed the salutary influence of "traditional education." Once this group flexed its Teachers College muscles, Allen believed, more and more teachers and educators were "prepared to use the schools to introduce a new social order."[76]

For God and Country

The image of Teachers College as the headquarters of progressive education had developed long before the Rugg textbook controversy and lasted long after. Similarly, the American Legion had long exemplified the desire for greater conservatism and patriotism in American education. Though Augustin Rudd initially had to pull some strings in order to interest the national leadership in the Rugg textbook issue,[77] once the national leadership entered the fray it devoted its considerable influence and energy to the cause. But the American Legion cared deeply about broader issues in American education before, during, and after the Rugg battle. In order to make sense of the conservative side of this school controversy, we need to take a wider look at the American Legion's vision of proper education.

The Rugg controversy prodded Legion leaders to articulate their vision of proper schooling. For instance, R. Worth Shumaker, at the time Chaillaux's assistant director in the National Americanism Commission, insisted in 1941 that America's "great public school system" must be understood to be America's "first line of defense."[78] Only by making sure the teaching in such schools reinforced traditional ideas about religion, family, and patriotism could Americans be sure that their home front was secure. As would many Legionnaires, Shumaker attributed enormous influence to the school system. Throughout American history, Shumaker insisted, the social problems of the nation had been solved through educational reform.[79]

In a four-pamphlet series analyzing the dangers of the Rugg books, Shumaker expanded on this theme. The goal of education, Shumaker repeated, was not to teach students to question established truths. Rather, Shumaker insisted, "All textbooks should inculcate in the

Youth of our Nation a genuine love for America and a desire to protect and defend our priceless ideals, institutions, and heritage."[80] The first function of America's precious public school system, Shumaker argued, had been to defend freedom. Schools could do this by conserving "the proven values and traditions of our American heritage." Shumaker indicted the "so-called progressive, the liberal, or the radical group" for willfully misunderstanding this central goal of American education. Instead of training students to tear down, Shumaker insisted, to doubt and question, proper education should instead "bequeath upon each child his priceless legacy of liberty." Rugg's books hoped to transform American society from the bottom up. The books sought to inculcate a feeling of scorn for American tradition. In proper education, Shumaker argued, schools would do the opposite. Proper schools, Shumaker wrote, "should conserve and create, not revolutionize and destroy."[81]

Shumaker claimed that this vision of the proper role of schooling was widely shared by the "so-called conservative or traditional element" of society.[82] Indeed, among American Legion activists and leaders, this vision of both the importance of public schooling and schooling's proper goals seemed so widely shared as to be usually accepted without explanation. Throughout the Rugg controversy, Legion writers referred to this vision of the proper role of schooling, sometimes explicitly, sometimes by implication only. In one widely read 1941 article, for example, Legionnaire Hamilton Hicks insisted that for most right-thinking Americans, public schools existed precisely to teach patriotism. The notion of Rugg and his Frontier Thinkers that schools could challenge traditional patriotic notions struck such regular folks, Hicks wrote, as simply absurd.[83] Another Legion writer quoted with approval a speech by Dartmouth president Ernest Martin Hopkins at the commencement ceremony of 1940. Schooling, Hopkins told the group, had veered too far toward the inculcation of doubt and skepticism. Some "skepticisms," Hopkins warned, had been "allowed . . . to grow up unchallenged." As a result, Hopkins warned, too many young people "take liberties with things that are vital and venerable in our American way of life."[84] This sort of result could be expected, conservative Legion activists agreed, when schooling set out to puncture the traditional values of American society. Rugg's books were only one example of the way the proper role and function of schooling had been perverted. Of course, many Legionnaires noted, skeptical inquiry and reasonable questioning lay at the heart of good education. But by promoting an attitude that all traditional values must be cleared away to make room for truly modern thinking, Rugg and his ilk had birthed a dangerous innovation in

traditional values

American education. Instead of pulling down all the traditional values, schools ought to train young people in the importance of those values. Instead of lampooning traditional thinking as old-fashioned, schools must first ground young Americans in the home truths of patriotism, religion, and morality.

Whether articulated or left implicit, this vision of both the importance and the proper goals of schooling animated many conservative Legion activists throughout the 1930s and early 1940s. And unlike some of the Legion's less prominent allies, the Legion had the power to defend this vision of school. Both friends and foes agreed on the influence of the Legion. Just as the Rugg controversy leaped into the headlines in 1939, one Seattle activist praised the Legion's long educational activism. Along with other groups such as the Daughters of the American Revolution, the writer claimed the American Legion had "for years tried to arouse our people to the trend of these present educational policies but the people having been so absorbed with the novelty of the expression 'Progressive Education' have followed along and pleasantly accepted the derisions cast at our patriotic groups."[85] One American Legion writer, looking back from the vantage point of the late 1950s, concluded that the Legion's educational activism had been its leading public activism since its inception in 1919.[86]

Even opponents credited the Legion with leadership. Rugg himself blamed the American Legion, along with the Daughters of the American Revolution and the Veterans of Foreign Wars, for the unfair targeting of his textbooks.[87] One analyst from the Harvard Business School insisted in 1932 that the Legion's unofficial influence in so many aspects of American public life made "Al Capone a piker as a racketeer."[88]

Historians have agreed with contemporary partisans. William Pencak, for instance, has argued that the Legion deserves either credit or blame as one of the leading supporters of "traditional Americanism."[89] Similarly, in her history of 1950s anti-communism, Ellen Schrecker noted that Legion members "were among the most steadfast carriers of the traditional countersubversive ideology."[90]

Some of this immense influence resulted from the Legion's unique connections among government organizations. For instance, as Schrecker documented, by the 1950s the Federal Bureau of Investigation worked closely with the Legion to ferret out communists.[91] Even at the time of the Rugg book fight, the Legion and its activists commanded enough respect among government leaders to receive direct communication from the US Senate about educational matters of interest to the Legion.[92] Such courtesies from the highest levels of federal

gov Conn to Legion

government demonstrated both the political pull of the Legion and its extensive network of powerful connections.

In the anti-Rugg fight, as in much of the Legion's anti-subversive activism, the Americanism Commission played a leading role. This commission had been established in 1919 to "foster the teaching of Americanism in all schools" and to "combat all anti-American tendencies, activities and propaganda."[93] However, throughout the Rugg ordeal and long after, the Legion as a whole officially endorsed the work of this aggressive commission.[94]

Such official endorsement, however, does not mean that the Legion was ever unanimous in its antagonism to the Rugg books or other supposedly subversive school materials. As William Pencak has noted, several local posts insisted on their support for the Rugg books, most notably the Willard Straight Post in Manhattan.[95] Even before the Rugg battle, a group of Legion educators joined together to form the Legion Schoolmasters. This group, founded in 1936, hoped to assert an explicitly progressive vision for Legion teachers and parents. Instead of schools that drilled student in patriotic orthodoxy, Schoolmasters leader Walter B. Townsend argued, Legionnaires should promote the teaching of both sides of every issue, encouraging students to make up their own minds. There was no love lost between the leaders of these internal Legion factions. As Townsend once said of Americanism Commission leader Homer Chaillaux, "Homer knows that I hope he gets run over or dies."[96]

For progressive Legionnaires such as Townsend, Chaillaux made a tempting target. As head of the Americanism Commission since 1934, Chaillaux exerted significant influence in maintaining the Legion's status as an aggressively anti-subversive organization. Chaillaux had been a Legion leader in Southern California, coming to national attention for his violent strike-breaking efforts in the region. William Pencak has argued that Chaillaux's tireless energy and leadership helped account for the Legion's shift in a conservative direction in the 1930s.[97]

For Chaillaux, defense of American traditions required energetic commitment to the cause of American education. In 1934, for instance, Chaillaux warned Legionnaires of a looming "Crisis in Education." Only the Legion, Chaillaux argued, had the resources to combat widespread educational subversion. Such subversion did not limit itself to formal schools, and neither could the Legion, Chaillaux believed. Chaillaux praised the Legion's wide-ranging program of healthy activities for young people, including baseball leagues, military training in public schools, Boy Scout groups, citizenship classes, and school

= providing out of school activities

awards. However, Chaillaux warned of a range of "subversive activities" among young people. Groups such as the Young Pioneers, the International Economic Conference of Students, the Industrial Unions, the American Civil Liberties Union, and others, Chaillaux insisted, menaced America's gullible children both inside and outside of schools. The solution must be twofold, Chaillaux argued in a 1934 circular. The Legion must expand its own programs. But the Legion must also get more aggressive toward subversives. Every convicted radical, Chaillaux urged, should be punished in a new network of hard-labor camps.[98]

For Chaillaux and other conservative activists within the American Legion, digging out subversive teachers and textbooks formed only one part of effective educational activism. In order to save American society, Legion activists hoped to influence education in a variety of ways. Many local posts continued throughout the 1930s and into the World War II years to support a wide range of activities for young people, including Sons of the American Legion clubs, baseball teams, marching bands, and other activities. As one leader from Wausau, Wisconsin, put it in 1935, a local Sons of the American Legion squadron was "the best means . . . to combat the subversive teachings handed out to youngsters."[99]

These efforts to reach young people inside and outside of school continued a tradition of Legion counter-subversive efforts among young people. One Legion leader warned in 1930 that communists thrived on the "negative energy" of traditional Legion anti-communist campaigns.[100] Instead, this writer insisted, Legion activists could organize youth activities to offer positive options for youth vulnerable to communist influence. By organizing baseball teams and youth military-drill groups, the Legion could "win and hold the confidence of our boys." As this writer warned, when communist propagandists

> Scattered literature . . . to teach [youth] disrespect for parental authority, let us preach the doctrine of love of parents and love of home. While the communist ridicules the ethics of religion, let us teach its beauty and comfort and hope. While the communist preaches its cowardly philosophy of dissipating the fruits of labor and capital, let us strive to inculcate the manly principles of energy, ambition and thrift in the hearts of our people.[101]

This writer insisted the Legion must conduct a wide-ranging campaign to secure the loyalty and traditional values of young people nationwide. In his opinion, formal schooling must also be part of this program. The communist agent, the writer warned, "gathers up boys

ed for whom and for what purpose

and girls and sends them to colleges and universities of his own endowment for the purpose of making teachers of communism and atheism out of them." In response, the Legion should promote more widespread "patriotic and religious education." If all young people could receive such an education, the pamphlet concluded, "the schools and pulpits of tomorrow will be filled with right-thinking men and women."[102]

As this pamphlet urged, Legion educational activism throughout the 1930s focused on both formal and informal education of young people. The most prominent formal education program by the time of the Rugg book controversy was the Legion's co-sponsorship of American Education Week. This program, jointly run with the National Education Association, started in 1921 and continued through the 1950s.[103] The structure and themes of these education weeks changed along with changing times. In 1924, for instance, the program for education week suggested that all religious "ministers" participate by preaching a sermon on education. The slogan for Sunday, November 23, 1924, proclaimed, "A Godly nation cannot fail."[104] By 1938, the implicit Protestant theology of American Education Week had disappeared, in favor of a new theme appropriate for a Depression-wracked nation. In that week, the Legion and the National Education Association urged citizens to consider "Education for Tomorrow's America."[105] By 1939, the Legion insisted that Education Week could be used to counter "un-American activities in the schools."[106] In 1941, as the world roiled in bloody conflict, Legion planners had transformed the theme for Education Week's Sunday into the timely "Seeking World Order."[107]

In addition to support for Education Week, the American Legion also sponsored student contests aimed at promoting traditional patriotic values. In 1938, for example, the Legion began a national annual oratorical contest about the Constitution. In its first year, the contest attracted 4,000 participants.[108] In just two years, according to Homer Chaillaux, the number of participants climbed to 62,000.[109] In these contests, students were required to prepare a twelve-minute address on patriotic topics. In 1938, the theme was the Bill of Rights.[110] The winner, John Janson of Phoenix, Arizona, claimed his prize of a four-day educational tour of Washington DC for his address, "The Need for Government Reorganization."[111]

The Legion also hoped its student essay contests could encourage patriotic feelings among young people. Winning essays often articulated a sentimental patriotism coupled with an ardent anti-subversion. One winner from 1939 expressed typical sentiments. Its author, high school student Loraine Heit from Wisconsin, declared that looking at a map of the United States "gives me a thrill!" Even in this "free country," however, Heit warned, citizens must be on the lookout for "those who will criticize and tear down our ideals and laws." Criticism, Heit wrote in an oft-repeated theme, was a wonderful part of the American tradition of free speech. But subversives made only "a destructive criticism; hindering, instead of helping, our lawmakers."[112]

The Legion also awarded Legion Medals to students who displayed "patriotism and good citizenship in the schools."[113] During the time of the Rugg controversy, Legion leaders hoped these medals could serve as rewards for students who embodied the Legion's vision of proper education. National Americanism Commission leaders shared one letter from a Florida award winner. This young woman, Corinna Belle Gerhart, exemplified the goals and successes of the medal program. Gerhart wrote to her state Legion leaders to thank them for her medal. She explained that her family did not have a lot of money. She had to work hard for all of her accomplishments. She appreciated the Legion support. Thanks to her award, she reported, she was awarded a college scholarship.[114]

In the era of the Rugg book controversy, the Legion selected its medal winners according to a list of moral qualities, including responsibility, thoughtfulness, emotional stability, scholarship, and morality. The Legion distributed a rubric for proposed award winners to public schools nationwide. Teachers were asked to rank nominated students in ten categories, from "very weak" to "superior." For example, in one category, a student who "would cheat to win or to better his position" should be marked as "very weak," while someone with a "clearly defined sense of right and wrong; unswerving in his allegiance" could be marked "superior."[115]

These efforts to promote patriotism, hard work, and traditional values among America's youth did not start only with the advent of the tough times of the 1930s. Long before Legionnaires complained about the subversion of Rugg's social-studies books, before they began oratory competitions or patriotic student awards, the Legion had sponsored a patriotic school history textbook of its own. One legionnaire, Frank Samuel, remembered discussions about such a book as early as 1922. Samuel recalled in 1928 that the Legion had resolved in 1922 to sponsor its own textbook for United States history. Too many textbooks, the Legion had concluded, "contain misrepresentation of American history." In 1922, at least according to Samuel's recollection, the Legion had condemned "any attempt at un-American propaganda or misrepresentation in our school text books."[116]

one united national story [handwritten annotation]

Legion leaders contacted Charles F. Horne, a professor of English at City College of New York. As the Legion's U.S. History Textbook Committee claimed in 1925, the Legion wanted a book that would accomplish four main goals. First, a proper textbook should tell one united national story, not a story of state or sectional history. As the Textbook Committee claimed in their 1925 pamphlet, "As young Americans 'over there' our Legionnaires learned the heart-warming fact that Americans are really brothers." Children in Maine should learn the same US history as children in Texas, and that story should value the contributions of both.[117] Second, a good textbook must also be scrupulously accurate, this pamphlet explained.[118] At the same time, a good book must be "brave" enough to confront and discuss controversial issues.[119] Finally, and most important, a good textbook should build "character."[120] Too often, the Legion brochure lamented, young people "grow up ignorant or anarchistic or otherwise 'destructive,'" and such youth would not preserve a healthy society. The proper teaching of history, the Legion brochure argued, must teach, despite "occasional mistakes," that American history has been "so glorious that its proper study must inspire any child to patriotism."[121]

Patriotism despite few mis. [handwritten annotation]

The new two-volume text appeared in a preliminary draft in 1925 and was published in its final form the next year. *The Story of Our American People* earned some instant praise from conservatives who had long fretted about the deplorable state of most history textbooks. Walter M. Pierce, for example, in 1926 the Klan-backed governor of Oregon, dashed off a letter to Professor Horne. The new volumes, Governor Pierce gushed, represented "the finest history of early America that we have ever had."[122] Similarly, a past state Legion leader from Kansas, Theodore Gardner, predicted the books would be enthusiastically embraced by "the loyal and liberty-loving people of our country." Another fan praised the books for defending so vigorously "the spirit of American patriotism."[123]

However, critical readers both inside and outside the American Legion soon offered harsher reviews. Writing in the pages of *Harper's Magazine,* historian Harold Underwood Faulkner blasted Horne's books as "perverted American history." No professional historian, Faulkner sniffed, would have produced such drivel. The books represented nothing more than a "bombastic eulogy of all things American."[124] They could not even be criticized on historical grounds, Faulkner claimed, since the books did not really constitute a history. Worse, the books were intended to "produce a bigoted and stereotyped nationalism . . . a deplorable subservience to the rule of ignorance."[125]

If such harsh criticisms had come only from a few scattered left-ists, the Legion might have brushed them off. But before the books were released to the public, an internal Legion investigative committee offered an equally harsh review. This special committee concluded that the text was "filled with incomplete and inaccurate statements."[126] In addition, the style of the books did not seem likely to appeal to twelve- and thirteen-year-old students. Worst of all, the tone of the book seemed unnecessarily provocative to the committee. In the investigators' opinion, the text would "subject the LEGION to unfavorable criticism." The patent anti-immigrant tone, the committee concluded, would make the Legion look bigoted and parochial.[127]

For these reasons, even before the Horne textbooks hit bookstores, the Legion withdrew its official support. National Commander John R. McQuigg agreed that the Legion would not receive any revenue from sales of the book. McQuigg also committed the Legion to correcting any and all historical errors before the book reached American classrooms.[128]

In the end, the Horne textbook series never appeared in any number. Even Legion leaders soon forgot about the embarrassing episode entirely. Though Homer Chaillaux recalled the precedent in 1937,[129] by 1949 one Legion writer suggested in apparent innocence that the Legion should sponsor its own two-volume school textbook. Such a book, this writer suggested, could replace boring textbooks with "the rich and meaty story of American history."[130] A few years later, in 1951, a legionnaire from Los Angeles wrote to the National American Commission to inquire about the forgotten Horne textbook effort. George Nilsson remembered taking part in the deliberations in 1925, but in the long years since he had not heard a whisper about the books.[131] The Legion apparently hoped that its wall of silence would erase as much of their humiliating effort in school publishing as possible.

With the passage of time, however, the memory of the Horne texts lost some of its bitterness. In 1963, the new assistant director of the National Americanism Commission defended the Legion's efforts with the Horne book. Ed Wieland claimed the Horne textbook had hoped only to "tell the truth fearlessly, preserving old tales of devotion and heroism, but not ignoring national errors." Wieland made no mention of the quick abrogation of Horne's Legion contract. Instead, Wieland emphasized the textbooks' laudable goals of diminishing sectional animosity and inspiring confidence and loyalty to government.[132]

Throughout its educational campaigns, this notion that schools and school textbooks ought to increase patriotism and inspire students with traditional morality remained central among American Legion activists. By sponsoring its own textbook years before most Legionnaires had heard of Harold Rugg, Legion leaders hoped to influence the stories told in most American classrooms. Similarly, the Legion's intense and varied activism among youth inside and outside of schools hoped to shape American culture along traditional lines. The alarm with which Legion leaders viewed the Rugg textbooks must be understood as an outgrowth of the Legion's fundamental belief that America's schools represented the "first line of defense."[133] Legion leaders shared the confidence of Rugg and the Frontier Thinkers that society could be formed by deliberate school reforms. And Legion members nationwide worked hard to be sure that those reforms would push schools and youth in the direction of traditional religion and patriotism.

The Struggle to Define Democracy

In September 1939, the Legion's long campaign for greater traditional values in America's schools gained an influential new ally. In that month, publisher Bertie Forbes took a seat on the school board of Englewood, New Jersey. Forbes's main reason for getting involved in local educational politics was his concern with the potential influence of the Rugg textbooks. "If I were a youth," Forbes wrote privately to the president of the Englewood board of education,

> I would be converted by reading these Rugg books to the belief that our whole American system, our whole American form of government, is wrong, that the framers of our Constitution were mostly a bunch of selfish mercenaries, that private enterprise should be abolished, and that we should set up Communistic Russia as our model.[134]

Once on the school board, Forbes did not waste any time. He denounced Rugg's books as threats to America's welfare. In response, Professor Rugg crossed the Hudson to Englewood for a confrontation in November 1939. The Parent-Teacher Association in Englewood arranged a meeting at the Cleveland School. Since Forbes did not attend, George West, an American Legion member from Haworth, New Jersey, represented the anti-Rugg side. Rugg told the assembly that he had repeatedly invited Forbes himself to speak face-to-face. Forbes's refusal to "use the old New England town meeting plan of talking things over and settling things face to face," Rugg accused, led Rugg to question Forbes's "sincerity and integrity."[135]

Rugg later recalled that his opponents turned the meeting into a raucous and anti-intellectual personal attack on him.[136] The opposition in general, Rugg said, were "authoritarians who are trying to censor American schools." Rugg assailed "the hate and ruthless determination which motivate the tiny minority who would rule our schools."[137] Rugg blasted Forbes as not a "true American"; Forbes's behavior was "destructive" and "unseemly."[138] The reason, Rugg implied in a moment of venomous nativism, may have been due to Forbes's "foreign birth."[139]

Though vicious, Rugg's accusation was true. Forbes had been born in New Deer, Aberdeenshire, Scotland, in 1880. He had worked as a "printer's devil" as a youth, eventually moving to South Africa and then New York City. He found jobs as a financial reporter and editor of the *Journal of Commerce,* then as the business and financial editor of the *New York American* before founding *Forbes Magazine* in 1916. His financial journalism had most influence through this successful publication and in his daily syndicated column, which Forbes authored until 1943.[140]

Forbes's quick success in the world of financial reporting led him to an enthusiastic patriotism for his adopted country. Forbes especially embraced the notion that capitalism and free markets had allowed America to become a free and powerful nation. Any idea that challenged those presumptions, Forbes believed, represented an acute threat to American greatness. During the years of the textbook controversy, Forbes often repeated a story about how he had first become concerned with the content and character of the Rugg books. When he visited a junior high school, he spoke with students who reported that their teacher had asked them if the government of the United States was or was not better than other governments. When some students said that the United States was the best, their teacher told them—reading instructions from her Rugg textbook teacher's guide—that the correct reply was "No." Several of the students remembered their teachers telling them, "There are several other countries that have as good a form of government as ours."[141]

Such teaching, Forbes warned, would derail the nation. In one of his syndicated columns, Forbes asked,

> Do American parents want their children taught such ideas? Do they want them to be inculcated with the idea that the United States is a second-rate country, that its form of government is open to question, that there are other countries more happily circumstanced and governed than ours?[142]

patriotism again

The danger seemed apparent to Forbes. Such teaching could never "inspire" young people with "burning loyalty . . . with ardor." In any time of crisis, youth raised with such negative teachings would fail to defend their country.[143]

In Forbes's opinion, proper education remained a strictly traditional process of information transmission. Young people received ideas from teachers. If teachers voiced skepticism, students would become skeptical. If, on the other hand, teachers spoke patriotically, students would internalize a necessary love for their country. Textbooks, too, could transmit good or bad ideas. Forbes wanted books more like the ones he recalled from his own childhood. Those books, Forbes wrote, "were strictly factual, not opinionative." Any negative opinions in those books, Forbes believed, would simply "poison our minds against our native land."[144] As Forbes wrote in 1940, books like Rugg's were "impregnating young America with their philosophy." Such books "subtly" presented young minds with a "jaundiced picture" of American government and economics.[145]

For Forbes, the connection was clear. The nature of education remained a transmission of information from teacher to student. With that understanding, Forbes concluded, the content of the curriculum became of vital interest to properly patriotic Americans. For Forbes, as for many of his anti-Rugg allies, proper classroom content must only reinforce positive conceptions of capitalism and existing government. What Rugg and other progressive educators viewed as a crucial training in the skepticism and intellectual engagement necessary in a modern democracy, Forbes viewed as "impregnating" young people with a deep scorn for the United States.

Given Forbes's acerbic and personal accusations against Rugg, Rugg took some personal satisfaction in noting that the board of education in Englewood outvoted Forbes four to one to keep Rugg's books in Englewood's schools. Even more satisfying, Forbes did not receive another appointment to the school board in 1941.[146] The entire Englewood episode, Rugg concluded, had become a "case study in democracy."[147] Unfortunately, Rugg lamented in retrospect, though the active, empowered, truly democratic citizenry in Englewood had stood up to Forbes's bullying tactics, too many teachers in Englewood schools remained "authoritarians."[148] Such teachers blocked their students from becoming full members of the democratic polity. In Rugg's opinion, the "strict disciplinarians . . . deny the democratic way, which is the hard way of tolerance, of opening the mind to all sides of a question,

[handwritten marginalia: what is the "right" view of US]

of searching for data and determining their validity, of undergoing the ordeal of group discussion and decision."[149] Such teachers refused to adapt their classroom methods to the pressing needs of modern democratic society, Rugg believed.

According to Rugg, Forbes encouraged this outdated authoritarian vision of schooling and society. Yet Forbes and his conservative allies often agreed with Rugg that the central issue at stake in the textbook controversy was the preservation of what everyone called "democracy." And all sides seemed to agree that education and schools remained central to the task. But the meanings of democracy, and the structure and content of the education needed to preserve it, remained the subject of an intense and vicious debate long after the Rugg textbooks had molded over on back shelves in lonely school district storerooms. For conservatives, a defense of democracy usually meant an adherence to traditional American values. To defend democracy, many conservatives insisted in the late 1930s and early 1940s, meant precisely fighting against the over-reaching "reconstructionism" of Rugg and his ilk. This struggle over the very nature of democracy took on very different contours from what historian Edward A. Purcell Jr. has called the "crisis of democratic theory" that occurred among leading social scientists in this same era.[150] In the battle over the Rugg textbooks, "democracy" meant either a training in skepticism and questioning or an inculcation with reverence for the values and traditions of the United States.

Rugg himself knew that his definition of democracy had come under attack. Yet he was resolute in his embrace of the term. In 1940, for instance, he told a reporter, "I try to sell democracy. I believe in it, and I make no bones about it."[151] In 1941, Rugg underlined his "profound admiration and deep loyalty to the historic American version of the democratic way of life."[152] Rugg insisted that his ideas remained the core of a "new education which could serve as the true implementation of democracy."[153]

Yet Rugg's repeated insistence on his adherence to the ideals of democracy rubbed along in constant intellectual tension with another central element of Rugg's educational and social philosophy. Just as he wanted students to learn a democratic skepticism, Rugg also insisted that the problems of society required the strong hand of "competent experts."[154] In 1933, Rugg had argued that his vision of social and educational reform would include both "scientific design by experts" and the guided, informed, "true consent of the people."[155] This consent would be educated by what Rugg called the "thinking minority."[156] Though Rugg consistently defended his right to call his vision of progressive education the voice of true democracy, the closest scholarly student of Rugg's philosophy concluded that Rugg never escaped an "autocratic ring . . . faintly audible in much of Rugg's work."[157]

Nevertheless, Rugg's notion that non-authoritarian classrooms had become a necessary, if not sufficient, condition of modern democracy was shared by many leading progressive educators. Boyd Bode, for example, in his widely read *Progressive Education at the Crossroads* (1939), argued, "A democratic program of education must necessarily rest on the perception that democracy is a challenge to all forms of absolutism."[158]

Similarly, leading progressive theorist John Dewey connected authentic democracy with his vision of good education.[159] Historian Robert Westbrook has argued that Dewey viewed democracy as "an ethical ideal [that] calls upon men and women to build communities in which the necessary opportunities and resources are available for every individual to realize fully his or her particular capacities and powers through participation in political, social, and cultural life."[160]

Philosopher Richard Bernstein has added that we cannot understand Dewey's ideas about democracy without putting them in context with Dewey's notions of "community life." For Dewey, Bernstein wrote, "the idea of community is intended to call our attention to the democratic virtues of active citizenship that are required to ameliorate the ills of rampant individualism of modern bourgeois life."[161] According to Bernstein, Dewey "felt that the laissez faire tendencies that he discerned in social and political life in the United States—and in much of modern life—were at once betraying and undermining what he took so essential for genuine democracy—a creative democracy in which 'all share and all participate.'"[162] Bernstein insisted that Dewey viewed the cure for the ills of democracy as always more democracy.[163]

In the years preceding the Second World War, as historians such as Edward Purcell and Andrew Jewett have argued, Dewey largely led the way in defining for a new and influential group of social scientists the meanings of democracy.[164] In these years, among leading academics and intellectuals, Deweyan democracy became, in Purcell's words, "a set of procedures for compromising diverse interests, none of which could be taken as absolute without endangering the whole system."[165] In other words, as Bernstein also insisted, Dewey's influential definition of democracy required a community committed to pluralism.[166]

This vision of democracy stood in sharp contrast to that of the conservative activists engaged in the Rugg controversy. At least among the American Legion, the Advertising Federation of America, and their influential allies such as B. C. Forbes, democracy meant nearly exactly the opposite. For most of these conservative educational activists, democracy implied the freedom to pursue individual goals within a traditional network of laissez faire economics. Moreover, for many conservatives, an ardent defense of "democracy" also included an insistent defense of traditional non-pluralist American culture, a culture that gave explicit pride of place to white Protestant capitalism.

For example, in 1935 one American Legion writer warned that the public schools had become caught up in "the cross fire of conflicting propaganda" over the nature of democracy.[167] Though the youth of the 1920s and early 1930s at first "seemed strange to us," this Legionnaire wrote, schools had done a good job in inculcating each recent generation with a veneration for the traditions of democratic society.[168] The lesson was clear, at least to this Depression-era Legionnaire. The world teetered between democracy and dictatorship. Public schools could easily tip the balance. In the end, this writer argued, "Preserve the schools and you preserve democracy."[169] Any change in schooling meant an abandonment of democracy, an abandonment of the American tradition.

As the Rugg textbook controversy neared, National Commander Daniel Doherty echoed this Legion sentiment. Subversive teaching in schools and colleges, Doherty warned in 1938, had become "the menace that exists to our democracy."[170] Tinpot despots and armchair socialists hoped to exploit the gullibility and idealism of youth, Doherty warned. All citizens must fix a gimlet eye on their local schools to be sure no such anti-democratic subversion took place.[171]

Some Legionnaires took this notion of democracy to an extreme. In early 1939, for instance, the Jersey City Legion post warned any and all leftists that they would be violently stopped. This violence the Jersey Legionnaires called "a lesson in democracy that you and your kind will never forget as long as you live."[172] For these activists, democracy could be taught with baseball bats and iron bars. Democracy meant a stern, even violent defense of traditional values, especially against notions of socialism or collectivism.

Doubtless John Dewey and other progressives would have been horrified at this traditionalist understanding of democracy. Yet the idea of democracy as a stand-in for traditional capitalist American society had wide currency among conservative activists at the time. Alfred Falk, for instance, casually equated "traditional American ideals" with what Falk called "our democratic private enterprise system." Falk believed that Rugg intended his books to undermine those ideals, to replace them with "alien philosophies and the principles of collectivism."[173]

For its part, the leadership of the National Association of Manufacturers argued that free enterprise was a necessary attribute of true democracy. In 1939, a private memo from NAM's Committee on Educational Cooperation warned that "free private enterprise" and "religious liberty" were both "inseparable concomitants" of democracy. Neither teachers nor textbooks, the NAM committee insisted, ought to claim freedom to "undermine the vital concept of representative democracy."[174] Indeed, the NAM committee believed that teachers must teach more about the benefits of private enterprise. Such teaching would be "essential to the continued existence of representative democracy and religious liberty."[175] The NAM committee insisted it did not want teachers to whitewash the past. Teachers and textbooks could and should point out "the defects of private enterprise." But those defects should not diminish the status of private enterprise, the committee concluded, as "an essential element in the preservation of representative democracy and religious freedom."[176]

As the Rugg book controversy heated up, conservative activists grew more explicit about their meanings of democracy, and more insistent that their vision of democracy must triumph over Rugg's. In 1940, Merwin Hart disputed Rugg's use of the term. In the mouths of Rugg and his allies, Hart argued, "'Democracy,' then, is the rallying cry under which the American system of government is being prepared for despotism." Hart argued that this sort of democracy had begun as a Soviet strategy to redefine the term. By 1940, according to Rugg's memoir, Hart warned, "If you find any organization containing the word 'democracy' it is probably directly or indirectly affiliated with the Communist Party."[177]

Legionnaire Hamilton Hicks agreed. Leftist calls for democracy, Hicks insisted in 1940, merely represented an underhanded tactic to crush true democracy. "The Communist," Hicks wrote, "pleads for more democracy with which to smother democracy."[178] Rugg's books in particular, Hicks argued, demonstrated a particularly dangerous example of this sort of sneaky attack. According to Hicks, Rugg's ideas "would destroy the Constitution *and* democracy."[179]

Journalist George Sokolsky warned readers that the works of Rugg and other Frontier Thinkers threatened to undermine American democracy. Books such as Rugg's made it more difficult to "maintain a democracy in the face of world pressure," Sokolsky insisted.[180] Too often, "democratic principles [were] disappearing from our schoolbooks," Sokolsky wrote.[181] Unless parents took immediate action, democracy as a whole would likely disappear, first from schools, then from American society.

By 1941, conservative Legion leader R. Worth Shumaker combined these warnings in a comprehensive defense of the conservative vision of true democracy and schooling. Teachers in public schools must teach the "sacred legacy" of democracy in their classrooms. The "fine, loyal corps of teachers" had long guarded this legacy by inculcating the traditions of democratic America into every new generation. As a result, "Young America" had always embraced "those ideals and aspirations true to the American tradition." The name for this sort of education, Shumaker wrote, was "the democratic processes of education."[182]

No one should be fooled, Shumaker argued, by the false definitions of democracy emanating from Teachers College. Shumaker believed Rugg's close colleague George Counts had dismissed the true tradition of American democracy in his popular book *Dare the School Build a New Social Order* (1932). Counts had disparaged the Constitution and the electoral traditions of American democracy, Shumaker charged.[183] Rugg was no better. The textbooks Rugg hoped to foist on American youth hoped to graft a "socialistic state" onto the traditions of American democracy.[184]

If Americans hoped to perpetuate their system of "constitutional democracy," the schools had to help, Shumaker concluded. But they could not help if they were perverted by "Dr. Rugg's philosophy of 'accelerated change.'"[185] Instead, there was only one "truly American way of educating boys and girls," Shumaker wrote. In order to preserve true democracy, schools must use "the traditional, time-tested, and accepted method, based on our ideas and institutions."[186]

In 1942, Shumaker again critiqued Rugg's new definition of democracy. Rugg and his colleagues, Shumaker noted, insisted that American traditions had failed. The solution, these leftists argued, must be "more democracy."[187] What Rugg and other leftists meant by that term, Shumaker wrote, was the abandonment of American society, economy, and government in favor of some "form of collectivism." Those who paused to look closely at what such subversives meant by democracy would be "amazed to learn that their concept of it is nothing more nor less than Marxian Socialism."[188] Such leftists used the term "democracy" only as a tactic to distract Americans from their true intentions. In recent years, Shumaker warned, Rugg and other "Frontier Thinkers" strategically abandoned using terms such as "communism" and "socialism." By calling their subversive socialist scheme "democracy," Teachers College radicals placated the too-trusting American people. As Shumaker explained, "As everyone likes to be progressive, and everybody wants democracy, little opposition developed."[189]

Shumaker and other conservative activists hoped to use their agitation against Rugg's textbooks to thwart that trend. By asserting a traditionalist definition of democracy, conservatives hoped to reclaim the term for their side. Most conservatives agreed with Rugg that classrooms could teach students the basics of democracy. Indeed, conservatives agreed that without such instruction, democracy could not be sustained. But they contended—sometimes even violently—with Rugg's vision of the meanings of modern democracy. For conservatives, "democracy" meant reverence for American traditions of laissez faire economics, religious liberty, and constitutional law. Young people would be taught to defend democracy only when they were inculcated with a deep love for those traditions, and a zeal to defend them against new definitions, especially including those allegedly on display in Professor Rugg's textbooks.

Burning Garbage

These different definitions often spoke past one another. Progressives accused conservatives of authoritarianism in their traditionalist zeal to crush a truly democratic outpouring of patriotic criticism of American history and institutions. Conservatives accused progressives of subverting democracy to teach its authoritarian, socialist, totalitarian opposite.

The two contending conceptions echoed in local battles over the Rugg books nationwide. In Binghamton, New York, for instance, the controversy over Rugg's books took off in December 1939. Merwin Hart, the Utica attorney and leader of the conservative New York State Economic Council, told an audience at the Binghamton Exchange Club on December 13 that Rugg's books represented a clear and present danger to American society. The books, Hart insisted, promoted socialism and attacked capitalism. Worst of all, Hart told the gathering at Binghamton's Arlington Hotel, was Rugg's "subtle, sugar-coated" approach. Young people would be convinced of the faults of "the American system," Hart claimed. Schoolchildren would learn that "a new system, which in plain words is Socialism, should be substituted in its place." Why had this far-ranging plot been so successful? Hart explained that Rugg's scheme was "one of the shrewdest and probably one of the most effective of the Communist Front efforts now being made in the United States—all the more dangerous because carried out under the high respectability of our great American school system."[190]

Binghamton reporters sniffed a story and rushed to interview local school officials. Superintendent Daniel Kelly would not engage. There was nothing subversive about Rugg's books, Kelly insisted.[191] But editor Thomas Hutton of the *Binghamton Press* would not be put off. After the "aerial bomb" dropped by Hart, Hutton asked in an editorial, why could Binghamton schools not conduct an investigation? After all, Bertie Forbes's home district of Englewood, New Jersey, was carrying out just such a probe, Hutton pointed out. Such an investigation would be nothing more than a display of the "processes of democracy as we teach them in the schools."[192]

As winter warmed slowly into spring, the Binghamton Parent Teacher Association investigated Rugg's books. The PTA chairman concluded that Hart's accusations were "justified to a degree," but that there was no cause for immediate alarm. Superintendent Kelly remained convinced of the books' worth. "Personally," Kelly claimed, "it's the kind of book I want my children to have. To say it is subversive is absurd."[193]

Nevertheless, Kelly decided to remove Rugg books from Binghamton schools. Kelly had not changed his opinion of the books, but decided to "stop the controversy" by ordering the books out.[194] Tom Hutton of the *Binghamton Press* approved. Rugg himself was "collectivistic," Hutton insisted. Though Binghamton teachers were good and loyal to American tradition, Hutton wrote, "the loyalty of Dr. Harold Rugg . . . isn't above question." In the end, Hutton approved of Kelly's removal of the books. "We don't think it is fair," Hutton wrote, "to use taxpayer money in a democracy to teach the glory of collectivism to the budding citizens of a democracy."[195]

The vigorous protest of Binghamton leftists only convinced Hutton further. Hutton told *Press* readers of an angry letter he had received from one frequent letter writer. This person called the removal of the Rugg books nothing less than an episode of "capitalist terrorism." Worse, this sort of conservative censorship, in the letter writer's opinion, equaled a "book burning."[196]

Such protests had little effect in Binghamton. By mid-April, the school board unanimously approved of Superintendent Kelly's decision to remove the books. One board member, Mrs. Howard R. Swartwood, even confirmed the fears of the angry anti-conservative letter writer. In order to remove the threat of the Rugg books, Swartwood suggested "a bonfire be made" of the removed titles. Two other board members agreed.[197]

This sort of talk attracted national attention. John Dewey wrote in the pages of the *New York Times* that Binghamton's action had been the result of nefarious "pressure groups." Groups such as Hart's New

York Economic Council exploited the "prejudice, bigotry, and unenlightenment" of average people in places such as Binghamton, Dewey warned.[198]

Nor was Binghamton the only city to threaten to pile Rugg's books into bonfires. In late 1940, *Time Magazine* reported burnings of the Rugg books in small towns in New Jersey.[199] Some of the burnings took place far out of the view of such national publications. Years after the Rugg controversy, one historian spoke with a school official in Marshfield, Wisconsin. This informant divulged that the Rugg books had been secretly taken from the shelves of their school district warehouse and burned surreptitiously.[200]

As the Binghamton letter writer made clear, to be a "book burner" in the era of Nazi power seizures and book burnings seemed an obviously un-American charge. Yet conservatives in the Rugg controversy did not shrink from advocating such burnings. B. C. Forbes insisted that if parents were aware of the true threat represented by Rugg books, they would "cast these obnoxious volumes into the furnace."[201] Similarly, Merwin Hart defended his attacks on the Rugg books in Binghamton and nationwide. The dangers from the Rugg books must be combated vigorously, Hart insisted. The books did not simply discuss socialism, Hart complained, they "actually aim to indoctrinate the pupil with collectivist ideas." Students must never be exposed to such an ideological threat, Hart argued. Activists must take any necessary action to protect such immediately threatened youth.[202]

In Binghamton and nationwide, conservative critics demanded that any books by leftist ideologues must be removed, if not destroyed. Editor Tom Hutton had worried that the loyalty of Professor Rugg could not be assured.[203] Hutton did not feel a need to say any more than that. By implication, Hutton suggested, any book by a disloyal author would necessarily constitute a severe ideological threat.

Many anti-Rugg activists argued from a similar perspective. They sought to discredit Harold Rugg personally. By proving that Rugg was a socialist, a leftist, a radical determined to reconstruct American society and schools, many conservatives felt that his books would automatically be proven dangerous. American Legion activist Hamilton Hicks, for instance, believed that the first step in understanding the dangers of the Rugg books lay in understanding that Rugg himself had a "political purpose" in writing them.[204] Rugg's ultimate goal, Hicks warned, was "totalitarianism."[205] Though Rugg did not admit as much in the textbooks themselves, an examination of Rugg's other works made it clear, Hicks believed. Books such as Rugg's 1933 *Great Technology* demonstrated Rugg's true philosophy, Hicks argued. That book, Hicks claimed, was "Rugg's *Mein Kampf*."[206] In *The Great Technology*, Rugg laid out his true philosophy of education. Rugg had planned since 1933 to use schools to undermine traditional faith in government and religion, Hicks insisted.[207] Though Rugg later denied such a goal, Hicks warned that Rugg's "academic double talk" should not fool the unwary.[208] According to Hicks, Rugg's earlier publications proved that Rugg wanted revolutionary change in America. And he planned to achieve it by insidious manipulation of children's minds through their textbooks. As did other conservative activists, Hicks believed the problem with the Rugg textbooks started and ended with their author's proven disloyalty. "Is this a man," Hicks asked, "on whom you may rely to give your children a sound, unbiased education? Is he qualified to impart a knowledge of intellectual and moral issues to the very young?"[209]

The answer, for R. Worth Shumaker as for Hamilton Hicks, was an obvious no. From his post as assistant director of the National Americanism Commission of the American Legion, Shumaker agreed that the discussion of the Rugg textbooks must begin with an examination of Rugg himself. Shumaker believed "the background of the author" plays a determining role "in the fashioning of the plastic minds of immature pupils."[210]

Other leading Legionnaires seconded this direct attack on Rugg himself. Augustin Rudd, the Legionnaire who started the controversy, warned that Rugg had "for years advocated a 'new social order' to be based on collectivism, to replace our traditional American institutions." This long leftist activism proved not only Rugg's disloyalty, but by implication proved the dangers of Rugg's textbooks, Rudd insisted. Even if Rugg had been completely loyal, and not a dangerous "Left Wing educator from Teachers College," Rudd worried about concentrating educational power in any one writer's hands.[211]

For Legion leaders and other conservatives, Rugg's leftist intellectual record proved Rugg's suspect goals. Even if Rugg had not been demonstrably committed to the subversive undermining of America's government and institutions, however, Rugg's textbooks themselves demonstrated a woeful misunderstanding of what schools ought to be doing, according to many leaders of the anti-Rugg campaign. Augustin Rudd argued that schools must devote themselves to "instilling an understanding and respect for our American form of government." With Rugg's books, however, schools would be committed instead to "sabotaging this traditional policy."[212]

The Legionnaires of Haworth, New Jersey, close allies of Bertie Forbes's anti-Rugg fight in nearby Englewood, similarly worried that the Rugg books would derail the true purposes of public education. Legionnaires on the Haworth school board issued a bitter minority report attacking the Rugg textbooks. The proper goal of schools, this minority report insisted, was "that the youth of our school have instilled in them in their formative years" notions of "love of and loyalty to our country."[213] The Rugg textbooks were "UNAMERICAN," this report concluded, in that they failed to emphasize "the lives, heroic struggles, and aims of the founders . . . as examples to be emulated." These ideas were "passed on to us as a sacred heritage," the Haworth conservative faction claimed. Rugg's books must be ousted, since the books misunderstood the vital importance of passing on that heritage to every new generation.[214]

Alfred Falk concurred. Besides the obvious dangers of Rugg's patent left-wing ideology, Falk believed Rugg's books misunderstood the fundamental goals of education. Not only Rugg, Falk wrote privately to Homer Chaillaux, but the "whole progressive-education movement" had made this immense mistake. For "old-fashioned believers in mental discipline," Falk wrote, this misapprehension on the part of Rugg and his allies loomed just as dangerous as intentional subversion. Too often, naïve "progressive educators" got mixed up with "the spreaders of radical un-American doctrines." So mixed up, Falk wrote, that the two camps often became "the same people and they mix their two products together and wrap them up in one package."[215] Like other conservatives, Falk worried that such mistaken attitudes about the proper nature of education made Rugg's books dangerous, even if Rugg himself had not schemed to use the books to promote revolution.

Many conservatives argued they did not need to cite specific chapter and verse in which Rugg's textbooks promoted collectivism or anti-Americanism. It was enough, Shumaker claimed, to prove that Rugg's books failed in their proper task. "All textbooks," Shumaker wrote, "should inculcate in the Youth of our Nation a genuine love for America and a desire to protect and defend our priceless ideals, institutions, and heritage."[216] Even the most ardent defenders of Rugg's textbooks did not claim Rugg's books did that.

Conservatives did not end their anti-Rugg arguments there. In addition to discrediting Rugg personally, in addition to claiming that Rugg's books misunderstood the basic principles of proper public education, several conservative activists also offered specific criticisms of the books and of their likely effects. Augustin Rudd warned that American students were learning "socialistic ideas and theories." This sad state of affairs, Rudd argued, did "not just happen." Textbooks, especially Rugg's hugely influential series, promoted such anti-American ideas.[217]

Hamilton Hicks predicted the gruesome future of an America weaned on Rugg textbooks:

> When enough of the tots grow up (they've been reading them for over ten years) to take over the Government, abolish the Constitution and establish a collectivist dictatorship, it would not matter if the parents caught on to what had been happening. Should they object then, their children could send them to a concentration camp.

Hicks admitted that Rugg did not advocate such a terrifying future. Nevertheless, Hicks claimed that such a result was the "logical outcome" of Rugg's educational and social philosophy.[218]

Merwin Hart warned audiences that no amount of parental influence could counter the subversive influence of the Rugg books. The majority of American parents, Hart claimed, "depend on private enterprise for a living." Yet in school, the Rugg books were teaching children that "private enterprise should go and some kind of socialistic scheme should take its place." In a situation like that, parents had little chance of raising their children right.[219]

Working together as the "Guardians of American Education," Hamilton Hicks, Augustin Rudd, and Alfred Falk warned parents that Rugg books would have a predictably terrible result. "This Rugg brand of 'progressive' education,'" the Guardians argued, " . . . sets up a destructive influence in the training of children as useful members of American society."[220] One unpleasant result of this subversive training, according to the Guardians, had been a "growing disrespect among students for school authority and discipline."[221] Such trends were not accidental, but rather a deliberate product of years of leftist teaching and textbooks, the Guardians claimed.

Throughout the controversy, conservatives also produced long, exhaustive lists of specific passages in the Rugg textbooks that exemplified conservative claims. It was important, Legion writer O. K. Armstrong noted, to take a close look at the textbook series as a whole. Even if certain parts of certain texts seemed unobjectionable, Armstrong claimed, seen as a whole the books *"form a complete pattern of propaganda for a change in our political, economic, and social order."*[222]

In particular, Alfred Falk worried in 1939 that Rugg's books "describe advertising more or less as an instrument for exploitation by unscrupulous business."[223] Page by page and text by text, Falk warned, Rugg presented American society and economy as a battle between scheming business and helpless American victims. The books carefully avoided "outright denunciation," Falk admitted, but nevertheless the slanted tone could convince innocent young readers that advertising and business could only be tools of oppression.[224]

Augustin Rudd offered chapter and verse. In the teachers' guide to *Our Country and Our People,* Rudd warned—a guide "not available to parents"—Rugg suggested asking students if the United States was really a land of opportunity for all people. The answer, Rugg told teachers, was an obvious no. Too many Americans did not have a chance to earn any income whatsoever. The differences between rich and poor created a cruel class system, and most people had no real security.[225] Rudd admitted that many parts of many of Rugg's books seemed fair and balanced. But the overall effect of the books tipped decidedly toward the subversive left. "Time after time," Rudd wrote, Rugg "uses half-truths, partisan references, and an amazing liberty with historical facts, the net effect of which is to undermine the faith of children in the American way of life. The constantly recurring theme is an effort to sell the child the collectivist theory of society." Worst of all, any criticism of the Rugg books, Rudd believed, risked an accusation that the critic was "un-progressive."[226]

George Sokolsky also offered readers a list of specific criticisms. In Rugg's *March toward Democracy,* Sokolsky claimed, Rugg called the founding fathers gamblers with public lands and public money. In a passage on page 110, Sokolsky wrote, Rugg denounced the founders as greedy capitalists. A few pages later, Rugg's book told impressionable youth that the founders feared democracy.[227] Such doctrines taught students a false vision of both the past and the present. By undermining students' faith in the nation's founders, Sokolsky charged, Rugg hoped to weaken students' faith in their own government. According to Sokolsky, Rugg's ultimate goal was to create a generation friendlier to the Soviet Union than to the United States.[228]

Occasionally, rank-and-file Legionnaires asked their conservative leaders to explain the threat of the Rugg textbooks. Eugene Lathe, a Legion member from Hammond, Indiana, wrote to the national headquarters to ask for a specific critique, something Lathe could take to his local school board. R. Worth Shumaker sent Lathe a long summary of Shumaker's reasons. "The Rugg books," Shumaker wrote Lathe, are based on his philosophy which opposed individual enterprise and free competition. Rugg would set-up a collectivist state in which private capital would be controlled by bureaus or government. The books place far too little emphasis on our American heroes and our great tradition. They emphasize those things in our history which can be painted as a dark picture. . . . He (Rugg) used the Soviety [*sic*] Union as an example of collectivism and he speaks of the progress of the Soviety [*sic*] Union in very commendable terms. In fact, his references to the Soviet Union prove decisively that Rugg believes in a form of socialist state.[229]

Shumaker expanded on this sentiment in his four-pamphlet analysis of the Rugg books. In volume two of this pamphlet series, Shumaker warned that teachers could not do their job if only given Rugg books with which to work. The books "tend to destroy the child's faith in America and . . . seek a 'change' in our basic institutions."[230] If teachers only had proper textbooks, Shumaker wrote, "loyal and patriotic" teachers could do their jobs: teachers could instill in young people the glories of America's "illustrious past." Such youth would be proof against "alien influence."[231] Rugg's books, however, conveyed the idea that the only worthwhile moral goals were change and reconstruction. The books consistently derided the United States as "a 'depressed society.'" The textbooks gave up on teaching traditional history and geography, and taught instead a tendentious "political, social and economic discussion" aimed at convincing students of the dangers of tradition and capitalism.[232]

"Communist" and "Communistic"

As the school year began in the fall of 1940, the *American Legion Magazine* published another broadside against the Rugg textbooks. Not only the Rugg books, Legionnaire O. K. Armstrong warned, but a long list of curricular materials threatened to undermine students' patriotism. Armstrong attacked magazines such as *Scholastic,* the *Civil Leader,* the *Junior Review,* and the *Weekly News Review.* Such magazines, Armstrong insisted, must be removed from public schools immediately. Textbooks, too, worried Armstrong. In addition to Rugg's textbooks, Armstrong warned about textbooks by historians such as Carl Becker and Charles Beard.[233]

Coming as it did in the middle of the fight over the Rugg textbooks, Armstrong's article raised hackles on all sides. Edward Kenerson, director of Ginn & Company publishers, wrote to Homer Chaillaux to demand an immediate retraction of this "libelous campaign."[234] Augustin Rudd privately admitted being the source of Armstrong's list of dangerous titles, but told Chaillaux he had never meant for the list to be made public.[235] Ruth Myer, associate editor of *The American Observer*, a magazine on Armstrong's blacklist, lamented that they had lost 15,000 subscriptions due to Armstrong's article. As a result, Myer told Chaillaux, her magazine faced "utter ruin."[236] In the end, the American Legion and Armstrong retracted their denunciations of a few magazines, including *The American Observer*.[237]

But in spite of similar protests against overly broad denunciations of subversive school histories, conservative leaders never retreated from treating Rugg's books and other books by left-leaning authors as inherently subversive. When Rugg or other authors protested that they were not communists or socialists, or even sympathetic to the movements, conservatives were not impressed. Authors did not need to be active communists or socialists for their books to be dangerously subversive, in the viewpoint of many conservative activists. Rugg's books showed sympathies and tendencies in the direction of communism, many critics felt. Such tendencies were enough.

Other readers with a different perspective disagreed. Many found compelling Rugg's explicit denial of any affiliation with communism or subversion. In his 1941 memoir, Rugg hoped to clear the air. "I am not a Communist," Rugg wrote.

> I have never been a Communist. I have never been a member of or affiliated with the Communist party, directly or indirectly, in any way whatsoever. I am not a Socialist. I have never been a member of or affiliated with the Socialist party. Nor have I taken part in the work of that party.[238]

Some readers of Rugg's books were convinced. For example, the Legion post of North Canton, Ohio, reported in the aftermath of Armstrong's article that they had inspected the books carefully and found nothing wrong with them. As long as teachers taught patriotically, these legionnaires concluded, the Rugg books would be a fine addition that would not undermine "traditional religious faiths."[239] One newspaper in New Jersey came to similar conclusions. The *Red Bank Register* reported that most of the people in town agreed that Rugg and his books presented no threat. The Red Bank school superintendent reported, "There was nothing in the books tending to make children Communistic." As the newspaper's editors concluded, the books taught "reverence for American institutions . . . in a most interesting manner."[240]

Legion posts in Fairfield, Connecticut,[241] and Rapid City, South Dakota, agreed. There was nothing subversive, Rapid City adjutant Walter McDonald wrote in 1941, in teaching children about communism. That was all the Rugg books did, McDonald believed. "The American Legion," McDonald argued, "owes an apology to the schools of the United States."[242]

To Rugg himself and these satisfied inspectors of Rugg's books, a book or author must purposefully set forth to spread communist or socialist propaganda in order for the book to be considered subversive. The subversive content would be patently obvious to any casual reader. But many conservative critics throughout the Rugg controversy used a much broader definition of subversion. For many conservatives, it was enough for a book or author to tend toward leftist ideas, to promote a sympathetic viewpoint or even an openness toward socialist or communist ideas. Such authors could even be unaware of the tendencies of their own works. Or, worse, authors could use an insidious, extremely subtle sort of propaganda, one that could escape the notice of all but the most active and skilled patriots.

In the late 1930s, this broad understanding of the threat from leftist subversion had considerable cultural and political support. In 1938, the US House of Representatives voted by an overwhelming margin to empower Texas representative Martin Dies to root out such devious dangers. Dies led the Special House Committee on Un-American Activities (HUAC), popularly known during the 1930s as the Dies Committee.[243] This committee, led by the energetic and controversial Dies, immediately began rooting out communist influence in unions and government agencies.[244] In its early years, the committee and its leader, Martin Dies, worked closely with the activists on the American Legion's National Americanism Commission.[245] This national hunt for hidden reds attracted a great deal of attention. According to historian Walter Goodman, reporting on the committee's work filled more than 500 column-inches in the New York Times in the first six weeks of the committee's existence.[246]

The Dies Committee represented only one of a spate of legislative investigative bodies. In New York, the Rapp-Coudert legislative committee expanded its mandate from an initial goal of investigating New York City's school finances to a much broader investigation of subversive activities in schools and colleges.[247] In New York and nationwide, many investigators believed that schools would be a primary target of subversive agents. As conservative activist and journalist Walter S. Steele told the Dies Committee in 1938, "There has probably been as much if not more 'red' activity in this field [education] than in any other excepting among the working class."[248]

It must come as no surprise, then, that conservatives in the late 1930s remained on the lookout for sneaky socialist subversion in America's schools. As political scientist Michael Paul Rogin has argued, many such red hunters delved deep into a tradition of "political demonology" to feed a "counter-subversive imagination."[249] Such activists often believed a set of stereotypical assumptions about communists and subversive leftists, as historian Ellen Schrecker has noted.[250] Communists, many conservative educational activists believed, remained hidden. Such hidden communists worked by injecting coded information into newspapers, textbooks, films, and other cultural artifacts. Once right-thinking Americans cracked the code, such subversive messages became obvious. But many Americans remained, at best, naïve dupes of a worldwide subversive network.[251]

Activists in the Rugg controversy demonstrated this broader understanding of the possible threat from subversive propaganda. It was not enough, many conservatives insisted, to remove the open, explicit communist materials from schools. Rather, Americans must be on the lookout for materials designed to seem harmless, but that in fact carried subtle messages undermining traditional American values such as capitalism, religion, and true democracy. In 1936, Frederick Palmer warned his fellow Legionnaires of the subtle nature of this communist threat. Palmer told readers of the *American Legion Monthly* that communists actively targeted young Americans with a devastatingly effective psychological campaign.[252] Just as Americans came of age, communist agents promised them the world if only the youth promoted a communist revolution. "In short," the communist agent promised gullible students, "anything you want is yours once America goes Red." Communists did not make such promises in the open, where conservatives could fight them. Rather, Palmer wrote, subversive agents snuck into existing clubs and schools, making their promises "by the whispered word." This "virus for injection," Palmer worried, could soon turn the heads of naïve and impressionable youth.[253]

From the very beginning of the Rugg controversy, conservative leaders adopted this understanding of the broad danger from implicit tendencies of textbooks. Augustin Rudd first appealed to the national leaders of the American Legion in 1938 by warning them that the dangers from the Rugg books were always "very subtle." It would take a properly trained expert to "expose the purpose and technique of these collectivists."[254] In public, Rudd warned that the Rugg books did their work through their seemingly harmless nature. "Never was there a more perfect propaganda set-up," Rudd concluded, "never a more subtle one."[255] Alfred Falk noted similarly that the Rugg books had been "cleverly designed to destroy the child's faith in traditional American ideals."[256] Though the material in the Rugg books might seem innocuous to inattentive readers, Falk believed that "it was put there in pursuance of a deliberate plan worked up by a well-defined group of left-wingers and educators, collaborating for a number of years on this huge project of reconstructing our society."[257] B. C. Forbes agreed that the books might seem fine to the untrained eye. However, though the books were "extremely subtly" written, Forbes told the president of the board of education in Englewood, yet they were "shot through . . . with the kind of propaganda championed by Communists."[258] For Forbes, Falk, Rudd, and other conservative leaders, only a careful and informed examination of the textbooks would yield the proper conclusion. This was no accident, but in fact served as further proof of the books' danger. The fact that the books' rampant communist propaganda could seem neutral or even patriotic demonstrated to many conservatives just how threatening the Rugg books really were.

R. Worth Shumaker argued that the books' true purpose only became clear when Rugg himself was understood as an assiduous and devious leftist agent. Shumaker told one skeptical correspondent that reading only one or two of Rugg's books could, indeed, make it seem as if the books contained no subversive material. In order to expose Rugg's true purpose, Shumaker insisted it was necessary to "go back of the scenes." Such investigations revealed Rugg's "very clever" scheme. Once an earnest investigator learned of Rugg's left-wing associations and read Rugg's endorsement of the Soviet Union, suddenly one could see "how clearly these things are written in the textbooks and the even-more-than-dangerous teachers' guides and keys."[259]

As did Shumaker, many conservative activists saw Rugg's undisputed intelligence as more proof of his complex and expansive propagandistic scheme. The Guardians of American Education, led by Rudd, Hamilton Hicks, and Falk, warned that the danger of Rugg's books came precisely from the fact that Rugg's method was "extremely clever." Young readers would be approached by "stealth." The books led children "with gentle language and a pedagogic smile . . . through the successive stages of indoctrination." Most patriotic readers, the Guardians conceded, could read the books without finding any threat.[260] Such seeming innocence only made the case for vigilance that much stronger.

As B. C. Forbes wrote, these "subtle subverters" used "finesse." Unlike public communists such as Earl Browder, Forbes warned, this sort of "oily propaganda" threatened to spread "contempt for America and Americanism." Only by carefully reading such material with a trained eye could readers see the true threat.[261]

Conservative activists often portrayed themselves as the specially trained and experienced readers who could inform the average American of this concealed threat. As Legionnaire Hamilton Hicks admitted, it was entirely possible for "intelligent people" to read one or two Rugg books without finding anything objectionable. The true goal of the books only became clear, Hicks wrote, when someone like Hicks examined the book series as a whole. After all, Hicks insisted, "Dr. Rugg is far too adept a propagandist to disclose his real purpose in any one textbook."[262] Similarly, Legion activist O. K. Armstrong noted that the poison pill of subversion came "wrapped in the cloak of accepted progressive methods." It would be easy—far too easy—to dismiss the possible subversive threat from such progressive-seeming curricular materials. Only when given close and expert scrutiny, Armstrong implied, would the theme of leftist subversion become clear.[263]

As the Rugg controversy proceeded angrily in towns and cities across the country, both defenders of the books and their conservative opponents insisted that the real meanings of the books could only be seen as a whole. Rugg supporters in Philadelphia, for example, reported that the Rugg books contained "no taint of subversion." The accusations against the books, this board concluded, all came from "single passages isolated from context."[264] But Homer Chaillaux warned one correspondent that any one Rugg book could seem harmless if read alone. Once a reader examined the entire series, the subversive goal became clear.[265] As R. Worth Shumaker concluded in his Legion-published critique, it was not enough to read just one or two of the books. In order to sniff out the truly terrifying subversive implications of the Rugg books, any reader must take the time and effort to find out the true story of the books. Given Rugg's earlier statements against American traditions and government, given the content of the series as a whole, and given the instructions provided to teachers in supplementary materials, the books' true nature soon became clear. The fact that some readers—even patriotic, conservative readers—could find nothing subversive in the Rugg books did not dissuade ardent activists that the books contained ideological poison.[266]

Big Business and the Promise of Capitalism

By early 1941, the textbook controversy had entered its final months. However, at the time the fight seemed as ferocious as ever. In late February, the lead author of a textbook survey funded by the National Association of Manufacturers garnered front-page headlines by denouncing the content of social-studies textbooks.[267] Economist Ralph Robey of Columbia University had agreed to investigate the content of America's textbooks. In this public comment, Robey criticized a "substantial proportion" of contemporary textbooks. Most books, Robey explained, tended to be overly critical of the American government and economic system.[268] In Robey's opinion, students should first be taught the fundamentals of American traditions. Only when young people had learned such basics could they safely be taught about America's problems. The textbooks Robey examined did not contain out-and-out Soviet propaganda, Robey explained, but a more subtle "critical attitude" toward the United States.[269]

Robey had not been speaking specifically of the Rugg textbooks, but in the context of the Rugg controversy, Robey's public comments aroused immediate opposition among publishers.[270] Though the National Association of Manufacturers had initiated and funded Robey's survey, NAM leaders quickly backed away from the controversy.[271] By this time, NAM had transformed itself from its nineteenth-century roots into a conglomeration of elite big-business leaders.[272]

NAM scrupulously avoided public controversy, and its leaders energetically denied any connection to Robey's denunciations. As NAM president W. D. Fuller told Edmund Brunner, a professor at Teachers College, Columbia, Robey's comments were his alone. Robey, Fuller told Brunner, did not represent NAM or big business. The survey Robey had conducted had indeed been a NAM project, but Robey's public comments had been solely an expression of Robey's personal opinions, undertaken after his contract with NAM had expired. No one, Fuller assured Brunner, cared more about "preserving freedom of discussion in schools" than NAM, whose goal had always been to present "controversial issues . . . in the proper balance."[273] In a public letter to educators, Fuller emphasized that the newspapers had given "distorted impressions of the project and of our opinion of the patriotism of American teachers." NAM had not set out to denounce the loyalty of textbooks or teachers, Fuller insisted, but only to offer informative abstracts about the nature of textbooks.[274]

Yet in spite of such public protestations, NAM had indeed envisioned Robey's survey as a way to sniff out subversive, anti-capitalist teaching in America's textbooks. As leaders planned to conduct a textbook survey in the summer of 1940, NAM administrator John C. Gebhart worried that any attempt to discover which textbooks "contain subversive doctrines" would be a "difficult and ticklish subject."[275] Gebhart described the danger to NAM leader C. E. Harrison a week later: "The American people are pretty strong for academic freedom and might resent any attack by this Association on the professors."[276] As Harrison wrote NAM executive vice president W. B. Weisenburger in late July 1940, NAM needed more specific evidence before it accused textbooks of anti-business bias. If NAM accused books simply of a leftist tone, it would seem subjective and publicly indefensible. As with the Rugg books, Harrison explained, though all sensible readers agreed that the books were "unfairly biased," without enough specific evidence, it was difficult to make a "convincing case" against them.[277]

NAM leaders picked Ralph Robey as a suitable academic expert to front the research project precisely because of Robey's ideological compatibility. NAM would hire research assistants to review hundreds of textbooks. Robey and his team would prepare a short abstract for each title. "Particularly if the author's general thesis is unfairly prejudiced against private enterprise," NAM planners agreed, Robey's team would provide specific offensive passages as evidence.[278]

Though NAM leaders quickly backed away from Robey's public statements in February 1941, NAM had worked for years to promote similar traditionalist notions in public schools. Even before NAM leaders conceived of this ambitious textbook survey, they had worked to promote such ideals. In the summer of 1938, NAM leaders prepared a private memo to Dean William F. Russell of Teachers College. This memo outlined the educational vision of NAM leaders at the time.[279] The "American Way," this private memo explained, could only be maintained if schools taught it explicitly and successfully.[280]

This sort of proper education must be a transmission of wisdom and knowledge from one generation to the next. "Modern America," the NAM committee argued, "must benefit from the experience of past generations."[281] The way to accomplish this lofty goal was to create a patriotic set of textbooks in what the committee suggested could be called "The Roots of Liberty." Such curricular materials would emphasize "the historical and spiritual foundations of the American system of government, free enterprise and religious liberty."[282] The *religion*

most important element of American education, the NAM committee argued, was to inspire each new generation with an appreciation of
these "fundamental concepts of freedom" that had motivated the first
generation of Americans.[283]

Unfortunately, the committee warned Dean Russell, too many teachers taught socialism, communism, and the desirability of restructuring
the American economy. The academic freedom of these teachers and
textbooks must end as soon as they began to "undermine the vital concept of representative democracy—with its inseparable concomitants—
free private enterprise and civil, especially religious liberty."[284] Teachers
must be free to teach the problems and struggles of private enterprise,
but they must also instill in young students a faith that such capitalism
also remained a central building block of democracy and freedom.[285]

In 1939, Charles Hook, at the time president of American Rolling
Mill Company and chairman of the National Association of Manufacturers, made a public statement in favor of these NAM educational
goals. At a speech to an annual assembly of Missouri's public school
teachers on November 16, 1939, Hook endorsed NAM's "Roots of
Liberty" dream curriculum.[286] Unfortunately, too many teachers had
adopted "alien philosophies [that] . . . would tear down the capitalistic
system."[287] Teachers, like those in Hook's St. Louis audience, had the
duty and privilege to help each student understand his or her responsibilities as a citizen. As nations around the world teetered "on the brink
of totalitarianism," Hook warned, "sound education can help avoid that
peril here."[288] Teachers could save America, Hook enthused, if they
added to their teaching of "material facts and skills" a broader "emphasis upon the philosophic concepts on which the maintenance of our
republic demands."[289] Only if teachers and textbooks actively embraced
and explicitly taught a studied loyalty to capitalism and American tradition could the nation be saved from the threat of socialist takeover.

Leaders of NAM did more than simply advocate a capitalism-friendly
school environment. Beginning in 1939, NAM supplied thousands of
classroom teachers with booklets promoting the democratic benefits of
capitalism. By the end of 1940, according to an internal NAM survey
in 1941, 17,000 teachers and school administrators had received some
form of NAM educational literature. NAM claimed to have distributed
more than 175,000 classroom posters and fielded teachers' requests for
3,500,000 more copies of the pamphlet *You and Industry*.[290]

In order to gauge the effectiveness of this massive literature-
distribution campaign, NAM assigned pollster Henry Abt to investigate. Abt traveled to eleven unspecified cities in six unspecified states,

power of teachers

visiting forty-four classrooms and meeting with eleven school administrators. Abt was pleased to report that teachers and school principals
from his select group seemed overwhelmingly appreciative of NAM's
classroom materials. Most teachers, Abt concluded, "think of NAM
primarily as an informational service; an authoritative source of economic and social data."[291] From NAM's perspective, nothing could
be better. Abt recommended that the wide classroom use of NAM
materials promised to influence enormous numbers of impressionable
young people. If these high school audiences could be "inculcated with
a measure of appreciation for private enterprise," Abt recommended,
the future of American capitalism and big business seemed politically
secure.[292] In general, most of the teachers Abt spoke with seemed to
Abt to be embracing explicitly conservative ideas. Among forty-nine
teachers Abt surveyed, thirty said they had not recently changed their
opinion toward capitalism and big business. Sixteen had become more
sympathetic. Only one interviewee reported having recently lost faith
in American capitalism, due precisely to the Rugg textbook controversy. This teacher told Abt he was "perturbed about the activities of
the Advertising Federation of America, NAM, and American Legion
(which he lumped together as representative of industry) in respect to
textbooks."[293]

No Rugg, No Reconstruction

For years, NAM had dedicated its educational efforts to the promotion of a specific vision of capitalism as a pillar of American freedom
and democracy. Although NAM later made efforts to distance itself
from Robey's inflammatory public comments, Robey's project originally planned to demonstrate the dangers of leftism in American textbooks. It must have been sheer coincidence that the *New York Times*
carried Robey's attack on textbooks just as Rugg himself prepared to
confront his foes face-to-face in Philadelphia. As we've seen, that confrontation on February 22, 1941, between Rugg, Merwin Hart, and
Alfred Falk made no pretense to civility or decorum. Rugg accused
his accusers of being the enemies of America's children.[294] Falk called
Rugg a liar.[295] In coming months, the Philadelphia school board battled
back and forth over whether or not to ban Rugg's books.[296]

Despite the heat and anger of that meeting, however, by early 1941
the public phase of the Rugg controversy had largely spent itself. Historians have disagreed about the ultimate impact of conservative activism
in the Rugg battle. Charles Dorn has argued that the anti-Rugg crusade

fizzled, since ultimately conservatives failed to get control over public education.[297] Jonathan Zimmerman agreed that organizations such as NAM and the American Legion effectively withdrew their larger ambitions and retired satisfied to see Rugg's titles removed.[298] In the end, these historians argued, what seemed like an epochal conservative uprising against the Rugg textbooks had very limited results.

Rugg himself insisted that the opposition to his books was never a "popular protest."[299] It had been initiated by a few "false patriots"[300] who stoked contrived fires of public outrage. Yet even Rugg conceded that the late 1930s represented a time of "general retreat to orthodoxy."[301] Certainly, the historical evidence demonstrates that conservative anti-Rugg leaders managed to attract eager support among a wide segment of the American population. Within the sprawling American Legion organization, for instance, local posts led the charge against the Rugg books, dragging reluctant national leaders in their wake. In local school districts nationwide, administrators found themselves besieged by parents and local citizens who demanded the removal of the Rugg books and all they represented. The best evidence for this local conservative support remains the dramatic drop in sales of Rugg's books. These decisions were made in local school boards. They reflected the wishes of local communities. In a sense, whatever their reasons, those local officials voted with their budgets, demonstrating the broad opposition to the bundle of ideas that "Rugg" came to represent.

Indeed, the true significance of the Rugg controversy was precisely this broadly supported demonstration of outrage against not only the Rugg books themselves, but everything the books came to symbolize. Conservatives who mobilized to remove Rugg's books from America's public schools engaged, consciously or not, in the continuing tradition of educational conservatism. Like every sort of school reformer, these activists believed that the ideas taught in schools mattered beyond the schoolhouse door, exemplified by subversive so-called experts who might attempt to reconstruct American society in leftist directions. Conservative activists became alarmed precisely because they agreed with progressive reformers that changes to schooling would lead to changes in society. What distinguished conservative educational activists from their progressive foes was not their faith in the power of schooling to transform America. What distinguished conservatives in this controversy was their vision of the proper directions both schooling and society should take. In stark contrast to progressive reformers such as Rugg and his Frontier-Thinking comrades at Teachers College, conservative school reformers involved in this textbook controversy hoped to make schools and society more patriotic, more friendly to capitalism, and more supportive of traditional visions of home and family.

Viewed from this perspective, conservative activism against Rugg's books can be judged a success. Anti-Rugg activists succeeded in making a convincing case about the proper purpose of education. Good schooling ought to focus on a transmission of ideas from one generation to the next, conservatives argued. Those ideas must include a bundle of traditional notions, including the vision of "democracy" as an umbrella term for traditional American values; the value of free enterprise and big business as pillars of American freedom; a vaguely defined but nonetheless powerful notion of proper manners and subservience among young people; and an ideological defense of home and nation.

Conservative critics succeeded in portraying Rugg as a subversive activist intent on changing those traditional social values by changing traditional education. The protest against Rugg's books demonstrated a widespread hostility to Rugg's presumed goals. The true importance of the conservative protest lay in its successful demonstration of such hostility. If Rugg planned to introduce students at a young age to the subversive notion that proper thinking meant ruthless skepticism toward received wisdom in culture, religion, economics, and politics, the anti-Rugg protest showed that a significant proportion of American parents disapproved.

The ultimate effectiveness of this broader conservative protest can be seen in the shocking naïveté of Rugg's 1941 vision of the future of American schooling. As Rugg reflected on the tumultuous years of textbook controversy, he confidently concluded that the social-frontier thinking of Rugg and Rugg's Teachers College colleagues had "already begun to shake the old and inadequate out of our educational system."[302] Barring a "major cultural catastrophe," Rugg predicted, nothing could stop the "progressive advance" of American schools. The progressive victory remained "utterly inevitable," Rugg promised.[303]

The wide-ranging conservative activism against the Rugg textbooks represented the sort of "cultural catastrophe" Rugg failed to foresee. From the conservative perspective, this "catastrophe" heralded the tremendous success in heading off the takeover of American public schools by Rugg's reconstructionist ideology. There may have been other books like Rugg's still in use. Many school districts may have even kept Rugg books on back shelves. But just as Rugg noted, the controversy itself was largely about him, not his books. It was a protest against a coterie of self-assured experts headquartered at Teachers College and other teachers colleges. It was a protest against the goal of rebuilding

American society in progressive directions by reshaping American education. And the protest worked.

To the continuing chagrin of progressive educators, protests against the Rugg textbooks demonstrated conclusively that power over American education did not reside solely in the hands of progressive leaders. Patriotic groups such as the American Legion, business groups such as the Advertising Federation of America and the National Association of Manufacturers, and journalists such as Bertie Forbes and George Sokolsky all wielded their influence outside the reach of experts from Teachers College. Both sides insisted they represented the forces of true Americanism, true democracy. In the Rugg textbook fight, as in so many educational battles, this tendency to use the same words to mean opposite things fueled the ferocious and durable cultural controversy over the most basic meanings of education and schooling.

CHAPTER FOUR

Rich, Republican, and Reactionary

Pasadena's Revolt against Progressivism

Maybe they were feeling surly after a visiting Ohio State football team walloped the University of California Golden Bears in 1950's Rose Bowl. Or maybe Pasadenans felt nervous in an uncertain post-World War II era about the "crisis in education" that announced itself from nearly every popular magazine and newspaper.[1] Or, maybe, a large number of Pasadenans simply relished the chance to see their opinions in the newspaper. Whatever the reason, when managing editor T. G. Wood of the *Pasadena Independent* asked readers for their criticisms of progressive education, Pasadenans jumped at the chance.[2]

Some of them just wanted to blow off steam. As one mother noted at the end of her blistering attack on progressive education, "Writing this has relieved some of the pent-up feeling I've had toward the present school system."[3] Perhaps most of the letter writers would have been satisfied to vent some "pent-up feeling" and let the issue go at that. As we will see, that was not to be the case. Complicated ideas about the nature of progressive education mixed with deeply held feelings about race, religion, patriotism, subversion, and taxes to produce another school controversy that attracted the attention of the entire nation.

Conservatives in Pasadena articulated anxieties about education that had long exercised activists nationwide. As had earlier conservatives, Pasadenans in 1950 accused progressive educators of belittling parents in favor of experts from "Columbia University." They called for the "assurance of the three R's" and more "whipping . . . when the situation calls for such punishment."[4] One writer claimed that "no true American" could find out the truth about progressive education "without his blood boiling."[5]

Some assumed that progressive education wasted children's class time "painting and daubing" instead of mastering "the basic three R's"[6] while others insisted it really meant an intentional conspiracy to dumb down American kids. One writer, "S.R.," claimed that progressive education aimed at confusing students so that they would eventually become "easy prey to propaganda leaders."[7]

Even more vaguely, conservatives articulated a hazy but powerful nostalgia, a feeling that schools had strayed from tried-and-true educational standards. As it had done since the 1920s and would continue to do into the twenty-first century, this nostalgism became a powerful motivator in 1950s Pasadena. Parents complained that progressive schools led to a modern rudeness, laziness, surliness, and insouciance. They insisted that progressive education lacked the stern but fair absolutes parents remembered from their own childhood schools.

These furious letter writers clearly felt their city had had enough progressive education, though they did not seem entirely unified on what exactly that kind of education entailed. By the time the 1951 Rose Bowl parade swept through the tidy streets of Pasadena—heralding another shameful defeat of California's Golden Bears, this time by the Wolverines of Michigan—this complicated public perception of progressive education had catapulted the city into the national limelight.

Their well-known superintendent Willard Goslin had been ignominiously fired. As in Dayton, Tennessee, and Philadelphia, throughout the months-long controversy, Pasadena found itself welcoming more than just college football fans. As in every other prominent school controversy, activists from around the nation involved themselves in the Goslin case in order to press home the claims of conservative school reform. In Pasadena, as elsewhere, conservatives agreed with progressives that the content and structure of schooling would determine the fate of America as a whole. In the Pasadena case, conservatives blasted left-leaning progressive reform as an attempt to move society in socialistic directions. The urgent threat posed by such progressive subversion, in the opinion of conservative reformers, required urgent action, even if such action invited accusations of hysteria or red-baiting.

In Pasadena, conservative "pressure groups" weighed in on the attack on Goslin and progressive education. Progressive education, such activists told locals, meant less learning and more communism. It meant racial desegregation and higher taxes. Red-baiting politicians swept into town, hoping to make their careers by ferreting out the subversive influence of such progressivism on the unwitting schoolchildren of Pasadena. Other national organizations, most notably the

National Education Association, rallied to the defense of Goslin and progressivism.

The controversy in Pasadena served as a testing ground of sorts. Conservative battles against a complex and shifting enemy known as "progressive education" relied for decades on tropes honed in the struggle against Willard Goslin.[8] In addition, looming battles over race and desegregation found an early field of battle in this foothill city. Decades before "busing" and the "Silent Majority" became buzzwords for conservatives, anti-progressive activists in Pasadena used what historian Matthew Lassiter has called "an ethos of color-blind individualism" to fight against Goslin's brand of progressivism.[9] As historian Arthur Zilversmit concluded, "What happened in Pasadena became a symbol of the turmoil in American education in the postwar period."[10] This chapter will explore the ways conservatives rallied round new visions of ideology and activism in this controversy at the start of the Cold War era.

Welcome to the Athens of the West

Although the activists involved would look back at the beginning of Goslin's tenure as Pasadena's school superintendent and find evidence of the coming storm, Goslin's first year in office appeared boringly mundane at the time. The movers and shakers in Pasadena had wanted the very best school administrator in the nation. Goslin fit the bill. He was president of the American Association of School Administrators and had served as an award-winning superintendent of Minneapolis and of Webster Groves, Missouri. The National Education Association had labeled Goslin "one of the country's outstanding superintendents."[11] The school board was overjoyed to have Goslin accept their offer in April 1948.[12]

When he came to town in July, looking something like an earnest Barney Fife in a rumpled suit, the Pasadena that welcomed him was growing fast. By the time Goslin left office, the total population of the school district had grown by over 50,000 people in just ten years.[13] For school administrators, that demographic bulge meant a desperate need for funding. The schools would have to be expanded and updated. Those new kids would all need teachers, books, desks, walls, and ceilings. It was not necessarily financially impossible. The city had plenty of resources. One contemporary survey concluded that Pasadena in 1949 enjoyed the sixth-highest per capita income in the nation.[14] The problem seemed more likely to be one of political will. Pasadenans were not known for their eagerness to fund public expenditures. As journalist

David Hulburd noted at the time, Pasadena was said to have its own set of three Rs: Rich, Reactionary, and Republican.[15]

Indeed, the most pressing problems for the new superintendent had nothing to do with progressivism and all it implied. Most of Goslin's first months in office were spent in the agonizingly humdrum process of estimating the size of the coming school-age population and struggling to raise money for new schools to accommodate the newcomers.[16] And if Pasadena parents had one leading concern about what their kids might bring home from school in 1948, it was polio, not progressivism.[17]

Nevertheless, while Goslin spent most of his time worrying about demographics, disease, and school funding, he also raised some typically progressive issues. For instance, in his first public speech to the assembled teachers of Pasadena's public schools, Goslin warned that traditional report cards did more harm than good. "Keep hammering home each six weeks the idea that a child is a failure," Goslin told Pasadena's teachers, "not up to the standards of his classmates, and in 10 or 12 years, you will convince him that he is a failure."[18] If the three Rs were all there were to teaching, Goslin told the crowd, then he'd get out of the field "before noon."[19] Those fundamentals were important, Goslin told them, but the real job of a teacher was to help develop students' appetites for freedom and democracy. Only by grooming well-educated, activist citizens, only by raising a generation that looked to international organizations such as the United Nations to usher in a new peaceful age, could America hope to survive in 1948's new world of atomic weapons.[20]

It would be understandable if Willard Goslin saw no foreboding signs in this first meeting. Indeed, as a local reporter described, "the room shook with the burst of applause that followed."[21] But while teachers thundered their applause for Goslin's approach to education, a powerful cocktail of notions, loosely collected as a conservative anti-progressivism, gained influence among other Pasadenans. Some parents worried that without report cards, their children would never be able to learn.[22] Others passed around pamphlets from anti-communist activists, pamphlets that warned of the insidious methods of educational subversives. One of the first—seemingly innocent—moves these communist dupes would make, parents read, was the elimination of report cards and academic competition in public schools. By training young people not to compete, parents in Pasadena read, progressive education prepared students only for adult life in a "socialist society."[23] As a result, these pamphlets warned, young people would become susceptible to a "terrifying social delinquency," open to pernicious socialist ideas, a "more terrifying menace to all America and to our free life than any external menace."[24] Not only that, such miseducated young people, without the benefits of a traditional education including report cards and healthy competition, became subject to a lamentably predictable "moral disintegration," all "directly traceable to the fatal lack of the right kind of instruction in our schools."[25]

Moreover, such conservative activists warned one another and anyone who would listen about the creeping internationalism of such bodies as the United Nations. What Goslin saw as the only hope for lasting world peace, conservatives in Pasadena and around the nation saw as a sinister international conspiracy hoping to transform patriotic Americans into weak-willed socialistic internationalists.[26]

Goslin may have enjoyed the hearty applause of that warm late summer afternoon. But as he lauded the benefits of abolishing traditional report cards, as he planned to eliminate school zoning preferences that allowed racial segregation, as he inaugurated a series of summer workshops to expose Pasadena's teachers to the latest in educational thinking, he may not have heard the low rumble of conservative discontent that would soon lead to his very public ouster.

But that gets ahead of the story. In the fall of 1948, Goslin had every reason to believe he was fulfilling the high expectations of Pasadenans. After all, he succeeded at the hardest job of any school superintendent, shepherding through a new bond issue worth just over five million dollars. The new kindergarten class of 1948–49 revealed the coming baby boom.[27] Goslin managed to convince Pasadenans that such numbers needed new schools and classrooms. The editors of Pasadena's *Star News* concluded just before the October bond issue vote that support for the new bond issue was "strikingly unanimous." Goslin, the editors felt, had quickly "inspired a high degree of public confidence."[28] The Pasadena public demonstrated that confidence by showing up in record numbers to vote in favor of the new bonds, voting yes in a crushing six-to-one majority. As a result, the city schools would be able to add over a hundred new classrooms, install new lights in all the schools, build a new school for what they called "handicapped children," and more.[29]

Flush with success, Goslin introduced the next of his major reforms in January 1949. In order to involve all employees more authentically in the school district's decision-making process, Goslin established "vertical groups" of teachers, staff, and administrators. These groups of roughly twenty employees would meet regularly to make sure that all employees understood the curricular plan for the entire district. Each group would choose a leader who would receive extra training in running these sorts of meetings. In Goslin's telling, these working groups would ensure a truly democratic power structure. Unfortunately for Goslin, however, the meanings of democracy became just as problematic in Pasadena as they had during the Rugg textbook controversy.[30]

Goslin also introduced his plan for summer workshops for teachers. These would serve to keep teachers up to date with the latest educational thinking, Goslin claimed. Summer workshops would also help ease a long-term transition to year-round schooling. In Goslin's opinion, long summer vacations had clearly outlived their usefulness; they lingered only due to unexamined habit and intellectual laziness.[31]

Shadow Boxing

By the end of his first academic year as superintendent, Goslin realized that Pasadenans might not embrace his reform plans as eagerly as he had hoped. Too many Pasadenans, Goslin believed, resisted the notion that the public schools were everyone's business. "People around town," Goslin told one audience in May 1949, "are pulling at my coat tails and talking about 'my' system of education, but I want to test my system with 'you,' because if what I think won't stand up among the people, then I better get another system." In fact, Goslin warned, such delegation of authority had almost killed public schooling in America. Goslin's only plans, he insisted, were to involve more Pasadenans with their public schools. He did not want to impose any kind of school administration that did not have public support. If people in Pasadena continued what Goslin admitted was public "resistance" to being included in the schools, Goslin feared that the whole project might end up on the "ash heap."[32]

Contrary to Goslin's claims, conservatives in Pasadena did not seem hesitant to assert control over the public schools. Indeed, by the end of the 1948–49 school year, those conservative complaints became the dominant tone in the public conversation about Pasadena's schools. One of the first complaints lodged by conservatives was that Goslin had brought a parade of left-leaning educational experts to town in order to brainwash Pasadena's teachers.

For instance, in December 1949, Goslin invited Eldridge T. McSwain to deliver some "provocative thought in new things in education."[33] McSwain was not a wild-eyed leftist radical. At the time, he served as dean of Northwestern University's School of Education. His research focused on elementary school curriculum and child development, rather than on using schools to transform American society in progressive directions.[34] Nevertheless, McSwain's talk on "Education for Living in 1950 to 2000" emphasized dominant progressive notions about the nature of formal education. According to McSwain, schooling needed to do more than teach fundamental academic skills, the "three Rs." Rather, schooling done right meant the transformation of lives, the opening of children to the possibilities of better living.[35]

Even worse, in the eyes of conservatives, was Goslin's welcoming of the famous Teachers College professor William Heard Kilpatrick. Kilpatrick had been a close associate of progressive godfather John Dewey. Earlier activists who had fretted about the influence of Harold Rugg and the Social Reconstruction movement had often included Kilpatrick in their rogues' gallery. By 1949, Kilpatrick had become best known for his advocacy of the "project method" of education.[36] Kilpatrick had been the star attraction of Goslin's teacher workshops in the summer of 1949, where he lectured on the theme "We Learn What We Live." As conservatives later fumed, this workshop hoped to convince Pasadena's teachers that the nature of morality must be determined not by reference to transcendent moral norms, nor by consulting religious traditions, but rather solely by "group action."[37] Kilpatrick's workshop, one conservative activist insisted, was nothing more than a "super-duper indoctrination course" for Pasadena's teachers.[38] Some teachers, she wrote, "have completely fallen under his spell and are working feverishly to follow his guidance with something akin to fanaticism."[39]

By the late 1940s, Kilpatrick had become something of a symbol of the vaguely defined "progressive" movement that so exercised conservative reformers. Though he had retired from active teaching at Teachers College in 1938, his prolific public scholarship since the 1920s maintained his reputation as the embodiment of educational progressivism.[40] Indeed, around the time of the Pasadena blow-up, John Dewey himself insisted that "progressive education and the work of Dr. Kilpatrick are virtually synonymous."[41]

Kilpatrick doubtless would have taken issue with the way conservative school reformers caricatured his work. As one sympathetic early biographer gushed, the "million-dollar professor" never shied away from a fight.[42] Yet Pasadena's conservatives did not simply create a progressive bogey out of whole cloth; in their critiques they focused on issues and themes that truly had been central to Kilpatrick's career. Conservatives, for instance, accused Kilpatrick of insisting that moral values could never be fixed, never be understood in the abstract. As conservative investigators later charged, Kilpatrick had asked Pasadena's teachers in the summer of 1949, "Does good vary from place to place, from time to time? The only answer we can give you is yes."[43]

Kilpatrick might have defended such talk as simply the bare truth. Throughout his career, Kilpatrick had insisted that education must change radically in order to meet the changing needs of modern civilization. In 1926, Kilpatrick had argued that the old education model had based its authority on crude appeals to external authority. Parents and teachers told children, Kilpatrick lamented, "certain things were wrong because 'the Bible says so' or because their church so taught."[44] Such external appeals, Kilpatrick argued, no longer worked. The simple reason, he asserted in 1933, was what he called the "fundamental collapse of authoritarianism."[45]

As he traveled from New York to Pasadena to address the district's teachers in 1949, Kilpatrick repeated his long-held notion that old educational notions no longer sufficed.[46] By that time, Kilpatrick had begun calling the old educational system "Alexandrian." This outmoded vision of education, Kilpatrick argued, had originated in Alexandria in the third century BCE. This "old type of school, dedicated to 'learning about,'" Kilpatrick insisted, could not prepare young people to function in the modern world.[47] In this ancient tradition, education consisted of collecting and passing along "accumulated wisdom" from one group to another, across the generations and across the centuries.[48]

This sort of education, Kilpatrick believed, only included recitations of dry facts, empty rehashings of dusty memories. In the wake of World War II, Kilpatrick argued that education must make bolder claims on students. Students must learn more than just a catalog of traditional information. In order for American society to function as a true democracy, as an ethical society, students must learn to behave in ways that fundamentally respected the full citizenship of all persons.[49]

As he had for decades, in 1949 Kilpatrick laid out a compelling case for the necessity of schools to adapt to fit a changing civilization. For Kilpatrick, such radical change represented the best hope—indeed the only hope—for society to survive. As he put it in a 1926 lecture, "Our youth no longer accept authoritarian morals. We must develop then a point of view and devise a correlative educational system which shall take adequate account of this fact of ever increasing change. Otherwise civilization itself seems threatened."[50] But what Kilpatrick saw as pragmatic flexibility, conservative school reformers saw as a terrifying example of pernicious moral relativism. Such notions, conservatives accused, denigrated American traditions, mocked American values, and betrayed America's free enterprise system.[51]

Such freewheeling notions of morality, many conservatives charged, would lead America's youth into a devastating moral ambiguity. In order to force such ideas down the throats of America's schoolchildren, conservatives charged, radicals like Kilpatrick planned to use schools to diminish parental authority. As investigators later publicized, Kilpatrick had allegedly warned Pasadena's teachers to expect misguided resistance from conservative parents. "Many, many parents," conservatives accused Kilpatrick of saying,

> form their ideas about school by having gone to school a generation ago. They are afraid of anything different. Many of those parents have a very inadequate social outlook, especially when you come to human relations and group relations. Many parents, otherwise excellent, have very inadequate group attitudes, and so teach their children in advance wrong ways to think and feel.[52]

And, indeed, Kilpatrick had a long history of questioning the proper relationship between school, child, and parent. In the 1920s, Kilpatrick worried that members of the "older generation," himself included, would have trouble adjusting to the moral turbulence of the modern world.[53] Young people would likely have less difficulty recognizing the inadequacy of older traditions of external authority. But parents would lag behind.[54]

By the 1930s Kilpatrick had become even less sanguine about the role of parents in a changing educational system. In a good "modern-type school," Kilpatrick assumed, young people would learn about real social problems. In proper schooling, Kilpatrick argued, students would spend time concocting collaboratively "a desired change in the social practice."[55] When they brought this vision of social reform home, it would undoubtedly cause tension between stuck-in-the-mud parents and progressive children. To Kilpatrick, this inevitable family tension could only be fairly solved by including parents in the educational project as well. Instead of assuming that parental visions of proper society should be given precedence, Kilpatrick assumed that modern schooling must extend its intellectual and moral influence to change parental notions.[56]

Kilpatrick had long recognized that such efforts had been pilloried as propaganda. In the wrong hands, he admitted that such efforts to change the morals of American communities could indeed degrade into "propaganda or indoctrination."[57] But such errors of commission should not discourage teachers from guiding communities toward the new educational mode. Even if a properly educated teacher found himself in a "backward community," Kilpatrick argued in 1933, he or she must recognize the inherent rights of that community as "freemen." Though the educator may be "further along in his own thinking," he must not impose proper choices on a local community. Rather, a good educator must help locals choose "what to reject from their hitherto accepted ideas as well as what to accept from the new ideas."[58]

Kilpatrick never seemed to doubt that his vision of modern thinking and schooling represented a necessary improvement. The old system of education fit an older society, Kilpatrick believed. A modern age required a new way of understanding education and schooling. As he reflected on his talk in Pasadena in 1949, Kilpatrick certainly had no inkling that his vision of proper education would prove so galling to so many conservatives. As he wrote in his diary following his talk to Pasadena's teachers, "They all seemed to feel that the Conference has been a success. . . . Not in a long time have I had a group work with such discernment."[59]

Conservatives saw it differently. Not only did they profoundly disagree with Kilpatrick's denunciation of educational and cultural traditions, they deeply resented any suggestion that they represented any sort of "backward community." Throughout the Pasadena controversy, moreover, conservatives used Kilpatrick's ideas and reputation to attack Superintendent Goslin. Conservatives accused Goslin, like Kilpatrick, of hoping to split children from their parents' traditional values. They insinuated that Goslin's school plans hoped to rob students of their sense of transcendent values, of good and evil. As one journalist later observed, Goslin himself had not actually publicly supported "these deeper social philosophies." Nevertheless, by ferreting out the radical nature of ideas coming from guest speakers such as Kilpatrick, alert conservatives could discover that such ideas run "through the entire progressive pattern."[60]

As conservative Pasadenans grumbled about the nature of Goslin's plans, T. G. Wood of the *Pasadena Independent* asked readers at the end of January 1950 if progressive education was "leaving children little better than high grade imbeciles after months of modernistic 'training.'"[61] Wood invited readers to weigh in. The resulting newspaper debate about the meaning and value of progressive education signaled the public phase of Pasadena's school controversy.

But this timing raises difficult questions. When Pasadenans started their fight over Goslin and progressive education, they lived in a city that had famously led the nation in progressive education for decades. As a leading historian of progressive education noted, Pasadena was

These children were packed into an unapologetically progressive classroom. Yet their "activity program" in 1929 never attracted attention from conservative critics. Image from the 45th Annual Report of the Pasadena City Schools, 1928–1929, p. 16. (Courtesy Pasadena Unified School District)

"well known in the period before World War II for the progressivism of its public schools."[62] Goslin's predecessor, the long-serving John Sexson, had introduced a progressive structure to the system, offering six years of elementary education, four years of what twenty-first-century Americans would call "middle school," and four years that combined two years of high school and two years of junior college.[63]

Indeed, a school survey in 1931 praised Pasadena for managing even in economic hard times to maintain a thoroughly progressive educational philosophy and structure.[64] The district itself promoted its progressive image, trumpeting in 1929 its use of the progressive favorite, the "activity program" of early education. The original caption to the image shown above proudly proclaimed, "The Activity program eliminates failures and disciplinary problems."[65]

Nor was racial desegregation—an issue that seemed to spring out of nowhere in the Goslin controversy—necessarily new in 1950. The same school district report of 1929 proudly showed children of apparently

Neither progressive activity nor racial desegregation was new to Pasadena in 1950, as this publicity photo shows. Image from the 45th Annual Report of the Pasadena City Schools, 1928–1929, p. 31. (Courtesy Pasadena Unified School District)

different ethnic backgrounds working together happily. The 1929 report enthused that the multi-racial group of kindergartners shown in the photo above could succeed only when each child "first learns to interpret his experiences, to join the group, to share with others, and to work with his hands."[66]

As any of Goslin's fierce critics would have insisted in 1950, such claims smacked of progressive education. Yet Pasadena did not sack its progressive superintendent in 1930. Conservatives in 1929 or 1939 did not rally against these patently progressive-sounding innovations. Yet by 1949 it had become a bitterly contested issue. Why then?

The Crisis in Education

Perhaps one reason for the timing of Pasadena's explosion of conservative anti-progressivism was the broader cultural context. As we have seen, every decade in the twentieth century offered conservatives plenty of fodder for energetic public activism. But as historian Andrew Hartman has noted, such concerns rose to another frenetic peak in the late 1940s and early 1950s. As he argued, "Cold War anxieties over children translated into Cold War concerns for the schools."[67] Similarly, Adam Golub has noted that the national mood in 1949 included new protestations of anxiety about the "crisis in education."[68]

Like Americans nationwide, conservatives in Pasadena were keenly tuned in to a conversation about the pernicious nature of progressive education. They read and discussed the work of journalists, scholars, and politicians who insisted that such notions of education must be combated. Some of the most prominent critics of progressive education focused on the fact that progressive education had failed to teach American children. Mortimer Smith, for example, a businessman who attracted widespread attention with his 1949 book *And Madly Teach,* criticized progressive education as a pedagogical cop-out. True education, Smith contended, required the painstaking transmission of "the whole heritage of man's progress through history." In effective, traditional schools, young people learned "spiritual and moral standards."[69]

Unfortunately for American society, according to Smith, most teachers could not achieve that daunting goal. Teachers settled instead for the "easier" task of helping students toward a progressive "self-realization."[70] No one learned a thing, Smith argued, but everyone went home happy. In the end, however, Smith believed progressive education was more dangerous than this. In its inability to educate its students, a progressive school encouraged them to abandon an ethos of individual achievement, to adopt instead a group-centered ideology, an "un-American" approach that edged ever closer "along the road to totalitarianism."[71]

Bernard Iddings Bell praised Smith's "thoughtful complaints" about progressive education.[72] Bell himself attracted his share of public attention with his 1949 book *Crisis in Education.*[73] Bell, an educator and Episcopalian clergyman, felt American education had failed in its unique task of "democratic education." Instead of educating the American masses in the best academic traditions, Bell believed mass public education had created "the uneducated Common Man . . . the perpetually adolescent Common Man . . . blatantly vulgar, ill-mannered, boorish, unsure of himself, hungry for happiness." The fault lay not with students, in Bell's opinion, but squarely with the public education system.[74] Even the "modern educators," Bell felt, had been trapped in a system of "spiritual malaise," unable to do more with their students than hope for a minimum level of technical proficiency.[75]

Bell avoided such terms as "progressive" and "traditional" in his critique of education. Indeed, he prided himself as someone who approached the "crisis" in education "from a philosophical angle which is neither 'progressive' nor 'traditionalist' but only 'realistic.'"[76] Nevertheless, he blasted the "poisonous notion" that education should follow the inclinations of children. Instead, true education must transmit the best elements of "the race's wisdom . . . in the tried and tested folkways." Schooling for young people, Bell insisted in 1947, must drill students in basic subjects such as reading, writing, and arithmetic. In addition, Bell felt that public schooling had gone awry when it had abandoned traditional "reward and deprivations." Schooling must remain competitive, or it would teach all students that effort did not matter. Similarly, Bell hammered the traditionalist notions that school must teach "decent manners" and a sense of transcendent truth. He lamented the modern "cleavage between religion and secular learning," though he agreed that public schools must not favor any single denomination or religious tradition.[77]

In the end, Bell argued, modern education failed when it overreached. The home and family must be the primary influences on children. But due to the harried nature of American life in 1948, Bell believed, "overworked and unskilled instructors" had taken responsibility for "the whole child." This sad situation, promoted by lazy parents, unrealistic school administrators, and overzealous education professors, left little time in public schools for their proper work: "a thorough mastery of the old-fashioned school subjects."[78] Conservative activists in Pasadena read and discussed Bell's trenchant criticisms of modern education.[79]

Pasadena's anti-progressive activists also read Albert Lynd's stinging critique of progressive education.[80] Lynd, a businessman and school board member in Sharon, Massachusetts, vented his bile at the "pedagogical cult" of modern education in an early 1950 article in *Atlantic Monthly*.[81] Lynd's rant, "Quackery in the Public Schools," which he soon expanded into a book of the same name, attacked progressive educators for leaching the intellectual content out of public schools. It would not be unusual in 1920, Lynd insisted, for the principal of a high school to be the "most learned fellow in town."[82] But since the triumph of progressivism, spurred on from the "Vatican of the cult" at Teachers College, public school teachers and administrators no longer cared about academic learning.[83] They did not need to, Lynd claimed, since they only listened to one another. Instead of relying on the "traditional education system," in which students were pumped full of "objective information," the new schools allowed students to follow their "natural inclinations." Instead of receiving "rigid drillings in reading, writing, and arithmetic," according to Lynd, students in progressive schools were taught vague "'skills' for 'socially useful' results."[84]

In addition to such denunciations of the moral and pedagogical failings of progressive education, conservatives in Pasadena and around the nation warned that progressivism in education promoted communism. As we've seen, conservative activists had been warning of such a connection for decades. In the early 1930s, for example, professional anti-communist Elizabeth Dilling blasted John Dewey as "the atheistic 'Progressive Education' head and idol of the Reds."[85] Her 1934 screed *The Red Network* denounced such educational organizations as the American Federation of Teachers as socialist, communist, and atheist.[86] It blasted the "radical" National Education Association[87] and indicted progressive education's leaders, including William Heard Kilpatrick,[88] John Dewey,[89] George Counts,[90] progressive school superintendent Carleton Washburne,[91] and of course Harold Rugg.[92] Such radicals, Dilling charged, denied their own involvement in this subversive plot, hoping to confuse and soothe the "non-radical" American public.[93]

Dilling's book, ironically, inspired a vigorous network of anti-communist activists vitally interested in progressive education. Such activists, like those in Pasadena, fretted that subversive organizations used "progressive education" as a cover for their left-wing campaigns. As historian Ellen Schrecker has argued, by the late 1940s, anti-communists had created a "loosely structured, but surprisingly self-conscious, network of political activists who had been working for years to drive Communism out of American life."[94] Just as the tense times of the Great Depression lent anti-communists added urgency in the 1930s, so the developing Cold War deadlock sent a jolt of anxious energy to these later red hunters. Throughout the late 1940s and early 1950s, this network continued its goal of protecting America's public schools from the subversive threat of progressivism.

The background of some of these activists has left only the faintest traces in the archival record. For example, a barrage of anonymous newsletters seems to have filled the mailboxes of conservative activists. One such document accidentally preserved in the archival record warned of the dangers of "Progressive Education." Such education, this anonymous manifesto declared, "is impairing the moral fibre of the United States. It has and is producing a generation of selfish, lawless individuals." Through the abandonment of corporal punishment and Christian values, the letter charged, progressives sought to undermine the stability of the American republic itself.[95]

Other educational conservatives in this network gained more prominence. For instance, retired US Army major general Amos Fries, former head of the army's Chemical Warfare Service, built a second career in the 1930s denouncing communist subversion in public schools. In the 1920s, while still an active military officer, Fries and his associates created and distributed the "Spider Web Chart" of suspect women and women's organizations. This widely distributed graphic charged numerous organizations of connecting in a sinister-seeming web of left-wing influence.[96]

After his retirement, Fries created a new organization, Friends of the Public Schools, to continue his anti-subversive activism. In the 1940s, Fries denounced progressive bugbears such as the Frontier Thinkers of Teachers College and the Progressive Education Association. In order to combat the creeping communism of such front groups, Fries warned, public schools must "teach fundamentals." True patriots, Fries believed, must fight the triple threat from progressives. Progressive dupes introduced dangerous changes including centralization of education at the federal level, dumbing-down of curriculum with the introduction of inane "progressive" practices, and an unhealthy disrespect for patriotic American symbols and traditions.[97]

Fries's educational jeremiads resonated powerfully within an expansive network of conservative educational activists. Leaders of the American Legion eagerly shared copies of his works.[98] Prominent Daughters of the American Revolution quoted Fries approvingly.[99] Indeed, Mrs. Amos Fries had long been an active DAR leader.[100] Augustin Rudd, the anti-Rugg leader, subscribed to the Fries newsletter.[101]

This activist network expanded to include other pundits convinced of the threat of communist subversion in America's public schools. For instance, Fries lent his anti-communist, anti-progressive education prestige to the work of Lucille Crain. Beginning in 1949, funded in part by William F. Buckley Sr., Crain edited the *Educational Reviewer*.[102] This newsletter exposed the workings of subversives in all aspects of America's educational system.[103] Though the newsletter never reached more than 2,000 subscribers, it helped mobilize and motivate a national network of anti-communist school activists.[104]

Crain also helped expand and strengthen the reach of anti-communism in educational circles. In early 1950, just as Pasadenans vented their anger against progressive education in the pages of the *Pasadena Independent,* Crain introduced John Flynn to the dangers of subversive progressivism in education.[105] By 1950, John Flynn had built a complicated career as a journalist and activist. He bounced between popularity and obscurity, trumpeting first an ardent liberal denunciation of big business, then shifting by the mid-1940s to a virulent anti-communist conservatism.[106] Though his political ideology shifted, his work ethic did not. Throughout his career, Flynn remained a prolific writer and an energetic activist. His books, articles, and weekly radio program reached millions of Americans in the 1940s.[107]

By far the most popular of Flynn's books was *The Road Ahead* (1949). In this book, Flynn denounced the "sneak attack" being carried out by the political left.[108] Under the cover of promoting a patriotic "Planned Economy," subversives had been preparing the United States for socialist oppression.[109] The danger, Flynn warned, was not mainly from open communists and socialists—though such folks were indeed traitors—but rather from sneaking leftist trade union officials, college professors, and government economists.[110] Flynn denounced the creeping influence of socialism in civil rights organizations, liberal Protestant churches, publishing houses, and higher education faculties. His strident tone helped introduce the term "creeping socialism" into common parlance in the late 1950s.[111]

The Road Ahead reached a wide audience. In its first month, it sold 20,000 copies. By the time Pasadena's conservative activists had wrangled the firing of Goslin, the book had sold well into the millions.[112] Conservative activists in Pasadena remembered Flynn's stirring denunciations of "a number of influential educators," progressives who "have for twenty years been trying to use the public schools to shape the minds of children in support of socialist theories."[113]

Pasadena's conservative anti-communists also drew inspiration from the ardent anti-communism of government agencies. Such institutional anti-communism thrived across the political spectrum. For example, President Truman—not known as a strident conservative in most of his political life—set the tone. In early 1947 he issued Executive Order 9835. Henceforth, communists, along with fascists and other totalitarians, could not work for the federal government. This order also included in its wide anti-subversive net all those guilty of "sympathetic association" with such subversive groups.[114]

Members of the US Congress helped turn the focus of this anti-communist crusade to the nation's schools. In 1948, for instance, the House Un-American Activities Committee published a pamphlet describing the dangers of subversion in schools. As we've seen, HUAC had been a leading investigator of domestic communism since the late 1930s. Unlike other leading anti-communists in government, HUAC's activism had been tied to a recognizably anti-New Deal, anti-liberal conservatism.[115] Its 1948 pamphlet warned that much of what passed as progressive reform signaled the onset of a long-standing communist conspiracy to wreck America through its public schools. One sign of this menace, HUAC warned, was a breakdown in teachers' authority. When communists had inflicted their schemes on schools, "classrooms became madhouses of disorder."[116]

Like other anti-communist activists, the members of HUAC also warned that textbooks had become riddled with pro-Soviet ideology.[117] HUAC encouraged all patriotic Americans, in Pasadena and around the country, to root out such nefarious influence. Get involved in local schools, HUAC encouraged. Educate yourself about the code words and secret schemes used by communists and their dupes. And be ready to be attacked. The "standard smears" used against alert patriots, HUAC warned, included "accusations of 'witch-hunting,' 'Red-baiting,' 'textbook-burning,' and 'strangling academic freedom.'"[118]

Closer to home, Pasadenans could look to the energetic Tenney Committee of California's state senate for support and guidance. Though it had originally been established in 1941 to investigate welfare fraud, under the leadership of state senator Jack Tenney the committee soon became what historian Ellen Schrecker has called a "HUAC clone."[119] The Tenney Committee achieved some notable success in its brief history. In 1946 the committee attempted to have two Los Angeles-area teachers fired for subversion. All told, the committee proposed eight anti-subversion bills, one of which eventually became law.[120]

As we'll see, conservative activists in Pasadena soon prevailed on the Tenney Committee and its spin-off Dilworth Committee to bring their pressure to Pasadena and to Goslin. In the meantime, conservative educational activists in Pasadena supported the work of HUAC and Tenney. As HUAC had requested, they read widely from the growing library of anti-progressive and anti-communist publications. They formed local organizations and joined national ones. They pushed the agenda of anti-communist conservatives nationwide onto the agenda of Pasadena's local school debates.

One of the most influential conservative organizations in 1949 Pasadena was Pro America. This national group claimed most of its organizational robustness along the West Coast.[121] It had humble origins in one garden club's reaction to the 1932 presidential election.[122] By the late 1940s, Pasadena's patriotic women could claim a proud recent history of serving as the national headquarters of the expanded organization.[123] Before the Goslin controversy, Pasadena's chapter had also interested itself intensely in local politics.[124] Because most of its members were

female, Pro America was often treated condescendingly in the Pasadena press. For instance, in early 1949 the Pasadena chapter hosted the
organization's three-day national conference. Although the conference
focused on political and cultural issues of national importance, the *Pasadena Star News* covered the meeting initially on its society pages.[125]
News of another Pro America meeting, in which the members mostly
reviewed national legislation, was relegated to the *Star News*'s "Woman's World" pages.[126]

Nevertheless, for the 300 attendees of the February 1949 conference, Pro America meant more than just a "ladies'" social club. Former
US senator Alfred Hawkes, father of Pasadena leader Louise Padelford, addressed the conference about the importance of active citizenship and free markets. Only by fighting to maintain "free enterprise,"
Hawkes warned, could Americans continue to "make a living under
free government and with attention to the individual rights of man."[127]
Congregational pastor James Fifield lectured about the importance of
religion in combating communist subversion. And journalist Waldo
Drake harangued the attendees about the fumbling US policy in China
that had led to the "loss" of China to Mao's communists.[128]

At this February 1949 meeting, Pasadena leader Louise Padelford
handed over the presidency of the national organization. In her farewell
address, Padelford warned that the biggest dangers to traditional American government and society were "ignorance and consequent apathy."
The dangers of communist subversion, she said, resulted largely from
an American population too comfortable in its postwar abundance to
confront creeping subversion. The *raison d'etre* for organizations such as
Pro America, Padelford believed, was to organize energetic resistance
to all such "destructive influences."[129]

Padelford defied some of the stereotypes of Cold War red hunters.
As one skeptical journalist admitted with surprise, Padelford was anything but the typical angry right-wing crank. Instead, the journalist
described an activist with "clear blue eyes that look out at the world
with wide-open frankness; her ear is keen, her wit quick, and her smile
enchanting."[130] Her background also belied the expectations of some
progressives. She came from an elite background, daughter of a US
senator. She had been educated at Vassar and Columbia University and
had earned a PhD in romance languages. She had spent two years as
an assistant professor of French literature after marrying and moving
to Pasadena in 1934.[131]

By 1949, Padelford's conservative activism had come to focus primarily on what she perceived as the threat of progressive education.

Her leadership of Pro America in the fight against Goslin became her method to oppose this danger. As Padelford later reflected, progressive education made fundamental philosophic mistakes that would, if allowed free rein, cripple education and American society. For one thing, progressive educators misunderstood that education, at its heart, meant imposing knowledge systematically upon children.[132] The only way to maintain a strong, patriotic society, Padelford believed, was to teach "American History with pride and love of country."[133] Anything else would weaken America's strong resolve. Similarly, Padelford insisted that Goslin's support for federal aid to education would lead "inevitably to Federal control." Such control would undermine the ability of parents to have a voice in their children's education. It would allow progressive educators in far-off ivory towers to impose destructive methods on America's public schools nationwide.[134]

Under Padelford's leadership, the Pasadena chapter of Pro America became actively involved in educational issues. At the national conference held in Pasadena in February 1949, one speaker told an appreciative audience that public schools were the best place to defend against communist subversion. If schools taught patriotic values, youth could lead the fight.[135] At a Pasadena chapter meeting in the summer of 1950, George Benson, president of Claremont Men's College (today's Claremont McKenna College), insisted that public schools would fall apart if they continued to ignore "the three R's." Neither American schools nor American society could last long, Benson warned, if the schools abjured their responsibility to teach patriotism. Too many progressive schools, like those under Goslin's leadership in Pasadena, blithely abandoned "established values." Like many of the conservative activists in his audience, Benson believed that traditional pedagogy and traditional cultural values remained inextricably linked. Progressive education, he believed, threatened to break that link and weaken America's anti-communist spine. "Harder drilling on writing, on reading, and on mathematics in secondary school," Benson told the Pro America audience, "would make far better citizens of all of us and guarantee the future of our American tradition."[136]

In addition to hosting conservative speakers such as Benson, Pro America leaders also shared literature with other Pasadenans concerned about the direction of the public schools. Activists would later remember reading and sharing the works of Mortimer Smith, Albert Lynd, Bernard Iddings Bell, and John Flynn.[137] But no conservative pundit had more ideological influence on Pasadena's conservative activists than Allen Zoll.

A Thorn in the City of Roses

In the Pasadena controversy, the level of Zoll's influence became a matter of intense debate. Progressives claimed that Zoll represented the takeover of Pasadena's schools by outside extremists. Conservatives admitted to having read Zoll's work, but denied any connection to Zoll's extremist background. As always, it is notoriously difficult for historians to untangle claims of intellectual influence. But in at least one episode, we can see the ways Zoll's ideas influenced local debate in the Pasadena controversy. In December 1949, one activist confronted Goslin about an issue that may not have seemed particularly relevant to Pasadena, but had exercised Zoll and other conservative pundits nationwide. Unaware of the planned confrontation, Goslin had agreed to attend a meeting of the School Development Council. By that time, Goslin was aware of the rumblings of conservative opposition to his policies but he apparently did not understand the depth of conservative anger. By attending the meeting, Goslin hoped to defuse any lingering tension.[138]

Later reports differed as to the roots of the School Development Council, or SDC. According to journalist David Hulburd, the SDC had been founded just that winter, with about seventy original members.[139] Later investigators from the National Education Association disagreed. They concluded that the SDC had not been formed until June 1950.[140] That late date seems extremely unlikely, since by then the SDC had taken a leading role in organizing conservative protest in Pasadena. Two local conservative leaders remembered it differently. According to Louise Padelford and Cay Hallberg, the SDC had existed as a loosely organized citizens' group since early 1949. It was only when the public outpouring of anger at the perceived sins of progressive education hit the newspapers in February 1950 that the group became reinvigorated with a new, earnest, well-organized steering committee under the chairmanship of local businessman Frank Wells.[141]

In whatever state it existed, by the time the SDC hosted Goslin at their meeting in December 1949, some SDC members had determined to force Goslin's suspected progressivism into the open. Members had been reading a pamphlet by right-wing activist Allen Zoll, *They Want Your Child!* Zoll warned readers that progressives pushed federal aid for schools as a first step toward communist takeover. "We had better stop smiling," Zoll warned. "There IS a conspiracy."[142] Communists, Zoll insisted, used well-meaning schoolteachers and administrators as dupes. Such subversives promised more federal funding for education as part of their calculated plan to undermine local conservative watch-dogs. The only way to ferret out such subversion, Zoll told anxious readers, was through energetic and aggressive purging of all such front men and sympathizers.[143]

At their December meeting, SDC members planned to confront Goslin over the issue of federal aid to Pasadena's schools. Predictably, when activists asked Goslin if he supported federal aid to education, the somewhat surprised Goslin admitted that he did. Indeed, he had a public record as an outspoken proponent of such assistance. In Goslin's opinion, only federal dollars could equalize educational opportunity in the United States and lift American schools out of the trap of "medioc-rity" in which they flailed.[144]

The different meanings of the issue of federal aid to schools demonstrate some of the cultural distance involved between Pasadena's conservatives and progressives. For Goslin, the issue was a non-issue. Federal money simply represented an unobjectionable resource to improve Pasadena's schools. However, for many members of the SDC, Goslin's support of federal aid for local schools served as proof positive of Goslin's menace. SDC leaders agreed wholeheartedly with Allen Zoll that Goslin's support for federal aid served as an effective sign that Goslin had become an agent of creeping communism.[145]

Given the influence of Zoll's pamphlets among Pasadena's conser-vative activists, an examination of Zoll's career will offer some clues into the intellectual universe of educational conservatism in this con-troversy. By 1949, Zoll had established himself as a central figure on the rightward edge of the conservative education reform movement. In the 1930s, his group, American Patriots Incorporated, sought political and financial support for its campaign to ensure "that the only 'ism' . . . tol-erated in America is 'Americanism.'"[146] Through the years, Zoll kept in close contact with a conservative anti-communist network of activists, including Lucille Cardin Crain, Augustin Rudd, and Amos Fries.[147]

Perhaps spurred by the torrent of conservative interest in the dan-gers of progressive education, Zoll had shifted his focus by the late 1940s. His National Council for American Education (NCAE) warned of the subversive threat to America's public schools. The NCAE proved most influential through its pamphlets, like the ones that surfaced in Pasadena. However, along with his colleague Verne Kaub, Zoll had hoped to establish himself as a conservative leader in other ways as well.[148] For instance, Zoll had offered in his pamphlets to provide detailed lists of subversive textbooks to anyone who requested them. Many local activists took him up on it. Zoll's NCAE fielded requests for textbook lists from conservatives planning to enter the teaching field,[149] from activist members of the Daughters of the American Revolution,[150] and from conservative parents from across the nation.[151] However, Zoll never followed through.[152] The NCAE never distributed its promised definitive guide to subversive textbooks. Though Zoll's colleague Verne Kaub reviewed several school textbooks and compiled a draft master list of dangerous books, the NCAE never managed to produce its promised guidebook.[153] Kaub privately complained that he simply did not have time to maintain an adequate compendium of all the books on the market.[154] The difficulty of the task and its lack of profit convinced Zoll to move out of the field of education activism by 1953.[155]

Before he could do so, however, Zoll's extremist tone and history of involvement with extremist organizations discredited him in the eyes of much of the mainstream conservative movement. Liberal activists from Pasadena and from the investigating committee of the National Education Association uncovered some unsavory details. The Reverend Max Merritt Morrison, for example, denounced Zoll's right-wing extremism in a sermon at Pasadena's Westminster Presbyterian Church. Morrison related a tale of his visit to an SDC meeting. The tone at the meeting shocked Morrison by its angry, extreme tone. In the sermon, which was reprinted as a full-page paid advertisement in Pasadena's newspapers, Morrison worried that he "heard good American citizens . . . ridiculed, labeled with detestable un-American names." Anyone who spoke up in favor of Goslin or progressive education, Morrison said, was "yelled down or told to go home."[156]

Morrison noted that many SDC members quoted Zoll approvingly at this angry meeting. Afterwards, Morrison did a little digging. He found some newspaper reports that denounced Zoll as a right-wing "Hate-monger." In the 1930s, Zoll's organization, American Patriots, Inc., had been listed as "fascist and subversive" by Attorney General Tom Clarke. At a House Un-American Activities Committee meeting in 1939, according to these reports, Zoll had been attacked as anti-Semitic for his opposition to Justice Felix Frankfurter's elevation to the US Supreme Court.[157]

Similarly, the Pasadena Education Association (PEA) distributed a pamphlet highlighting Zoll's extremist background. The PEA pamphlet warned against the SDC's use of Zoll's "propaganda." It highlighted Zoll's "Fascist Taint" and concluded, "This is strange company for sincere friends of free, democratic public education."[158]

The National Education Association took an even harsher line. Zoll, one NEA leader insisted, served as a "general, or chief-of-staff" for right-wing attacks on Pasadena's schools. Zoll's methods included a "Hitler technique of repetition" to pound home propaganda points.[159]

One journalist sympathetic to the NEA's position ominously denounced Zoll as an "insidious virus" that was "infecting" the brains of Pasadena's citizens. Under Zoll's influence, this author concluded, Pasadena's conservatives engaged in some "fascist-style moves" to take over the schools. There should be no doubt, however, that Zoll remained responsible; Zoll was the "leader of a movement to ruin American public schools."[160]

Some conservative leaders affected, at least, to ignore these attacks on Zoll's character. As historian Jonathan Zimmerman has noted, William F. Buckley Jr. insisted in 1951 that Zoll was doing a "splendid job." Buckley encouraged fellow conservatives not to listen to such "leftist smear organizations" as the ones that had denounced Zoll.[161] Buckley's loyalty makes sense. After all, it was to established leaders such as Zoll that Buckley turned for advice when starting his career as a conservative activist.[162]

In Pasadena, conservative activists showed less assurance when it came to Zoll. After Morrison's attack on Zoll, SDC president Frank Wells offered a two-part defense. First of all, Wells insisted that the SDC was not part of Zoll's NCAE "or any other national organization." The SDC's concerns, Wells claimed, were purely local. The SDC, he told reporters, was an organization made up of concerned Pasadenans with every right to take charge of their public schools, not the patsy of some national right-wing extremist group. Furthermore, the SDC publicly repudiated "any organization found guilty of subversive activities or propaganda, whether fascist or communist."[163]

Skeptical journalist David Hulburd claimed Wells originally told him of being in touch with Zoll. Later, however, Wells changed his story and said they had not spoken directly.[164] By the time the California state senate investigating committee came to town, Wells insisted he had not had any direct contact with Zoll.[165]

But that did not mean that Wells disagreed with Zoll's ideas. Indeed, in his public repudiation of the NCAE, Wells insisted that the SDC agreed strongly with Zoll's ideas. Even if Zoll might have an unsavory extremist past, Wells declared, his writing was "about as subversive as the American Constitution and the Bill of Rights. It quotes Thomas Jefferson, Christian principles and the Uniform Crime Reports of the Department of Justice."[166]

Similarly, W. Ernest Brower, a Pasadena physician and Wells's successor as SDC chairman, insisted that the SDC was not part of any national right-wing organization. According to Brower, SDC leaders came across some of Zoll's pamphlets and "agreed thoroughly" with their sentiments. The SDC, Brower testified, did not look closely at Zoll's history, but felt that his work "would be proper literature for us to use at our meetings." Though hesitant to embrace Zoll's reputation as an anti-Semite and violent extremist, Brower concluded that Zoll's writings still expressed the feelings of the SDC very well. "Insofar as the content is concerned," Brower maintained, "we have nothing to find wrong with it."[167] Neither Brower nor Wells disputed the accusation that the SDC had distributed Zoll's *Progressive Education Increases Delinquency*, in addition to Zoll's *They Want Your Child!*[168]

As have other leading educational conservatives,[169] Zoll began his critique of contemporary American education by comparing it to a lost golden age. In *Progressive Education Increases Delinquency*, Zoll insisted that early American schools and society found their cultural and intellectual sources in Christianity.[170] In the nineteenth century, Zoll argued, public schools trained students in more than the three Rs. Those early schools "sought also to bind the minds and hearts of childhood and youth to the moral principles basic to our peculiar and distinctive society."[171]

Like other conservative educational activists before and after him, Zoll believed that the bundle of notions called "progressive education" made fundamental mistakes about the nature of culture and education. Real education, Zoll wrote, must not suggest a mere pragmatic understanding of the nature of truth and of knowledge. Instead, education must instill in young people a belief that there is a transcendent truth; there are eternal values of right and wrong. In the past, Zoll believed, American schools did just that. Nineteenth-century schools did not fill students' heads with notions that "mankind is composed of clever animals." On the contrary, early public schools taught "that the life we live on earth should be lived in the light that streams upon us from God Himself, and that man was made for an eternal destiny."[172]

In addition, golden-age schools taught a healthy skepticism toward government interference and control of Americans' affairs. Traditional American schools instilled the notion that government was something created to serve the needs of citizens, not the other way around. At the same time, early schools taught true patriotism, "the passionate love for a land which, more than any other land on earth, offered rewards for courage, intelligence, and hard work."[173]

As a result of all this, Zoll argued that Americans in the 1840s were not only more moral and patriotic than Americans in the 1940s, but "the level of public intelligence . . . was very materially higher" as well.[174] In Zoll's vision of American educational and cultural history, John Dewey and his ilk shattered this happy past. Since the time Dewey gained pernicious influence over the institutions that trained American teachers, American education had embraced Dewey's "tragic and terrifying" philosophy. That philosophy, at its root, insisted on the utter absence of any "binding moral code." Since Dewey, Zoll wrote, American educators had been forced through "a fundamental revolution in human thinking of the first order." Such teachers had embraced Dewey's "mental and ethical nihilism."[175] This dangerous thinking had taken over American schools, Zoll believed. If conservative activists did not stop it, such ideas would certainly lead to "the disintegration and final extinction of the American society."[176]

Progressive educators, Zoll maintained, did not simply stumble into these dangerous notions. Instead, progressives had explicitly planned to cripple students intellectually. By cranking out of America's public schools "a tragically misshapen generation . . . without the ability to think for themselves, filled only with the desired herd ideas," progressive educators would achieve their sinister long-term goals. Such warped young people would grow into subjects, not citizens. They would be unable to read, unable to cipher. They would be unable to vote intelligently. In the end, they would succumb gladly and gratefully to the demands of an "authoritarian state."[177]

Indeed, in Zoll's telling, the greatest threat to American society came not from "Marx, Lenin, Trotsky, [former Communist Party USA leader Earl] Browder or any of that ilk."[178] The much bigger threat loomed from progressives such as Harold Rugg and his Social-Frontier colleagues. The Frontier Thinkers, Zoll concluded, were the ones eroding America from within.[179]

Zoll continued the theme of communist subversion in *They Want Your Child!*, which focused on the dangers of federal aid to education. The plan, Zoll warned in the pamphlet, was to consolidate control of education at the federal level.[180] Once communists had achieved that goal, through the assistance of well-meaning dupes and front men, they would begin to implement their plan to destroy America. Zoll described "the infiltration and control of American education" as the "number one objective" of communists in America.[181]

Once communists gained control of schools, they would start their campaign by attacking the idea of "truth as something absolute and timeless."[182] If America's schools taught an enervating moral relativism, as progressive educators insisted they should, communists would be able to raise a generation of Americans unable to defend themselves. Similarly, as communists urged, progressive educators derided the notion that children should compete academically. Progressives, as their secret communist controllers demanded, taught that an undue emphasis on competition made children "un-social."[183] As a result, Zoll argued, "progressive education has produced millions of little victims who know next to nothing and who have never been taught even how to learn anything."[184]

Little Old Ladies from Pasadena

At least some of Pasadena's conservative activists agreed heartily with Zoll's analysis. Of course, the level of zeal with which local conservatives embraced these ideas varied. One of the most ardent anti-progressive activists in Pasadena at the time was Mary Allen. Allen would eventually write for a local conservative newsletter, *FACTS:* "Fundamental Issues, Americanism, Constitutional Government, Truth, Spiritual Values."[185] After the dust had settled from the Goslin controversy, she also collected her thoughts about progressivism, subversion, and education into a book, *Education or Indoctrination.* Allen wondered why American schools, even in "such conservative cities as Pasadena," had turned into "the center of confusion, emotional wrangling, and extreme differences of opinion."[186]

Most of Allen's analysis echoed the arguments of Zoll and other leading activists such as John Flynn. The roots of the problem, Allen argued, lay with the philosophic roots of progressive education. Since the time of Dewey, progressive educators had eliminated the notion of permanent truths or values.[187] Since the 1930s, Allen believed, the Frontier Thinkers of Columbia University had worked to derogate free enterprise and the American way of life through a transformation of public schooling. Dangerous sociopaths such as Harold Rugg, George Counts, and William Heard Kilpatrick, Allen argued, had hoped to spread "distaste for the American way of life and approval of the socialization of Soviet Russia."[188]

As did the New Deal, in Allen's telling, such insidious educational progressivism hoped to promote a collective, anti-capitalist lifestyle.[189] One of the first ways progressives approached their goal, Allen believed, was by teaching children that they were citizens of the world, not of any particular nation. The United Nations, Allen argued, and its organization, the United Nations Educational, Scientific, and Cultural Organization (UNESCO), had "attached itself to progressive education"[190] in order to achieve its ultimate goal of "world domination through education."[191] The danger was real and immediate. If alert citizens and parents failed to keep close tabs on the goings-on in their local schools, "communist infiltration" would certainly spread.[192]

As Superintendent Goslin promoted his plans to eliminate competitive grades, as he argued for more federal aid to local schools, as he defended the importance of the United Nations as an institution, conservatives in Pasadena read and discussed the works of activists such as Allen and Zoll. They read or heard of the anti-progressive notions of writers such as Albert Lynd, Mortimer Smith, Bernard Iddings Bell, and John Flynn. When Pasadena's conservatives asked Goslin if he supported federal aid to schools, they did so as a litmus test, not as a policy discussion. For conservatives in Pasadena, Goslin embodied almost all of the tropes conservative pundits warned them about.

And local anti-progressives hastened to put in their two cents about the nature and threat of progressive education. When T. G. Wood of the *Pasadena Independent* asked readers to share their opinions of progressive education in late January 1950, he tapped into a deep and energetic vein of local discontent. As did national writers and activists, conservative Pasadenans had a variety of reasons for disliking progressive education. Writers in the *Independent*—sometimes anonymous, sometimes not—articulated the kaleidoscopic nature of progressive education and its critics in 1950's America.

When Wood called for a public discussion about the nature of progressive education in early 1950, he tipped the tables heavily in favor of its critics. Though he included a few defenses of progressive education, he published more community voices who agreed that the issue at hand was "the failure of the public schools."[193] Clearly, we can't know from Wood's partisan selection of letters how the majority of Pasadenans felt at the time about Goslin and the nature of progressive education. But these letters do offer a unique and telling window into what some of Pasadena's angry anti-progressives thought was wrong with progressivism in schools.

Many writers started their assaults on progressive education by critiquing its educational effectiveness. One "mother" complained that her children made it to the third grade in Pasadena's public schools without learning to read. When she complained to her children's teachers, she wrote, she "was told the old methods of teaching the three R's were outmoded, and gently but firmly made to feel ridiculous for having even mentioned the subject." The same was true in mathematics. Her children were not forced to memorize arithmetic tables, so they "struggled along miserably." If only her children had practiced the three Rs, this writer felt, "as we did," they would have learned much more easily.[194]

One writer who identified herself as a Pasadena teacher agreed that progressive education meant the abandonment of the only pedagogical methods that really worked. Under the tenets of progressivism, this teacher complained, teachers were not allowed to require any memorization by their pupils. More emphasis was placed on making the learning environment pleasant. As a result, students did not actually learn much.[195]

Another anonymous "mother" blasted the "look-say" method of reading instruction. In this method, students are taught to recognize whole words, instead of breaking down words into their component sounds. This writer complained that her daughter always received very good grades, even though she could not read. The daughter would mistake similar words, such as "family" and "familiar." Instead of learning through phonics to read every sound of each word, her daughter had been taught a ridiculously ineffective reading method. As a result, the daughter was too embarrassed to read anymore.[196]

One of the most pressing educational failures of progressive education, many writers argued, came with its abandonment of the principle of competition. The traditional evaluation of students with letter grades and report cards, many felt, gave students some reason to push themselves. Without such public markers of accomplishment, progressive education threatened to allow students to relax into a dangerous sloth. One letter writer described this tendency as "the fallacy of the whole system." In her opinion, without traditional grades and report cards, "there is no incentive for the average student or the exceptionally bright student to do any better than the slower ones." All students will coast along, developing "indolent habits," until it is too late for them to master the basic academic skills and attitudes that would have led them to success.[197]

One correspondent argued that the effect of abandoning report cards was the dumbing-down of schooling for all. In progressive education, this writer insisted, "The standards of education are being gradually lowered to the level of slower children."[198] Without competition for grades, no students bothered to work at all. One writer posed a rhetorical question: "What, may I ask, do these dear people think that life consists of?" It was competition that made the US "the greatest country in the world today," he insisted. In order to prepare students to "enter into the world of commerce and industry for which they are supposedly being trained," schools must give them basic practice in competition.[199]

Competition and grades mattered both as markers of achieve-ment and as shapers of personalities. But it was not only laziness anti-progressives worried about. One writer believed that progressive educa-tion could be blamed for the "sassiness and disobedience" she detected in her children.[200] The non-progressive teacher quoted above agreed that progressivism taught students "arrogance, hostility and defiance, even vandalism."[201] Due, perhaps, to the ministrations of progressive education, one writer complained that the youth of her day only "want to rush to the radio and listen to the degenerative radio programs put out for them."[202]

These anti-progressive writers may have represented only a small but vocal segment of Pasadena's population. Other sources, however, also suggest a stark divide between teachers and the general population about the suitability of progressive education for Pasadena's schools. One survey commissioned by the Pasadena Education Association (PEA) pointed to a glaring distinction between most adults and Pasa-dena's teachers. The surveyors conducted 1,150 interviews in the sum-mer of 1950. They found just over half of Pasadena's adults thought that school discipline was satisfactory, while eighty-three percent of teachers did. Similarly, only about a third of the general public thought that Pasadena's schools spent enough time teaching "the fundamental subjects," while just under three-quarters of teachers thought they did. Perhaps most remarkably, among those who thought teaching was not the same in 1950 as it was "when they went to school," only around twenty-nine percent of the general public thought schooling in 1950 was better. In contrast, nearly seventy-two percent of teachers found their own teaching better than what they had experienced.[203]

Of course, none of these opinions were merely academic in Pas-adena in 1950. The target of anti-progressive ire was Willard Goslin. Many writers agreed with "H.G.B.," who blamed "Goslin and his gang" for the woefully "progressive" state of Pasadena's schools. Worst of all, teachers, "and apparently Mr. Goslin concurs," treated parents who lobbied for more traditional pedagogy as "a bunch of crackpots." For H.G.B., the pedagogical proof was in the pudding. He claimed that his son could not read at the end of the third grade. H.G.B. hired an "old-fashioned teacher" who quickly taught the boy to read in three months.[204] His wife, at least, agreed. "Mrs. H.G.B." had hoped, she wrote, "that when Mr. Goslin took over the position of Superintendent of Schools here there would be some changes made, but it seems it was a vain hope, as he is also a progressive."[205]

Though he tried at times to dispute the accusation, Goslin stood charged with all the crimes of progressivism. Yet as this brief sampling of letters from anti-progressives in 1950 Pasadena has shown, the nature of progressive education was by no means simple to define. With the benefit of hindsight, conservative Pasadena activist Mary Allen tried to sum up the differences between proper, traditional education and the progressive doppelganger rearing its head in Pasadena's schools.

Allen drew up a list of contrasting visions of Pasadena's schools. She called one side what "the people" wanted and the other "what they were offered" by progressive educators such as Willard Goslin. According to Allen, the people wanted the three Rs and traditional pedagogy. They wanted their children to be drilled in phonics and math tables. Instead, they were force-fed a "100% experience curriculum with no stress on the fundamentals." The people wanted a fixed curriculum, but they got only a loose, undefined schooling. They wanted firm, adult-imposed discipline in schools, but instead children were offered "freedom in the classroom." They wanted schools to stress civics and American history, but instead students received nothing but world citizenship training and indoctrination in "living democracy in the group."[206]

Allen thought parents wanted higher achievement standards. Instead, they got schools with no grades, no failures, and no competition. She believed parents also wanted their children to learn moral and spiritual values. Instead, children were taught that the only eternal truth was the concept of "change with no permanent moral and spiritual values."[207]

Finally, Allen insisted parents wanted schools that would teach children the values of the parents. Instead, Goslin's schools taught that the parents needed re-education. Even worse, instead of bringing in outside speakers who would aggressively "support the American way of life," Goslin invited dangerous subversives who taught adults and children alike that socialism and communism offered significant improvements over America's tottering traditions.[208]

Piling On

By the spring of 1950, the battle lines had been drawn. On one side stood Goslin and progressive education. Fairly or not, in the eyes of conservatives, progressive education came to connote a witches' brew of dangerous notions. Progressive education, from the conservative perspective, included sympathy for socialist or communist ideology, an embrace of United Nations-style internationalism, a greater role for the federal government in local decision making, and an educational method that eschewed classroom discipline, a method that did not demand rigorous academic achievement. As we will see, "progressivism" soon also came to include higher taxes and an enforcement of racial desegregation in schools. Standing opposed to such notions meant embracing traditional rote learning in schools, opposing communist subversion, encouraging schools to teach traditional moral and spiritual values, maintaining established racial schooling patterns, and claiming a leading role for parents as non-experts.

Once the issue in Pasadena came to be defined as one of conservatism against progressivism, conservative activists piled on other simmering issues from beyond the confines of Pasadena's immediate controversy. For instance, conservatives in 1950 and 1951 hastened to examine the textbooks used in Pasadena's schools. As we've seen with the controversy over the Rugg textbooks, conservatives had long remonstrated against the tone of America's textbooks. California conservatives had been no exception. The target of conservative frustration in the late 1940s was *Building America,* a series of social-studies textbooks and pamphlets published by the curricular arm of the National Education Association. The NEA published the textbook series in 1947. By 1948 California conservatives had forced the state to reject the books.[209]

In the first months of that year, the California state senate held hearings to uncover the subversive intent of the textbook series. Red-hunting senators on the Investigating Committee on Education, led in 1948 by Nelson Dilworth, insisted that they were not accusing the NEA of communist subversion. However, they suggested that the organization had fallen prey to "Soviet sympathizers." There was no organization, no matter how loyal, the senators concluded, that such subversives "will not try to infiltrate and make use of." It would be difficult for the NEA to defend itself, the senators insisted, since "Education and schools are [subversives'] Number 1 target in the United States."[210]

Nor should casual readers be fooled by the seemingly harmless academic tone of the *Building America* books, California watchdogs warned. In the opinion of the senate investigators, the amount of historically accurate, ideologically neutral material included in the books did not disprove the accusation of subversion. Such good—and even patriotic—historic content only served as "confidence winning bait" in subversive textbooks. It was only included by a subversive agent "to conceal his poison."[211]

As with the Rugg textbooks a decade earlier, senators accused the *Building America* series of an improper sympathy for the Soviet Union.[212] Worse, the series combined a flattering portrayal of communist Russia with critical indictments of American heroes such as Abraham Lincoln[213] and Thomas Jefferson.[214]

For its research, the senate investigating committee hired analysts such as Louis Samuel Nast Phillipp and R. E. Combs. They also consulted earnest volunteer red hunters such as Edwin C. Mead. Phillipp had served in the army during World War I, then attended Lane Seminary in Cincinnati. Between the wars he worked as a Presbyterian pastor in Ohio and Indiana until he returned to active duty in Asia during World War II.[215] Phillipp warned the committee that young Americans must be trained to see America's republican system of government as "the most enlightened and constructive development of the efforts of sentient human beings to live together in peace and harmony." If students were not properly taught this notion, America would soon lose that government to totalitarianism. The problem with the *Building America* series, Phillipp argued, was that it snuck its "serious attempt to subvert the mind" into the books as "the continual presentation of half-truths under the guise of progressive thought."[216]

Mead had a similar military background. He had retired from active service after World War II as a lieutenant colonel and became active in the American Legion and the Sons of the American Revolution. Like Phillipp, Mead warned the committee that the textbooks taught unwary young people a skewed vision of American government and history. Instead of celebrating our democratic heritage, Mead insisted, *Building America* taught that "our Constitution was just born to enslave . . . the working classes."[217]

R. E. Combs had a different professional background. Instead of a retired pastor or military man, Combs had worked since the 1930s as legal counsel for various legislative committees. To build a case against *Building America,* Combs painstakingly connected 113 alleged communist front organizations to 50 authors included in the textbook series.[218] The conclusion Combs offered the committee was that, overall, "The majority of the books are slanted in such a manner that they pointedly disparage the American way of life by criticizing the defects and failing to devote commensurate attention to the benefits."[219]

Remembering the recent successful outcry against *Building America,* conservative activists in Pasadena determined to investigate the books used under Goslin's watch. Louise Padelford and Catherine "Cay" Hallberg, leaders of both the SDC and Pro America, uncovered a junior high textbook with similar subversive tendencies. With its echoes of the Communist International, it is likely the title itself caused Padelford and Hallberg some dismay as they examined lists of approved textbooks for Pasadena schools. But the title was not their only objection. According to Padelford and Hallberg, *Living in the Peoples' World* by Lawrence V. Roth (1949) repeated many of the crimes of *Building America*. Roth's book informed young Pasadenans, Padelford and Hallberg charged, that the world was dramatically different in 1949 than it had been in the past. "The hint," these critics accused, was "strong that such fluidity must and should lead to political internationalism."[220] Instead of teaching junior high students to love America and embrace its traditions, such books encouraged them to consider "*only the imperfections of our society.*"[221]

By making these connections between the textbooks used in Pasadena's schools and the beleaguered *Building America* series, conservatives in Pasadena managed to associate Goslin and his purportedly progressive policies with earlier struggles against subversion. Similarly, Goslin came to be accused of another sinister plot to subvert the minds and spirits of Pasadena's young. By the end of his tenure in Pasadena, all commentators agreed that Goslin had planned to begin a program of summer camps for Pasadena's schoolchildren. The origins of this widely shared belief are not clear. Goslin had, indeed, made summer workshops for teachers one of his flagship reforms, but he never publicly announced any plan to include a summer camp for children.

Nevertheless, just as Goslin was lumped in with the alleged subversive tendencies of the *Building America* series, so he soon stood accused of a nefarious plan to spirit Pasadena's children off to the woods for weeks of socialist indoctrination. The fact that the school administration did not in fact propose any such plan did not satisfy conservative critics. One local parent thought that the administration's lack of discussion of the imagined summer camp plan merely demonstrated a typically conspiratorial left-wing tactic of "hush-hush planning." She asked in outrage, "Why should a plan as new and startling as an experimental mountain boarding school camp be kept under cover?"[222]

Commentators outside of conservative circles were bewildered by the intense backlash against the merest accusation of a summer camp for children. Journalist David Hulburd found it strange that "many Goslin opponents seemed to have attached undue importance" to the alleged plan. This made no sense to Hulburd, not only because such a plan had not been a central part—if any part at all—of Goslin's reform plan, but also because of the "harmlessness of the idea itself."[223] NEA investigator Robert Skaife also failed to see the threat from summer camps. As Skaife told Goslin privately, the innocuous camp proposal was "misinterpreted" by conservative activists, but Skaife could not understand why.[224] To Hulburd, Skaife, and others who did not speak the language of mid-century conservatism, the notion of a summer camp for children was about as harmless as one could get.

But among conservative school reformers, the idea had distinct sinister overtones. Such camps had long been feared as pastoral brainwashing centers. As historian Paul Mishler has described, the summer camps and educational programs of America's small, divided communist community did not in actuality pose the dire threat many conservatives imagined. Most of the children in the communist summer camp network came from families already dedicated to the communist ideal.[225] Nevertheless, there did exist what Mishler called a "substantial network" of communist summer camps,[226] and just as fear of polio led some frightened parents to restrict their children's summer activities far more than might have been medically necessary, so fear of summer camp communist subversion had a strong pull on the conservative imagination.[227]

Many sources fed this belief. For instance, in the early 1950s, famed ex-communist Bella Dodd confirmed that during her time as legal representative for the Communist Party in New York City, most of the party's income had come from a string of summer camps for young people. During the 1940s, when she was actively involved in communist activism, Dodd insisted that such camps had become an integral part of American communism.[228]

Soon after Dodd's exposé, this deep conservative anxiety about communist summer camps prompted the New York legislature to investigate charges of widespread subversion via a network of communist children's camps.[229] In 1955, the Joint Legislative Committee on Charitable and Philanthropic Agencies and Organizations of the State of New York began an investigation of the camps. To their alarm, they found a "real danger" that even patriotic American parents might be fooled into sending their children to Communist summer camps,[230] where the impressionable youth would be "brain washed with a roaring crescendo of myths and perverted history."[231] In their hunt, they dug up twenty-seven such camps.[232]

These conservative anxieties about communist summer camps were not new to the 1950s. Elizabeth Dilling had warned in the 1930s that such camps churned out thousands of "young Communists" every year.[233] Journalists such as Elliott Arnold confirmed in 1937 the widespread belief that such camps served to promote "the business of revolution."[234] In 1930s California, concern over communist summer camps led to conservative intervention. As historian Ellen Schrecker has documented, American Legion posts raided a local camp to disrupt its subversive work.[235]

Other patriotic activists reinforced the legend. The staunch anti-communist organization Daughters of the American Revolution—as we'll see, a group some SDC members believed to be one of the only educational activist groups that could be trusted—had insisted for decades that communists hoped to make off with American children to fill their minds with ideological poison. For example, in a radio broadcast in early 1927, national leader Grace Brosseau warned of the spreading influence of communist Young Pioneer camps.[236]

Accordingly, in 1928, the Women's Patriotic Conference on National Defense resolved to encourage all its members to investigate any local groups who might be operating such camps. This conference included the DAR alongside such groups as the American Legion Auxiliary, the United Daughters of the Confederacy, the Service Star Legion, and a clutch of smaller conservative women's organizations.[237] In their 1928 resolution, these patriotic groups pledged to investigate every local organization for signs of subversive intent. Among the warning signs were plans of "so-called liberals" to organize "'betterment meetings,' 'international programs,' 'fellowship discussions,' and the like." Another sign of local subversive activism, members learned, was the organization of "student tours . . . summer conferences and camps, and . . . youth caravans."[238]

By the time of its 1929 conference, this coalition had grown to include thirty-eight anti-communist women's groups. Flora Walker, an ardent anti-subversive activist and chairperson of the DAR's National Defense Committee, warned the assembled delegates that they must watch for "various movements" that assiduously wormed their way into every community. Such groups hoped to undermine the Christian roots of American society, to involve young people "in a vortex of swirling sex agitation," and to lure American children to their "radical headquarters, various centers of occultism, and race settlements." Walker recognized that such radical changes could not easily be accomplished when children lived at home with alert parents. However, communists often overcame this obstacle by having children "taken from the arms of their mothers and placed in institutions designed to foster the collective instincts."[239]

Such "institutions" always included a purportedly vibrant network of communist summer camps. For years, activist groups such as the

DAR kept alive this message that summer camps were often the first stage of communist plans to take over children's minds.[240] Small wonder, then, that conservatives in Pasadena seized upon the notion as yet another of Goslin's progressive crimes. It is difficult to determine the exact root of the rumor that Goslin planned youth summer camps. He made no public statement to that effect, but he may have mentioned such a plan at some point in the long controversy. However, the first recorded public appearance of the charge that Goslin intended to lure children away to indoctrination centers came from a journalist's accusation in the early summer of 1950. John Copeland of the *Los Angeles Times* penned a series of articles denouncing Goslin's radical plans. In one article, Copeland described a camping program from nearby San Diego. In these camps, Copeland charged, students were forced to learn the suspicious-sounding skills of "social living," "group process," "intercultural relations," and a "learning-from-experience curriculum." Moreover, San Diego had come to its plan from none other than Teachers College expert William Heard Kilpatrick, whom Copeland reminded readers was a "long-time friend of Supt. Goslin."[241]

This attack on San Diego's camp plan is the first mention in the historical record of any such plan for Pasadena. Copeland did not claim that Goslin actually intended to start such camps on his own, but he clearly insinuated that Goslin approved of the plan. In spite of this tenuous connection, conservatives in Pasadena uniformly accepted this legend as fact. Mary Allen, for instance, denounced Goslin's plans to force children away from parental influence. In these summer camps, Allen charged, students would be forced to "learn 'group-cohesive-living.'"[242] In Allen's view, the goal was nothing less than to practice "Socialism . . . in the mountains, away from home influence."[243] Dorothy Higby, another Pasadena conservative, agreed that the expensive summer camps would do nothing more than train Pasadena's youth in "group living and thinking."[244] SDC leader Frank Wells charged that such "costly summer youth camps" would mean the indoctrination of students with "'social' training . . . away from family and 'old-fashioned' parents."[245]

Race and the Struggle against Progressive Education

Goslin may never have hoped to lure students out to summer camps to indoctrinate them in woodcraft and socialism, but in April 1950 he did introduce a new policy guaranteed to ignite controversy. Just as conservatives in Pasadena issued their fiery denunciations of Goslin and the many-headed threat from progressive education, just as the SDC reorganized itself as the strong new voice of anti-Goslin conservatism, Goslin announced a plan to rezone the school district. The new zones would make it harder for white parents to continue sending their children to white-majority schools. Earlier zone boundaries had sidestepped the issue by leaving areas with high populations of Latinos and African Americans as "neutral zones." White parents living in those areas could easily arrange to have their children bused to white-majority schools. Goslin's plan would change that.

Conservatives reacted with predictable fury. Throughout their protests, however, they insisted that their objections were not about race. Pasadena's progressive community contended, on the contrary, that the fight was exactly about race and racism. Goslin dodged. The only issue he cared about, he insisted, was logistical efficiency.

In the wake of World War II, the meanings of race and racism in American culture had undergone significant transformation. As we have seen, white conservatives in the 1920s rarely wondered about the racial meanings of their school reform plans. As Chapter 2 argued, the explicit white Protestant chauvinism of the Ku Klux Klan jostled along compatibly, if not always comfortably, with less melodramatic expressions of white conservatism in the 1920s.

By the 1950s, white conservatives had developed a more complicated attitude toward race. As a group, white conservatives after World War II paid more explicit attention to the specifically "conservative" meanings of racial issues than did the previous generation. Time and again, white conservatives fought off charges of racism. White conservatives tried to shift racial discussions to questions of creeping communism and progressivism instead.[246] Even those conservative groups most closely identified with racism and white supremacy often denied racist intentions. White segregationists in Mississippi, for example, claimed their activism would "preserve and promote the best interests of both races."[247]

The desegregation battles in the years immediately following World War II were different from the ones that garnered the nation's attention later in the 1950s. In those later fights, conservatives in the former Confederacy and some border states reacted to the *Brown v. Board of Education* decision with a ferocious crusade of "Massive Resistance."[248] In Pasadena, on the other hand, as in northern urban centers, the fight over race, progressivism, and education played out differently. It began in the immediate aftermath of World War II and lingered in ugly disputes over busing, housing, and citizenship well into the 1970s and beyond.

With all the public anger over his progressive policies, Goslin did not plan to provoke this decades-long battle. Nevertheless, he quickly learned in April 1950 that his plan would be met with "violent opposition." The need for the new zones, Goslin explained, came from the district's two new junior high schools. These schools, La Canada and Temple City, would mean that students formerly attending the mostly white Linda Vista Junior High would be split between different schools, some of which would likely be majority African American. Goslin tried to soften the impact by allowing students currently attending any junior high to remain there.[249]

Though the new zones quickly won the unanimous support of the school board, protesters packed each board meeting to demand repeal.[250] Whatever protesters, school board members, progressive community members, or Goslin might say, all recognized that Pasadena's schools had to deal with a rapidly changing population. Between 1939 and 1951, new manufacturing jobs in Pasadena attracted thousands of new residents, many of them non-white. In 1940, non-whites made up four percent of the school district's population. By 1950, that number had increased to just over nine percent.[251] In 1934, the school district included 703 African American students. By 1950, that number almost doubled, to 1,344.[252] In 1920, Pasadena included 240 African American households, roughly 1,000 people. By the late 1940s, this had grown to a population of 6,500.[253] As a direct result, the face of Pasadena's schools changed dramatically. In 1946, for example, Washington Elementary was ten percent African American. By 1958 it had become fifty-two percent African American.[254]

The policy of "neutral zones" had dissipated some of the nervousness about these demographic changes among white Pasadenans. Though in theory any parent could request a transfer for his or her children, in practice the district only honored white requests.[255] Similar contests had emerged in the immediate postwar years in cities such as Baltimore and Detroit, as African Americans moved into industrial cities to take wartime jobs and sparked angry conflicts over housing and education.[256]

As in those cities, Pasadena's racial progressives did not doubt the meaning of the zoning changes. When conservatives insisted the issue was not race, local racial progressives insisted that it was. Adophus R. Traylor, for instance, president of the local National Association for the Advancement of Colored People (NAACP) used his time at a school board meeting to ask conservatives if they would object to new school zones if the issue was not racial desegregation. Why would property values go down, Traylor challenged Pasadena's conservative community, if whites did not want their children to go to school with blacks?[257] The Pasadena NAACP lauded the new school zones as a move toward "true democracy." Local African American attorney Isaac H. Spears similarly endorsed the new school zones as a move toward ending racial discrimination and segregation. Bob Jones, a student leader of local anti-racist organizations, praised the school board as "courageous" for its willingness to fight racism with the new boundaries.[258] The Reverend Felix Manley, of the Pasadena Council of Churches, concluded that the new school zones "represented a forward move in bringing democracy to Pasadena."[259]

Similar accolades poured in from Pasadena's racial progressives, including such organizations as the American Association of University Women, the League of Women Voters, the Pasadena Interracial Club, the Pasadena Jewish Community, and the Interdenominational Negro Ministers. All lauded Goslin's plan to fight racism by rezoning the school district.[260]

Goslin dodged their fulsome praise. The change, he insisted repeatedly, was not about race. It was not about democracy. It seems Goslin hoped to keep the new zones as quiet as possible. When community members declared the new zones to be a culmination of their work toward ending racism and segregation in Pasadena, Goslin demurred. The changes, he claimed, were not about desegregation, only about geography and efficiency.[261] When protesters attacked the plan, Goslin repeated that it was not about desegregation, only streamlining. With the new zones, Goslin argued, students would no longer need expensive busing.[262]

No one bought it. Conservatives would not even agree that the issue was race. Instead, they claimed only to be interested in the new law's impact on local property values. For example, at one angry, overcrowded school board meeting, John S. Moore of the Pasadena Realty Board agreed that people who would not pay as much for homes due to the school zone change were "in error." Nevertheless, Moore insisted, the fact remained that since a large percentage of home buyers did hold such beliefs, the downward pressure on home prices would become inexorable. One protester presented a petition from her neighborhood, signed by "her Negro, Mexican and Oriental neighbors" as well as whites. All of them, she noted, opposed the new zoning rules. The issue, she insisted, was not race. As more proof, she invoked what would become a cliché of postwar racial debates. She could not be a racist, she said, because she had quickly become friends with one of her new neighbors, a "Negro physician."[263]

This debate in Pasadena echoed similar postwar debates in other cities. In Baltimore in 1945, for example, white homeowner associations protested moves by African Americans into previously white neighborhoods. The protest, insisted Baltimore's Fulton Improvement Association, was "not directed against colored citizens," even though it hoped to stop their incursion. These sentiments attracted the unanimous support of the white city leadership. In Baltimore, only the local African American press called such arguments racist.[264]

Such battles over housing and race also consumed postwar Chicago and Detroit. In each city, African Americans squeezed for housing moved into previously all-white neighborhoods. In each case, resistance often centered on an ostensibly non-racist defense of property values. By 1945 in Chicago, large majorities of whites believed that African American residents led directly to the entire loss of value in their homes.[265] In Detroit, as in Chicago, such beliefs led to widespread racial violence.[266] Local "homeowners" groups formed to combat the racial transformation of their neighborhoods, leading to hundreds of attacks on African American homeowners.[267]

In the 1940s, Pasadena managed to avoid this kind of widespread terror. But the language of anti-zoning in Pasadena echoed that of Baltimore, Detroit, and Chicago. Pasadena's segregationists insisted they were not racist, even as they fought against the new school zones. Racial progressives, however much Goslin attempted to dodge the issue, put race and racism at the center of the public debate. Historians have recently explored the complicated meanings of such segregation arguments in closer detail. They have offered more nuanced analyses of segregationism, ones that avoid the overly convenient dismissal of such attitudes as simply racist. Though the attitudes of many whites may indeed have been formed by racism, we must also recognize the complexity of such beliefs. For instance, in some cases, as in Detroit, affluent African Americans allied with conservative whites to fight against public-housing projects.[268] And in Baltimore, the blockbusting policies of real estate promoters really did lower property values. Whites sold under pressure at prices up to fifty percent under market value. African Americans with little financial capital were forced to use high-interest loans that cost up to fifty percent above market value.[269] Though white segregationists may have been racist, they also had apparently legitimate fears about the changing values of their homes.

As Ronald Formisano has argued, dismissing segregationist activism because it included racism does not help us to understand it. This does not mean that the racism included in such "reactionary populist" movements should be excused or denied.[270] Rather, the racism of these segregationists should be understood as part of a complex way of understanding themselves and society. As historian Thomas Sugrue argued about white segregationism in Detroit, the fight for white property rights in an era of desegregation "was a malleable concept, one that derived its power from its imprecision."[271]

In the case of Pasadena, segregationism in the postwar years had a unique career. As in other cities, it attached itself to a loudly color-blind rhetoric of property values. But unlike in other cities, since the new zones had been imposed by Goslin, the entire fight over race and schooling became another marker of the many meanings of educational conservatism and progressive education. The opponents of Goslin's rezoning initiative engaged in what historian Matthew Lassiter has called the "middle course," between open racism and egalitarianism, based on "an ethos of color-blind individualism that accepted the principle of equal opportunity under the law but refused to countenance affirmative action policies designed to overcome metropolitan structures of inequality."[272] Moreover, the Pasadena controversy stamped the debate in racial terms. Conservatives, though they might have denied it, became the side of racism and white privilege. Progressives became the side of racial liberalism and desegregation.

Paying for Progressivism

The fight against school desegregation was not an incidental or minor part of the conservative school campaign in Pasadena. Along with tax questions, this question of racial segregation turned a cranky dispute about pedagogy and classroom practice into something far more tumultuous. Just as Goslin introduced his new zoning policies, he also requested a new school tax hike. Since 1937, Pasadena's schools had operated with a rate of ninety cents per one hundred dollars of assessed property value for school taxes. In April 1950, Goslin announced his plan to increase that tax rate to a dollar thirty-five per hundred dollars. The city would vote on June 2 about the new tax rate.[273]

Conservatives seized on the issue as yet another reason to oppose Goslin and progressivism in Pasadena's schools. At first, the SDC requested a delay in the June tax election. Goslin refused.[274] Forced to respond quickly, conservatives rolled their anti-tax animus into their existing anger at the perceived crimes of progressive education.[275] Conservative leaders did not separate out taxes from race and progressivism. Instead, they combined all these issues into a politically powerful conservative impulse. This multi-issue protest movement was enough to defeat the tax increase and drive Goslin out of town.

Conservative activists proved adept at connecting the progressive dots. For instance, Frank Wells, president of the SDC, tried to turn the June 2 tax vote into a referendum on all of the meanings of progressive education. At a tumultuous school board meeting in late May, just a few days before the tax election, Wells blasted taxes and progressivism as part of the same sordid scheme. Wells's speech appealed to the established and politically potent tradition of educational conservatism. Both in classroom practice and political ideology, Wells charged, Goslin's purported progressivism represented an urgent threat. Wells never doubted that school reform mattered. He assumed that progressive change to schools would have devastating effects on Pasadena and all of America. Proper school reform—conservative school reform—had the urgent duty to stop progressive plans and replace them with traditional values.

Progressive education, Wells charged, sought "to make guinea pigs and future socialists out of our children." One way to fight back, he insisted, was to defeat the new tax request.[276] Taxes and progressivism, Wells explained, were part of the same subversive strategy. "The tax levy," he told the crowded auditorium of the John Madison School, "is not needed to make the education of our children better, but instead is needed for excessive costs of the progressive system." Progressive education, according to Wells, meant an education that dismissed traditional moral values. It meant a decrease in authentic thinking by students. It meant a promotion of socialism and a diminution of individualism. It led directly to an increase in "social delinquency," including the recent rise of violent youth "Wolf Packs" in the Los Angeles area. Progressive education, Wells charged, cut out parents' rights and replaced them with subversive "educational theory." The solution, Wells concluded, was to "cut out the frills and the wasteful use of tax money. Let's vote NO!"[277]

Wells was not alone in his articulation of the tradition of educational conservatism. Ernest Brower, Wells's successor as SDC president, later recalled that the SDC's opposition to the tax rate increase did not mean they were "tax haters." Rather, Brower's SDC concluded that the most effective way to fight the many meanings of progressive education was to "cut off funds."[278] This simple method, Brower felt, could fix many of the "symptoms of the disease" of progressivism in Pasadena. The litany, by this point, had become familiar. Brower described the dangers of progressive education as including "a definite elimination of parental authority, undermining of parental influence, aiding and abetting immorality by the use of immoral and amoral textbooks on sex, [and] destruction of patriotic attitudes of students, such as pride in America."[279] Pasadena voters, Brower could have pointed out, had supported tax increases in the recent past when such increases led to improvements in traditional schooling.[280] But they should never approve a tax increase that would feed the beast of progressive education.

The rhetoric of educational conservatism proved politically unstoppable. Voters turned out in record numbers on June 2, 1950, and dealt the tax increase a killing blow. By a margin of over two to one, they decisively defeated Goslin's requested tax increase.[281] The SDC called this result a referendum against all of the tenets of progressive education. They moved quickly to drive a stake through its heart. In yet another packed meeting in a hot auditorium, members of the SDC laid out their post-election demands. For the first time, they publicly called for Goslin's resignation. Only such a move would satisfy their demands that Pasadena's schools eliminate "progressive education" and return to "the teaching of fundamentals."[282]

The next day, the triumphant SDC presented a list of demands to the school board. In addition to Goslin's ouster, the SDC insisted that all school employees take a loyalty oath. Furthermore, as a measure to safeguard Pasadena's schools from the subversive nature of progressive education, the SDC called for an "ideological investigation" of the school district. The SDC did not trust the school board itself to carry out this investigation, so it demanded that an outside group direct the inquiry. The only groups the SDC trusted were "patriotic organizations" such as the American Legion, the Sons of the American Revolution, or the Daughters of the American Revolution.[283]

In the eyes of conservative organizations like the SDC, such outside groups were the only ones with credibility. We have seen the ways the American Legion established its credentials as a conservative, traditionalist watchdog over public education. They were not alone. Organizations such as the Sons of the American Revolution had played a role in investigating the threat of communist subversion in schools nationwide.[284] But by the time the SDC came looking for conservative educational investigation and oversight, the Daughters of the American Revolution (DAR) had established their reputation as among the most formidable conservative school reform organizations in America. By the late 1940s, for instance, leading anti-subversive investigators in the Federal Bureau of Investigation considered the DAR one of the few organizations it could trust.[285] A digression into the DAR's educational accomplishments will help us understand why the SDC called for their assistance in Pasadena's hour of crisis. It will help us see what it meant to be an educational conservative in the America of 1950.

Cheerleaders for America

For decades, the DAR had made itself a national leader in conservative educational activism. That record continued in the late 1940s. For instance, at the time Willard Goslin quietly accepted the job as Pasadena's superintendent, President General May Talmadge of the DAR was pressing every member to "constitute herself a committee of one to oppose by every means within her power the infiltration of communistic teachers in our schools."[286] Talmadge practiced what she preached. A native Georgian, while working as president general she took an active role in her Washington DC neighborhood schools. She helped the local Webster School establish an Americanization program to help teach young people the value of American traditions.[287]

By the time Goslin had come under fire for his purported progressivism, the DAR claimed that it had achieved a banner year in ideological investigations of American schools. In 1950, hundreds of DAR chapters had conducted independent inquiries into their local schools and textbooks. In Indiana, the state DAR had succeeded in its effort to establish a three-person committee to evaluate the potential subversive content of all textbooks used by young Hoosiers.[288] This signaled the fulfillment of a state DAR pledge in 1949 to investigate all history textbooks used in Indiana public schools.[289] Similar DAR pressure in West Virginia and Texas had successfully controlled the types of textbooks used in state schools.[290] The District of Columbia DAR conference resolved in 1950 that it, too, would fight any "introduction of subversive ideas in American education" in DC public schools.[291] Other state conferences had begun their campaigns earlier. In Iowa, for example, the state DAR conference resolved in 1948 that every member must investigate local high schools and colleges, on the lookout for activity of "eighty-five subversive groups" at work in those schools.[292] In 1951, the active Texas DAR continued to scan textbooks to make sure they "taught the principles embraced by our forefathers." More impressive, the Texas leaders bragged that 1,695 of its members had visited history classes to investigate teaching.[293]

Throughout 1950 and 1951, the DAR continued such involvement in public education nationwide. In Alabama, for instance, a majority of local chapters distributed anti-communist pamphlets and booklets to their local public schools. In Colorado, local DAR chapters took it upon themselves to enforce loyalty oath laws among teachers. In Delaware, a local DAR activist contacted a sympathetic high school teacher to ensure DAR's patriotic, traditional, anti-communist message was heard in his classroom.[294] DAR chapters conducted similar campaigns across the nation, including in California. After the Goslin controversy, the California DAR conference resolved to spend more time assisting public education officials "for more effective exclusion of subversive material."[295]

This ardent educational activism inspired Pasadena's conservatives to look to the DAR for trustworthy leadership in traditional, patriotic, anti-subversive education. The DAR's reputation by 1950 included its ardent ideological activism as well as its reputation for snobbish antiquarianism. Perhaps the best-known articulation of this aspect of the DAR mystique was Grant Wood's satiric 1932 painting, *Daughters of the American Revolution.*[296] Wood's Daughters were birdlike spinsters, ossifying as they sipped tea and congratulated themselves on their superior heritage.

By the time of the Great Depression, that image of the DAR was only one face of its complex public persona. The organization began its long life in 1896 as an elite heritage society for women, modeled on the Sons of the American Revolution.[297] By World War I, the national leaders of the organization had imposed a more explicitly conservative, "America First" ideology on the organization.[298]

This conservative turn did not take immediate hold among all members or supporters of the organization. Along with the starched, decorous elitism of the early DAR, many members saw themselves as part of a more generic women's club. Many members felt the organization ought not restrict itself to conservative activism. In its early decades, these tensions occasionally erupted into national controversies. For instance, in the wake of the distribution of the "Spider Web Chart" of subversive women's organizations by Amos Fries, well-known suffrage leader Carrie Chapman Catt published "An Open Letter to the DAR" in *The Woman Citizen.* Catt accused the DAR of irresponsible witch-hunting in its publications. The malicious spirit of the Spider Web Chart had influenced the DAR's work, according to Catt, who particularly denounced one DAR-distributed pamphlet, *The Common Enemy,* which had condemned several organizations for serving as dupes or fronts for communism. In short, anyone to the left of political center had been accused of promoting communism.[299] President General Grace Brosseau attempted to brush off Catt's accusations, but DAR members expressed their disapproval of the DAR's alleged smear.[300]

The following year, 1928, prominent Boston DAR member Helen Bailie Tufts accused DAR leaders of circulating a blacklist of speakers for DAR meetings. The list, Tufts charged, included such prominent Bostonians as Dean Roscoe Pound of Harvard Law School and such nationally known personalities as former president Taft.[301] President General Brosseau denied the existence of any such list, but defended the right of state DAR leaders to "advise for or against speakers to appear before the organization."[302]

Another very public controversy a decade later again demonstrated the increasingly fractious nature of the DAR membership. In April 1939, organizers of a Howard University concert series attempted to book famous African American contralto Marian Anderson for an engagement at the DAR's Constitution Hall, the largest auditorium in Washington DC. The DAR leadership, claiming to be observing District law, refused the use of their hall for a racially integrated performance. Among the many protesters against this decision was First Lady Eleanor Roosevelt, who resigned her DAR membership in protest.[303] Among the diverse membership of the DAR, the issue of race and racism continued to cause division throughout the 1940s.[304]

Other DAR members contested the ideological turn of the organization in more subtle ways. One meeting of a local chapter in 1928 described the kind of activism that many DAR members associated with the organization. There was no mention of communism or defense of traditional family structures. There were no calls for increased military spending or teachers' loyalty oaths. At the September 1928 meeting of the Major Isaac Sadler DAR Chapter of Omaha, Nebraska, the members were more interested in other projects. They dedicated a decorative birdbath with an historical marker for the village of Belleview, Nebraska. They earnestly discussed and debated their plans for beautification and maintenance of the birdbath. They eventually agreed that "Old fashioned, low-blooming flowers will be planted there in the spring."[305] By maintaining a primary interest in purportedly non-ideological projects, such DAR members asserted their own identity for the women's organization.

In such a sprawling organization, this continued devotion to a vision of the DAR as primarily a social heritage organization lasted for decades. In one telling example, one Florida DAR member described her vision of DAR ideology: "I don't pay any attention to what they say in Washington [DAR headquarters]. I like the women and enjoy our meetings."[306] Although her comment came from a later generation, it seems to have been representative of some members' feelings in an earlier period as well.

Such DAR members did not think of their organization primarily as a conservative one. They were more interested in marking local historical monuments and enjoying social occasions. Nevertheless, the national leadership of the DAR repeatedly claimed that their ideological views represented those of the entirety of the DAR membership. During the 1920s and early 1930s, the membership numbers slowly increased from roughly 110,000 to nearly 180,000. Numbers dipped during the Depression years, but throughout the 1940s membership climbed from roughly 140,000 to just under 170,000 by early 1951, with a quick spike in the immediate aftermath of World War II.[307]

Such membership numbers were respectable, but still not enough on their own to claim the undivided attention of national politicians. Yet DAR leaders proudly noted that they were received at the White House by Presidents Coolidge[308] and Hoover.[309] President Roosevelt addressed their national gathering in 1938,[310] as celebrity Will Rogers had done in 1931.[311] During and after World War II, presidents tended to greet the annual DAR Continental Convention by letter instead of by personal appearance.[312]

But other prominent politicians and leaders continued to court DAR members. J. Edgar Hoover, for instance, praised DAR's "right-thinking American women" for recognizing the need to begin the fight against crime and subversion by maintaining traditional American homes.[313] Fresh from his success in World War II, Dwight Eisenhower appealed in person to the patriotic, anti-subversive DAR for help in opposing communism's advance.[314] And as anti-communism fever gripped the nation, an array of red-hunting politicians came to the DAR for support.[315] Echoing the flattery of the rest of these prominent men in public office, Senator Karl Mundt of South Dakota praised "the courageous, clear-thinking women of the DAR" for their conservative leadership.[316]

Yet unlike Mundt and other male politicians, the female leaders of the DAR felt compelled to justify their public activism. As did other political women, they used existing gender norms to do so. From "Republican mothers" in the eighteenth century to "maternalist" activism in the twentieth, activists have consistently used gendered notions of politics and culture in order to justify women's participation.[317] These arguments have been particularly effective in rationalizing women's right to public activism in issues related to childraising. In the twentieth century, for instance, women successfully used these traditional gender norms to legitimate their roles as professionals in the field of education.[318]

Conservative women activists have often found themselves in a double bind. They have committed themselves to traditional gender roles. Yet they have used the prerogatives of those roles to articulate reasons for their active leadership in the traditionally male field of politics.[319] For instance, President General Grace Brosseau told attendees at the 1928 annual DAR Continental Congress that they needed to get more politically active. But Brosseau wrapped this unmistakable call to activism in a thoroughly gendered passivity. What America needed, Brosseau told the delegates, was some "cheer leaders for America; we need some fearless citizens to sit on the side lines and do a little talking in the interest of this country."[320]

For decades, DAR leaders and members had done more than sit on the sidelines of American public life. Especially in their role as educational activists, DAR members established themselves, along with the American Legion, as the most aggressive voices for traditionalism and patriotism in America's public schools. The DAR had long combated the intellectual underpinnings of progressive education. As would the activists in Pasadena's controversy, DAR leaders had long connected such progressive ideas to the threat of communist subversion and the dangerous abandonment of traditional American cultural norms.

And like other national conservative organizations such as the 1920s Ku Klux Klan or the American Legion, DAR leaders had worked for decades to depict their organization primarily as an educational one. President General Edith Magna, for example, liked to describe the DAR as "an educational society." The need to police the public education system, Magna argued in 1934, provided plenty of "work for every member."[321] In 1945, new President General May Talmadge seconded this vision of schooling as the DAR's "greatest concern." The DAR, Talmadge insisted, "should make it our business to see that the conditions in our schools and our communities are such that only the right kind of citizenship may be developed."[322] These were not isolated voices among DAR leaders and members. For decades, the DAR had insisted that its primary public mission was to police the public schools. DAR leaders throughout the early twentieth century appointed themselves the spiritual and ideological guardians of America's public school children.[323]

The ultimate goal of their educational activism, DAR leaders agreed, was the never-ending battle to protect traditional values and teaching techniques. In order to maintain proper schooling, DAR members emphasized the need to combat any tendency toward subversion or progressivism in American education. As did other conservative educational activists, most DAR leaders assumed that progressive education served mainly as a stalking horse for communist subversion. DAR leaders also firmly believed that traditional values must form a bulwark of anti-progressive, anti-subversive education.

Perhaps no DAR leader made this point more forcefully than did President General Anne Minor. In the early 1920s, Minor insisted that subversives hoped to use schools, the "fountainhead of the Republic," for "leading astray our young people." In order to fight such attacks, Minor called for "teachers of high character, high ideals, and *unimpeachable loyalty to America*." Better a loyal mind than a brilliant mind, she insisted. What schools ought to be doing, Minor noted, was "training" students in "Character and patriotism and obedience to the law." Instead, although Minor did not use the word "progressive," she warned that too many schools taught a dangerous moral ambivalence. The DAR, Minor intoned, "want no teachers who say there are two sides to every question." Such instruction, hiding behind the shield of "'academic freedom of speech' and opinion (so called)," had no place in shaping the "unformed minds" of America's children. Instead, Minor said, schools must instill in every student a deep love of country and respect for its traditions. If the DAR did not "guard well" the schools, Minor warned, "the life of the nation [would] be poisoned at its source."[324]

A few years later, President General Grace Brosseau emphasized similar themes. When schools taught modern "theories" and "fallacious atheistic doctrines," such schools struck a "deadly blow at civilization."[325] Elsewhere, Brosseau agreed with Minor that young children ought not to be harmed by "the decrepit theory that both sides of the question should be presented to permit the forming of unbiased opinions." Such modern theories of education, Brosseau insisted, fundamentally misunderstood the nature of childhood and the responsibilities of education. As she explained in 1929, "One does not place before a delicate child a cup of strong black coffee and a glass of milk; or a big cigar and a stick of barley candy; or a narcotic and an orange, and in the name of progress and freedom insist that both must be tested in order that the child be given the right of choice." Instead, parents and teachers must give students only what students need to develop the "delicate and impressionable fabric of the mind." The proper education, Brosseau argued, must tell students the right answers, not force them to question all answers. It must include spiritual truths. It must be kept safe from the preaching of atheism, socialism, or anti-Americanism.[326]

DAR leaders continued to emphasize these themes during the Great Depression years. President General Edith Hobart complained in 1931 about the threat from modern teaching techniques. Modern teachers, Hobart warned, conspired to "rob my child of his belief in God, his respect for parental authority and his confidence in our form of Government." Every public school, Hobart added, must pay "customary attention to the desire of parents and of community direction."[327]

From her roles as chairperson of the National Defense Committee and eventually as president general in the 1930s, Florence Becker agreed. She offered a traditional definition of proper education as a body of ideas that "shall be transmitted by us to our children."[328] Becker lambasted the progressive education model. Such "self-expression"-based education, Becker charged, had "left empty houses into which have come evil spirits bent upon destruction." The modern, progressive impulse to encourage young people to "grow up unrestrained and undirected" led to "unprecedented . . . lawlessness and crime." Without traditional "moral training and acceptance of individual responsibility," progressive ideas had led young people "from the moorings of Christian government, home and church, and Public Schools from their purpose of training citizens for life in a Republic."[329] Becker warned ominously that the "fungi and parasites" that attacked those traditions must be "cut away."[330] The goal of education, Becker observed, must instead be something in which young people's "spiritual nature" is "trained as is the intellectual, the social instinct developed." The DAR, Becker explained in a speech she gave to DAR audiences nationwide, had a critical role to play. If the DAR exerted its "powerful influence in leading the youth of today," the organization could effect "a revitalization of basic moral and spiritual values which alone can save the nation."[331]

For Becker, as for other DAR leaders before and after her, progressive education mistook the basic nature of public education. Such education must include a rigorous training in accepted wisdom and knowledge. It must include the transmission of both morals and information from the older generation to the younger. By substituting notions such as "self-expression" and moral ambiguity, progressive education threatened to tear apart the fabric of American society, culture, and politics.

By the 1940s, DAR leaders had begun to mobilize on specific issues that would erupt in the Pasadena controversy. For example, DAR members in 1943 received warnings about the dangers of federal aid to education. If the federal government paid for education, it would simply mean the US Office of Education taking over the intrusive role that had long been played by the experts of Teachers College. Such federal aid created nothing, one DAR writer warned, but "another huge arm of the Federal Government . . . more chains . . . forged to shackle the unthinking." This writer quoted conservative activist Amos Fries with approval. Fries had denounced federal aid to schools as nothing but another gambit by "socialist-minded educators" hoping to overthrow traditional values and methods in public schools.[332] The national organization passed repeated resolutions against such encroachment by the federal government throughout the 1940s.[333]

How did rank-and-file members receive these calls for conservative activism in schools? Many local chapters reported their efforts to combat un-American tendencies by distributing "Good Citizenship Medals" to teenagers who embodied the values the DAR supported. Some members got more involved. In 1929, one high school principal in New York City asked for DAR help to combat the aggressive proselytizing of a communist group in his school. Several DAR members agreed to spend time at the school, "talking to the pupils upon patriotic subjects." There was no report of the success of their efforts.[334] One chapter, in Elizabeth, New Jersey, started what they called the Boudinot Club. This club offered students a patriotic alternative to what DAR leaders thought were aggressive communist and atheist youth groups. Members of the DAR-sponsored Boudinot Club spent their after-school hours singing patriotic songs, conducting group chants about the responsibilities of citizenship, and praying.[335]

An educational cause nearer to the hearts of many DAR members was the DAR schools. The DAR ran two schools of its own throughout the first half of the twentieth century, Tamassee School in South Carolina and Kate Duncan Smith School in Alabama. They also financially supported a number of other schools—eighteen in 1920, dropping to fifteen in 1949. These supported schools met DAR standards for conservative education, but were independently run. Most of these schools were in the Southern Appalachian region, intended to uplift the region's isolated population. In 1923, one national DAR leader wrote that Tamassee would be an answer to DAR's educational prayers, "a monument to real Americans, for real Americans, by real Americans."[336] As another DAR leader put it in 1925, the people of those southern mountains were "those of the purest Anglo Saxon strain." If left in their isolation, under the eye of the "feudist and the moonshiner," such "mountaineers" could never prosper. Given proper education in DAR schools, where they learned the value of hard work, patriotism, and

Protestantism, such children could turn into "loyal people . . . a great reserve against a time of need."[337] DAR members responded to such calls throughout the interwar period. They donated funds to maintain the schools; some even visited the area to see the patriotic schools in action.[338]

DAR schools were one concrete way the organization hoped to combat distressing trends in American culture. National leaders such as President General Lora Haines Cook boasted in 1925 that by controlling such schools, DAR members could be sure the schools would "serve the needs of the time" and noted that "the conditions of teaching are sound and just." She promised DAR members that "if we find among the teaching force in any one of our institutions of learning, progenitors of half-baked radicalism, bolshevism, or socialistic communism, imposing their dangerous doctrines upon our youth, we shall as speedily scourge them out, as we would a virulent plague."[339] Some state leaders agreed. New York DAR leader Frances Tupper Nash hoped that the students at Tamassee, "the purest of Anglo Saxons . . . may yet be the means of preserving our American ideals and principles as set forth and battled for by their forefathers and ours." With the host of modern ills plaguing America, it made sense to Nash to support such schools vigorously.[340]

When Nash articulated her support of Tamassee in 1923, she hoped that DAR support of Tamassee School would produce some "sturdier types" who could help the DAR in the fight against all of its foes. As did national leaders, Nash offered a complex list of cultural dangers that Tamassee graduates could face. They included "the enemy within and the enemy without." They also included "false propaganda." Beyond such standard anti-subversive terms, however, Nash warned against a dangerous modern plague of "indifference" and "ease."[341] Tamassee graduates would be patriotic, Christian, hardworking, and polite. They would be racially and morally pure. They would embody, Nash and other DAR members hoped, the DAR's conservative vision for America.

Among most DAR leaders, the explicit racialization of this patriotic vision died away after the 1920s. But other aspects of the educational goals of DAR schools remained fairly consistent through the 1940s. For instance, one Tamassee student was invited to address the 1942 DAR Congress in Chicago. In her address, she exhorted her fellow young Americans to embrace the Bible and the Constitution. She warned young people of the dangers of "false propaganda" and celebrated the patriotic education she had received in her years at the DAR school.[342] During the World War II years, the national chairmen of the DAR committee responsible for their schools emphasized the value of "Christian education." Such schools, Chairman Harriet Simons claimed in 1943, were like educational victory gardens. Each school helped the local community as well as giving "vital nourishment and strength" to the national cause of patriotism and anti-subversive activism.[343]

In the years following World War II, President General Gertrude Carraway praised DAR-supported schools as providing the kind of education all young people needed. In DAR-supported schools, Carraway claimed, "We seek to foster better citizenship, to give a little training in patriotism and to develop character and religious faith." If more schools were like that, Carraway noted, there would be no need to fret about the direction of modern education.[344]

In addition to supporting the DAR's patriotic, traditional schools, local DAR chapters and their state organizations also rallied to the cause of teachers' loyalty oaths. In the 1920s and 1930s, this had been one of the leading policy goals of DAR national leaders. They hoped such oaths would guarantee the loyalty and adherence to traditional American values of schoolteachers. One such call came from the 1929 DAR Continental Congress. Members passed a resolution in favor of state laws mandating loyalty oaths.[345] Grace Brosseau made such oaths one of her programmatic goals for the DAR in her 1929 annual message.[346] President General Florence Becker agreed. In 1935, she repeated the call for DAR activism in support of mandatory oaths. "If any one teaching in public institutions of learning," Becker insisted, "cannot pledge loyalty to American principles for the duration of his service, he should not be instructing American youth."[347]

Such state laws had varied success. By 1949 twenty-five states and Washington DC, Alaska, Puerto Rico, and Hawaii all had such laws, most passed in the 1930s.[348] When the push for laws did succeed, key support often came from DAR members.[349] In Indiana, for instance, when the state legislature first considered a teachers' oath law in 1926, the text of the bill they considered had been drawn up by the state DAR conference. When Indiana finally passed such a law in 1929, the governor used the pen of Indiana DAR leader Electa Chase Murphy to sign the bill.[350] Similarly, when Michigan became the seventh state to pass such a law in 1931, state and local DAR leaders claimed credit.[351]

Laying Blame

It might have been this leading role in advocating for teachers' loyalty oaths that had attracted Pasadena's conservative activists to the DAR's brand of conservative educational activism. After the SDC scored its resounding victory in the June 1950 tax election, its leaders called for Goslin's resignation. They also demanded that all Pasadena teachers take a new loyalty oath, written by the SDC and greatly expanded.[352] Many states had passed laws mandating such oaths for teachers in the 1930s, a crusade that has still not received its due share of attention from historians. But California had passed its original loyalty oath legislation during the Civil War.[353] The California law required teachers to pledge the following:

> I solemnly swear that I will support the Constitution of the United States of America, the Constitution of the State of California, and the laws of the United States and the State of California, and will, by precept and example, promote respect for the Flag and the Statutes of the United States and of the State of California, reverence law and order, and offer undivided allegiance to the Government of the United States of America.[354]

Progressive teachers in Pasadena agreed only to repeat the oaths they had already taken.[355] Because of a recent controversy about loyalty oaths for faculty in the University of California system, many Pasadenans likely did not understand that public school teachers had been required to take such an oath for generations.[356]

More challenging was the SDC's call for Goslin's resignation. The school board waffled. No member of the board likely forgot that the SDC's original demand in June had been for a clean sweep, an ouster of Goslin and the entire board. By the end of the hot summer of 1950, the target had been unofficially narrowed to Goslin. One teachers' group filed a petition in support of Goslin, signed by just under 200 teachers out of a total faculty of 1,200.[357] Other district employees[358] and community voices[359] supported the SDC's call for Goslin's immediate resignation.

By November, the divided school board agreed to a clumsy tactic. While Goslin attended a meeting in New York, the school board requested his resignation by telegram.[360] In the telegram, the board explained that Goslin had become too controversial due to his identification with increased taxes, his expansion of programs to include expensive summer workshops for teachers, his overly aggressive nature in hiring administrators without board approval, and his promotion of the phantom student summer camp program without consulting the board.[361]

Four of five board members had consented to this maneuver. They hoped that Goslin's resignation would clear the air and allow Pasadena to concentrate on issues of real importance. Goslin, the majority of the board agreed, had become a monumental distraction. Pasadenans who had reliably voted for tax increases in the past would no longer do so, the board explained, as long as Goslin represented Pasadena's public schools. The best solution for Goslin and Pasadena, the board members told Goslin, would be for Goslin to stay quietly in New York for a while.[362] The need for immediate action, according to dissenting board member Gladys Rinehart, came from a rumor that the SDC planned to meet Goslin's returning plane to demand his immediate departure.[363] Some sources confidentially suggested that the SDC had a much fiercer plan. According to Goslin aide Blair Nixon, the SDC had planned to meet Goslin's plane with a subpoena from the California State Senate Investigating Committee on Education. Nixon's source had intimated that Goslin would be indicted on charges of subversion, incompetence, cronyism, and corruption.[364] Whatever the SDC's plan had been, the other board members felt that an ugly public confrontation could only make the situation worse.

Goslin was willing to retire, but he refused to make a quiet exit. He immediately contacted a loyal aide in Pasadena and instructed him to publish the telegram.[365] When he returned to Pasadena, Goslin remained pointedly good natured. Whatever the outcome of this dispute, he told reporters, he would have "no hard feelings."[366]

By the time the California State Senate Investigating Committee on Education came to Pasadena on November 15, 1950, Goslin and the board had agreed to a settlement, in principle. They soon finalized the details. Goslin would take a cash buyout of the remaining eighteen months of his contract, with a lump-sum payment of $23,250.[367]

The school board hoped this generous settlement would dissipate the sour spirit of controversy that had come to plague Pasadena's schools. They might have hesitated if they could have seen just a few years into the future. In 1957, another Pasadena superintendent lost his job and progressive teachers again felt "attacked and vilified."[368] As one Pasadenan privately lamented, schooling in Pasadena remained "a highly controversial matter with the battle fronts lining up with 'liberals' on one side and 'conservatives' on the other."[369] Into the 1960s and 70s, city leaders in Pasadena squirmed uncomfortably as the city became the location of California's first school desegregation lawsuits in the aftermath of *Brown v. Board*.[370]

The school board might also have refused such generous terms if Goslin had not received a hero's welcome at the senate committee hearing. The committee, a 1947 spin-off of the red-hunting Tenney Committee led by former Tenney assistant Nelson Dilworth, had made itself a leader in California's quest to protect its schools from communist subversion.[371] As we've seen, the committee had led the fight in 1948 against the *Building America* textbook series. The senators came to town in 1950 to investigate the many-layered phenomenon of "progressive methods of education." Those methods, the committee charged, included the abandonment of report cards, the use of textbooks "which were subversive in character or tended to ridicule American fundamentals," and the use of subversive speakers.[372] Goslin's supporters suggested that this investigation of progressivism in Pasadena resulted from backroom dealing by prominent SDC members.[373]

If such had been the SDC's plan, it backfired badly. When Goslin arrived at the school auditorium in which the hearings took place, the room had been packed well beyond its 750-person capacity. Conservatives later charged that the room had been packed by Goslin-friendly stooges.[374] Such tactics, conservatives claimed, reflected further evidence of communist subversion, since conservatives believed left-wingers consistently manipulated parliamentary procedure to ram through communist-friendly policies.[375] If administrators had hoped to make a show of public support for Goslin, they succeeded. When Goslin walked into the room, the crowd erupted in a huge ovation. Someone shouted, "Here he comes!" Then almost everyone stood and applauded for several minutes. As a reporter from the *Pasadena Star News* described, the crowd "shouted, cheered, and greeted him with wild applause."[376]

In response to senators' questions, Goslin quietly insisted that there was absolutely no communist subversion going on in Pasadena's schools.[377] He understood that he had been condemned as a progressive, but he denied the label. "I do not class myself as a progressive," Goslin told the senators and the packed auditorium. "I was never called a progressive educator until I came to Pasadena."[378]

In spite of such protestations, commentators from around the nation insisted that the heated controversy in Pasadena had been precisely about the nature of progressive education. As both progressive and conservative educational activists rushed to analyze the meaning of Pasadena's controversy, both sides showed a surprising unanimity about the nature of the battle. Commentators of all backgrounds agreed that the fight had been foisted upon Pasadena by scheming outsiders. And the main issue, almost everyone agreed, was the fight over progressive education.

However, pundits writing with the benefit of hindsight could no more agree on the meaning of progressivism than could the angry activists involved in Goslin's ouster. Conservatives accused subversives from the National Education Association, Teachers College, and the Communist Party of forcing progressive education on Pasadena in order to weaken America from within. Progressives charged that right-wing agitators used Pasadena as an arena to test their extreme, paranoid, anti-democratic educational witch-hunting.

The National Commission for the Defense of Democracy through Education (Defense Commission) of the National Education Association (NEA), for example, concluded that the attacks on Goslin were nothing more than "a 'test-tube' for attacks on public schools by certain nationally organized groups who are striking at public-school philosophy, curriculum, textbooks, and personnel."[379] The worst culprit, in the Defense Commission's opinion, was Allen Zoll and his extremist National Council for American Education.[380]

Robert Skaife, field secretary for the Defense Commission, thought the Pasadena controversy was only one part of a "nationwide campaign . . . to wipe out many of the advances the schools have made in the past fifty years."[381] Though privately Skaife doubted whether Zoll alone was responsible for the controversy in Pasadena, publicly he argued that Zoll's pamphlets had played a leading role.[382] Skaife warned that Zoll's tactics were similar to other extremists. First they inundated a town with inflammatory propaganda. Then they moved in to engage in a "heavy pressure campaign."[383]

Other liberal voices agreed. The Reverend Eugene Caron Blake of Pasadena described the nature of the controversy as a fight between "the three R's" and "progressive class rooms." Though Blake denounced "rabidly progressive" excesses, he insisted that all Pasadenans agreed that they wanted fundamentally modern, pluralistic schools. Blake did not mention race or taxes, but he agreed that the controversy came from outside the community. It was only when confronted with ideologies from "forces largely outside our community," Blake argued, that Pasadenans attacked Goslin and his purportedly progressive style.[384]

Goslin himself blamed Zoll. Speaking at Pasadena City College a few weeks before his resignation, Goslin accused Zoll's National Council for American Education and another national organization, the Constitutional Education Committee, of promoting education only for "the limited few." Goslin himself hoped education could become "functional for all." According to Goslin, Zoll and his ilk had spread their poison throughout the nation. They encouraged local conservatives to take up arms against modern education. Goslin did not mention taxes or race. Rather, in his account, the debate arose solely between modern educators and "those who favor the traditional form of education, called 3R's."[385]

Similarly, the progressive Committee on Public Education (COPE) warned Pasadenans that outside "troublemakers" had embroiled local schools in a "phony debate." Such outsiders, COPE argued, wrapped everything they disagreed with in the label "progressive education." Right-wing agitators blamed progressive teachers for "socialism, irresponsible academic freedom and the moral breakdown of youth." COPE noted that conservatives blamed the influence of Teachers College for such pernicious "revolutionary philosophies." However, like other commentators, they did not mention desegregation or taxes as part of the cause of the conflict in Pasadena.[386]

One reporter from the *New York Times* identified the main issue in Pasadena as a "row" between "the stark three R's and the mysteries of hyper progressive education." The primary elements of the controversy, she reported, were the new racial zoning scheme, the teacher workshops, the phantom student summer camps, the abandonment of traditional report cards, the use of a sex education film, and the adoption of suspect textbooks.[387]

Surprisingly few other observers noted the central role of racial desegregation in the Pasadena story. Robert Skaife of the NEA put race, along with taxes, at the center of his analysis. In Pasadena, Skaife concluded that the issue of progressive education was only a red herring. In fact, Skaife argued, conservatives hated the notion of racial desegregation. The simplest way to oppose it, he believed, was by mounting a mean-spirited crusade against Goslin and progressive education. Similarly, when Pasadena "businessmen" balked at higher taxes, instead of fighting against taxes as such, they publicly attacked progressive education instead. In Skaife's view, such bigoted, penurious conservatives faked their animosity to progressive education since they lacked the courage to fight honestly against new taxes and racial desegregation.[388]

Most other analysts did not see the issue that way. Progressive teachers in Pasadena complained that Skaife had placed too much emphasis on desegregation.[389] Even the leaders of the National Association for the Advancement of Colored People (NAACP) did not focus on the desegregation fight in Pasadena as one of their national priorities. In the aftermath of Goslin's firing, the editors of the NAACP journal *The Crisis* agreed that school segregation was a "burning issue." But for those editors in 1951, the "forefront of the fight" was not California, but rather "Maryland, Virginia, South Carolina, Georgia, Texas, and Oklahoma."[390]

Conservative analysts ignored the role of race even more point-edly. To a greater degree than had liberal commentators, conservatives insisted that the issue in Pasadena had been only that of progressive education and outside agitation. Of course, conservatives targeted a different set of outsiders with a different set of political goals. The red-hunting state senators of the California State Senate Investigative Committee implied that Goslin had brought in outsiders to take over local schools. In addition to speakers such as William Heard Kilpat-rick, the senators accused Goslin of packing the district office with left-wing propagandists. The most egregious example, they thought, was the new assistant curriculum coordinator in charge of public rela-tions, George Gerbner. Goslin had hired Gerbner in late 1950, hoping to streamline communications between the central office and the wider community.[391] The senators implied that Gerbner was nothing but a communist plant. They pressed Gerbner to explain his connection with leftist publications such as *Progressive Citizen*. It seemed obvious to the investigating committee that Gerbner hoped to insinuate himself into Pasadena schools in order to propagate the subversive agenda of the world communist movement.[392]

Local conservative leaders found similar evidence of outside influ-ences in Pasadena. Louise Padelford and Cay Hallberg of the SDC and Pro America accused communist activists from Los Angeles of packing Pasadena school board meetings with leftist dupes. Such tactics, Padel-ford and Hallberg charged, were typical of the "left-wing crowd." By filling school board meetings with outsiders, their "loud and aggressive voices" could drown out local folk. The real conspiracy, according to these SDC leaders, was the leftist rush to bring in journalist David Hulburd. Only through conspiracy, they charged, could Hulburd have found a publisher so quickly for his progressive account of the Pas-adena battle. Like Hulburd, though, Padelford and Hallberg defined the contest as one about progressive education. The conspiracy they denounced did not involve new taxes or racial desegregation. Rather, the goal of the outsiders was only to drown out the legitimate protest against progressivism, the opinions of "those of us who believe educa-tion has been taken off the track."[393]

Frank Wells agreed. In Wells's telling, the uproar in Pasadena had been caused by a "latent, national 'Education Party' directed by pro-gressive educators at New York and Columbia Universities." He claimed to have uncovered "daily and hourly evidence" that this national con-spiracy had come to Pasadena in order to test its national program of "thought control." Wells described the four-point program of this national conspiracy. First, the "Education Party" planned to extend its progressive ideology from a base in the public schools. Second, through unwitting children, this ideology would insinuate itself into American homes. Third, this ideology would claim more and more control over students' daily activities, eventually extending even into the phantom summer camps. Finally, this ideology would be dominant throughout the nation. Soon, only a few "old-fashioned" protesters would dare complain. By then, it would be too late. The scheming national education leaders would have taken over the mind of America, children first.[394]

Conservative school board member Lawrence Lamb explained that the "Battle Royal" in Pasadena was started as part of a wider "blueprint for nationalization of our schools." He told an audience of Sons of the American Revolution that such fights would become more common as "sinister influences and ideologies" probed the defenses of traditional, patriotic America. Such left-wing organizations, Lamb bitterly proclaimed, used sympathetic liberal journalists to spread their distorted version of such battles. Those who stood up for traditional education and society, he warned, would be derided as "villains, idiots and stupid fools."[395]

Perhaps the most thorough conservative analysis of the causes and nature of the Pasadena controversy came from Mary Allen. Allen called the defense of traditional education in Pasadena "our Maginot line."[396] "Alien influences" such as the National Education Association, the Anti-Defamation League of B'nai B'rith, the American Education Fellowship, and the John Dewey Society had conspired to invade Pasadena.[397] Allen considered this assault "a full-scale invasion." The goal of progressives, she warned, was to try their hand in Pasadena as a "testing ground" for their subversive policies.[398] The fight was "not accidental, but planned." Progressive educators hoped to provoke the battle to see if conservatives would defend their traditional values. If progressives could succeed in Pasadena, they'd carry their fight to the rest of the nation.[399]

The nature of the battle, as Allen and the other analysts all agreed, was over the true nature and meaning of progressive education. As scholars such as Adam Golub[400] and Andrew Hartman[401] have pointed out, historians and activists have too often accepted this truncated analysis. A more careful look at the historical record shows that the meanings of progressive education, in Pasadena and nationwide, became ineluctably tied to other cultural debates. The battles over racial desegregation, taxes, the nature of childhood, the purpose of education, and the need,

full scale invasion

D.d not provide much analysis of racial segregation. Most examples from elsewhere.

for vigilant defense of American traditions—all these elements combined to form a complex and politically powerful conservative impulse.

In the end, it does not clarify the issue to conclude that the battle in Pasadena was—at its core—only about one or the other issue. In places such as Pasadena, the conservative appeal did not need to break itself down into discrete components. Conservative activists did not lay out a clear program with distinct and strategic planks, such as racial segregation, lower taxes, patriotic anti-communism, and traditional pedagogy. Rather, the power of the conservative school reformers' program came precisely from the vague blending of all those themes. When conservatives fought for schools the way they ought to be, the way they always had been, readers and listeners could fill those promises with their own meanings. They could assume—correctly—that the anti-progressive side meant support for continued racial segregation in schools. They could also assume that such traditionalism meant lower taxes, a purge of subversive texts and teachers, and a return to traditional classroom practice. They did not need to announce their preferences in order to side with more traditional schools. If they supported continued racial segregation, they could do so without publicly coming out as racists. If they wanted lower taxes, they could do so without seeming cheap or heartless. And if their main worry was creeping communism, they could oppose it without acceding to charges of witch-hunting.

One way to make sense of this complex bundling of ideological threads is to look at a specific example. When Theodore Brameld came to Pasadena in February 1950, conservatives attacked him as the embodiment of all that was wrong with Goslin's schools. Brameld in 1950 was at the peak of his career as an educational philosopher and activist. At the time, he worked as a college professor in New York, not at Teachers College, but at the equally suspect New York University. Brameld was an unapologetic leftist, anti-racist, and social reconstructionist. He ardently believed that public schools could and must be used to make American society more egalitarian, less racist, and more open to internationalism. By 1950 his publications included titles such as "Karl Marx and the American Teacher" (1935), "American Education and the Social Struggle" (1936), and *Minority Problems in the Public Schools* (1945).[402]

Conservative activists blasted Brameld as just another part of the sinister progressive education hierarchy. In many ways, conservative attacks on Brameld illustrated the ways the tradition of educational conservatism played out in the Pasadena controversy. Mary Allen, for instance, declared that Brameld was "known for his pro-Marxist views."[403] Louise Padelford and Cay Hallberg denounced Brameld as a collectivist.[404] Frank Wells connected Brameld to higher school taxes. Progressives such as Brameld, Wells charged, wanted to double taxes to pay for their vision of subversive, socialist, ineffective schools.[405] One anonymous member of the SDC claimed that Brameld had built his career on his success at "intensive indoctrination of socialism" among unwitting high school students.[406] According to such conservative activists, Goslin defended Brameld as an expert in "interracial relations."[407] When Brameld spoke to Pasadena's teachers, conservatives claimed, he forced them to read pamphlets such as "Civil Rights—Barometer of Democracy."[408]

So what did Brameld mean to conservatives from Pasadena and around the nation in 1950? How did educational conservatives in 1950 see Brameld's vision of school reform? Brameld embodied progressive education, in all its meanings. Brameld and his ilk reached out from their calculating, disdainful ivory towers in New York. They pushed white kids together with black and brown, deliberately using schools to transform American culture, society, and politics. They indoctrinated defenseless schoolchildren with collectivism, ignoring the fact that kids weren't learning to read and cipher. Even worse, progressives planned precisely to limit the learning of public school children; a duller populace would allow for an easier conversion to socialism. To pay for it all, progressives doubled taxes in a sinister attempt to move wealth from private wallets to government coffers. This progressive scheme forced right-thinking Americans to pay extra to have their schools subverted and their society undermined. Conservatives in Pasadena and around the nation could embrace all, some, or any one of these meanings and feel themselves a part of a conservative educational campaign. Were those campaigns about race? Yes. Taxes? Yes. Socialism, phonics, manners, nostalgia, juvenile delinquency, and a host of other cultural and educational issues? Yes, yes, and yes again.

CHAPTER FIVE

Save the Children

Kanawha County in the Age of Malaise

Like Willard Goslin, Superintendent Kenneth Underwood resigned under intense pressure from conservative school reformers. But Underwood did not just lose his job. He spent September 1974 in hiding, fearing for his life. He had moved his family out of town for their protection. He no longer worked in his office, but moved constantly to keep one step ahead of incessant death threats.[1]

Nor were these empty threats. In the school controversy that engulfed Kanawha County, West Virginia, in 1974, shootings, bombings, and violence became nearly daily occurrences. Underwood himself eventually had to fight off a physical attack at a school board meeting.[2] He was also arrested by conservative local politicians and charged with contributing to the delinquency of a minor. His crime? Approving textbooks that included the work of writers such as Eldridge Cleaver, Sigmund Freud, and e.e. cummings.[3] Underwood described his experience as similar to driving "a runaway locomotive."[4]

These startling events captured the attention of the nation. The ferocity of the protest mystified many outsiders. The National Education Association's investigators concluded in 1975, without much factual basis,[5] that support for the protest came mainly from "rural areas" in Kanawha County, "led by fundamentalist ministers."[6] Such rural fundamentalists, the NEA declared, had been egged on by right-wing extremist groups from around the country, especially the John Birch Society.[7]

In the decades since, the Kanawha County textbook protest has continued to receive a great deal of attention from scholars and activists. Some have explained this intense controversy as the birth of a

"New Right,"[8] the direct progenitor of twenty-first-century "tea party" conservatism.[9] Others have dismissed the protest as a mysterious eruption of "agnosis," a deliberate desire not to know the truths of life in Modern America.[10]

Most of the facts of the story, however, are not in dispute. In brief outline, the controversy began in April 1974. At a school board meeting, Kanawha County school board member Alice Moore objected to the purchase of a new textbook series. The books, Moore insisted, promoted poor grammar and anti-American sentiments. The rest of the school board, despite popular protest during the summer, decided that the books had already been approved and must be used in the county's schools. Otherwise, students would have had to use their old books for five more years. In response, local conservative activists called for a boycott of public schools in the fall of 1974.

The county had always been a complicated place. Home to the state capital, Charleston, Kanawha County has long hosted some of the most productive coal mines in the nation. The county sprawls over hundreds of square miles of hills and valleys. Besides Charleston, it is dotted with cities such as Nitro and Dunbar, towns such as Belle and Cedar Grove. In 1970, the county was home to just over 200,000 people, most of them clustered in the cities and towns.[11] The mining industry had brought some share of prosperity to the region, but it had also brought a history of intensely violent labor conflicts in the early decades of the twentieth century.[12]

It is dangerous to assume too much from this local history of labor conflict, but the tones of the early miners' strikes echoed throughout the 1974 protest. Soon after activists declared a school boycott, local coal miners and bus drivers joined the picket lines in sympathy strikes. The protest marches provided fodder for newspapers nationwide, with memorable signs and frightening violence. Protesters blocked school buses and mysterious assailants shot holes through schools, buses, and police cars. The school board proposed a middling solution that satisfied no one: All sides would agree to a thirty-day cooling-off period. A citizens' committee would examine the books. Children would return to school. Picket lines would clear up.

But the boycott resumed. Dynamite bombs rocked the offices of the school board building. Protesters continued to shoot at empty school buses. School buildings became, in some cases, empty shells, blocked by angry pickets of protesters. Charleston and surrounding Kanawha County remained mired in angry and tumultuous conflict. In November 1974, the majority of the citizens' committee reported that

the textbooks were unobjectionable. But a minority splinter committee issued a detailed, blistering 500-page denunciation. In the end, the
school board returned almost all the books to schools, but parents had
to sign a permission slip to allow their children to read some of them.

As in 1920s Dayton, 1940s Philadelphia, and 1950s Pasadena, the
Kanawha County school protest drew together local and national conservative activists. It forced them to articulate their distrust and disgust
at some aspects of contemporary schooling. In many ways, the West
Virginia controversy embodied the continuing force and appeal of the
tradition of educational conservatism. By mobilizing conservatives to
assert control over the ideological content of public schooling, this prolonged dispute pushed conservatives to explain what they wanted school
to look like and what they feared school might become. As with earlier
school controversies, the strength and vehemence of Kanawha County's outrage typified nationwide pressure that moved America's schools
in profoundly conservative directions. By examining what conservative
activists wanted in Kanawha County in 1974 and 1975, we can get a
deeper understanding of the developing nature of twentieth-century
conservative activism in education.

Sweet Alice

By all accounts, the woman most nearly at the center of this conservative protest was school board member Alice Moore. In April 1974,
Moore provided the spark that set the school controversy alight. At a
board meeting on April 11, Moore asked if the recently purchased set
of English textbooks could be put on hold. She was worried that some
of the textbooks might emphasize "dialectology"—improper English
taught in what Moore considered a misguided attempt to be welcoming
to other cultures. She told the board that this approach was opposed
by thoughtful commentators, including the National Association for
the Advancement of Colored People.[13] Only later, Moore has told interviewers for decades, as she exited that April meeting, did her husband
point out to her how truly dreadful the texts were. During the meeting,
he had been flipping through some of the display copies and had found
what he considered to be shockingly violent, degrading, sexualized
sentiments.[14]

At that April meeting, Moore was told the county had very little
choice. The board could either purchase the approved books or keep
the old books for another five years. However, Moore successfully
demanded that the board reserve the right to inspect the books and

*Alice Moore presents her objections at an over-packed
school-board meeting, June 27, 1974. (Courtesy Charleston
Gazette)*

delete objectionable sections.[15] As she undertook a closer inspection of
the books, her dismay at the contents of the books launched the protest movement. Though the diffuse and many-faceted controversy can
claim no single leader, Moore's personality and ideology left their mark
on the conservative side. Though some of her political campaign material insisted that Moore was mainly a non-partisan "mother" hoping
only to inject some common sense onto the school board, Moore's history shows that she had long embraced a complex conservative ideology
in tune with national trends.[16]

   As a conservative school reformer, Moore echoed many of the
themes of that long tradition. Schools must not be run by distant
experts, Moore insisted. Schoolbooks and teachers must not set out
to undermine traditional values. And schools must not allow students
merely to amble along in an intellectual jaunt, picking up ideas here and
there as they seemed appealing. Rather, schools must provide structured environments in which young people imbibed the best of both

no experts

knowledge and the values of their culture. In 1974, as they had since at least 1925, such ideas of conservative school reform proved enormously influential in Kanawha County and nationwide.

Even her opponents in the 1970s conceded that Moore had earned their respect.[17] After interviewing Moore for her 2009 book about the Kanawha County controversy, scholar Carol Mason agreed that Moore "was indeed charming, smart, and very generous."[18] In 2011, when Moore consented to be interviewed yet again during the research for this chapter, she remained witty, engaging, and insightful.[19] Yet the notion that she had somehow only stumbled into this textbook controversy does not do justice to her history as a dedicated conservative activist. Moore herself always insisted that she was drawn into cultural and educational politics because of her opposition to sex education in public schools.[20] But Moore's opposition to sex ed was not the deciding factor in the 1970 school board election. Instead, Moore distinguished herself by her comprehensive conservative political agenda. Her dramatic come-from-behind electoral victory owed itself to Moore's ambitious and wide-ranging cultural and pedagogical conservatism, not merely to Moore's public opposition to sex ed in Kanawha County.

After all, out of the seven candidates for the Kanawha County school board in the 1970 election, Moore was one of three who ran on an anti-sex ed platform.[21] Of the four who supported sex ed, two of the contenders ran explicitly as progressives. Lawrence Barker, for instance, a former mayor of the town of Dunbar, claimed he had always held a "progressive concern in the interests of youth."[22] Incumbent C. Carl Tully ran on his record of support for a "progressive educational program."[23]

In the days leading up to the election, local polls put Moore far behind Tully.[24] But Moore campaigned energetically against rampant progressivism in Kanawha County's schools. For instance, she accused the school board of allowing inappropriate psychological testing in public schools. Surveys of children, Moore charged, had asked for "information concerning themselves, their religion, their sexual feelings and their family."[25] No school, Moore insisted, had the right to insert itself into students' and families' personal lives in this way. The survey, Moore charged, demonstrated the woefully out-of-touch nature of contemporary schools. What school, she asked, would ask a thirteen-year-old if he feared being sexually impotent? How intelligent he considered his mother? How often his mother went to church? Such interviews, Moore claimed, were symptomatic of a school system in which progressive notions ran wild.[26]

Moore told a local newspaper that the "experts" behind progressive educational programs seemed intent on "destroying our children's patriotism, trust in God, respect for authority and confidence in their parents." If elected, Moore promised to turn this sorry situation around by returning Kanawha County's schools to "the three R's of education." Moore appealed to all the "concerned parents, overworked taxpayers and citizens who are tired of seeing their religious and moral convictions trodden under foot in the name of 'academic freedom.'"[27]

It worked. Moore came from far behind in polls to defeat Tully decisively.[28] At the time, Moore credited her surprise victory to her strong stance against sex education. But she also believed she received support "from those opposed to the school system in general."[29] If Moore owed her victory to a widely shared feeling that the public schools needed more conservative leadership, then her actions on taking office must have pleased her constituency. One of Moore's first moves as school board member was to inspect a new progressive middle school. The Andrew Jackson Junior High School had been created to break down the walls of traditional education. And like many open-concept schools at the time, the school building literally broke down classroom walls. The school encouraged a looser sense of student discipline and a more open curiosity about learning. As one teacher and enthusiastic progressive educator remembered, the school originally encouraged typical progressive teaching, including "Learning Fairs, Applied Field Day, and wonderful games."[30] When Moore came to visit, this teacher remembered, she "strode blindly through [the school and] said, 'I will close you down.'"[31]

Moore remembered Andrew Jackson much differently. The school, Moore recalled, was not a proper learning institution. It had become a cesspool of unrestrained sloth and lust. The students, she recalled, did "whatever they wanted to." As she walked in for her first inspection, a young couple stood in the doorway, wrapped in each other's arms. She had to ask them to move out of her way, which they did only with notable resentment. Other students wandered around the school and neighboring fields, smoking and engaging in all kinds of sexual activity in nearby barns. When Moore asked the principal to explain this sort of behavior, he informed Moore that the school hoped to do more than simply transmit information to students; it hoped to transform them into agents of social change. Teachers should see their roles as co-learners, not as dictators. This sort of progressive shibboleth exasperated Moore.[32]

Some local parents, too, balked at the breakdown of traditional discipline at the new school. Marceline Parsons transferred his daughter out of Andrew Jackson, dismayed at the lack of academic rigor. Parsons had also been perturbed at the high crime rate in the school. His wife, Zelma Parsons, claimed that the school's anything-goes policies had left their daughter ignored and isolated. Mrs. Parsons felt that young people "need to be pushed a little and have something expected of them."[33] By the end of the 1970s, opposition from Moore and parents like Mr. and Mrs. Parsons transformed Jackson back into a more traditional middle school.[34]

Nor was Moore's opposition to the progressivism of Andrew Jackson Junior High her only conservative activism before the 1974 textbook controversy. In 1971, Moore supported the fight against sex education in Kanawha County schools. Such education, Moore argued, did more than simply offer health information to students. In ways both subtle and overt, such education undermined students' belief in religious absolutes. "God's law," Moore protested, "is absolute!"[35] In addition, in 1973, Moore argued in favor of adopting a "California-style" approach to the teaching of evolution. That is, in order not to offend religious conservatives, Moore argued that Kanawha County public schools ought to teach both scientific creationism and evolution.[36] A few months later, Moore bemoaned the nation's "mass slaughter of innocent babies" in abortion clinics.[37] Her role as member of the Kanawha County Board of Education, Moore insisted, put her in a position to raise public awareness of all these issues.[38]

In every way, Moore distinguished herself as a thoroughly conservative politician and activist. The notion that she was some sort of political ingénue, an average mother and housewife, blindsided by the shockingly inappropriate materials she found in the set of textbooks adopted in Kanawha County in April 1974, does not stand up against the evidence. Rather, Moore came to the office of school board determined to use her influence to push Kanawha County schools and culture in conservative directions. She opposed more than sex education. Sex education, in Moore's opinion, was only one way progressives undermined students' faith in God's absolute values. More than just single issues such as sex ed, Moore fought against progressive education broadly understood. She wanted traditional teaching and discipline in Kanawha County schools. She wanted evolution out. She campaigned against abortion and sexual license. With the issue of inappropriate school textbooks, she finally found a cause that resonated intensely among local parents. It also brought Kanawha County to the attention of more prominent conservative educational activists. However, those national leaders did not simply descend upon a local controversy.

Rather, Moore had been reading conservative writers such as Max Rafferty since at least 1970, as we will explore in more detail below.[39] Her first move at the start of the 1974 textbook controversy was to reach out to another set of nationally known conservative activists.

The View from Longview

Moore's impulse to contact Mel and Norma Gabler makes sense. By 1974, the Gablers had over a decade of experience as conservative educational activists in Texas. They had attracted national attention as tireless critics of progressivism and leftism in textbooks.[40] Like Alice Moore, the Gablers insisted they had never wanted to become involved in educational politics. As the Gablers tell the story, their eldest son Jim complained to them in 1961 that his US history and government textbooks told a biased story of America's roots.[41] Mel and Norma were skeptical. The family had lived in Hawkins, Texas, since 1958 and had been active supporters of the public schools.[42] When Mel reluctantly agreed to look over Jim's books, he "couldn't believe his eyes."[43] The books denigrated traditional patriotism, endorsed one-world government, and seemed to deride traditional morality and religion. The Gablers searched for a way to address this depressing situation. As they told the story to writer James Hefley, the Gablers hoped to find some organization that could stop this sort of left-wing ideological takeover of America's schoolbooks. The Texas Daughters of the American Revolution had long been on the case, the Gablers discovered, as had a group calling itself Texans for America.[44] Such groups, though the Gablers fully supported their efforts, had been tarred with accusations of extremism.[45]

Inspired by the victories of Max Rafferty in California, the Gablers decided to take action themselves.[46] Mel wrote and Norma presented a detailed list of grievances to the 1962 Texas special legislative investigative committee on textbooks. The public school, the Gablers told the committee, had been turned into a subversive "propaganda agency." Parents had a right and a duty to protest.[47]

Throughout the 1960s, Norma did most of the traveling and public speaking for the couple. Mel held down his full-time job as a clerk for a pipeline corporation, in his spare time handling paperwork, reviewing textbooks, and writing detailed critiques of books. As their fight against creeping leftism in textbooks expanded, they moved to Longview, Texas, in 1965.[48] Mel took an early retirement in 1975 and the couple incorporated as Educational Research Analysts.[49] By the mid-1980s, they employed a staff of eight at their home office.[50] Throughout the decades of the Gablers' activism, their mission remained the same. They hoped to fight against the propagation of leftist ideas in school textbooks. They wanted to help parents like themselves take cultural control of their public schools. And they hoped their work would transform the nation back into a religious, polite, patriotic society.

As the Gablers explained it, America had a dire need for conservative activism in schools. They shared stories like that of "Geri." Geri had contacted the Gablers in the early 1980s to beg for help. Geri's ten-year-old daughter had begun displaying worrisome behavior. The daughter talked back, acted impolite, and no longer respected her parents' wishes. Geri searched for a cause. She ruled out television and Sunday school teachers. Finally, as the Gablers tell the story, Geri had a revelation. *"You dummy!"* she told herself. *"Who has your kids more than anyone else? The school!"*[51] Geri worked hard to convince hostile teachers and school administrators to talk with her. She finally got her hands on her daughter's textbooks. The books disgusted her. At a loss as to what to do next, she contacted the Gablers for help.[52] Geri was not alone. One parent told the Gablers that her child had committed suicide because of his depressing textbooks.[53]

Such tragedies, the Gablers believed, could be prevented. The root cause of the problem, the Gablers argued, was "progressive education's grand scheme" to transform America.[54] The long-term goal of such progressives was to transform a religious, independent, patriotic, capitalistic populace into a self-hating, group-thinking, atheistic herd.

This trend energized the Gablers to take action. Throughout the 1960s, '70s, and '80s, the Gablers submitted detailed lists of complaints to the Texas authorities in charge of textbook adoptions.[55] Before 1975, Norma traveled alone to hearings of the state board of education and its textbook selection committee. She detailed the shortcomings of the textbooks for every board member. At a hearing called by the Texas commissioner of education, September 18, 1973, Norma insisted that Allyn & Bacon's *Inquiries in Sociology* did more than simply teach students the basics of social science. Instead, Norma insisted, the book hoped to change the "beneficial values of students." This kind of text, Norma told the committee, threatened to transform America's public schools into "mass experimental centers to develop humanistic citizens of the future."[56]

The Gablers also worked to rally conservative supporters to their textbook cause. Not surprisingly, some prominent Texas business leaders agreed that textbooks must not promote socialism or denigrate capitalism. In 1963, for instance, the Gablers enlisted Morgan J. Davis, chairman of the board of Humble Oil and Refining Company, in their campaign against McGraw-Hill's *Economics for Our Times*. Davis wrote to the Texas commissioner of education and to the governor that the book was "an out-and-out advocate of the welfare state."[57] The same business leaders, however, tended to avoid any involvement in other conservative complaints, such as the Gablers' anti-evolution campaign.[58]

The activity that absorbed most of the Gablers' efforts, however, was the dissemination of detailed critiques of textbooks to an ever-growing mailing list of parents and educators.[59] By the 1970s, Educational Research Analysts had assembled a bullpen of writers to contribute reviews for each newsletter.[60] As they did in Kanawha County, the Gablers sent such reviews to parents and teachers nationwide who wanted evidence against certain textbooks.

In some cases, these direct communications with local activists and school districts had a significant impact on textbook sales. Under the Texas system, the state adopted a short list of books from which local districts could choose. When the Gablers failed to have offensive textbooks dropped from the list of adopted texts, they often wrote directly to parents and school districts, warning of the left-leaning nature of certain books.[61] In some cases, as with Allyn & Bacon's *A Global History of Man*, those warnings crippled sales for books the Gablers did not like, even when the title had been adopted by the state.[62]

These tactics often made the Gablers decidedly unpopular among textbook salesmen in Texas.[63] Among journalists and politicians, however, the Gablers wielded great influence.[64] In 1970, for instance, the Texas state board of education approved three policies that the Gablers had long advocated. First, any science book would need to carry a statement "on an introductory page that any material on evolution is presented as a theory rather than as a fact." Second, no textbook could contain "blatantly offensive" language. Third, all textbooks under consideration would have to be made available for public viewing in advance.[65] In 1974, textbook publishers agreed to remove 26 of the 163 specific objections listed by the Gablers.[66] In the early 1980s, Robert D. Fitzgerald, vice president of Allyn & Bacon, admitted to a reporter, "We're all certainly very much aware of [the Gablers.]"[67] The decisions made in Texas, after all, had a much wider impact than most of the other states with statewide adoption policies. Since the market in Texas is so large, Texas's demands have long tended to push publishers to edit out any material that might be perceived as anti-patriotic or anti-religious.[68] The Gablers' outsized influence in Texas gave them an even broader influence nationwide on textbook publishers' editing and publishing decisions.

In spite of their influence, the Gablers always presented themselves as "ordinary parents."[69] But like Alice Moore and earlier generations of conservative educational activists, their activism and influence gave their ideas about education more weight than those of the average PTA member. Throughout their career, the Gablers articulated a deeply conservative vision of proper schooling and curriculum.

In many ways, the Gablers' educational philosophy echoed that of earlier generations of conservatives. They laid the blame for the decline of America's schools on John Dewey and his ilk. Dewey, whom the Gablers referred to as a "declared atheist," could be understood by the Humanist Manifesto of 1933, the Gablers explained. That manifesto declared the need for a new understanding of humanity's place in the cosmos, as part of nature.[70] By the 1930s, Dewey had seized control of teachers' colleges such as Teachers College, Columbia, and promoted "progressive education," based on the notion that "there was no absolute transcendental God, Bible, or system of beliefs."[71] But other progressives shared the blame. In the Gablers' vision of American educational history, educational insiders such as the leaders of the National Education Association made it their mission—and had done so since at least the 1930s—to replace capitalism and traditional values with a new secular socialism.[72]

In language that both echoed and influenced the rhetoric of Kanawha County's protesters, the Gablers combined a belief in their own rock-solid majority among right-thinking Americans with a claim for the rights due an aggrieved minority group. The Gablers believed that conservative Protestants had foolishly avoided politics during the 1930s and 1940s.[73] But by the 1980s, they explained, "the Judeo-Christian mainstream is awakening to the Humanist minority's takeover of the public school curriculum."[74]

In all their critiques of textbooks, the Gablers focused on the specific ways this conservative majority could excise the rot from the nation's schoolbooks. First of all, conservatives must watch for books that denigrated traditional patriotic stories. For instance, the Gablers described the problems with *American Adventures,* an eighth-grade text by Scholastic. This book left out Ethan Allen, Nathan Hale, John Paul Jones, David Farragut, and George Washington Carver. At the same time, the book crammed in Bob Dylan, Janis Joplin, Gertrude Ederle, Bobby Jones, Joan Baez, W. E. B. Du Bois, "and many others dear to liberal hearts."[75]

Many textbooks also promoted a distorted and debased vision of human sexuality. Books under consideration in Texas encouraged masturbation,[76] abortion,[77] and what the Gablers scornfully called a "Liberated" sexuality.[78] And as had been a leading theme of Kanawha County protesters, the Gablers also decried many textbooks' tendency to promote a broad and subversive immoralism. Books included "graphic accounts of gang fights; raids by wild motorcyclists; violent demonstrations against authority; murders of family members; rape."[79] The Gablers repeatedly insisted—as did protesters in Kanawha County—that the language and content of some textbooks was so obscene it could not be read in polite company. For example, the Gablers' official early biography told a story from the early 1960s in which Norma Gabler showed some of the content of offensive textbooks to Alf Jernigan, the assistant manager of the East Texas Chamber of Commerce. Jernigan expressed skepticism, but—according to the Gablers' story—when he read the books, he could not believe the filth.[80] Similarly, when a woman read excerpts from textbooks to the Texas state legislative investigating committee in 1962, according to the Gablers' biographer, "The obscenities and explicit descriptions of sexual intercourse and perversions shocked listeners. Some clapped hands over their ears. Others cried for readers to stop."[81]

In addition to specific offensive passages, the Gablers insisted that many books promoted broader themes of alienation, hate, immorality, disrespect, and skepticism.[82] The moral equivalent of this type of education, the Gablers argued, was putting students into lifeboats in choppy and dangerous seas, and telling them simply to steer wherever they thought was right. Teachers knew the dangers, but scrupulously avoided helping children steer away from the reefs and crashing waves.[83] Too many textbooks, the Gablers believed, presented a false image of life. For instance, in their critique of English language-arts books in 1970, the Gablers asked the Texas adoption committee, "Couldn't half of the stories in this series tell about people living together in harmony, love, understanding, and helpfulness?"[84]

Woven throughout the Gablers' specific criticisms of specific textbooks ran a vision of the proper role of school and the nature of childhood. Progressive educators, the Gablers believed, went wrong when they assumed that children were naturally good. The Gablers argued, to the contrary, that "qualities such as morality must be taught. They do not come naturally."[85] Children, the Gablers believed, ought not to be asked to decide moral questions on their own. Instead, schools must transmit such values directly to young people.[86]

Schools had not only been failing to teach positive values, the Gablers believed. Under the influence of progressive educators, schools had begun actively teaching pernicious ideas. The schools, the Gablers argued, had taken upon themselves the mission to transform children's traditional values. As Norma explained to the Downtown Kiwanis Club in Tyler, Texas, in 1971, schools tried "to teach the child that there are no absolutes, no certain values, that what he learned from his parents and his church is to be discredited or at least discouraged."[87] On the contrary, since the very beginning of their activism, the Gablers had insisted on the rights of parents to have schools that transmit the parents' values to their children.[88]

The Gablers did more than support Alice Moore and the Kanawha County protesters from a distance. In October 1974, the couple traveled to Charleston for a six-day tour of the region. They spoke at a rally on October 6, telling thousands of protesters that their cause was shared by right-thinking parents nationwide.[89] They met with members of the appointed textbook review committee for hours.[90] Even after the Gablers returned to their headquarters in Longview, they maintained close contact with Moore, sending reviews and policy suggestions.[91]

"I Don't Need Those Dirty Books"

Long before the Gablers journeyed to Charleston, local parents and activists mobilized to block the use of the new textbooks in Kanawha County schools. At a meeting of the school board on May 23, 1974, Moore denounced the content of the books in public. The books, she accused, did more than simply butcher the English language. The texts promoted an effete anti-patriotism, a new anti-white racism, a sexualized, bestialized immorality, and a corrosive, anti-religious vision of the nature of humanity. Moore won—for a short while—the support of board member Matthew Kinsolving. She also attracted enough attention to the issue to pressure the rest of the board of education to set another meeting in a month's time to discuss the charges.[92]

In the meantime, Moore spoke widely in the community. She typically read a few excerpts of the books, then noted that she dared not read the rest, as a woman speaking to a mixed audience. The books, she explained, simply contained too much sex and violence to be shared in public. The school board made the entire list of books available for public inspection at a local public library.[93]

If Moore's titillating excerpts had been a calculated ploy to raise community interest in the issue, it worked. Over 1,000 people jammed the board's public meeting on June 27. Nearly 500 attendees had to sit outside in a bitter rain, listening in at windows as best they could.[94] Feelings ran high. Board president Albert Anson had to threaten several times to clear the room, due to repeated outbursts from the audience. Perhaps it is not surprising that neither side seemed able to understand what the other was saying. Just as William Jennings Bryan and Clarence Darrow had spoken past one another nearly fifty years before, supporters and opponents of the textbooks seemed to make such radically different assumptions about the nature and purpose of education that they could barely understand one another. Richard Clendenin, president of the Kanawha County Association of Teachers of English, insisted that the textbooks did a good job of teaching students about other cultures. To a single loud "boo" from the crowd, Clendenin explained that the opposition must come from "uninformed and ill-informed" citizens. The books would help teachers perform their primary duty, Clendenin felt. When pressed by Moore, Clendenin explained this duty as guiding each young person through "the challenge of thinking for one's self."[95]

Similarly, textbook supporter Ronald English explained to the meeting that the new books would allow Kanawha County schools to remain "on the cutting edge of progressive education." The books promised to help complete the racial desegregation of the county's schools, "not in terms of bodies being integrated but in terms of awareness and lifestyles." The opposition to the books, the Reverend English felt, came from "the kind of tyranny that seeks to control the minds of youth."[96]

Michael Wenger, a former teacher and the father of two children in Kanawha County public schools, explained to the packed meeting that the books did exactly what they should be doing. The books challenged students "to think for themselves," Wenger argued. Wenger conceded that the books contained some explicit material about human sexuality and challenging ideas about morality. But that was precisely the purpose of education. The literature selections, Wenger believed, included a wealth of beautiful, inspiring, provocative resources. Such things as violence and skepticism, Wenger argued, were crucial parts of life, and Wenger told the crowd, "we cannot hide it from our children." In short, Wenger exhorted the board to purchase the books, since their approach "brings us out of the dark ages and into the twentieth century."[97] For Wenger, as for Clandenin, English, and other book supporters such as Betty Hamilton of the West Virginia Human Rights Commission, the books promised to push Kanawha County teachers and schoolchildren to do exactly what schools ought to do: confront prejudice, expose children to new ideas, and help students overcome inherited bigotry.

Those who opposed the books had a vastly different understanding of the purpose of schooling. School ought to pass along inherited knowledge and moral values. These books did the opposite. As Donald Dobbs complained, the books dangerously abandoned standards, both moral and grammatical. Not only should students be taught that it is incorrect to say "he done did it," but they must be taught that their own tendency to evil must be tightly constrained. The real standard, the Reverend Dobbs maintained, must come from the Bible. Anything else threatened utter "moral degradation." The crowd applauded wildly.[98]

But neither pro- nor anti-textbook advocates seemed able or willing to understand one another. Under questioning by Alice Moore, for example, Reverend English bemoaned the fact that she did not seem to grasp any of what he had been trying to say. For English, the desirability of textbooks that celebrated the value of a multi-racial, multi-ethnic society seemed obvious, beyond the need for proof. Moore similarly seemed frustrated that book supporters kept returning the discussion to racial issues. She insisted that she supported the inclusion of more African American voices. However, she pointedly asked each book supporter if they thought textbooks and teachers had the right to encourage third-graders, eight- and nine-year-old students, to abandon their religious faith. To Moore, as it had to Dobbs and other textbook opponents, it seemed equally self-evident that textbooks had no right to challenge students' religious beliefs.[99]

As they had since the days of Darrow and Bryan, these interchanges played on stereotypes held by each side. Book supporters assumed that conservatives acted out of ignorance, closed-mindedness, and racism. Conservative activists protested each accusation. It was not racism or ignorance that compelled them to act, they argued. The real issue, conservatives insisted, was that the books sought to undermine children's morality. Worst of all, they fumed, was the supercilious attitude of distant educational elites. It did not make one ignorant, conservatives retorted time and again, to claim control over the proper education of one's own children, to ensure those children learned the home truths of piety, loyalty, and hard work. These books, conservatives claimed, would wreck the faith of readers in family, country, and religion.

In spite of these protests, the school board voted to use the texts in schools, excepting only eight pieces of supplemental material.[100] Those eight supplements contained some of the most objectionable material, including excerpts from Eldridge Cleaver's *Soul on Ice*, e.e. cummings's "i like my body," and Freud's "Character and Anal Eroticism."[101]

Outraged conservatives doubled their efforts to demonstrate the dangers of the texts. Some activists circulated flyers containing excerpts from the books. One flyer included chunks of an included poem, "Speaking: The Hero," by Felix Pollak. The poem described the efforts of a military inductee to avoid service. The speaker refused to fight, yet was killed accidentally in the line of duty. "I died a coward," the poem concludes. "They called me a hero." The flyer also contained bits of Freud that described the roots of feelings of sexual inadequacy. It included a poem by Yusef Iman, in which the brutalities of African American life were ironically contrasted with the call to "Love Your Enemy." The makers of the flyer wanted readers to see that these textbooks promoted thoroughly anti-patriotic, sexualized, racially offensive themes. This flyer also included a call to arms; it asked readers to "wake up Americans! It is your fight for freedom, too!"[102]

The new organization Christian American Parents (CAP) circulated similar selections from the textbooks. In one excerpt, CAP claimed, daredevil Evel Knievel told a subversive story of his childhood. Knievel explained how to blow open a safe, how to escape from police. The police, Knievel recounted, could never catch him. "They're too goddam lazy," Knievel wrote, "or too busy chasing goofballs and homosexuals." Another bit from "Allen Ginsberg at Columbia" included a particularly inflammatory description of a prostitute:

> A tall, red-headed chick. She had been mainly a whore, actually, with very expensive Johns, who would pay her a hundred dollars a shot. And she was a very lively chick, who took a lot of pot. Really a remarkable, beautiful, good-hearted, tender girl. I had a special regard for her, because she had really put herself out to straighten me out and here she was like a big, expensive whore.[103]

Activists often repeated and reproduced these sections of text in a burst of mimeographed flyers.[104] Similar charges of rampant sexualism, drug use, criminality, anti-patriotism, reverse racism, and violence appeared in each. Some of the excerpts commonly reproduced did not even appear in the textbooks under review. The most egregious example of this was a two-sided insert attached to some distributed flyers.[105] This inserted document included excerpts from books not on the list of adopted texts, such as illustrated instructions in the use of condoms and selections from Sol Gordon's *Facts about Sex for Today's Youth* (1973).[106] In this excerpt, Gordon explained, "Some 'street' words for vagina are 'box,' 'snatch,' 'cunt,' 'hole,' 'pussy.' It is not polite to say any of these expressions. However, since they are sometimes used, there is no need to be embarrassed by not knowing what they mean."[107] Though this passage did not actually appear in any of the textbooks under consideration, this widely distributed insert implied that it did. Parents and activists in Kanawha County often thought they were taking action to prevent what they saw as lurid material from falling into their children's hands.

The culmination of these specific claims against the adopted textbooks came only later. In November 1974, a minority of the appointed citizens' committee issued a thick, 500-page report that listed the specific passages to which they objected. Their detailed critique ranged from broad religious and cultural objections to commentary on contemporary current events. For instance, the minority concluded that the adapted story of Jack and the Beanstalk was "more sadistic and gruesome than usual with the giant discussing the eating of children in the most casual manner." Even worse, the discussion guide encouraged children to question the morality of Jack stealing from the giant. In the minority's opinion, these questions amounted to "another discussion of situation ethics which should be condemned." In one fourth-grade text, the minority argued, students were asked to make up a myth to explain the origins of different languages. The committee insisted, "The question why men do not speak the same language is answered in the book of Genesis. The inference that the answer can be classified as a myth again presupposes that the Bible is based on a myth." The minority report also objected to specific examples of the use of dialect. They derided some articles about yoga as mere "religious indoctrination." And they objected that segments about the My Lai massacre and Charles Manson could cause students to "become confused."[108]

All in all, from the protesters' point of view, this exhaustive, detailed catalog did the job. Anyone who wondered how these textbooks could offend could browse through this comprehensive indictment. But conservative opposition to the adopted texts went beyond specific objections to specific selections from the books. Many conservatives articulated the idea that one could object to the textbooks even if one had not read the books themselves. As local conservative businessman Elmer Fike put it, "You don't have to read the textbooks. If you've read anything that the radicals have been putting out in the last few years, that was what was in the textbooks."[109]

Critics have interpreted this attitude as a bewilderingly deliberate ignorance. James Moffett, an editor of some books under review who later analyzed the controversy, insisted that this conservative stance represented a lamentable "agnosis," a "not-wanting-to-know."[110]

Certainly, an insistence that protesters need not actually read the books sounds like a head-in-the-sand reaction.

But from the protesters' perspective, this insistence that one need not read the specific textbooks resulted from the broader roots of the textbook controversy. Many protesters had wider concerns, beyond the specific objectionable passages in these specific textbooks. They felt that progressive educators had seized control of publishing and education. Progressives, many protesters felt, used their outsized influence to change the character and ideas of America's schoolchildren in ways parents would not approve. In the mid-1970s, the cultural atmosphere surrounding education and schooling remained so foul that many conservatives did not need to see specific examples to believe that an educational establishment wanted to promote abhorrent values.

As we have seen in the Rugg controversy and in the Pasadena battle, conservative school reformers often assumed that the levers of educational power had been seized by a usurping clique of self-described experts. Such experts, many conservatives in Kanawha County believed, could be counted on to produce skewed and subversive materials. Right-thinking school reformers did not need to examine every jot and tittle to know that such evil trees would produce pernicious fruit. Examples of this broader protest sentiment abounded. A. K. Boyd, a conservative Baptist from Kanawha City, had not read the books. But he protested against them after he heard his pastor describe the "low-down rottenness that our children are being taught." In Boyd's opinion, this rottenness came as no surprise. After all, higher education had long taught young people the demeaning doctrines of evolution, that humans resulted from "monkeys or . . . one living cell in the ocean." Even worse, this kind of dictatorial public policy, Boyd argued, represented just another example of the millennia-old persecution of Christians. In the end, Boyd warned, the board of education must repent. His advice for them? "Read Psalm 46:1–11."[111] God would punish all those who thwarted His will.[112]

One "agonized parent" complained of utterly losing faith in the educational establishment. This parent explained that with every new "innovative, progressive craze," progressives asked parents to "trust us." First it was sight-reading, then the new math. In the current debate, this parent explained, the dangers became so vast and so immediate that parents did not dare to trust again. This parent's complaints were so illustrative of the broader educational and cultural issues at play that they are worth quoting at some length:

Now, once again, we hear, "Parents, trust us!" This time the radical program is brazen enough to ridicule and undermine God and our beloved America, tampering with the values which have made our Judeo-Christian society the greatest in the history of world civilization. "Trust us," while we turn your precious heirs into animals, reduced to the basest nature, with no convictions of their own, who will be unable to make individual value judgments, relying upon group thinking and decision making.[113]

Parents like this believed that the makers of textbooks had a long history of aggressive anti-traditionalist propaganda. Like Elmer Fike, this parent did not think it necessary to read the textbooks to find specific objectionable passages. Rather, the entire educational establishment had proven itself time and again to be incompetent and immoral.

In some cases, observers tied the 1974 controversy explicitly to earlier school battles. One journalist noted that Alice Moore seemed to rehash "the 1930 indictments brought by those who stood in terror of Harold Rugg."[114] Though the journalist got the dates wrong, the sentiment made sense. By the 1970s, the history of educational controversy had soured some conservatives on the entire educational establishment. The tradition of educational conservatism had been firmly established. Once rumors of offensive textbooks began, conservatives did not need to be convinced in specific detail.

For instance, one petition that gathered over 12,000 signatures did not pick out specific passages from the textbooks under review. Rather, the "Magic Valley Mother's Club" petition simply demanded the elimination of any books which "foster disbelief in the institutions of the United States and in western civilization." In their opinion, those institutions included traditional heterosexual marriage as the basis of the family, support for public religion, constitutional government, free enterprise, and pride in the history of the United States."[115] It was a symptom of the hostile atmosphere surrounding public education in 1974 Kanawha County that many people simply assumed that the textbooks under consideration flouted all these traditional values.

Many protesters objected to the "secular humanism" that ran throughout the books. Speaking to the investigating body of the NEA in December 1974, for instance, teacher and activist Karl Priest defined the problem as one of creeping humanism.[116] Richard Neely, a conservative West Virginia State Supreme Court justice, identified "secular humanism" as the root cause of the "apparent inflexibility of the public school system."[117]

By the time of the Kanawha County controversy, creeping "secular humanism" had come to be a common worry among conservative activists. The secular humanist ideology, as evangelical intellectual Francis Schaeffer defined it in the early 1980s, consisted of a set of ideas that placed humanity at the center of all things, and made humans the "measure of all things."[118] The Gablers had denounced it as "a religion with an anti-biblical, anti-God bent."[119] Fundamentalist author Tim LaHaye blamed secular humanists for training young people in public schools to be "anti-God, antimoral, antifamily, anti-free enterprise and anti-American."[120]

Scholar Carol Mason has suggested that the Kanawha County controversy marked the beginning of a discursive shift among American conservatives from traditional worries about "communism" to a focus on the threat of "secular humanism."[121] It is important to remember, however, that this did not mean a simple one-for-one replacement of bogeymen for the textbook protesters. Protesters certainly warned of the dangers of secular humanism. But activists in Kanawha County also used other terms to describe the problem. For instance, protesters often continued to denounce the "communistic" origins of the textbook problems. Superintendent Underwood complained that textbook supporters were called a host of names, including anti-American, anti-religious, and communistic.[122] Similarly, the Reverend Graley told an interviewer that he thought the books resulted from a "Communist conspiracy."[123] Protest signs throughout the months of school boycott emphasized the communistic nature of the books. For instance, at one December rally, protest signs read, "No Peaceful Coexistence with Satanic Communism."[124] Writing for the Heritage Foundation, at the time a fledgling conservative think tank, Onalee McGraw warned that secular humanism was really simply the "latest manifestation of the so-called progressive life-adjustment philosophy that has dominated our schools and teacher education for decades."[125] For McGraw as for protesters in Kanawha County, "Secular Humanism" joined the jumble of terms used to explain and interpret the problems with schools and textbooks. The use of one explanation for the dangers of the textbooks did not rule out the use of others.

Some protesters offered their own idiosyncratic explanations of the dangers of the books. For instance, one anonymous thirty-year-old mother warned that the books merely joined the rest of rotten American popular culture. Along with the books, children in 1974 had to experience "soap operas and other shows . . . displaying adultery, drunkedness [*sic*], rape, arguing amongst parents, breaking up of homes, murder, stealing, taking God's name in vain and many others." Like these television shows, the textbooks suffered from their incessant immorality.[126] For this parent, the protest against the textbooks incorporated her feelings of helpless anger about much broader cultural issues.

Similarly, long-simmering feelings of resentment apparently provoked some local protesters. More than simply a protest against the content of the texts, some protesters seemed outraged at their long history of being dismissed by a perceived cultural elite. Camay Ward of Kanawha Falls penned a sarcastic letter to the *Charleston Daily Mail*. The protesters, Ward explained with his tongue in his cheek, "live in the coal camps 'n minin' towns 'n uster-be-whistle stops what don't know nothin' 'bout nothin'. We don't get eddicated like them city-folk."[127]

Teacher Karl Priest, for whom the 1974 protest sparked a lifetime of conservative activism, complained to the NEA investigating committee in December that the school board meant "to insinuate that [the protesters] are not sincerely offended; or are not capable of knowing when they *are* offended; or are not worthy of being considered." On the contrary, Priest argued, many of the protesters had received extensive formal education. He himself had earned both bachelor's and master's degrees at secular schools. The problem, Priest believed, was not the prejudices of the conservative protesters. Many shared Priest's education and open-mindedness. The real problem, Priest insisted, was that self-satisfied progressives failed to examine their own prejudices; they failed to consider other viewpoints as of equal merit to their own.[128]

Local leader Elmer Fike agreed. The textbook protest, Fike wrote in his newsletter, was often portrayed as an "argument . . . between a group of red-neck, ignorant, fundamentalist preachers and the well-educated Board members who are trying to modernize the educational system."[129] The real protest, Fike argued, lay between out-of-touch "avant-garde liberals and the conservatives who want to preserve American heritage." The reason one did not need to read the books to know they were dangerous, Fike believed, resulted from the fact that the textbooks themselves were not "the sole point of protest." In reality, the textbooks were only a "last straw." The real issue was a "nationwide" campaign for "a return to fundamental and basic education."[130]

As one local teacher complained, "the books have a definitely 'Leftist' lean."[131] The books were the product of a rotten system. As such, one did not need to find specific offending passages to condemn the books overall. The problem was the books' desire to indoctrinate young people. Specific objectionable passages merely illustrated this pernicious tendency. Similarly, the local John Birch Society insisted that the problem with the books went far beyond the specifically objectionable passages. Those passages, one flyer sponsored by the local John Birch Society bookstore argued, were merely symptomatic of the aggressive tendrils of the "one world-liberal establishment," a sinister organization that had "long ago planned our destruction." The offensive passages in these specific books represented the educational wing of this comprehensive liberal strategy, a strategy that included breaking down traditional manners and religion, as well as hooking kids on drugs and luring them away from their parents' control and example.[132]

As with much else in the controversy, Alice Moore offered perhaps the clearest articulation of these ideas. The specific content of the books, Moore told one audience of local Kiwanis, was not as important as the menacing intent of the books to transform the ideology, religion, and morals of Kanawha County schoolchildren. "People send their children to school to learn reading, writing, and arithmetic," Moore warned, "but too many educators think their job is to change the students' attitudes and values."[133]

For Moore and for many other protesters, this broader educational effort remained the true object of the protest. Protesters attacked more than these specific books. They demanded protection from the entire perceived progressive educational project. Thus, some protesters called the textbooks anti-biblical. Others called them one-world/socialist. Others—at least one other—compared them to smutty soap operas. The specific complaints reflected the diverse nature of the conservative protesters. But they also demonstrated the broader tradition of protest that informed the events of 1974. Conservatives often needed no proof to believe that textbooks contained material deeply offensive to their core values. After all, given the history of educational culture wars since the Scopes trial of 1925, conservatives had come to see themselves as confronting an educational elite dedicated to transforming their children's values and beliefs.

Some evidence indicates that the broader suspicions of conservative activists had a basis in fact. James Moffett, an editor of the *Interaction* series that drew most of the fire from conservative protesters, later defended the series. In Moffett's telling, the book series really did intend to shake up students' and families' moral traditions. The reading series, Moffett explained, bravely flouted some of the traditions of language arts textbooks. Despite pressure from "our increasingly jittery publisher," the devoted teachers who put the series together remained committed to repudiating conventions.[134]

As Moffett remembered, the *Interaction* series called for more than just a different set of excerpts from possibly offensive sources. The reading series demanded a radical break from "conventional classroom management." Moffett and his colleagues intended for their series to shatter the notion of a teacher-centered traditional classroom. Classrooms that used *Interaction* selections and activities, Moffett hoped, would become "student-centered." Until the Kanawha County protest, Moffett believed "the country was still riding the crest of progressive energy that had wrought so many changes in the 1960s and seemed to mandate further innovations in schooling."[135] Moffett and the protesters agreed on one thing: this reading series hoped to transform the morality and worldview of students. It planned to change radically the nature of schooling to create a generation of young people who would not accept the rote dictates of traditional morality.

"If We Don't Protect Our Children from Evil We'll Have to Go to Hell for It"

Yet despite the ferocious summer activism of Kanawha County protesters, the books remained in schools as the days shortened and leaves began to fall. Local leaders called for a boycott of all schools until the school board removed the texts. Starting on September 3, 1974, parents and activists kept their kids home. The next day, local coal miners walked off their jobs in a sympathy strike.[136] By the end of the first scheduled week of school, Charleston's public bus drivers joined the picket lines. In spite of a request to return to work by United Mine Workers president Arnold Miller, Kanawha County's miners stayed away.[137]

Overall, Kanawha County schools saw a spike of twenty percent absenteeism, compared to the usual eight percent. But this number does not fairly represent the town-by-town and neighborhood-by-neighborhood nature of the boycott. Some schools, such as Cedar Grove Community School, stood nearly entirely empty, with only 9 of its 900 students showing up.[138] At Dupont High School, only 423 students came to school, of an expected 745. East Bank High welcomed only 186 students of an expected 800. But Charleston High found that most of its students repudiated the boycott. Of an expected 1,000 students, 957 came to school on September 3, a higher attendance rate than usual.[139]

In order to pressure more families to honor the boycott, picketers blocked school buildings and school bus routes. By the end of the first week of the protest, Kanawha County Circuit Court judge John

Charnock issued an injunction forbidding protesters from interfering with schools or buses.[140] State police resolutely refused Superintendent Underwood's requests for help. The fifty deputies of the sheriff's department reported they did not have the manpower to provide security for all the schools and all the buses.[141]

Much of the press coverage at the time focused on protester violence. Images of cars with windows smashed and school buses riddled with bullet holes seemed to confirm that tale. As we will discuss in more detail below, the violence and coercion associated with this school protest need more careful examination. Similarly, the protests themselves included many counter-protests and micro-protests that must be recognized as currents within the wider pattern. For example, at the height of the first boycott, students at George Washington High School staged a pro-textbook walkout. As one student explained, "We see nothing wrong with the books. So we asked for them back."[142] Elsewhere, parents at Ruthlawn Elementary successfully incorporated a call for the removal of an unpopular school principal into their school picket.[143] Parents and teachers had struggled unsuccessfully for months to have the principal removed. They felt their complaints to the board of education had fallen on deaf ears.[144] These parents not only kept their kids at home, but they seized the opportunity of the boycott to take direct action against the leadership of their children's school.

After a week of tumultuous protests, the school board offered a lukewarm solution. They would remove the books from the schools and appoint an eighteen-member citizens' committee to review the books. Each board member, including new chairman-elect Douglas Stump, would appoint three citizens. All sides would agree to a thirty-day review period.[145] Protest leaders initially condemned the plan, since the school board members would likely appoint commissioners friendly to their own views. With a three-two split in favor of the books among school board members, protesters feared a similarly biased decision by the citizens' committee.[146] Nevertheless, boycott leaders eventually agreed to respect the thirty-day examination compromise.[147]

Among those emerging leaders, local ministers played a prominent role. Their involvement pushed them to articulate the reasons for their objections to the books. The Reverend Marvin Horan, for example, took on a role as a leader of the protest when he called for the boycott at a Labor Day rally on September 2, 1974.[148] After becoming disillusioned with the temporary compromise in September, Horan would call for a second boycott in October 1974. "No education at all," Horan would insist, "is 100 percent better than what's going on in the schools now. If we don't protect our children from evil we'll have to go to hell for it."[149] The protesters, Horan argued, "never have had the coverage from the news media that we deserve." The protest, Horan told a local television reporter, ultimately planned to do more than simply reject the textbooks. The final goal, Horan insisted, was to return schools "to the old standard of teaching."[150]

Ezra Graley, another conservative Protestant minister who took on a leadership role, later explained that he, too, felt the news coverage at the time of the protest misrepresented the protesters. He believed that reporters focused on isolated violent acts by protesters, when the same reporters did not report on the fact that school officials had confiscated "truck loads" of Bibles from public schools.[151] The books, in Graley's opinion, represented the worst sort of "anti-family, anti-authority" messages.[152] This type of filth, Graley argued, resulted from a "Communist conspiracy."[153] The clear goal was to shatter American morality, leading to an increase in crime and disorder.[154]

As for many protesters, to Graley the book campaign represented a broad cultural and political protest. Inspired by his role in the textbook movement, Graley eventually ran for governor. His platform incorporated the complex conservatism that motivated many textbook protesters. Some of the planks, such as an end to compulsory school attendance laws, prayer and Bible reading in schools, more classroom discipline, and a school voucher plan, concerned schooling and education directly. But Graley also promoted a much broader ideology, one that called for "Honesty, Decency, [and] Integrity." One that called for more protection from crime, more capital punishment, lower taxes, and an end to abortion and euthanasia. Graley's platform opposed welfare and the Equal Rights Amendment, as well as a perception of increased drug use in America.[155] For Graley, the 1974 textbook protest became part and parcel of this broader conservative activism.

Another protest leader and Protestant minister agreed. The problem with the books, Avis Hill told one interviewer, was their "philosophy of . . . secularism." It was not only the specific objectionable passages that outraged Hill. Rather, he felt the books as a whole promoted "the attitudes of evolution and all that."[156] To another interviewer, Hill reported that the protest resulted from resentment against being treated like "third- and fourth-class citizens."[157] He himself complained of being "looked on as a nobody; I was spoken of as a backwoods fundamentalist Bible-toting, foot-stomping, Bible-thumping preacher."[158]

Not all the protest leaders had backgrounds in the ministry. Elmer Fike owned a local chemical plant. Among other things, Fike objected to the textbooks' disparaging tone toward capitalism and the free enterprise system.[159] But as Fike told James Moffett, "It wasn't just the textbooks. They brought it to a head and made clear what the so-called progressives in the educational system were trying to do."[160] As Fike argued in a 1976 essay, traditionalism and progressivism stared at each other across a seemingly unbridgeable divide. Traditionalists, Fike argued, understood education to be a simple process of transmitting information and skills from teacher to student. "The job of the schools," in Fike's articulation of the traditionalist philosophy, "is considered to be the transmission of the tradition of the parents to the children in order to preserve society." Progressives, on the other hand, wanted children to experiment with a variety of philosophies with a minimum of guidance. The progressive goal, Fike argued, was to empower young people to make their own intelligent decisions.[161]

During the hottest days of the school boycotts, Fike bought space in the *Charleston Daily Mail* to explain his objections to the books. The books, Fike insisted, failed to promote "the legitimate purpose of education." That purpose had been articulated properly by the NEA's 1918 Commission on the Reorganization of Secondary Education, Fike believed. The commission had identified seven "Cardinal Principles" of education, including health, command of fundamental processes (which Fike clarified as "the three R's"), worthy home membership, vocation, citizenship, worthy use of leisure, and ethical character. The textbooks promoted none of these things. In fact, the books undermined ethical character and "social values of home and community accepted by a large majority of the people." Use of the books, Fike believed, would lead to a further increase in crime and delinquency. It would lead to anti-patriotic sentiments among the young and even more "antisocial behavior."[162]

When Fike issued his denunciation, the protest had entered its most tumultuous phase. Though leaders had initially agreed to the school board's thirty-day cooling off period while the citizens' committee debated and analyzed the books, protesters soon decided to renew the school boycott. On October 6, flanked by Mel Gabler, Marvin Horan called for a renewed boycott.[163] Soon, protest leaders Ezra Graley and Avis Hill found themselves in jail for almost ten days, on a charge of interfering with bus routes.[164] In spite of Alice Moore's pleas to end the renewed boycott,[165] students stayed home throughout the month of October.[166]

The intense political turmoil led board member Albert Anson to retire. Anson hoped his retirement would cool the dispute, since he had supported the textbooks.[167] With Anson out, anti-textbook board member Douglas Stump took his seat on the school board. Stump's vitriolic attacks on Superintendent Underwood soon led Underwood to announce his own retirement.[168] The fight had become so bitter, however, that announcing his upcoming retirement did not mean the end of controversy for Underwood. In November, Underwood was symbolically arrested on warrants drawn up by the Upper Kanawha Valley Mayors Association. One of the association's leaders, Cedar Grove's mayor, John Lee Hudnall, had tried and failed to have Underwood arrested earlier.[169] Though Underwood immediately obtained release on bond, the arrest for Underwood's contribution to the delinquency of minors was a humiliating reprisal for the arrests of Graley, Hill, and other anti-textbook leaders. It was also a stark reminder of the feuding tradition in West Virginia, in which competing parties used loyal judges to harass the other side.[170]

Bloody Hills

Nor was such symbolic harassment the worst of Underwood's worries. Throughout the school boycotts, Underwood received incessant telephone threats. By late September, he had moved his family out of their home. He no longer worked at his office, but rather moved around from school to school.[171] One letter that had circulated around Charleston, purportedly from a group calling itself the Vigilante Committee for Decency in Our Schools, urged textbook supporters to "flee this county and burden someone else somewhere else." Not too long ago, the flyer warned, "insects on the order of Underwood, [school board members] Anson, Issacs, Stansbury and [US District Judge] Knapp would have been lynched for less than their present activities just to rid the earth of their foul presence." Though the flyer ended with a disclaimer that it did not advocate this sort of violence, since "these creeps are not worth going to jail for," the implication was indeed ominous.[172]

The history of the region, especially over mining disputes, had long been punctuated by episodes of intense violence and strife.[173] Perhaps this tradition of violent protest contributed to the intense and unremitting violence associated with the school boycott. Of course, the mountain location does not explain away the persistent and dramatic violence. We must not dismiss the shootings and bombings as mere eruptions of an Appalachian folk tradition, as mere continuations of Hatfields and McCoys. However, the context is important. Activists evoked that tradition explicitly, and it loomed implicitly as a significant presence throughout the school boycott and its aftermath. Nor is it enough to understand the boycott violence as a relic of Kanawha County's rugged labor history. In some ways, the boycott picket lines resembled labor lines, and much of the violence stemmed from an effort to enforce the boycott, but not all. A careful catalog of the violence associated with this school controversy reveals more of a violent free-for-all than a concerted campaign of violence by only one side.

For instance, the protest witnessed two shootings on September 12, 1974, and both victims came from among the ranks of the protesters. First, Everett Mitchell, a janitor at Smith's Transfer Corporation in Belle, pushed through a picket line in order to get to work. He was jostled and shoved by protesters. In response, he pulled out a pistol and fired several shots into the crowd. One protester suffered minor injuries. Mitchell, however, was not so lucky. The surrounding protesters disarmed him and beat him severely.[174]

The second shooting also took place at the scene of a contested picket line. Bill Noel tried to get to his United Parcel Service delivery truck. Blocked by angry pickets, Noel shot and wounded protester Philip Cochran. Noel fled the scene, but soon surrendered to police. Noel told police he had fired in self-defense.[175]

We might also include in this list of anti-protest violence the targeting of the leadership for legal and extra-legal coercion. Alice Moore, for instance, claimed to have received threats from textbook supporters. She told one interviewer that she heard warning shots fired outside her house.[176]

It is easier to confirm the legal coercion applied to leaders of the protest. Both Ezra Graley and Avis Hill spent time in prison, charged with leading illegal blockades of schools and school buses.[177] In early October 1974, three protesters—Mary Thompson, Loraine Atkinson, and Helen Slack—were each sentenced to thirty days and fined five hundred dollars for blocking school buses at the bus garage in Dickinson.[178]

Eventually, in April 1975, US District Judge K. K. Hall sentenced protest leader Marvin Horan to three years in prison for encouraging the worst of the school bombings.[179] Horan was not accused of planting any bombs or planning any bombings directly, but rather of encouraging the violence. According to the indictment, Horan had told protesters that they could "do anything they wanted to" when it came to blocking the functioning of schools.[180] In laying down the harsh sentence, Judge Hall called Horan "the leader of the conspiracy."[181] Horan's treatment became a cause célèbre among the textbook activists. Protest leaders agreed that Horan had been "railroaded," punished extravagantly as a symbol to the other protesters.[182]

Judge Hall may have felt such a warning was necessary. Protesters maintained a steady drumbeat of violent action through the months of the school boycotts. In mid-September 1974, during the period of the first boycott, a never-identified protester shot out the windows of the board of education building, without any casualties.[183] A few weeks later, on the night of October 8, bombs exploded in two elementary schools. At one of the schools, in Midway, a dynamite blast knocked out two doors and most of the windows. At the other school, Wet Branch, a firebomb thrown through a window caused smoke and fire damage. During the same period of the second school boycott, protesters routinely threw rocks at school buses. Bus drivers reported constant threats.[184] Later in October, Midway Elementary again sustained a dynamite blast, damaging one room severely.[185]

The pattern of violence continued throughout the fall of 1974. Protesters hoped the violence would enforce the school boycott. Any non-boycotting parents or school workers became targets. Similarly, the schools themselves and the board of education building were subjected to a series of bombings. Some were serious, some less so. For instance, on October 10, Chandler Elementary School in Orchard Manor was hit with a series of fire bombs. A car drove by and an occupant threw three homemade gas bombs. Only one exploded, causing only minor damage. The same day, an anonymous phone caller threatened John Clay, a janitor at Belle Elementary School. According to Clay, the caller warned him to stay home from work. When he reported to work the next day, Clay claimed, a mysterious assailant hit him in the back with a chair. Clay fell down a set of stairs, sustaining only minor injuries.[186] Even without actual bombings, the atmosphere disrupted school functioning. One local school principal reported that he had fielded twelve bomb threats in three weeks. Without being able to sort the real from the fake, the resulting evacuations made schooling distinctly less efficient.[187]

The biggest blast of the protest period came on October 30. During the night, fifteen sticks of dynamite rocked the board of education building. One worker was still inside at the time, but he was unhurt.[188] In the coming weeks, protesters threw rocks at cars of parents taking their children to school. In mid-November, picketers blocked students and teachers from entering Cedar Grove Community School. The car of one family who continued to send their children to school was fire-bombed. Since school buses became regular targets of gunfire, armed sheriff's deputies filled in for school bus drivers.[189] Even police cars escorting school buses received gunfire on at least one occasion.[190] In late November, one school bus driver reported that someone shot his pickup truck's radiator during the night.[191] Again in early December, a stick of dynamite exploded outside of Mary Ingles Elementary School in Tad during the night. The blast smashed several windows but inflicted no other damage.[192] During the days, protesters continued to block entrances to schools and even to industrial sites, usually unsuccessfully.[193]

Even when bombs failed to go off, or when bomb threats turned out to be false, or when attempts to blockade school entrances failed, the atmosphere surrounding schooling in Kanawha County became decidedly poisonous in the last months of 1974. It was made more so by the threats and rumors of threats by protest leaders. As we have seen, one widely circulated flyer warned that protesters might return to the tradition of lynching their foes.[194] Another flyer, authored by Glenn C. Roberts and published by the local John Birch Society bookstore, refuted charges by Episcopal minister James Lewis. Lewis had become a leader of the pro-textbook side. He had denounced the protests as racist and ignorant. In his rebuttal, Roberts warned Lewis "to please releave [*sic*] us of the burden of his presence, and to go back whence he came right quickly!" Roberts added ominously, "There are too many of [Lewis's] evil kind around here already."[195] Given the context of bombings, shootings, and assault, Roberts's rhetoric loomed as a reminder of the extralegal violence to which protesters might resort.

Religious leaders were also accused of encouraging protest violence. As we have seen, Judge Hall eventually sentenced the Reverend Marvin Horan to a stiff jail sentence for Horan's role in inciting violence. Horan admitted he had preached to a protest meeting on a well-known passage from the biblical book of Ecclesiastes. According to the original indictment, Horan's use of the passage—"A time to kill, and a time to heal; a time to break down, and a time to build up"—implied that protesters could use violence to eliminate the textbooks.[196] Similarly, the Reverend Charles Quigley attracted attention for his baleful prayer request. During the September protest, Quigley called on local Christians to pray for the deaths of those school board members who had supported the textbooks. "I am asking Christian people," Quigley asked, "to pray that God will kill the giants that have mocked and made fun of dumb fundamentalists."[197] Quigley later admitted to making the request, but he claimed never to have prayed personally for violence to the school board. Rather, Quigley hoped that he could divert attention from actual violence to prayer.[198]

In all the charges of violence and incitement, it is necessary to remember that much of the protest passed by without violence on any side. School bombings and bus shootings attracted the most attention, but they did not encompass the entirety of the boycott. For instance, in the very early days of the protest, acting principal Paul Boggess of Ruthlawn Elementary noted that the picketers at his school remained universally cordial. He invited them into the school for coffee and to inspect the books.[199] Even when protesters and school officials could not maintain this level of civility, much of the picket action limited itself to verbal "tongue lashing," not to physical violence or blockades of students or school buses.[200]

Other instances that contributed to the tumultuous atmosphere must be recognized as incidental to the protest itself. For instance, two young students from St. Albans High School admitted to making fake bomb threats to close down their school. These students were not motivated by anti-textbook sentiment. Rather, they merely took advantage of the situation to escape from a few days of schooling.[201]

Outside Agitators

If we are to understand the motives and ideology of the anti-textbook protesters, we need to take this kind of boycott opportunism into account. Just as some local parents used the protest to attack an unpopular school principal, so some students took the opportunity to close down their schools. Similarly, conservative groups converged on Charleston in an effort to shape the protest to fit their agendas. Some commentators have ascribed overwhelming influence to these outside activists. For instance, the investigative committee of the National Education Association concluded that the John Birch Society and its allies intensified and prolonged the protest.[202] James Moffett concluded that outside activists turned "a spontaneous local revolt [into] part of a national network long in operation but just fully savoring its power."[203]

As with the violence of the protest, the role of outside activists needs a closer look. There can be little doubt that the interest and influence of outsiders contributed to the protest in significant ways. As we have seen, Alice Moore quickly contacted the Gablers for help and advice. A steady stream of interested conservative pundits trickled through town in the fall of 1974. For instance, the Reverend Carl McIntire talked at a rally in late November. McIntire had built an empire of separatist Presbyterian fundamentalism from his New Jersey headquarters.[204] His popular radio show had long been carried on a local station.[205] Other conservative voices weighed in on the textbook fight. In the pages of the segregationist Citizens' Councils newsletter, for instance, George Shannon claimed that the protesters mainly opposed racial integration.[206]

But not every outside group had equal influence. If we hope to understand the conservative educational activism involved in this controversy, we need to avoid two errors. We must not assume that the protest was defined by outside activists. As did the NEA report, this kind of conclusion ignores the leading role played by local actors. It also leads to overly simplistic characterizations of the protest as embodying one national group's ideology or another's. We must also resist the temptation to conclude that outsiders played no significant role. Instead, we must draw a finer line. We need to test the competing claims about the various national groups involved. In some cases, such as the whistle-stop activism of Carl McIntire or the hapless grandstanding of the Ku Klux Klan, outside activists had little demonstrable impact on the events in Kanawha County. Attributing outsized influence to such outsiders more often served as a way to discredit or pigeonhole conservative school reformers than as a genuine attempt to understand the contours of the controversy.

In other cases the connection between locals and out-of-towners was significant and undeniable. As we've seen, local activists cooperated closely with the Gablers to form strategy and goals. In the end, as we will see, the school board largely adopted the Gablers' recommendations for resolving the boycott.

In addition, the ideas of the former superintendent of public instruction for California Max Rafferty had a direct impact on the thinking of at least some of the conservative leaders in Kanawha County. In order to make sense of the events and ideas at play in Charleston, we need to understand Rafferty's career and contributions to educational conservatism. By 1974, Max Rafferty no longer served as California's education leader, but he managed to exert sizeable influence on conservative educational thinking nationwide during the 1960s and 1970s. Though his bid for the US Senate flopped in 1968, with his syndicated newspaper column Rafferty held the attention of the nation long after his term as superintendent of public instruction in California ended in 1971.[207] As did a multitude of conservative celebrities and activists, Rafferty made a stop in Kanawha County during the textbook protest. At a rally in January 1975, Rafferty explained that textbook publishers did not care about the morality of their books. The publishers, Rafferty warned, just wanted "to make a buck. . . . They have no particular desire to reform anybody, do anybody any good or find a pathway to heaven." The publishers, Rafferty noted, did not set out to hurt or mislead America's schoolchildren, but unless kept on a tight leash by conservative activists, that is exactly what textbook publishers would do.[208]

Unlike some of the luminaries who made appearances in Charleston or Kanawha County during the tense months of the boycott, Rafferty's ideas enjoyed broad influence among conservative educators nationwide. For instance, the leading Protestant fundamentalist textbook publisher, A Beka Book, recommended Rafferty's work as a guideline for conservative parents and school administrators looking for resources in starting traditionalist Christian schools.[209] At least one of the start-up Christian private schools in Kanawha County adopted A Beka's curriculum, directly or indirectly following Rafferty's prescription for healthy conservative schools.[210] Not every conservative educational leader embraced Rafferty, however. Walter Fremont, in the early 1980s the long-serving dean of the fundamentalist Bob Jones University School of Education, warned his fellow religious conservatives against Rafferty's work. Fremont agreed that Rafferty's call for "a return to traditional education" would doubtless improve public schools. But as "an Episcopalian, an evolutionist, and certainly not one who claims to be born again," Rafferty ought not be taken as a model for Christian schools, Fremont argued.[211]

Also unlike some of the conservative pundits who descended upon Charleston during the controversy, Rafferty's ideas had long been decisively influential with Kanawha County's conservative school reformers. Alice Moore, especially, had long considered herself a student of Rafferty's. It is indisputably difficult to trace intellectual influence, but in this case we have convincing evidence that Moore was guided by Rafferty's work. As we have seen, since her election to the school board in 1970, Moore worked to promote a variety of conservative causes in schools and society. Her platform in that election explicitly echoed Rafferty's ideas. For instance, when asked in 1970 to describe her program, Moore endorsed Rafferty's suggested program of "education in depth" for healing Kanawha County schools.[212] Decades later, she remembered reading Rafferty's work as she began her school board career in 1970. Rafferty's books such as *Classroom Countdown* had a decisive impact on her thinking about the nature of education.[213] In Moore's case, at least, we can conclude that Rafferty's educational philosophy played a formative role. If we can understand Rafferty's ideas about education, tradition, and transforming American culture, we can get a better sense of the thinking of conservative activists in Kanawha County in the tumultuous fall of 1974.

Rafferty liked to present himself as a moderate. He critiqued knee-jerk traditionalists who planned to return American schools to an imagined "dear, dead past." Proper schooling, Rafferty argued, must certainly focus on the "'three R's,' . . . but only as a springboard for vastly more complex subject matter." Rafferty hoped traditionalist education could be about more than empty nostalgia. Proper, effective conservatism meant absorbing what is good from progressive education and removing what is ineffective. Corporal punishment, for instance, must be eliminated.[214] And the "new math" must be embraced.[215] Even some ideas of arch-progressive John Dewey ought to be accepted, Rafferty believed. As Dewey advocated, students ought to solve problems and engage in real-world thinking, not simply recite rote passages from memory.[216]

But at its core, Rafferty's vision rejected progressive education, as Rafferty defined it. Though some of its innovations were to the good, Rafferty explained, the core elements of progressivism threatened to crush American education. For Rafferty, the essential problem with progressivism in education was its emphasis on the relativity of all values. Progressivism in schools, Rafferty insisted, was merely a symptom of a "pervasive, all-inclusive twentieth-century disease: the passing of the absolute."[217] Without teaching young people simple, traditional, inclusive lessons about good and evil, America threatened to bring upon itself both moral and literal destruction.

To Rafferty, progressive education was not simply inefficient. Rather, it was nothing less than "a recipe for national suicide." Only those educated with traditional notions of absolute right and wrong, good and evil, Rafferty argued, became able to fight evil.[218] Progressive education robbed Americans of that sort of resolution. As John Dewey led the "new cult" of progressive education, Dewey discouraged students from actually learning the hard facts of mathematics, literature, geography, history, as well as morality.[219] Rafferty blamed Dewey and his Teachers College cohorts such as Harold Rugg, William Heard Kilpatrick, and George Counts for foisting an enervating relativism on America's schools.[220]

In 1963, Rafferty argued that this pernicious misunderstanding of the proper nature of education threatened "the survival of our country."[221] True education was an accumulative cultural process. Each generation ought to add its bit of knowledge and experience to the cultural stockpile. Education meant passing along that cultural treasure trove to the next generation. During the Cold War, Rafferty insisted that the loss of that heritage threatened to expose an underprepared America *traditional values*

moral reasons

to the "tyranny and vice . . . [of a] race of faceless, godless peasants from the steppes of Asia."[222] Beyond the Cold War struggle for survival against a relentless Soviet foe, progressive education threatened to undo all of America's traditional values.

Sex education was one example. In his typical folksy style, Rafferty opined in the heady days of 1968 that "today's children need instruction in sexual matters about as much as Custer needed more Indians."[223] Americans did not need to drill children in "the mechanics of sex."[224] Rather, American education and culture must embrace a return to traditional values. Americans in and out of schools must "recognize openly the ancient truth that illicit and premarital sex is an offense against both God and man, if only because of its chilling selfishness and complete disregard for others."[225] As with many of Rafferty's nostrums, this one reached far beyond the school walls. An authentic sexual education curriculum, Rafferty believed, would require all adults to set better examples of respect and self-restraint.[226]

A simpler way to heal American schools and culture, Rafferty believed, was to return local control to neighborhood schools. Rafferty chided "educational bureaucrats, resplendently sent among us from his Washington superiors to convert the heathen out in the hinterland."[227] Such out-of-touch educational elites had become "badly out of step with the rest of the American people."[228] And the American people deserved to be trusted. Rafferty believed in the "deep underlying instinct of the American people as to what was good for the children of the nation."[229] Local communities, Rafferty insisted, could solve any educational problem by working together "in the traditional American spirit of mutual tolerance and good will."[230] But thanks to the usurpation of educational decisions by far-off bureaucrats, regular parents and community leaders had no more voice in the kinds of classrooms their children would experience.

Those parents, Rafferty argued, could return "common sense" to American education.[231] As scholar Michael Apple has argued, by the twenty-first century conservatives had largely been able to "win the battle over common sense."[232] Rafferty led the way by promoting "common sense" educational solutions to America's cultural malaise. Common sense, Rafferty argued, could restore traditions of competition among students. It could return curriculum to such tried-and-true literature as Walter Scott, Arthurian legends, the Three Musketeers, and Mark Twain.[233] Common sense could invite a non-sectarian religion back into public schools.[234] Common sense would return phonics to a leading role in reading instruction.[235] It would teach young people American traditions[236] and clear definitions of right and wrong.[237]

Perhaps most importantly, Rafferty suggested that his common sense approach, what he called "Education In Depth," would restore the traditional understanding of the nature of childhood and education. Progressive education went wrong when it assumed too much for children. Children, Rafferty argued, were not capable of complex moral philosophizing. A child was the most important thing in the world, Rafferty noted, but "he is not the finished product. He is raw material, a potential adult."[238] Children were both more and less than adults, Rafferty argued. A child was "a being in transition and a lot closer to the raw simplicities of the primeval jungle than any of us will ever be again."[239]

By misunderstanding this central idea, progressive education made the mistake of thinking that the only way to teach adult behavior was to treat children as adults. Proper education, in contrast, set out a menu of correct notions to be mastered by young people. This meant that education might sometimes be unpleasant, as young people needed to master basic skills before they could move on to creative writing and thinking.[240] The goal of teachers, Rafferty explained, must not be to encourage young people to think for themselves. Young people will do that naturally. Formal education existed first to pass along the accumulated learning of civilization to young people.[241]

None of this, Rafferty emphasized, meant that schools should produce generations of mindless automatons. Indeed, it was progressive schools that hypocritically trained young people to thoughtless obedience. By sapping classrooms of any real content, by asking children to make meaningless decisions about meaningless hypothetical situations, progressive education cheated young people of any real education. Instead, by transmitting to young people the wisdom of preceding generations, traditional education could promise to produce generations of thoughtful, freedom-loving citizens with enough moral backbone to oppose immorality in all its guises.

Race to the Bottom

In many ways, the protesters in Kanawha County embodied—explicitly and intentionally, in the case of Alice Moore—Rafferty's ideas about education and culture. They protested against outside control of their children's education. They fought for greater traditionalism in education, greater "common sense." And all sides agreed that the stakes remained agonizingly high. Keen awareness of these stakes made the atmosphere tense when the school board hosted its next public meeting. On November 7, 1974, the board met to review the recommendations of the citizens' review committee. No one sitting in that packed meeting room could have forgotten that just one week earlier, a huge dynamite blast had rocked the building.[242] The citizens' committee had compounded the tension by offering two reports. The majority report found the textbooks unobjectionable. But, as we've seen, a minority committee that had splintered from the larger group presented a 500-page-long denunciation, listing page after page of specific examples of offensive language and ideas.[243] At that November 7th meeting, the board voted four to one—only Moore dissenting—to accept the majority report. Most of the books would return to Kanawha County's schools. Books from two series, a DC Heath *Communicating* series and a Houghton Mifflin *Interaction* series, would only be available in the library. Those most controversial books would only be available to students with a signed permission slip from parents.[244]

This decision did not end the outcry. Large majorities of parents in some schools refused to sign permission slips.[245] Elsewhere, the boycott continued. At DuPont High School, for example, in mid-November, police broke up a picket line of roughly sixty protesters. The protesters had hoped to block the entrance of the school. Even without their blockade, fewer than half of the school's students attended.[246]

In another attempt to tamp down public anger, the school board agreed to Alice Moore's guidelines for future textbook selection. Drawing on guidance from the Gablers, Moore dictated an ideological shopping list for all future textbooks.[247] No textbooks, the board conceded, could "intrude into the privacy of the students' homes by asking personal questions." Textbooks must emphasize such notions as the importance of the traditional family, loyalty to the United States, and the responsibilities of citizenship. Any adopted book must eliminate "offensive language." Each new book must encourage "traditional rules of grammar."[248] Nothing in adopted texts, Moore insisted, could promote racial animosity. Nor could they defame the traditional heroes of American history. Too often, Moore insisted, texts had focused on the "sexual exploits" of the Founding Fathers instead of celebrating their achievements.[249]

Nor was that the end of changes demanded by Moore. At a board meeting in December, Moore suggested a fact-finding trip to Charlotte, North Carolina. The school district there had established a traditional school, one that avoided any hint of progressivism. Moore also forced through an agreement that the board would approve a new private Christian school. In spite of the board's conciliatory mood, unnamed activists launched a physical attack on Superintendent Underwood, his assistant Robert Kittle, and board members Kinsolving, Stump, and Stansbury.[250] As Superintendent Underwood later explained, "some man" jumped out of the audience and attacked Stump. Stump had become the target of much protester ire in weeks before this attack. He had come to the board as a protester candidate, but had since moderated his anti-textbook position. Underwood told a reporter he went to Stump's aid, when "four or five" other audience members joined in the "scuffle." Underwood insisted he could not identify the assailants. There were no serious injuries and no charges were filed.[251] Nevertheless, the incident demonstrated the continuing anger and tension in the school district.

Though this altercation marked the end of the intense violence of the protest, at the start of 1975, the protest seemed to be rolling ahead at full steam. In January, for instance, the Ku Klux Klan promised a huge new rally to re-energize the protest movement. West Virginia Klan leader Ed Miller promised a crowd of thousands of hooded and robed Klansmen to join the fight against the textbooks.[252] On January 18th, however, the promised Klan rally fizzled.[253] For the next months, the visible Klan presence in Kanawha County petered out to tiny groups of Klansmen protesting textbook selections.[254] The group had been riven with internal rivalries and burdened with its recent history of racial extremism.[255]

damn been in it for a long time

Though the image of the hooded Klansman has always provoked intense controversy, the nature of the organization had changed radically since the days of the Scopes trial. In the 1920s, as we saw in Chapter 2, the Klan commanded the loyalty of millions of American men and women. By the mid-1970s, those numbers had withered to only around 1,500 members.[256] And the FBI claimed that one in every six of those remaining Klansmen worked as an informer.[257]

One meaning of the Klan for all observers, however, was its association with racial hatred. For many racial liberals, the support of Klan leaders for the textbook protest signaled the essential racism at the heart of the entire textbook protest. Leading textbook supporter Jim Lewis, for instance, told a television reporter that protesters repeatedly launched into racist and bigoted language. Protesters, according to the Reverend Lewis, repeated "anti-Semitic" slurs. Much of their distaste for the new books, Lewis felt, stemmed from protesters' hostility toward "black people."[258]

intersection of race + religion

Similarly, local NAACP member Ron English later remembered that the African American community blamed the entire protest on white racism. The African American community, English recalled, heard protesters denounce the "nigger books."[259] This did not mean that all African Americans embraced the content of the new textbooks. English noted that many African Americans in Kanawha County were "very conservative." Many of them, English explained, agreed that the textbooks included offensive "anti-Christian . . . unpatriotic" material. Such ideas, many conservative African Americans believed, ought not to be taught in Kanawha County's schools.[260] Nevertheless, from the very beginning of the controversy in April 1974, the Reverend English battled with Alice Moore over Moore's definition of the books. At the tumultuous board meeting in June 1974, English defended the inclusion of such African American authors as Eldridge Cleaver and George Jackson. Such voices, English insisted, represented an important tradition of Americanism, a true patriotism that challenged injustice in the system. Cleaver and Jackson, English argued, articulated a vital part of the American experience that stretched from Tom Paine through Martin Luther King Jr.[261] In December 1974, English told the NEA investigating committee that the root of the protest lay in the "integration of instructional materials and their content."[262] A few months later, English had become much bitterer about the racist, patronizing attitudes of protest leaders. In March 1975, English complained that such "white people" had showed decided "nerve . . . to suggest what is best for our children."[263]

Looking back from the perspective of the twenty-first century, the families of some protest leaders agreed that the protest had been fueled in large part by anti-black racism. Interviewed in 2010, Steve Horan, a member of Marvin Horan's family, remembered one Sunday in 1974 when a rumor spread among the protesters that "the blacks" planned a march into Kanawha County. The men all got their guns, the younger Horan recalled. Women and children gathered in churches. The situation was a racial tinderbox that never quite got the spark it needed to explode into a racial bloodbath, as Horan recalled. In spite of that lucky outcome, the motives of many protesters remained violently racist.[264]

Other analysts have agreed that festering anti-black racism lay at the root of the textbook protest. As one office worker in the Board of Education offices later told James Moffett,

> We all leafed through [the proposed textbook] and couldn't figure out why they were having such a fit over "Jack and the Bean Stalk."

. . . Anyway, when this board member came in, we asked him. . . . He took the book, and he put it down on the table. "It's not what's in the book—it's the *cover.*" . . . It was a collage of several different figures, on the cover, and in the foreground there are two children. . . . The little boy is black, and the little girl is white.[265]

It seems likely that many protesters, like many white Americans at the time and since, were motivated by such simple knee-jerk racism. But if we rest satisfied with that simplistic explanation as the root cause of the entire protest, we will misunderstand the complexity of the protest, including even the complexity of racial thinking among book protesters. Racial attitudes among white conservatives in the Kanawha County dispute had changed enormously since the days of the Scopes trial. As we have seen, in those days an implicit white supremacist ideology was often shared by both white progressives and white conservatives. By 1950, as we saw in the previous chapter, these racial attitudes had experienced a wholesale revolution. White conservatives in Pasadena worked hard to prove that their school reform plans were not based on any sort of anti-black racism.

Decades later, conservative school reformers in Kanawha County similarly insisted that their movement was not fueled by racism. Some of the protesters' claims seem legitimate. For example, every protest organization refused the request of the Ku Klux Klan for information.[266] Protesters were just as aware of the Klan's racist image as were textbook supporters. Protest leaders' refusal to associate with the Klan indicates an authentic desire to dissociate from such racist organizations. Despite offers of assistance from the Klan, all protest organizations refused to cooperate.[267]

Other claims by protesters stretch credulity. For instance, at a hearing in October 1974, protester Thomas Roberts denied using racist language. Roberts had been accused of insulting African American art teacher Gordon Roe at Washington Junior High. According to Roe, Roberts had interfered with students attempting to enter the school. When Roe looked out his classroom window, Roe testified, Roberts had shouted over a public address system, "Keep on looking out the window you black bastard." At the hearing in October, Roberts apologized. But Roberts insisted he had not used such racially loaded language. Instead, Roberts claimed, he had called to Roe, "I wish I had black men and white women to teach me when I was in school. This issue isn't black or white. Why don't you come out and talk with me?"[268] To be fair, without a corroborating witness, neither the court nor the historian knows which version to believe. However, given Roberts's willingness to apologize and the angry tone of most school picket lines, his remembered statement sounds more like what he may have wished he said, rather than what he actually said at the time.

In most other cases, protesters' attitudes on race and racism seem even more complex. Among religious protest leaders, many pointed to their racially integrated worship services as proof that they were not motivated by racism. Karl Priest, for instance, a teacher during the protest, remembered coaching a nearly all-black church basketball team at the time. His church supported the protest, yet represented a racially mixed conservative Protestant community.[269] Similarly, Avis Hill remembered his congregation including an even mix of white and African American members.[270] During the protests themselves, Ezra Graley described one of his nights in jail. During the long hours, Graley explained to a reporter upon his release, he prayed with four young inmates, including one African American. Graley's language likely offended many audience members—he referred to saving a "colored boy"—but from Graley's perspective, his willingness to pray with people of all races demonstrated his deep devotion to an anti-racist worldview.[271]

Alice Moore articulated a similarly complex racial understanding. Part of her inspiration for instigating the protests, Moore explained later, came from a conference she had attended in the early 1970s. At the conference, Arizona's African American state school board president, Stephen Jenkins, warned of an anti-black ideology masquerading as "multiculturalism." When textbooks included only African American voices from crumbling slums, or when only angry, violent black literature was included, Jenkins insisted, such "multiculturalism" actually meant anti-black racism.[272] When in June 1974 Moore raised her objections to the textbooks, she sounded honestly flummoxed that African American leader Ron English would want to include the voices of violent African Americans such as Eldridge Cleaver and George Jackson.[273]

Similarly, Elmer Fike explained that protesters should be considered the true anti-racists. The books themselves, by including violent African American voices, only "pit black against white." Instead of leading to multicultural harmony, Fike explained, such tactics "stirr[ed] up racial animosity." Fike himself attempted at a local NAACP meeting to invoke the support of conservative African American George Schuyler. The audience, Fike related, shouted him down. Such closed-mindedness on the part of textbook publishers and supporters, Fike believed, represented the true racism of the protest. "The protesters," Fike wrote, "do not object to authors because they are black, but they do believe convicted criminals and revolutionaries like Eldridge Cleaver should not be recognized."[274]

National conservative leaders at the time echoed this sentiment. From California, Max Rafferty concurred that the real racism came from progressives. He insisted that he hated "racial prejudice." But he felt programs that forced a racial balance in schools through busing missed the real point. The solution, Rafferty believed, lay in creating authentically diverse neighborhoods, not merely in coercing students to shuffle among schools.[275] Rafferty seems to have made some genuinely anti-racist moves during his years as state superintendent of public instruction in California. In one private letter, for instance, Rafferty pushed for textbooks that would include more text and images about African American life.[276] Rafferty opposed busing, yet he used his influence to make California's textbooks more racially representative.

As in Pasadena, the racial meanings of the Kanawha County protest defy easy categorization. For many white conservatives, a willingness to work with conservative African Americans served as proof against charges of racism. For Reverend Graley, or Karl Priest, or Reverend Hill, their dedication to praying with African Americans as equal before God signaled their innocence. For more secular protest leaders such as Moore and Fike, their embrace of conservative African Americans did the same. However, for many African Americans, even religious leaders such as Ron English, protesters' anger at the inclusion of African American authors sent a very different signal.

Yet as national conservative leaders such as Max Rafferty argued, a new conservative racial ideology was emerging by the mid-1970s. It is too simple to call this a unified or coherent way of thinking about race among conservatives. In Kanawha County, as in Dayton, Tennessee, Philadelphia, Pennsylvania, or Pasadena, California, ideology in action was a messy affair. As Steve Horan remembered, many white protesters believed in rumors of African American invasions. And in September 1975, unidentified, unreconstructed white racists burned a cross on the lawn of the board of education building.[277] Though protest leaders refused to work with the Klan, the Klan still came to work with the protesters.

Klan support demonstrated something about the protest that made many protesters squirm. The Klan came to fight, as did many protesters, to "return patriotism and Christianity to our schools." What the Klan wanted in 1975, leaders claimed, was to stop "the breakdown of morals among our children."[278] Though protest leaders may have disowned the Klan, they did share the Klan's embrace of traditional values. In the United States, those cultural traditions—even if a new generation of conservative activists did not approve—had long included white supremacy. Those leaders in Kanawha County and nation-wide who insisted on a post-racist conservatism had a difficult task. They hoped to assert a broader social conservatism, one that could be embraced by all conservatives regardless of race, gender, or creed. In Kanawha County, at least, conservative leaders failed. African Ameri-cans, though many shared a dislike for the anti-religious and anti-patri-otic tone of the textbooks, turned away from a protest movement still too closely linked with traditional white racism along with traditional social values.

Back to Basics

As winter turned to spring in 1975, the school protest ground into a bitter and indecisive stalemate. In April, protest leader Marvin Horan received his three-year sentence for encouraging the bombing of Wet Branch Elementary. The men convicted of the actual bombing itself received sentences ranging from three years to eighteen months.[279] This harsh sentence for a prominent protest leader struck many protesters as intensely unfair. After all, Horan had been convicted only of inspiring the violence, not of engaging in it himself. To many conservatives, it seemed a blatant attempt to punish all those who dared protest against the direction of public education.[280]

At the same time, one of the school board's attempts to allay conservative anger fizzled. The board had agreed to establish a new school, one that would include a "rigorous phonetic approach" to read-ing, training in formal grammar, "high standards of courtesy," and an intense program in patriotism. Teachers and administrators would enforce these goals with a dose of corporal punishment.[281]

The board developed this approach for an alternative traditionalist school after studying other such public schools nationwide, including two "Fundamental" schools in Pasadena, California.[282] Though such schools seemed to be succeeding elsewhere, Kanawha County's attempt failed. By June 1975, only 100 families had signed up, not enough to make the new traditionalist school a reality.[283]

Alice Moore herself had more success. In 1976, she again ran suc-cessfully for the school board. As in her 1970 campaign, Moore promoted herself as a thoroughly conservative candidate. Beyond the confines of educational politics, she won the endorsement of anti-abortion groups

*must conn to moral/relig.
of the home*

for her consistent anti-abortion rhetoric.[284] In educational terms, Moore presented herself as an experienced, dedicated conservative, fighting for traditional schools and back-to-basics curriculum. In one full-page newspaper advertisement, Moore articulated her conservative platform. First, she insisted that public schools must remain under the control of local taxpayers. Outsiders such as "Washington Bureaucrats . . . School Administrators . . . [and] National Education Organizations" must not be allowed to impose curricula. Second, she called for a drastic revision of the goals of schooling. Moore argued that schools must focus on "the best academic education possible with emphasis on basic skills." Schools must not challenge traditional beliefs of home, church, and family. Schools should "provide a disciplined and morally up-lifting educational climate" for students. Those "trouble-makers" who did not behave well must not be "coddl[ed.]" To accomplish these goals, Moore claimed, schools must be run as "efficiently as private enterprise."[285]

Throughout her 1976 campaign, Moore emphasized that "all change is not progress." Education, Moore believed, must be returned "to the purpose it once served, teaching basic skills to young people, passing on the traditional heritage of the nation." This was just as true of phonics and traditional math instruction as it was of patriotism and religion.[286] In 1976 as in the rest of the school protest, Moore articulated an ambitious, complex conservative educational ideology. In the 1976 election, her reputation for dedication to the cause won her a handy re-election. By 1976, Moore's brand of educational conservatism had become dominant. As her nearest 1976 rival conceded, "What Mrs. Moore says she wants—discipline and basic education—is what we all want."[287]

Moore's "back to the basics" rhetoric again demonstrated her harmony with national trends. By 1976, "back to basics" language had become hugely influential nationwide.[288] One 1978 survey found that ninety-six percent of all school board respondents had heard the issue discussed in their communities, and half reported that their districts had enacted some sort of back-to-basics reform.[289] In spite of such intense interest, in the mid-1970s the meaning of the "basics" remained unclear. For some back-to-the-basics advocates, the movement meant a rallying cry for improved, streamlined academic instruction. As one activist group from British Columbia argued, the "basics" meant a new emphasis on teacher quality, on fundamental academic skills, and on rigorous and extensive evaluation of student progress.[290] This sort of "back to basics" activism had a long history. Historian Arthur Bestor

Alice Moore runs for re-election on a conservative platform. (Courtesy West Virginia State Archives)

had founded the Council for Basic Education in the 1950s as an attempt to maintain academic rigor, academic skills, and high standards in American schools.[291] This kind of "basics" activism believed American schools ought to include only academic instruction, not a wider array of life skills. For many of these advocates of basic education, the main danger was an overzealous progressivism that left students without any grasp of basic concepts. As Lewis Spitz, dean of Stanford's School of Humanities and Science put it in 1975, many college professors "have begun to question the appropriateness of bestowing a bachelor of arts degree on people who are not sure whether the Greeks came before the

Romans. . . . The climate is right for the move toward a more structured liberal education."[292]

Other "basics" activists, like Alice Moore, included a far broader array of cultural traditionalism in their meanings of back-to-basics. By the 1970s, the "Fundamental Schools" of Pasadena combined an intense focus on phonics instruction with broader cultural policies such as dress codes, harsh discipline, and an emphasis on traditional character education.[293] As journalist Ben Brodinsky noted in 1977, back-to-basics education might include only a closer focus on "drill in the three Rs." In other cases, Brodinsky wrote, the basics included "patriotism and Puritan morality."[294]

For conservative school reformers like Alice Moore, the fight against progressive "frills" included both academic and cultural goals. For instance, during her 1976 campaign, Moore explained her opposition to student counseling in schools. Such add-ons threatened to water down the academic mission of proper education, Moore believed. But counseling also threatened to introduce hostile secular values to vulnerable children, Moore argued. "Parent-child conflicts often develop," Moore told the League of Women Voters, "when home values and counselor values clash."[295]

A Wrench in the Works

Moore's deeply conservative vision of back-to-basics education matched her broader cultural conservatism. A dedicated activist, Moore was no more simply a concerned, non-partisan mother than Rosa Parks was just another tired bus-rider. In the early 1970s, Moore had been looking for opportunities to promote a broad culturally conservative agenda. In the textbook protest, she seized her main chance. In many ways, "Sweet Alice" Moore and the controversy she instigated marked the culmination of generations of conservative educational activism. Moore combined anti-progressivism, anti-evolutionism, and anti-sex education with a firm commitment to traditionalist pedagogy, religion, patriotism, and morality. She fought for free markets and parental choice. She argued against abortion rights and irreligion. She insisted on a vision of schooling as primarily a place where teachers transmitted information to children. In all of these things, Moore's campaigns would likely have found sympathizers among conservative activists from other generations.

Indeed, in many ways the conservative protest movement in Kanawha County embodied the continuing tradition of educational conservatism throughout the twentieth century. Several commentators, both sympathizers and skeptics of the protest movement, have argued that the 1974 textbook protest marked the birth of a "New Right."[296] These claims have some justification, but they tend to ignore the many connections between the West Virginia controversy and those of earlier decades. For instance, the anti-racist rhetoric employed by many conservative leaders in Kanawha County had been part of the conservative tradition since the time of the Pasadena controversy. As they did in this school fight, conservative leaders from the late 1940s into the twenty-first century insisted that their movement had no truck with old-fashioned racism.

But in some ways, what emerged in the Kanawha County fight was profoundly new. Most telling, the Kanawha County experience midwived the birth of new organizations such as the Heritage Foundation, groups that remain influential institutional homes for conservative activists and intellectuals. The Heritage Foundation today occupies an impressive building in the center of Washington DC, just blocks from the Capitol. At the start of the twenty-first century, the Heritage Foundation expended an annual budget of over thirty million dollars and employed a staff of nearly 200.[297] At the time of the Kanawha County textbook controversy, however, it was a fledgling organization tucked away into a small second-story back office above a grocery store in a rough part of Washington DC. It had been started in 1973 by two conservative activists, Paul Weyrich and Edwin Feulner, funded by a quarter-million-dollar start-up grant from conservative beer mogul Joseph Coors.[298]

As leading Heritage Foundation writer Connie Marshner later remembered, the Kanawha County episode was one of the first causes to catch the attention of their new organization.[299] James McKenna of the Heritage Foundation traveled to Charleston, where he provided free legal counsel for the protesters. He also spoke widely during the school boycotts, encouraging protesters to see their cause as part of a vital national trend.[300]

The Heritage Foundation became in the 1980s what one analyst has called "America's most visible think tank."[301] Unlike some older think tanks, Heritage proudly and explicitly produced research and analysis with a conservative ideological slant. Much of Heritage's conservative educational ideology was profoundly influenced by the events in Kanawha County.[302] Though many of the prominent educational ideologues affiliated with the Heritage Foundation only articulated their ideas in the later 1970s and early 1980s, Kanawha County became a place to test and refine their conservative ideas about schooling and culture.

More than just as a birthplace of a new sort of conservative intellectual institution, the Kanawha County controversy directly influenced the mainstream of educational thinking and policy nationwide. For instance, in December 1974, the US education commissioner declared his support for the conservative goals of the textbook protest. As commissioner under President Ford and soon to become the secretary of education under Ronald Reagan,[303] Terrel H. Bell warned textbook publishers not to include any readings or material that might "insult the values of most parents." In a public statement, Bell agreed with the conservatives in West Virginia that textbooks must not inflict "blood and guts and street language" on young readers. Bell echoed the sentiments of Kanawha County's protest when he condemned the use of "violence and obscenity and moral judgments that run counter to tradition" in schoolbooks. Instead, Bell suggested, publishers ought to return to the values of such traditional schoolbooks as the Bible, *McGuffey's Readers*, and *The Wizard of Oz*.[304]

If the Kanawha County textbook controversy can be said to have pushed this kind of thinking to national notice, if the conservative thinking and strategy in West Virginia marked the maturation of this durable sort of late-twentieth-century conservatism, can they also be said to have had a lasting impact on local schools? In some ways, it appeared the entire bloody struggle had been entirely without effect in Kanawha County itself. At the end of the 1974–75 school year, the books were back in schools, protest leader Marvin Horan languished in jail, and an alternative traditional school flopped. Yet looking beyond the surface, the impact of the protest becomes clear. Teachers and administrators felt extremely cautious about what went on in their classrooms. With good reason. Conservative activists remained on high alert, sending a warning that local schools must avoid ideas and readings that threatened traditional notions. Perhaps most influential in the long term, the controversy sparked a rush to open a new independent network of Christian schools. Parents in Kanawha County would no longer feel trapped if they disagreed with the content and conduct of their local public schools.

The sudden burst in new Christian schools matched similar developments nationwide.[305] One school founder remembered that during the hottest days of the protest, "Christian day schools came into existence like wildfire."[306] Other leaders of new schools insisted the protest itself had only sped up a process they had already begun. The Reverend

Paul Warren, for example, told a reporter that his reasons for opening his new school stretched back before the controversy. However, Warren predicted that the publicity about the wretched nature of public education would boost his enrollment from its current 110 students to somewhere between 1,000 and 2,000.[307] Similarly, the Reverend David Kilburn of Fair Haven Baptist Church insisted that his church had planned its new school since 1970. Kilburn guessed the protest would boost his enrollment by three to five percent.[308]

Other Christian school founders admitted the role of the protest in their deliberations. The Reverend Jack Long of Christ Temple Church told one reporter he had made no plans to start a school, but with the advent of the 1974 protest, Long acceded to his congregation's demand for a safe educational harbor. Long's new school had already enrolled 150 students as of November 1974.[309] Similarly, three churches in Campbells Creek united to start the Kanawha County Christian School. As one leader explained, "We plan to continue classes until the dirty textbooks are out of the public schools." As of mid-November 1974, the school leaders claimed an enrollment of roughly 500 students.[310]

One reporter estimated that a dozen such schools opened in Kanawha County by early 1975. The deadlocked ending to the textbook battle left many students from protesters' families firmly lodged in their new Christian schools.[311] As it did elsewhere, the popularity of this kind of independent Christian institution led some local politicians to promote subsidies. In West Virginia, State Supreme Court justice Richard Neely promoted an amendment to the US Constitution to allow more public funding of private religious schools. Public schools, Neely argued in 1976, too often resemble "zoo[s]." Not only do such schools fail to control and educate children, Neely believed, but they promoted a destructive "secular humanism." It remained a basic American right, Neely insisted, for every child to attend a school that incorporated the values of the home.[312]

Though conservatives such as Neely insisted on the influence of anti-religious ideology in public schools, many public school teachers and administrators seemed more confused than ideologically committed in the wake of the controversy. Near the start of the protest in 1974, one woman who had considered taking a teaching job told a friend she had refused it. The situation, she explained, was "all chaos. . . . Nobody knows what to do."[313] School principal Tom Bunting of Cedar Grove Community School, soon to resign in disgust, told of a teacher who came to him in desperation. The teacher was slated to teach a unit in biology class about the asexual reproduction of mollusks. She asked the principal, "Can we defend teaching this in class?" Bunting felt exasperated by the endless confusion and self-censorship.[314]

One student explained later that he only remembered reading *Beowulf*. Teachers considered anything more recent than that—including such staples of high school literature classes as *The Grapes of Wrath*, *1984*, and *Brave New World*—far too controversial.[315] This intense self-censorship on the part of teachers and principals continued for years. One teacher remembered that even through the 1980s, teachers and administrators remained "very intimidated."[316]

And well they might. Though the bombings, shootings, and violent picket lines disappeared by the end of the 1974–75 school year, local conservative protesters remained active. Just before the start of the 1975–76 school year, for instance, twenty women occupied an auditorium in the board of education building. They had confronted John Santrock, the new superintendent, with a list of demands. The protesters wanted public funding to send their children to private schools. They wanted Santrock and the school board to resign immediately, with the exception of Alice Moore. And they refused to leave until their demands were met. In the end, after an overnight stay in the board of education building, the protesters were bodily removed by police.[317]

This sort of direct parental action continued, even if its goals changed. In March 1976, a group of parents again blocked school buses. In this case, the issue was dangerous road conditions. Parents demanded repairs to protect the safety of their bus-riding children.[318] The culture of protest, however, had been firmly established. Parents, teachers, and school administrators all knew that any hint of controversy would be met by loud and angry protest.

For protesters, the 1974 controversy often sparked a lifetime of activism, locally or nationwide. Protester Phyllis Harmon told interviewers decades later that the textbook protest had been the most important event of her life. The entire process had showed her that Satan "is a roaring lion; and he's out to steal, kill, and destroy our children."[319] Protest leaders reported similar impact from the protest. Teacher Karl Priest began a lifetime of activism against evolution and public education.[320] Alice Moore continued to fight against a broad array of progressive ideas. From her seat on the school board in 1977, Moore fought against a new series of science textbooks. The books, Moore believed, ought to teach both evolution and creationism, instead of insisting children learn an anti-religious evolutionism.[321] Moore's activism continued even after she moved away from Kanawha County. In 1982, Moore led a protest near Columbus, Ohio. She told a meeting of the Hamilton Township school board that a new health curriculum from Planned Parenthood would force third-graders to learn about contraception. The curriculum, Moore argued, would promote homosexuality and sexual promiscuity among young children.[322]

For Kanawha County, the 1974 battle marked the beginning of a new educational era. Parents insisted public schools teach values that did not conflict with their conservative beliefs. They demanded schools that stuck to traditional academic subjects, the "three Rs." And they insisted on the right to attend private schools at public expense. Anger at both the content of the new English language arts textbooks, as well as the perceived cavalier methods by which the school board adopted the books, led protesters to assert their power. Teachers, school administrators, and school board members had to recognize the protesters' demands.

It is too much to say that the events in West Virginia directly caused the rest of the nation to embrace such traditional ideas about the purpose and content of public education. But as in Dayton, Philadelphia, and Pasadena, what happened in Kanawha County symbolized a national struggle. Though the fight in Kanawha County attracted more than its share of notoriety, similar disagreements roiled communities nationwide.[323] Though the specifics of each school battle varied significantly, the trend of such struggles resembled in broad outline the fight in West Virginia. In each case, the language and strategy of local activists, especially as they cooperated with national conservative leaders and organizations, promoted a profoundly conservative vision of what American schools should be.

Conclusion

Conservatism and American Education

When I began my teaching career back in the 1990s, I was shocked to discover the influence of conservative ideas and activism on my school and on my classroom. I never expected parents to object to my goal of teaching their children to be skeptical thinkers and critical readers. I never expected parents to object to students questioning their faiths and examining their values.

Looking back, I'm surprised by my own naïveté about the profound influence of conservative ideas and traditions on schools. Why hadn't I expected conservative students? Conservative teachers? Why had I spent my time reading exclusively progressive visions of teaching and education? After all, the real world of teaching—at least in my experience—had a lot more to do with conservative notions of morals and authority than it did with progressive visions of empowerment and exploration. Conservative ideas and activists exerted a far more profound influence on my classroom than I had expected.

When I began my graduate research in American history a few years later, I looked for a satisfying explanation of this tradition of educational conservatism. I could not find it. I did find a great deal about American conservatives. American conservatives, I discovered, cared a lot about Jesus, about backyard barbecues, about foreign policy, and about family structures. But I couldn't find historical explorations of the traditions that tied together Jesus and phonics. I couldn't find books that examined conservative assumptions that sulky, ill-mannered students somehow lead to—or result from—combative communist-led labor unions.

source of culture

America's Other School Reformers

This book captures that complicated tradition. It argues that educational conservatism is a central part of both education and conservatism. Without understanding this tradition adequately, we will struggle to understand either one. This book insists that educational conservatism is fueled by something more than "unexamined institutional habits and widespread cultural beliefs."[1] Educational conservatism has been the agglomeration of school reform efforts by untold numbers of activists and individuals. As these pages have argued, those "other school reformers" have differed markedly from one another in their beliefs and policy prescriptions. But a vital ideological glue has held them together in all their different permutations. Educational conservatives have agreed that schools are the vital source of healthy culture. With conservative school policies in place, the nation can prosper. Without them, the nation is doomed.

has been many people

The ideas that are taught in America's schools have always been of central interest to conservative activists. If subversive or insidious ideas become part of the curriculum, young people will mature in unhealthy and perverted ways. They will grow into morally stunted adults, leading the nation into ruin. But when healthy truths form the basis of schooling, that process can be avoided or even reversed. Schools, conservatives have insisted for generations, must teach basic religious truths, or at least not denigrate religion. They must instill thoughtful patriotism in the young, or at least not deride students' love of country. They must help children to appreciate the capitalist traditions of America, or at least not teach that free markets are evil. Schools, conservatives have argued, must support parents' desires to pass along inherited values, or at least not step arrogantly between parent and child to impose a suspect system of sneering modern values.

The ways that schools and teachers do these things has been equally important to conservatives. If teachers assume that truth is something students must discover on their own, gullible and romantic young people will tend to choose rashly. Instead, teachers and schools must take responsibility to pass along the inherited wisdom of millennia of civilization. Schools must transmit truth, not merely act as facilitators for the bumbling inquiries of immature minds.

As the preceding chapters have explored, these themes have connected conservative educational activists across the generations. Educational conservatives in the 1920s wanted schools to remain bastions of traditional culture and religiosity. By the late 1930s, conservative school reformers battled to preserve schools that taught each new generation to love, cherish, and honor those who had come before. In the Cold War 1950s, conservatives fretted that Pasadena progressivism could be just the entering wedge of a sneaky and aggressive communist conspiracy. In West Virginia in the 1970s, activists from this conservative tradition drew a line in the sand against new efforts to transform the morals of a new generation of schoolchildren. In each case, conservatives agreed on a central vision of proper schooling. School, conservatives argued, must raise up each new generation in the best traditions of those who went before.

The State We're In

Things have changed since the dust settled in Kanawha County, West Virginia. In some ways, American conservatism has come in from the cold, with the election of a staunchly conservative president in 1980 and the sustained clout of self-consciously conservative institutions such as the Heritage Foundation. For the embattled activists of the Kanawha County fight in the 1970s, such things seemed almost too fantastic to hope for. The landscape of educational conservatism looks different in the twenty-first century than it did in 1975 and certainly different from the ways it appeared in the 1950s, 1930s, or 1920s. Yet the roots of today's conservatism remain firmly bound in the conservative tradition developed throughout those earlier decades.

These days, influential educational policies promote conservative or at least conservative-friendly ideas such as competition between schools and competition between students. The villains these days are often left-leaning teachers' unions or ivory-tower education schools. As education scholar Michael Apple has argued, schooling and school talk in the twenty-first century has been taken over by conservative themes of "markets, standards, God, and inequality."[2]

This conservative influence in contemporary American education reaches beyond the classroom issues of testing and privatization. The claims of cultural traditionalism are still strong in American schools. For instance, a recent survey of Texas public schools found that many of them teach a profoundly conservative interpretation of the Bible.[3] Nor is this only a Texas issue. Communities around the nation often assume that schools must impart a patriotic spirit in students. In 2012, for example, a public school principal in Brooklyn ignited a bitter controversy when she banned a popular patriotic song, "God Bless the USA," from a kindergarten celebration.[4] These local examples could be multiplied nearly endlessly. Beyond local controversies, national politicians with their finely tuned political antennae have consistently hoped to score points by proposing more religion and more patriotism in the nation's public schools.[5]

This does not mean that schooling has somehow remained strictly bound by conservative activism and pedagogical tradition. Important changes have been made in the structure and content of American education as a whole. To cite the most obvious examples, public schools are now legally desegregated by race; Protestant religiosity no longer dominates public schooling. On a day-to-day classroom level, traditional rows of bolted-down desks have been replaced by group tables and reading carpets, at least in many elementary schools. These are significant and lasting changes, progressive reforms that conservatives often tried unsuccessfully to block or eliminate. In some cases, these progressive reforms have become so thoroughly incorporated into the "grammar of schooling" that later conservative activists can defend them as part of America's great educational tradition.[6]

Yet in the face of these important progressive changes, generations of activists—the conservatives we've met in these pages—have successfully defended the notion of schooling as an institution primarily dedicated to the transmission of both knowledge and traditional values from one generation to the next. Though the content of public schooling has lost much of its explicit Protestant theology, it has retained a sense of traditional moral values. Patriotism remains an assumed part of most public education, as does reinforcement of traditional gender roles and family structures. Schools and textbooks rarely question the free-market premises of the American economy. Students and schools continue to compete with one another for rewards and funding. What's more, the structure of schooling has remained largely authoritarian and bureaucratic. Students mostly remain in classes with activities and lessons led directly by teachers. Bells ring at assigned times, and students move to assigned spaces to engage in assigned activities. The continuing strength of these educational traditions is not due only to some sort of vague cultural inertia. It cannot be dismissed as a sort of mysterious cultural lag, a lamentable gap between gleaming progressive visions and broken-down conservative realities. Rather, we must understand today's vibrant conservatism and traditionalism in American schools as the product in large part of generations of activism by conservative activists, the "other school reformers" described in these pages.

It may seem problematic to give credit or blame for today's school policies to conservative school reformers. After all, in the past few decades, conservative educational themes have been endorsed in different ways and with different emphases by politicians from across the political spectrum. As education scholars Chester Finn and Theodor Rebarber noted at the tail end of the twentieth century, "it has been hard to discern many systematic philosophical differences between Democrats and Republicans with respect to schooling."[7] In the twenty-first century, too, Democratic leaders such as President Obama and Secretary of Education Arne Duncan have been accused of simply continuing the education policies of conservative Republican George W. Bush.[8] Republican governors such as Scott Walker of Wisconsin[9] and Chris Christie of New Jersey[10] have built their careers on aggressive campaigns against teachers' unions. Even Democratic governors such as Andrew Cuomo of New York have proven friendly to privatization schemes that promote student testing, school privatization, and limitations on the power of teachers' unions.[11]

Beyond the ranks of elected politicians, self-styled reformers such as former chancellor of Washington DC schools Michelle Rhee have advocated similar policies. In order to clean up American education, Rhee has argued, schools must be liberated from the dead hand of teachers' unions. Parents and students must be given more choice beyond conventional public schools. Students must be tested and retested to be sure no child has been left behind and to clear out the deadwood of timeserving teachers.[12]

Proponents of these free-market competitive reforms might insist that the changes are somehow beyond ideology, that these changes will simply make schools better. Though leaders such as Michelle Rhee or Arne Duncan may not see their ideas as conservative, the fact remains that these policies have profoundly conservative implications. In politics, privatization reforms tend to weaken the power of both teachers' unions and conventional education schools. As we've seen, such institutions have felt the wrath of conservative activists for decades. Culturally, today's dominant reform rhetoric privileges a certain conservative vision of education. To improve schools, we hear, the market must be allowed to work its magic. As we've seen in these chapters, the vociferous pro-capitalist activism of groups such as the National Association of Manufacturers and the American Legion often dictated the contents of America's classrooms as far back as the 1920s. Into the twenty-first century, notions of parents-as-consumers and marketization of the public school system have become more powerful, not less. The leading reform measure of twenty-first-century schools has not been the public-service vision of progressives such as Harold Rugg. It has, instead, built on the market-loving conservatism of generations of the "other school reformers" stretching back nearly a century. Though Rugg himself optimistically predicted the impending triumph of progressivism, it has instead been the vision of conservative school reformers that has triumphed.[13]

This triumph can be seen in the glee with which self-identified conservatives embrace the current dominant language of education reform. Writing from the conservative American Enterprise Institute and Hoover Institution, for example, Frederick Hess and Michael Petrilli applauded Arne Duncan's and Michelle Rhee's "liberal" decisions to support President Bush's No Child Left Behind Act.[14] In essence, Hess and Petrilli crowed, that program "sketched a vision of reform informed by conservative intuitions and insights."[15]

Why were these conservative educational activists so happy? Their delight makes sense when we understand the long story of conservatism in American education. As we've seen again and again in these pages, since the 1920s conservative intellectuals and activists have considered themselves locked out of the elite circles of educational thinking. If it's true that self-identified liberals these days embrace conservative school reform ideas, then today's conservative activists have a good deal to celebrate.

Purifying the Well

We should only be surprised by such celebrations if we fail to understand the history of conservative educational activism. And we should only be surprised at the continuing strength of conservative ideas about schooling if we fail to recognize that those ideas have always had a decisive influence on American education. As we've seen throughout this book, the real world of schools and classrooms has been guided for generations by the energetic reform efforts of conservative activists. These "other school reformers" have never been a monolithic movement, never a single intellectual entity. Indeed, dominant "conservative" positions on key issues of race, religion, and the role of the federal government have often flip-flopped as the decades have passed. Yet we make a fundamental mistake if we ignore the unifying conservative impulse at the heart of disparate conservative activism across the generations.

The conservative activists we've gotten to know in these pages have insisted time and again that schooling remained the all-powerful key to culture. Schools, after all, were the public institution in which people formed their ideas about right and wrong, true and false. It was in schools, conservative activists believed, that the wellspring of moral society could be found. In most cases, conservatives did not make sharp distinctions between the sorts of conservative ideas they valued in American schools. After all, conservatives did not want children to be patriotic but not religious. They did not want children to be intelligent but morally monstrous. Rather, schools held the promise—for conservative activists—of combining all these vital social reforms in one institution.

Conservatives struggled repeatedly to express this unifying impulse, in contexts far removed from one another in time and space. They worked—sometimes awkwardly and sometimes with poetic grace—to articulate the ways schooling held the key to cultural renewal. In 1930, for instance, one American Legion member offered a passionate expression of the need to reform schools. Only such educational reform, he wrote, could ultimately defend young people from creeping communism. The communists themselves, this writer warned, made a sophisticated multi-level appeal to innocent young Americans. The solution was not only to fight communist influence in labor unions or street battles, but to launch a much broader campaign to "preach the doctrine of love of parents and love of home." Communists might tell Americans that labor must struggle with bosses. In contrast, right-thinking patriots must "inculcate the manly principles of energy, ambition and thrift in the hearts of our people." The only way to achieve this sweeping ambition, this writer argued, was to reform schools. In schools, the Legion writer warned, communists hoped to train students in communist tenets. But if schools taught more religious and patriotic notions, "the schools and pulpits of tomorrow will be filled with right-thinking men and women."[16] Clearly, for the American Legion in 1930, conservative education policy did not mean simply a laundry list of patriotic or religious curricular ideas. Instead, to heal American society, Americans needed to engage in a wholesale revolution in thinking and action. School reform was the way to achieve such a revolution. Young people must learn a totalized body of wisdom to counter the false appeal of the insidious communist.

As was often the case, in the 1980s the Gablers offered a compelling articulation of these ideas. "The basic issue is simple," the Gablers wrote:

Which principles will shape the minds of our children? Those which uphold family, morality, freedom, individuality, and free enterprise; or whose which advocate atheism, evolution, secularism, and a collectivism in which an elite governs and regulates religion, parenthood, education, property, and the lifestyle of all members of society?[17]

The Gablers assumed, as had preceding generations of conservative educational activists, that the ideas and attitudes with which children were educated would influence them profoundly. If those ideas reflected the proper traditions of patriotism, religion, and capitalism, then students could grow to be right-thinking adults. If, on the other hand, students learned leftist notions of big government, secularism, and socialism, both those students and America as a whole were doomed. Jesus and phonics, free markets and testing, patriotism and good manners—for conservative activists in the twentieth century, if school reform hoped to heal American society, all of these things must be united in proper education.

If we hope to make real sense of today's educational system, we must embrace a more thorough and coherent picture of what conservatives have wanted out of American education. We must acknowledge the significant influence of conservative activists on the structure and content of schooling. Too many teachers like the younger me stumble into schools poorly equipped to deal with the real world of teaching and learning. Similarly, unless and until we incorporate the tradition of educational conservatism into our historical understanding of conservatism as a whole, we will not achieve a complete grasp of what it meant to be conservative in America's twentieth century. Just as they worried about big government, or weakness in foreign affairs, or creeping secularism and socialism, American conservatives fretted about the course of American education. And their energetic activism changed the course of education in decisive ways, time after time. Yet too many scholars and activists see educational conservatism as only a curious but ill-fated exception. It has been much more. Indeed, the work of the "other school reformers"—the long tradition of defending tradition itself in American schools—has determined in many ways what goes on in America's schools. They might not garner the same recognition as names such as John Dewey, Harold Rugg, or Paolo Freire, but our other school reformers—folks such as Hiram Evans, Homer Chaillaux, Louise Padelford, and Alice Moore—have certainly had at least as much influence on the goings-on at schools across the decades, across the United States.

Notes

Acknowledgments

Index

Notes

Introduction

1. H. L. Mencken, "Mencken Finds Daytonians Full of Sickening Doubts about Value of Publicity," in *A Religious Orgy in Tennessee: A Reporter's Account of the Scopes Monkey Trial* (Hoboken, NJ: Melville House, 2006), 28–29 (originally in *Baltimore Evening Sun,* July 9, 1925).

2. David Hulburd, *This Happened in Pasadena* (New York: Macmillan, 1951), 59.

3. William Pencak, *For God and Country: The American Legion, 1919–1941* (Boston: Northeastern University Press, 1989), 240.

4. In 2010, Steven Horan remembered this racial tension in an interview with documentarian Trey Kay. See Trey Kay, Deborah George, and Stan Bumgardner, "The Great Textbook War," American RadioWorks. http://americanradioworks. publicradio.org/features/textbooks/index.html (accessed January 14, 2013); see also Catherine Ann Candor, "A History of the Kanawha County Textbook Controversy, April 1974–April 1975" (EdD diss., Virginia Polytechnic Institute, 1976), 156.

5. John Dewey, introduction to *The Uses of Resources in Education,* by Elsie Ripley Clapp (New York: Harper and Bros., 1952); reprinted in *Dewey on Education: Selections with an Introduction and Notes,* Martin S. Dworkin, ed. (New York: Teachers College Press, 1959), 129, 130, 131–132.

6. Michael Katz, *The Irony of Early School Reform: Educational Innovation in Mid-Nineteenth-Century Massachusetts* (Cambridge, MA: Harvard University Press, 1968), 3.

7. Arthur Zilversmit, *Changing Schools: Progressive Education Theory and Practice* (Chicago: University of Chicago Press, 1993), 169.

8. Michael W. Apple, *Educating the "Right" Way: Markets, Standards, God, and Inequality,* 2nd ed. (New York: Routledge, 2006), 4, 31, 53, 57.

1. What Does Jesus Have to Do with Phonics?

1. See, for example, Arthur Zilversmit, *Changing Schools: Progressive Education Theory and Practice* (Chicago: University of Chicago Press, 1993).

2. David Tyack and Larry Cuban, *Tinkering toward Utopia: A Century of Public School Reform* (Cambridge, MA: Harvard University Press, 1995), 88.

3. Daniel T. Rodgers, *Contested Truths: Keywords in American Politics since Independence* (New York: Basic Books, 1987), 11.

4. Kim Phillips-Fein, "Conservatism: A State of the Field," *Journal of American History* (December 2011): 723–743.

5. There have been significant exceptions. See, for example, Jonathan Zimmerman, *Whose America? Culture Wars in the Public Schools* (Cambridge, MA: Harvard University Press, 2002); Charles Israel, *Before Scopes: Evangelicalism, Education, and Evolution in Tennessee, 1870–1925* (Athens: University of Georgia Press, 2004); Milton Gaither, *Homeschool: An American History* (New York: Palgrave Macmillan, 2008); Andrew Hartman, *Education and the Cold War: The Battle for the American School* (New York: Palgrave Macmillan, 2008); and the author's *Fundamentalism and American Education in the Scopes Era: God, Darwin, and the Roots of America's Culture Wars* (New York: Palgrave Macmillan, 2010). In addition, some new dissertations will soon appear as books, including Natalia Mehlman-Petrzela, "Origins of the Culture Wars: Sex, Language, School, and State in California" (PhD diss., Stanford University, 2009); and Campbell Scribner, "The Exurban Exchange: Schools, Suburbs, and the History of Local Control" (PhD diss., University of Wisconsin–Madison, 2013). Hopefully these works have started a movement toward a more careful examination of the history of conservatism in American education.

6. Phillips-Fein, "Conservatism: A State of the Field," 723–743.

7. Ibid., 723.

8. Ibid., 726.

9. Ibid., 733.

10. Ibid., 729.

11. Bruce J. Schulman and Julian E. Zelizer, eds., *Rightward Bound: Making America Conservative in the 1970s* (Cambridge, MA: Harvard University Press, 2008).

12. Herbert M. Kliebard, *The Struggle for the American Curriculum, 1893–1958* (New York: Routledge and Kegan Paul, 1987), 8.

13. Ibid., 28–29.

14. William Torrey Harris, *The Theory of Education* (Syracuse, NY: C. W. Bardeen, 1893).

15. Michael John Demiashkevich, *An Introduction to the Philosophy of Education* (New York: American Book Company, 1935).

16. Arthur Bestor, *Educational Wastelands: The Retreat from Learning in Our Public Schools* (Urbana: University of Illinois Press, 1953).

17. Kliebard, *Struggle for the American Curriculum*, 28.

18. Anti-Rugg voices do show up briefly; see ibid., 206–207.

19. Jennifer Burns, "In Retrospect: George Nash's *The Conservative Intellectual Movement in America since 1945*," *Reviews in American History* 32:3 (September 2004): 455–456.

20. George Nash, *The Conservative Intellectual Movement in America since 1945*, 3rd ed. (Wilmington, DE: ISI Books, 2006), xx.

21. Donald T. Critchlow and Nancy K. MacLean, *Debating the American Conservative Movement: 1945 to the Present* (Lanham, MD: Rowman & Littlefield, 2009), vii, 1–2; see also Donald T. Critchlow, *The Conservative Ascendancy: How the GOP Right Made Political History* (Cambridge, MA: Harvard University Press, 2007).

22. See, e.g., Kim Phillips-Fein, *Invisible Hands: The Making of the Conservative Movement from the New Deal to Reagan* (New York: W. W. Norton, 2009), x; Bethany Moreton, *To Serve God and Wal-Mart: The Making of Christian Free Enterprise* (Cambridge, MA: Harvard University Press, 2009), 4.

23. David Farber, *The Rise and Fall of Modern Conservatism: A Short History* (Princeton, NJ: Princeton University Press, 2010), 10.

24. Ibid., 4.

25. Ibid., 5.

26. Allan J. Lichtman, *White Protestant Nation: The Rise of the American Conservative Movement* (New York: Atlantic Monthly Press, 2008), 1–2.

27. Leonard Moore, "Good Old-Fashioned New Social History and the Twentieth-Century American Right," *Reviews in American History* 24 (December 1996): 561.

28. Kim E. Nielsen, *Un-American Womanhood: Antiradicalism, Antifeminism, and the First Red Scare* (Columbus: The Ohio State University Press, 2001), 53.

29. Leo P. Ribuffo, "The Discovery and Rediscovery of American Conservatism Broadly Conceived," *OAH Magazine of History* 17 (January 2003): 8.

30. Burns, "In Retrospect," 455–456.

31. Nash, *Conservative Intellectual Movement in America since 1945*, 266–283.

32. John Lewis Gaddis, *The Landscape of History: How Historians Map the Past* (New York: Oxford University Press, 2002), 27–28, 123.

33. Jeffrey P. Moran, "The Scopes Trial and Southern Fundamentalism in Black and White: Race, Region, and Religion," *Journal of Southern History* 70 (February 2004): 113–115, 118–119.

34. Neil R. McMillen, *The Citizens' Council: Organized Resistance to the Second Reconstruction, 1954–64* (Urbana: University of Illinois Press, 1971), 17–18, 189–190, 199, 239.

35. Ibid., 16.

36. Adam Laats, *Fundamentalism and Education in the Scopes Era: God, Darwin, and the Roots of America's Culture Wars* (New York: Palgrave Macmillan, 2010).

37. Adam Laats, "Our Schools, Our Country: American Evangelicals, Public Schools, and the Supreme Court Decisions of 1962 and 1963," *Journal of Religious History* 36 (September 2012): 319–334.

38. Donald E. Boles, *The Two Swords: Commentaries and Cases in Religion and Education* (Ames: The Iowa State University Press, 1967), 74.

39. Duane T. Gish, *Teaching Creation Science in Public Schools* (El Cajon, CA: Institute for Creation Research, 1995), v.

40. Ronald L. Numbers, *Darwinism Comes to America* (Cambridge, MA: Harvard University Press, 1998), 91.

41. Adam Laats, "Many Educational Pasts: Conservative Visions and Revisions of the History of American Education," *Teachers College Record* 114 (2012): 1–25.

42. Andrew Jewett, *Science, Democracy, and the American University* (New York: Cambridge University Press, 2012), 6.

43. T. T. [Thomas Theodore] Martin, "The Evolution Issue" (speech, Los Angeles, October 28, 1923).

44. Laats, *Fundamentalism and Education in the Scopes Era*, 121–138.

45. Daniel Doherty, "Educators or Propagandists," August 15, 1938, typescript, Americanism Commission file, American Legion Archives, Indianapolis, IN. This speech also ran as an article in the *American Legion Magazine* (October 1938): 7–8, 52–53.

46. Mary L. Allen, *Education or Indoctrination: A Book for Educators* (Caldwell, ID: Caxton Printers, 1955), 36.

47. James Moffett, *Storm in the Mountains: A Case Study of Censorship, Conflict, and Consciousness* (Carbondale: Southern Illinois University Press, 1988), 70.

48. Anne Rogers Minor, "The Thirty-Second Continental Congress of the Daughters of the American Revolution," *Daughters of the American Revolution Magazine* 57 (May 1923): 268 (emphasis in original).

49. Ibid.

50. Ibid. (emphasis in original).

51. Ibid. (emphasis in original).

52. T. G. Wood, "Our City," *Pasadena Independent*, January 29, 1950, 31.

53. Ibid.

54. Ibid.

55. Mel and Norma Gabler with James C. Hefley, *What Are They Teaching Our Children?* (Wheaton, IL: Victor Books, 1986), 100.

56. Ibid.

57. Ibid.

58. Ibid., 98.

59. Ibid., 91.

60. William Jennings Bryan, *In His Image* (New York: Fleming H. Revell, 1922), 120.

61. Irene Corbally Kuhn, "Battle over Books," *American Legion Magazine* (October 1958): 37.

62. J. G. Harbord to Stephen F. Chadwick, 8 February 1939, American Legion dead-letter correspondence file, cited in Orville Eastland Jones, "Activities of the American Legion in Textbook Analysis and Criticism, 1938–1951" (EdD diss., University of Oklahoma, 1957), 10.

63. Frances B. Lucas, "National Defense," *Daughters of the American Revolution Magazine* 85 (November 1951): 925–928.

64. James C. Hefley, *Textbooks on Trial* (Wheaton, IL: Victor Books, 1976), 14–15.

65. Ibid., 15.

66. Gablers with Hefley, *What Are They Teaching Our Children*, 11.

67. Hefley, *Textbooks on Trial*, 15.

68. Gablers with Hefley, *What Are They Teaching Our Children*, 16–19.

69. Barbara Truesdell, "God, Home, and Country: Folklore, Patriotism, and the Politics of Culture in the Daughters of the American Revolution" (PhD diss., Indiana

University, 1996), 147–159; William Pencak, *For God and Country: The American Legion, 1919–1941* (Boston: Northeastern University Press, 1989), 3, 278–301.

70. Elisabeth Ellicott Poe, "Patriotic Women Take Stand for Adequate National Defense," *Daughters of the American Revolution Magazine* 62 (March 1928): 145–150.

71. "40th Continental Congress, NS, DAR," *Daughters of the American Revolution Magazine* 65 (May 1931): 261–271.

72. Carol Frank, "DAR Cheers Roosevelt in Defense Talk," *Washington Herald,* April 22, 1938, 1, 4.

73. J. Edgar Hoover, "How DAR Members Can Help in the FBI Drive against War Spies," *Daughters of the American Revolution Magazine* 84 (November 1950): 845, 895.

74. W. Alan Thody to American Legion, 21 April 1941, Americanism Commission Papers, American Legion Archives, Indianapolis, IN; Ellen Schrecker, *Many Are the Crimes: McCarthyism in America* (Princeton, NJ: Princeton University Press, 1998), 217.

75. Mrs. William Sherman Walker, "When Ideas Began to Grip," *Daughters of the American Revolution Magazine* 62 (May 1928): 300.

76. "Request School Loyalty Oaths Here," *Pasadena Independent,* July 12, 1950, 2, 20.

77. Hefley, *Textbooks on Trial,* 17–18.

78. Tyack and Cuban, *Tinkering toward Utopia,* 88.

2. Monkeys, Morality, and Modern America

1. For more on the Scopes trial, see Edward J. Larson, *Summer for the Gods: The Scopes Trial and America's Continuing Debate over Science and Education* (Cambridge, MA: Harvard University Press, 2001). See also the trial transcript, in *The World's Most Famous Court Trial:* State of Tennessee v. John Thomas Scopes (New York: Da Capo Press, 1971); original publication 1925.

2. Larson, *Summer for the Gods,* 203.

3. Ibid., 142.

4. *World's Most Famous Court Trial,* 287.

5. Ibid., 285.

6. H. L. Mencken, *A Religious Orgy in Tennessee: A Reporter's Account of the Scopes Monkey Trial* (Hoboken, NJ: Melville House, 2006), 45.

7. Ibid., 13.

8. Ibid., 11–12.

9. Ibid., 185.

10. Ibid., 187.

11. Quoted in Larson, *Summer for the Gods,* 179.

12. "Who's Who among the Convention Leaders," *New York Times,* June 22, 1924, XX5.

13. "Leopold and Loeb Plead Not Guilty," *New York Times,* June 12, 1924, 21.

14. "Mrs. Franks Heard as Counsel Fights for Son's Slayers," *New York Times,* July 24, 1924, 1, 7 (quotation on page 7).

15. Irving Stone, *Clarence Darrow for the Defense* (New York: Doubleday, 1941), 382.

16. Edward J. Larson and Jack Marshall, eds., *The Essential Words and Writings of Clarence Darrow* (New York: Modern Library, 2007), xii; Stone, *Clarence Darrow for the Defense*, 49–66; Andrew E. Kersten, *Clarence Darrow: American Iconoclast* (New York: Hill and Wang, 2011), 62–78.

17. "Mrs. Franks Heard as Counsel Fights for Son's Slayers," *New York Times*, July 24, 1924, 7.

18. Kersten, *Clarence Darrow: American Iconoclast*, 202.

19. Robert E. Crowe, "Capital Punishment Protects Society," *Forum* 73:2 (February 1925): 164.

20. Elmer Davis, "Mr. Darrow on Wealth," letter to the editor, *New York Times*, September 1, 1924, 12.

21. "Darrow for Liquor, Holmes against It," *New York Times*, December 15, 1924, 13.

22. "Darrow Offers Aid to Freethinkers," *New York Times*, June 11, 1925, 2.

23. So ran the title of a 1957 collection of Darrow's writings: Clarence Darrow, *Attorney for the Damned*, Arthur Weinberg, ed. (New York: Simon and Schuster, 1957). John Farrell's recent biography joined this refrain: *Clarence Darrow: Attorney for the Damned* (New York: Doubleday, 2011).

24. Guy T. Viskniskki to Bryan, 2 December 1922; Viskniskki to Bryan, 5 December 1922, Bryan Papers, Library of Congress, Washington, DC; *Commoner* 23 (April 1923): 1.

25. Michael Kazin, *A Godly Hero: The Life of William Jennings Bryan* (New York: Anchor Books, 2007), 45–79.

26. Ibid., 218–220.

27. Ibid., 234–238.

28. "Who Shall Control?," June 24 to June 30, 1925, typescript statement, file 3, Dayton trial correspondence, Bryan Papers.

29. William Jennings Bryan, "Letter to the Editor of the Chicago Evening Post," *The Commoner* 22 (February 1922): 5.

30. *World's Most Famous Court Trial*, 286.

31. Ibid., 287.

32. Frank L. McVey, "Address to the People of Kentucky," *Journal of the Kentucky Senate 1922*, 1031.

33. "Brands Darwin Bill Foes Apes," *Louisville Courier-Journal*, February 15, 1922.

34. Kentucky House Bill 191, *Journal of the House of Representatives of the Commonwealth of Kentucky 1922*, 1668–1669.

35. Amendment to Kentucky Senate Bill 136, *Journal of the Kentucky Senate 1922*, 1062.

36. George W. Ellis to William Jennings Bryan and J. W. Porter, 13 March 1922, Bryan Papers.

37. Richard David Wilhelm, "A Chronology and Analysis of Regulatory Actions relating to the Teaching of Evolution in Public Schools" (PhD diss., University of Texas–Austin, 1978), 323 [South Carolina 1922 Amendment].

38. Georgia House Resolution 58.246-B, *Journal of the House of Representatives of the State of Georgia 1923*, 353–354; Georgia House Resolution 93.390-C, *Journal of the House of Representatives of the State of Georgia 1923*, 553; Georgia House Resolution 93, *Journal of the House of Representatives of the State of Georgia 1923*, 1001–1002; Wilhelm, "Chronology and Analysis," 324–325 [Texas House Bill 97]; Texas House Concurrent Resolution 6, *Journal of the House of Representatives of the Third Called Session of the Thirty-Eighth Legislature of Texas 1923*, 73–74, 83; West Virginia House Bill 153, *Journal of the House of Delegates of the State of West Virginia 1923*, 743, 901, 1947; Tennessee House Bill 947, *Tennessee House Journal 1923*, 666, 694, 719; Alabama Senate Joint Resolution 55, *Alabama Senate Journal 1923*, 1211–1212; Iowa House File 657, *State of Iowa 1923 Journal of the House*, 758, 1048.

39. Florida House Concurrent Resolution 7, *Journal of the House of Representatives of the State of Florida 1923*, 482–483, 1176, 1853–1854, 1878, 2025–2027, 2200–2201, 2320, 3187–3190.

40. Oklahoma House Bill 197, *Oklahoma House Journal 1923*, 304–305; Oklahoma House Bill 197, *Oklahoma Senate Journal 1923*, 1718–1720; Oklahoma House Bill 197, *Session Laws of Oklahoma 1923*, 296; G. W. Moothart to Bryan, 5 December 1922, Bryan Papers; J. J. Walters [Governor of Oklahoma] to Bryan, 26 May 1923, Bryan Papers; Kenneth K. Bailey, "The Antievolution Crusade of the Nineteen-Twenties" (PhD diss., Vanderbilt University, 1954), 74.

41. "Science and Religion," *New York Times*, April 5, 1925, E4; Bailey, "The Antievolution Crusade," 67–68.

42. Ibid., 68–69.

43. Quote from Congress's D.C. teacher law is from "Evolution Battle to Go to Congress: New Law Is Sought," *New York Times*, July 24, 1925, 1; Congressional Record, 68 Congress, 1 Session, LXV, part 8, 7796.

44. West Virginia House Bill 175, *West Virginia Bills of the House of Delegates 1925*, 66; Texas House Bill 378, *Texas House Journal 1925*, 386; Florida House Bill 691, *Journal of the Florida House of Representatives 1925*, 1267, 1579–1580; "Anti-Darwin Campaigns Stir South and West," *New York Times*, June 10, 1923, X2.

45. Bailey, "The Antievolution Crusade," 71–72.

46. Tennessee House Bill 185, *House Journal of the Sixty-Fourth General Assembly of the State of Tennessee 1925*, 180, 201, 210, 248, 261, 268, 648, 655, 741; Tennessee House Bill 185, *Senate Journal of the Sixty-Fourth General Assembly of the State of Tennessee 1925*, 516–517; "Tennessee Bans the Teaching of Evolution," *New York Times*, March 24, 1925, 1; "Fights Evolution to Uphold Bible," *New York Times*, July 5, 1925, E1.

47. Larson, *Summer for the Gods*, 83.

48. Ibid., 67, 74.

49. Ibid., 88–91.

50. Ibid., 92.

51. Fred Inglis, *A Short History of Celebrity* (Princeton, NJ: Princeton University Press, 2010), 135–157.

52. Larson, *Summer for the Gods*, 113–120.

53. "Stop and Think," editorial, *Louisville Courier-Journal*, February 3, 1922.

54. Bryan to Sue Hicks, quoted in James Gilbert, *Redeeming Culture: American Religion in an Age of Science* (Chicago: University of Chicago Press, 1997), 32.

55. Bryan to Howard A. Kelly, 10 June 1925, Bryan Papers, Library of Congress, Washington, DC.

56. J. Frank Norris to William Jennings Bryan, June or July 1925, Bryan Papers.

57. Barry Hankins, *God's Rascal: J. Frank Norris and the Beginnings of Southern Fundamentalism* (Lexington: University Press of Kentucky, 1996), 119–120.

58. George McCready Price, "Modern Scientific Discoveries," *Christian Fundamentals in School and Church* 5 (October–December 1922); George McCready Price, "Present Predicament of the Evolution Doctrine," *Moody Bible Institute Monthly* 23 (July 1923): 517–519.

59. George McCready Price, "Modern Problems in Science and Religion," *Moody Bible Institute Monthly* 21 (February 1921): 256.

60. G. M. Price to Bryan, 27 February 1922, Bryan Papers.

61. Samuel Zane Batten, "The Battle within the Churches," *Searchlight* 6 (October 26, 1923): 1; also in *Christian Fundamentals in School and Church* 6 (October–December 1923): 8.

62. William R. Hutchison, *The Modernist Impulse in American Protestantism* (Cambridge, MA: Harvard University Press, 1976), 2.

63. Shirley Jackson Case, *The Revelation of John* (Chicago: University of Chicago Press, 1919); Shailer Mathews, *The Faith of Modernism* (New York: Macmillan, 1924).

64. William V. Trollinger, *God's Empire: William Bell Riley and Midwestern Fundamentalism* (Madison: University of Wisconsin Press, 1990), 16.

65. Ibid., 17–18.

66. Ibid., 159.

67. Ibid., 163.

68. William Bell Riley, in *Christian Fundamentals in School and Church* 8 (April–June 1926): 33, 43.

69. William Bell Riley, in *Christian Fundamentals in School and Church* 8 (January–March 1926): 18, 28.

70. George M. Marsden, *Fundamentalism and American Culture: The Shaping of Twentieth-Century Evangelicalism, 1870–1925* (New York: Oxford University Press, 1980), 4.

71. W. B. Norton, "Religious Poll Shows College Men Moderns: Nearly All Evolutionists, Report Reveals," *Chicago Daily Tribune*, January 8, 1925, 21.

72. Maynard Shipley, *The War on Modern Science* (New York: Alfred A. Knopf, 1927), 47.

73. William E. Leuchtenburg, *The Perils of Prosperity, 1914–1932* (Chicago: University of Chicago Press, 1958), 204–224.

74. H. L. Mencken, *A Religious Orgy in Tennessee: A Reporter's Account of the Scopes Monkey Trial* (Hoboken, NJ: Melville House, 2006), 44, 75.

75. "What Is a Fundamentalist?," *Forum* 76 (December 1926): 861.

76. Ibid.

77. Willard B. Gatewood Jr., *Preachers, Pedagogues and Politicians: The Evolution Controversy in North Carolina, 1920–1927* (Chapel Hill: University of North Carolina Press, 1966), 186.

78. Bess Davenport, "Scorching Epithets Bring Discord into Anti-Evolution War," *Raleigh News and Observer,* May 5, 1926, 1.

79. J. Frank Norris, in *The Searchlight* 6 (March 16, 1923): 1.

80. Congressional Record, 69 Congress, 1 Session, H 5748 (March 16, 1926).

81. "What Is a Fundamentalist?," 861.

82. Curtis Lee Laws, "Editorial Notes and Comments," *Watchman-Examiner* 13 (August 20, 1925): 1071.

83. James Gilbert, *Redeeming Culture: American Religion in an Age of Science* (Chicago: University of Chicago Press, 1997), 25–28; Burton Livingston to Bryan, 29 September 1924, Bryan Papers.

84. William Jennings Bryan, *In His Image* (New York: Fleming H. Revell, 1922), 69.

85. William Jennings Bryan, "God and Evolution," *New York Times,* February 26, 1922, 11.

86. Edwin Grant Conklin, "Bryan and Evolution," *New York Times,* March 5, 1922, 1.

87. Edwin Grant Conklin, *The Direction of Human Evolution* (New York: Scribner's, 1921), v–vi (emphasis in original).

88. Conklin, "Bryan and Evolution," 1.

89. William Jennings Bryan, *The Menace of Darwinism* (Louisville, KY: Pentecostal Publishing Co., n.d.), 10; Bryan, "God and Evolution," 1.

90. Bob Jones Sr., *The Perils of America, or, Where Are We Headed?,* from a sermon delivered at the Chicago Gospel Tabernacle, March 5, 1934, (n.d.), 13.

91. Ibid.

92. Norris quoted by James Gray, "Will the Christian Taxpayers Stand for This?," *Moody Bible Institute Monthly* 23 (May 1923): 409.

93. Bryan, *The Menace of Darwinism,* 4.

94. R. J. Alderman, "Evolution Leads to Sodom," *Monthly Bible Institute Monthly* 23 (September 1922): 12.

95. Jones, *The Perils of America,* 35.

96. Thomas Theodore Martin, *Hell and the High School: Christ or Evolution, Which?* (Kansas City, MO: Western Baptist Publishing Co., 1923), 10.

97. Not much is known about Martin's life, compared to his contemporaries in the 1920s school controversies. He published an autobiography, *Viewing Life's Sunset from Pike's Peak* (Louisville, KY: A.D. Muse, 1939), and has been the subject of a thesis: John Franklin Loftis, "Thomas Theodore Martin: His Life and Work as Evangelist, Fundamentalist, and Anti-Evolutionist" (Th.M. thesis, Southern Baptist Theological Seminary, 1980).

98. Larson, *Summer for the Gods,* 142.

99. Harold W. Fairbanks, *Home Geography,* rev. ed. (New York: Educational Publishing Company, 1924), 124.

100. T. T. Martin, *The Evolution Issue* (Los Angeles: Author, n.d. [1923?]), 34.

101. William Jennings Bryan to W. J. Singleterry, 11 April 1923, Bryan Papers; Bryan, "Letter to the Editor of the *Chicago Tribune*," *Chicago Tribune*, June 14, 1923; Bryan to C. H. Thurber, 22 December 1923, Bryan Papers.

102. Alfred Fairhurst, *Atheism in Our Universities* (Cincinnati, OH: Standard Publishing Co., 1923), 84.

103. Ibid., 92 (emphasis in original).

104. Martin, *The Evolution Issue*, 38–39.

105. James M. Gray, "The Sacred Cow of Evolution," *Moody Bible Institute Monthly* 29 (January 1929): 225.

106. William Jennings Bryan, *The Bible and Its Enemies: An Address Delivered at the Moody Bible Institute of Chicago* (Chicago: Bible Institute Colportage Association, 1921), 19.

107. William Jennings Bryan, *William Jennings Bryan's Last Speech: Undelivered Speech to the Jury in the Scopes Trial* (Oklahoma City, OK: Sunlight Publishing Society, 1925), 46.

108. William Bell Riley, "Reply to University Regents on the Evolutionary Controversy," *Christian Fundamentals in School and Church* 5 (July–September 1923): 51.

109. Mary Balch Women's Christian Temperance Union to Bryan, 26 May 1925, Bryan Papers; see also W. F. Garvin to Bryan, 19 May 1925, Bryan Papers.

110. Amendment to Kentucky Senate Bill 136, *Journal of the Kentucky Senate 1922*, 1062.

111. Gatewood, *Preachers, Pedagogues and Politicians*, 149.

112. Summers Amendment, Congressional Record, 68 Congress, 1 Session, H 7796 (May 3, 1924).

113. Gatewood, *Preachers, Pedagogues and Politicians*, 222 [text of Poole Bill, North Carolina House Bill No. 263]; North Carolina House Bill 263, *Journal of the House of Representatives of the General Assembly of the State of North Carolina 1927*, 85, 241.

114. West Virginia House Bill 264, *Journal of the House of Delegates of West Virginia 1927*, 104.

115. Florida House Bill 87, *Florida House Journal 1927*, 3000–3001.

116. John T. Scopes and James Presley, *Center of the Storm: Memoirs of John T. Scopes* (New York: Holt, Rinehart and Winston, 1967), 77.

117. "Cranks and Freaks Flock to Dayton," *New York Times*, July 11, 1925, 1–2.

118. Jeffrey P. Moran, *American Genesis: The Evolution Controversies from Scopes to Creation Science* (New York: Oxford University Press, 2012), 77.

119. Clarence Darrow, "The Problem of the Negro," *International Socialist Review* 2:5 (November 1901): 321 (from a speech May 19, 1901).

120. Ibid., 324–325.

121. Lynn Dumenil, *The Modern Temper: American Culture and Society in the 1920s* (New York: Hill & Wang, 1995), 207–210.

122. Henry Fairfield Osborn, *The Earth Speaks to Bryan* (New York: Scribner's, 1925).

123. Henry Fairfield Osborn, preface to *The Passing of the Great Race*, 2nd ed., by Madison Grant (New York: Scribner's, 1918), vii–ix.

124. Moran, *American Genesis*, 84–85.

125. Michael Kazin, *A Godly Hero: The Life of William Jennings Bryan* (New York: Alfred A. Knopf, 2006), 281.

126. James M. Gray, "Editorial Notes," *Moody Bible Institute Monthly* 23 (February 1923): 240.

127. J. Frank Norris, "Judge Wilson, K.C.'s. Ku Klux Klan and Bootleggers," *Searchlight* 4 (May 12, 1922): 1.

128. "Cranks and Freaks Flock to Dayton," 1–2.

129. Charles McD. Puckette, "The Evolution Arena at Dayton," *New York Times*, July 5, 1925, SM1, 22.

130. Jeffrey P. Moran, *The Scopes Trial: A Brief History with Documents* (Boston: Bedford/St. Martin's, 2002), 29; Larson, *Summer for the Gods*, 68–71, 79–80.

131. Beyond any attention he may have derived from his role in the trial, Sue Hicks claimed to have served as the inspiration for Johnny Cash's hit song "A Boy Named Sue." See "Johnny Cash Is Indebted to a Judge Named Sue," *New York Times*, July 12, 1970, 66.

132. Moran, *Scopes Trial*, 29.

133. *World's Greatest Court Trial*, 14.

134. Ibid., 10–45.

135. "Farmers Will Try Teacher," *New York Times*, July 11, 1925, 1.

136. *World's Greatest Court Trial*, 45.

137. Ibid., 56.

138. Ibid., 57.

139. Ibid., 75.

140. Larson, *Summer for the Gods*, 164–165.

141. *World's Greatest Court Trial*, 90.

142. Ibid., 93.

143. Ibid.

144. Mencken, *A Religious Orgy in Tennessee*, 73.

145. Larson, *Summer for the Gods*, 167.

146. Mencken, *A Religious Orgy in Tennessee*, 3, 72.

147. Adam Laats, *Fundamentalism and Education in the Scopes Era: God, Darwin, and the Roots of America's Culture Wars* (New York: Palgrave Macmillan, 2010), 36–37.

148. Larson, *Summer for the Gods*, 55.

149. See also the author's fuller treatment of this topic: Adam Laats, "Red Schoolhouse, Burning Cross: The Ku Klux Klan of the 1920s and Educational Reform," *History of Education Quarterly* 52:3 (August 2012): 323–350.

150. J. J. Walters to William Jennings Bryan, 26 May 1923, Bryan Papers.

151. House Bill 197, *Session Laws of the State of Oklahoma 1923*, 296.

152. "Donahey Defies Klan in Vetoing Bible Measure," *Cleveland Plain Dealer*, May 1, 1925, 1.

153. Larry R. Gerlach, *Blazing Crosses in Zion: The Ku Klux Klan in Utah* (Logan: Utah State University Press, 1982), 119 [Salt Lake City]; David Chalmers, *Hooded Americanism: The History of the Ku Klux Klan*, 3rd ed. (Durham, NC: Duke University Press, 1987), 99 [South Carolina], 260 [Long Island]; Jonathan

Zimmerman, *Small Wonder: The Little Red Schoolhouse in History and Memory* (New Haven, CT: Yale University Press), 76 [Illinois]; "Little Red Schoolhouse Brings Cheers," *The National Kourier* [*National Kourier*] 4 (December 5, 1924): 3 [Ohio]; "This Float in Mt. Sterling, Ill., Was Greatly Admired," *National Kourier* 4 (December 26, 1924): 8 [Illinois]; "Will Furnish Float," *Imperial Night-Hawk* 2 (July 2, 1924): 3 [Tennessee].

154. William D. Jenkins, *Steel Valley Klan: The Ku Klux Klan in Ohio's Mahoning Valley* (Kent, OH: Kent State University Press, 1990), 55.

155. Robert Alan Goldberg, *Hooded Empire: The Ku Klux Klan in Colorado* (Urbana: University of Illinois Press, 1981), 5.

156. Kathleen M. Blee, *Women of the Klan: Racism and Gender in the 1920s* (Berkeley: University of California Press, 1991), 2.

157. Wyn Craig Wade, *The Fiery Cross: The Ku Klux Klan in America* (New York: Simon & Schuster, 1987), 165.

158. See Shawn Lay, ed., *The Invisible Empire in the West: Toward a New Historical Appraisal of the Ku Klux Klan of the 1920s* (Urbana: University of Illinois Press, 2004).

159. See coverage in the official Klan newspaper: "Ku Klux Klan Receivership Suit Thrown Out of Court: Insurgents Are Defeated in Their Move to Wreck Great Order from Within," *The Searchlight* 3 (March 11, 1922): 1; "Wizard Charters Imperial Klan," *Searchlight* 3 (July 15, 1922): 1; "Clarke Resigns as Klan Official," *Searchlight* 3 (October 7, 1922): 1; "Dr. H. W. Evans New Imperial Wizard," *Searchlight* 3 (December 2, 1922): 1; J. O. Wood, "There Is Only One Klan and Simmons Is Its Head," *Searchlight* 4 (April 7, 1923): 1; William Joseph Simmons, "Emperor Gives Reasons for Resuming Active Control of Klan Affairs," *Searchlight* 4 (April 7, 1923): 1; J. O. Wood, "The Litigation Settlement," *Searchlight* 4 (April 28, 1923): 2; "Court Decree Defines Rights of Parties in the Klan Controversy," *Searchlight* 4 (May 5, 1923): 1; "Court Denies Klan Receivership," *Searchlight* 4 (November 3, 1923): 1. See also *Minutes of the Imperial Kloncilium: Meeting of May 1 and 2, 1923 Which Ratified W. J. Simmons' Agreement with the Knights of the Ku Klux Klan* (Atlanta, GA: Imperial Koncilium, 1923). See also Chalmers, *Hooded Americanism*, 101–107.

160. Hiram W. Evans, *The Public School Problem in America: Outlining fully the policies and the program of the Knights of the Ku Klux Klan toward the Public School System* (n.p.: 1924), 10.

161. Douglas J. Slawson, *The Department of Education Battle, 1918–1932: Public Schools, Catholic Schools, and the Social Order* (Notre Dame, IN: University of Notre Dame Press, 2005), 19–20.

162. Quoted in Slawson, *Department of Education Battle*, 136.

163. Hiram W. Evans, "Where Do We Go From Here?" in *Papers Read at the Meeting of Grand Dragons Knights of the Ku Klux Klan: Together with other articles of interest to Klansmen* (New York: Arno Press, 1977, orig. 1923).

164. Glenn Feldman, *Politics, Society, and the Klan in Alabama, 1915–1949* (Tuscaloosa: University of Alabama Press, 1999), 22–23, 27–28, 55.

165. Blee, *Women of the Klan*, 143–145.

166. Leonard J. Moore, *Citizen Klansmen: The Ku Klux Klan in Indiana, 1921–1928* (Chapel Hill: University of North Carolina Press, 1991), 38, 149.

167. Ibid., 179–183.

168. Ibid., 38, 148–149, 183.

169. Moore, *Citizen Klansmen*, 38–39; Blee, *Women of the Klan*, 160.

170. David B. Tyack, "The Perils of Pluralism: The Background of the Pierce Case," *American Historical Review* 74 (October 1968): 74–98; Slawson, *Department of Education Battle*, 108–114, 136, 138; Donald E. Boles, *The Two Swords: Commentaries and Cases in Religion and Education* (Ames: The Iowa State University Press, 1967), 303–306.

171. Tyack, "The Perils of Pluralism," 90.

172. David A. Horowitz, ed., *Inside the Klavern: The Secret History of a Ku Klux Klan of the 1920s* (Carbondale, IL: Southern Illinois University Press, 1999), 27.

173. George Estes, *The Old Cedar School* (Portland, OR: Luther I. Powell, 1922).

174. Blee, *Women of the Klan*, 143–145.

175. Bryan to G. M. Price, 7 June 1925; G. M. Price to Bryan, 1 July 1925, Bryan Papers. See also Ronald L. Numbers, *The Creationists: From Scientific Creationism to Intelligent Design*, exp. ed. (Cambridge, MA: Harvard University Press, 2006), 116–119; Larson, *Summer for the Gods*, 130.

176. Alfred W. McCann to William Jennings Bryan, n.d., file June 24–30, 1925, Bryan Papers.

177. Hankins, *God's Rascal*, 54–63; Leo P. Ribuffo, *The Old Christian Right: The Protestant Far Right from the Great Depression to the Cold War* (Philadelphia: Temple University Press, 1983), 100–101.

178. Numbers, *Creationists*, 88.

179. William Jennings Bryan to Howard A. Kelly, 10 June 1925; Kelly to Bryan, 15 June 1925; Bryan to Kelly, 17 June 1925; Bryan to Kelly, 22 June 1925, Bryan Papers.

180. Larson, *Summer for the Gods*, 172–173; *World's Greatest Court Trial*, 125–133. Ironically, as historian Adam Shapiro has pointed out recently, the legal case was not so cut-and-dried. Tennessee's 1925 law specified that the evolution of humanity could not be taught. Hunter's 1914 edition waffled on the issue of human evolution. See Adam R. Shapiro, *Trying Biology: The Scopes Trial, Textbooks, and the Antievolution Movement in American Schools* (Chicago: University of Chicago Press, 2013), 107–110.

181. Larson, *Summer for the Gods*, 174; *World's Greatest Court Trial*, 139.

182. *World's Greatest Court Trial*, 139.

183. Ibid., 146.

184. Ibid., 172.

185. Ibid., 174.

186. Ibid., 178–180.

187. Ibid., 181.

188. Bryan, "Who Shall Control?"

189. Mencken, *A Religious Orgy in Tennessee*, 89.

190. Ibid., 93.

191. *World's Greatest Court Trial*, 281.

192. Ibid.

193. Ibid., 172.

194. Ward W. Keesecker, *Legal Status of Bible Reading and Religious Instruction in Public Schools* (Washington, DC: United States Government Printing Office, 1930), 2.

195. W. S. Fleming, *God in Our Public Schools,* 3rd ed. (Pittsburgh, PA: National Reform Association, 1947), 143–144 (original publication 1942). The following states (with the year the law passed) required daily Bible reading: Massachusetts (1826), Pennsylvania (1913), Tennessee (1915), New Jersey (1916), Alabama (1919), Georgia (1921), Delaware (1923), Maine (1923), Kentucky (1924), Florida (1925), Idaho (1925), Arkansas (1930).

196. Adam Laats, "Monkeys, Bibles, and the Little Red Schoolhouse: Atlanta's School Battles in the Scopes Era," *Georgia Historical Quarterly* 95:3 (Fall 2011): 335–355.

197. Atlanta Board of Education, "Minutes, August 13, 1929," *Minutes: Board of Education, January 8, 1929 to February 11, 1930,* vol. 18, Board of Education Archives, Atlanta, Georgia.

198. James H. Weir, "The Power of God unto Salvation," *Moody Bible Institute Monthly* (May 1921): 423.

199. William Norton "The Gospel in Print," *Moody Bible Institute Monthly* (February 1921): 295.

200. Adam Laats, "The Quiet Crusade: The Moody Bible Institute's Outreach to Public Schools and the Mainstreaming of Appalachia, 1921–1966," *Church History* 75:3 (September 2006): 565–593.

201. "Coolidge Declares Bible a Bulwark," *New York Times,* April 4, 1927, 25.

202. "Hits Lack of Religion in the Public Schools," *New York Times,* November 13, 1926, 12.

203. Robert W. Lynn, "The Uses of History: An Inquiry into the History of American Religious Education," *Religious Education* 67 (March–April 1972): 91.

204. W. S. Fleming. *God in Our Public Schools,* 17 ["field force"], 90 [Ohio].

205. *World's Greatest Court Trial,* 283.

206. Larson, *Summer for the Gods,* 191.

207. Bryan, "Who Shall Control?"

208. *World's Greatest Court Trial,* 299.

209. Mencken, *A Religious Orgy in Tennessee,* 79.

210. Congressional Record, 69 Congress, 1 Session, LXVII, part 5, 5749.

211. Kazin, *A Godly Hero,* 294.

212. J. Frank Norris, "Bryan Wins Greatest Victory of His Career—Bible Triumphs over Infidelity: Commoner Outwits Darrow in Dayton Evolution Trial," *The Searchlight* 8 (July 24, 1925): 1.

213. T. C. Horton, "Bryan the Brave—'Defender of the Faith,'" *King's Business* 16 (September 1925): 1.

214. William Bell Riley, Editorial, *Christian Fundamentals in School and Church* 7 (October–December 1925): 52.

215. "Big Crowd Watches Trial under Trees," *New York Times,* July 21, 1925, 1.

216. Mencken, *A Religious Orgy in Tennessee,* 104.

217. Ibid., 105.

218. Ibid., 107.

219. Quoted in Larson, *Summer for the Gods,* 201.

220. Kenneth K. Bailey, "The Antievolution Crusade of the Nineteen-Twenties" (PhD diss., Vanderbilt University, 1953), 249.

221. Judith V. Grabiner and Peter D. Miller, "Effects of the Scopes Trial: Was It a Victory for Evolutionists?," *Science* 185 (September 6, 1974): 833.

222. George William Hunter, *Civic Biology* (New York: American Book Company, 1914), 195–196; George William Hunter, *New Civic Biology* (New York: American Book Company, 1926), 250–251. Historian Adam Shapiro has made it clear that these changes often proceeded in spite of Hunter's objections. See Adam R. Shapiro, *Trying Biology: The Scopes Trial, Textbooks, and the Antievolution Movement in American Schools* (Chicago: University of Chicago Press, 2013), 111–134.

223. "Texas Schoolbooks Omit Evolution," *New York Times,* July 13, 1926, 44.

224. Truman Moon, *Biology for Beginners* (New York: Holt, 1921), v.

225. Truman Moon, *Biology for Beginners,* rev. ed. (New York: Holt, 1926), v.

226. Gerald Skoog, "The Coverage of Human Evolution in High School Biology Textbooks in the 20th Century and in Current State Science Standards," *Science and Education* 14 (2005): 395–422.

227. Oscar Riddle, F. L. Fitzpatrick, H. B. Glass, B. C. Gruenberg, D. F. Miller, and E. W. Sinnott, eds., *The Teaching of Biology in Secondary Schools of the United States: A Report of Results from a Questionnaire* (Washington, DC: Union of American Biological Sciences, 1942), 7, 71.

228. Ibid., 76.

229. Ibid., 73–74.

230. Ibid., 73–74.

231. Lloyd P. Jorgenson, *The State and the Non-Public School, 1825–1925* (Columbia: University of Missouri Press, 1987), 135.

232. Kenneth M. Dolbeare and Phillip E. Hammond, *The School Prayer Decisions: From Court Policy to Local Practice* (Chicago: University of Chicago Press, 1971), 29; R. B. Dierenfield, *Religion in American Public Schools* (Washington, DC: Public Affairs Press, 1962), 51.

233. William Jennings Bryan, "Mr. Darrow's Charge of Ignorance" July 21 or 22, 1925, typescript, Bryan Papers.

234. *St. Paul Pioneer Press,* March 10, 1927, in Willard B. Gatewood Jr., ed., *Controversy in the 'Twenties: Fundamentalism, Modernism, and Evolution* (Nashville, TN: Vanderbilt University Press, 1969), 309.

235. William Bell Riley, "The Faith of the Fundamentalists," in Gatewood, *Controversy in the 'Twenties,* 75.

236. William Jennings Bryan, "Dr. Birge, Autocrat," *The Commoner* (May 1922): 1.

3. Pulling the Rugg Out

1. "Educators in Row over Rugg Books," *Philadelphia Inquirer,* February 23, 1941, B1, 9.

2. William A. Macdonald, "Dr. Rugg Defends Modern Histories," *New York Times*, February 23, 1941, 47.

3. Ibid.

4. Alfred T. Falk, *Does Advertising Harm or Benefit Consumers?* (New York: Advertising Federation of America, 1939).

5. A. T. Falk to Homer Chaillaux, 22 November 1939, copied in Orville Eastland Jones, *Activities of the American Legion in Textbook Analysis and Criticism, 1938–1951* (EdD diss., University of Oklahoma, 1957), 18. Jones copied verbatim correspondence that has since been lost or destroyed. See also Chaillaux to Falk, 1 December 1939, in Jones, *Activities of the American Legion*, 19.

6. "Educators in Row over Rugg Books," 9.

7. MacDonald, "Dr. Rugg Defends Modern Histories."

8. Benjamin Fine, "Un-American Tone Seen in Textbooks on Social Sciences," *New York Times*, February 22, 1941, 1.

9. Elmer Arthur Winters, "Harold Rugg and Education for Social Reconstruction" (PhD diss., University of Wisconsin, 1968), 91. Winters reported that the Rugg series as a whole sold 1,317,960 textbooks plus 2,687,000 workbooks between 1929 and 1939.

10. Ibid., 92. Winters interviewed Frank Moran of Ginn & Co., February 11, 1966.

11. Ronald W. Evans, *This Happened in America: Harold Rugg and the Censure of Social Studies* (Charlotte, NC: Information Age Publishing, 2007), 237.

12. "Rugg Textbooks out of Schools Officially by Order of Board," *Binghamton Press*, April 17, 1940, 3; Ellen Boesenberg and Karen Poland, "Struggle at the Frontier of Curriculum: The Rugg Textbook Controversy in Binghamton, New York," *Theory and Research in Social Education* 29:4 (2001): 640–671.

13. Jones, *Activities of the American Legion*, 41.

14. Ibid., 28.

15. "Iowa School Bars Rugg Books," *New York Times*, June 20, 1940, 25.

16. Charles Dorn, "'Treason in the Textbooks': Reinterpreting the Harold Rugg Textbook Controversy in the Context of Wartime Schooling," *Paedagogica Historica* 44:4 (August 2008): 469.

17. "Mt Kisco Bans Rugg Books," *New York Times*, November 15, 1940, 18.

18. Dorn, "'Treason in the Textbooks,'" 477; Jonathan Zimmerman, *Whose America? Culture Wars in the Public Schools* (Cambridge, MA: Harvard University Press, 2002), 79.

19. "Rugg's Books Barred from More Schools," *New York Times*, August 29, 1940, 17.

20. "Rugg's Books Are Upheld," *New York Times*, October 23, 1940, 21.

21. Evans, *This Happened in America*, 95.

22. Winters, *Harold Rugg and Education for Social Reconstruction*, 129.

23. Jones, *Activities of the American Legion*, 10.

24. Rudd to Stephen Chadwick (AL National Commander), 18 February 1939, in Jones, *Activities of the American Legion*, 12.

25. Augustin Rudd, *Bending the Twig: The Revolution in Education and its Effects on Our Children* (New York: Sons of the American Revolution, 1957), overleaf.

26. Jones, *Activities of the American Legion*, 10–14.

27. L. M. Bailey, "Weed Out the Communist Textbooks," *National Defenders Newsletter* (New York: National Defenders, n.d.). Copy in box 48, Billy James Hargis Papers (MC 1412), Special Collections, University of Arkansas Libraries, Fayetteville.

28. Harold Ordway Rugg, *That Men May Understand: An American in the Long Armistice* (New York: Doubleday, 1941), 95.

29. The six high school books included the following titles: *An Introduction to American Civilization; Changing Civilizations in the Modern World; A History of American Civilization; A History of American Government and Culture; An Introduction to the Problems of American Culture;* and *Changing Governments and Changing Cultures.* The eight middle school titles included the following: *The First Book of the Earth; Nature Peoples; Communities of Men; Peoples and Countries; The Building of America; Man at Work: His Industries; Man at Work: His Arts and Crafts;* and *Mankind throughout the Ages.* Rugg, *That Men May Understand*, 42–43.

30. Elizabeth Dilling, *The Red Network: A 'Who's Who' and Handbook of Radicalism for Patriots* (Kenilworth, IL: Author, 1934), 318.

31. Rugg, *That Men May Understand*, 205; Evans, *This Happened in America*, 55.

32. Evans, *This Happened in America*, 47; Harold O. Rugg, "A Preface to the Reconstruction of the American School Curriculum," *Teachers College Record* 27:7 (March 1926): 613 (emphasis in original).

33. "Archaic Texts Seen as School Handicap," *New York Times*, March 11, 1933, 15.

34. Peter F. Carbone Jr., *The Social and Educational Thought of Harold Rugg* (Durham, NC: Duke University Press, 1977), 57, 63, 68.

35. Carbone, *Social and Educational Thought of Harold Rugg*, 56–57. Quote is from Rugg, *Culture and Education in America* (New York: Harcourt, Brace, 1931), 255.

36. Lawrence Cremin, *American Education: The Metropolitan Experience* (New York: Harper & Row, 1988): 187–195.

37. Evans, *This Happened in America*, 110–111.

38. Earl Browder, "Education—An Ally in the Workers' Struggle," *Social Frontier* 1:4 (January 1935): 24.

39. C. A. Bowers, "Social Reconstructionism: Views from the Left and the Right, 1932–1942," *History of Education Quarterly* 10 (Spring 1970): 26.

40. Rugg, *That Men May Understand*, 10.

41. O. K. Armstrong, "Treason in the Textbooks," *American Legion Magazine* (September 1940): 8.

42. J. Frank Norris, "The Inspiration of the Scriptures: Sermon by the Pastor in Answer to a Book of Higher Criticism by Dr. John A. Rice of Southern Methodist University," *Searchlight* (May 21, 1921): 1.

43. See, for example, Richard Hofstadter's influential *Anti-Intellectualism in American Life* (New York: Knopf, 1963).

44. William Pencak, *For God and Country: The American Legion, 1919–1941* (Boston: Northeastern University Press, 1989), 241.

45. Phil Conley, "The Shifting Background: A Letter from an Old Classmate," *American Legion Magazine* (October 1935): 53.

46. Robert E. Pitkin, "The American Legion and the Schools," *American Legion Magazine* (September 1959): 24–26, 40–41; Pencak, *For God and Country*, 11, 162, 175, 265–266.

47. "Education Policy of Legion Scored," *New York Times*, November 24, 1935.

48. William Gellerman, *American Legion as Educator* (New York: Teachers College Press, 1938), 238.

49. Ibid., 241.

50. Ibid., 255.

51. William F. Russell to Daniel Doherty, 22 July 1938, Americanism Commission file, American Legion Archives, Indianapolis, IN. [Legion Archives]

52. "Doherty Disputes Charges," press release, 27 June 1938, Legion Archives.

53. Doherty to Edward McGrail, 6 July 1938, Legion Archives.

54. "Silly Harangue," *Des Moines* [IA] *Tribune*, July 22, 1938, clipping from Legion Archives.

55. "They're Both Right," *Staunton* [VA] *Leader*, July 22, 1938, clipping from Legion Archives; Doherty to Edward McGrail [AL National Publicity Officer], 22 July 1938, Legion Archives.

56. McGrail to Doherty, memo, 28 June 1938, Legion Archives; McGrail to Fred M. Fueker, 29 June 1938, Legion Archives.

57. Pat Kelly to Frank E. Samuels, telegram, 29 June 1938, Legion Archives.

58. Daniel Doherty, "Educators or Propagandists," typescript, 15 August 1938, Legion Archives. This speech also ran as an article in the *American Legion Magazine* (October 1938): 7–8, 52–53.

59. Doherty, "Educators or Propagandists."

60. Homer L. Chaillaux to Helen Silcox, 21 March 1939, Legion Archives.

61. A. T. Falk to Chaillaux, 22 November 1939, in Jones, *Activities of the American Legion*, 18.

62. A. T. Falk to Chaillaux, 4 December 1939, in Jones, *Activities of the American Legion*, 20.

63. Chaillaux to Falk, 1 December 1939, in Jones, *Activities of the American Legion*, 19.

64. Ibid.

65. Armstrong, "Treason in the Textbooks," 51.

66. Ibid.

67. R. Worth Shumaker, "No 'New Order' for Our Schools," *American Legion Magazine* (April 1941): 6.

68. Charlotte Wettrick, *Our American Schools: Shall We Keep Them Free?* (Seattle, WA: Author, 1939), Legion Archives.

69. B. C. Forbes, "Deplores Un-American Teachings in Colleges," box 7, folder: Memorabilia (Englewood Controversy), Forbes Papers, Syracuse University Special Collections, Syracuse, NY. [Forbes Papers]

70. Augustin G. Rudd, Hamilton Hicks, and Alfred T. Falk, eds., *Undermining Our Republic: Do You Know What the Children Are Being Taught in Our Public*

Schools? You'll Be Surprised (New York: Guardians of American Education, Inc., 1941), 17.

71. Ibid., 59.

72. *Teachers vs. Propagandists* (New York: Guardians of American Education, n.d.), single-sheet broadside, box 45, folder 49, Billy James Hargis Papers (MC 1412), Special Collections, University of Arkansas Libraries, Fayetteville.

73. Rugg, *That Men May Understand,* 13.

74. "Roscoe [illegible]" to "friend," 20 May 1943, Legion Archives.

75. Rudolf Flesch, *Why Johnny Can't Read, and What You Can Do About It* (New York: Harper & Row, 1955), 55.

76. Mary L. Allen, *Education or Indoctrination: A Book for Educators* (Caldwell, ID: Caxton Printers, 1955), 36.

77. Jones, *Activities of the American Legion,* 10–15.

78. Shumaker, "No 'New Order' for Our Schools," 5.

79. Ibid., 5–6.

80. National Americanism Commission [R. Worth Shumaker lead author], *Rugg Philosophy Analyzed,* Vol. II: *Statement of the Philosophy of Dr. Harold O. Rugg on Social, Economic, Political and Educational Problems, The Complete Rugg Philosophy* (Indianapolis, IN: American Legion, 1941), 3.

81. National Americanism Commission [R. Worth Shumaker, lead author], *Rugg Philosophy Analyzed,* Vol. IV (Indianapolis, IN: American Legion, 1942), 4.

82. Ibid.

83. Hamilton Hicks, "Ours to Reason Why," *American Legion Magazine* (May 1941): 6.

84. Bill Cunningham, "'Smearing the Minds of Kids': A Defense of Competitive Sports," *American Legion Magazine* (July 1941): 9.

85. Wettrick, *Our American Schools,* 9.

86. Pitkin, "The American Legion and the Schools."

87. Rugg, *That Men May Understand,* 80.

88. "Says Nation Needs a New Civilization," *New York Times,* May 18, 1932, 11.

89. Pencak, *For God and Country,* xii.

90. Ellen Schrecker, *Many Are the Crimes: McCarthyism in America* (Princeton, NJ: Princeton University Press, 1998), 61.

91. Ibid., 217.

92. W. Alan Thody to American Legion, 21 April 1941, Legion Archives.

93. *Summary of the Proceedings of the First National Convention of the American Legion* (Minneapolis, MN: American Legion, 1919): 39.

94. "Textbook Analysis," *Americanism Manual* (Indianapolis, IN: American Legion, 1953), 31.

95. Pencak, *For God and Country,* 274.

96. Ibid., 267.

97. Ibid., 222–238.

98. Homer Chaillaux, "Suggested Address on the National Americanism Program," December 4, 1934, Legion Archives.

99. "SOTAL Squadron in Every Post Is Committee's Aim," *The Badger Legionnaire* 13:5 (March 10, 1935). Copy in correspondence file, 1935, Joseph Hrdlick Papers, Wisconsin Historical Society Archives/Milwaukee Area Research Center, Milwaukee, WI.

100. *Americanism Handbook* (Indianapolis, IN: American Legion, n.d. [handwriting on cover notes 1930]), 8.

101. Ibid., 9.

102. Ibid.

103. Pitkin, "The American Legion and the Schools," 25.

104. "American Education Week: Program, November 17–23, 1924," Legion Archives.

105. *The Twentieth Anniversary Armistice Day Celebration, November 11, 1938* (Indianapolis, IN: National Americanism Commission, The American Legion, 1938), 8.

106. Homer Chaillaux, foreword to *American Education Week,* November 5 to 11, 1939, Legion Archives.

107. "1941," typescript plan, Legion Archives.

108. Pitkin, "The American Legion and the Schools," 26.

109. Homer Chaillaux, "Report of H. L. Chaillaux, Director/National Americanism Commission to the Annual Conference of Department Commanders and Adjutants, Indianapolis, Indiana, November 18, 19 and 30, 1940," American Legion Wisconsin Papers, Wisconsin Historical Society Archives, Madison, WI.

110. *First Annual National High School Oratorical Contest: A National Americanism Activity of The American Legion* (Indianapolis, IN: National Americanism Commission, American Legion, 1938), American Legion Wisconsin Papers, Wisconsin Historical Society Archives, Madison, WI.

111. Press release, June 13, 1938, from National Publicity Division, The American Legion, Indianapolis, IN, American Legion Wisconsin Papers, Wisconsin Historical Society Archives, Madison, WI.

112. Loraine Heit, "What America Means to Me," January 11, 1939, typescript essay, American Legion Wisconsin Papers, Wisconsin Historical Society Archives, Madison, WI.

113. *Report of the Special Committee to Investigate the Effectiveness of the Legion School Award, Department of California,* n.d. [committee appointed in February 1940], Legion Archives.

114. Corinna Belle Gerhart to Howard C. Rowton [FL state Adjutant], 9 July 1941, Legion Archives.

115. "Proposals for American Legion Award," n.d. [c. 1940], Legion Archives.

116. Frank E. Samuel to Halo Hibbard, 29 February 1928, Legion Archives.

117. "What School History of our Country Do We Want Our Children to Study? This Is What the American Legion Has Resolved to Do about It," n.d., 2. Legion Archives.

118. Ibid., 3.

119. Ibid., 4.

120. Ibid., 5.

121. Ibid., 6.

122. Walter M. Pierce to Charles Horne, 22 April 1926, Legion Archives.

123. *What the Nation's Leaders Think of* The Story of Our American People (New York: United States History Publishing Co., n.d.), Legion Archives.

124. Harold Underwood Faulkner, "Perverted American History," *Harper's* (February 1926): 345.

125. Ibid., 346.

126. Claude M. Fuess, Thomas F. Quinn, and Charles F. Herlihy, "Report of the Special Committee on the So-Called American Legion History," March 26, 1925, Legion Archives.

127. Ibid.

128. John R. McQuigg to W. F. Austin, 22 June 1926, Legion Archives.

129. Homer Chaillaux to Charles V. Falkenberg, 4 June 1937, Legion Archives.

130. John Dixon, "What's Wrong with American History?," *American Legion Magazine* (May 1949): 40.

131. George W. Nilsson to National Americanism Commission, 30 August 1951, Legion Archives.

132. Ed Wieland to Craig Comstock, 15 August 1963, Legion Archives.

133. Shumaker, "No 'New Order' for Our Schools," 5.

134. Forbes to Cornelius J. Westervelt [President Englewood Board of Education], 7 May 1940, box 2, correspondence 1940, Forbes Papers.

135. "Schoolbook 'Trial' Staged in New Jersey," *New York Times*, November 21, 1939, 25.

136. Rugg, *That Men May Understand*, 28.

137. Ibid., 28–29.

138. Ibid., 33.

139. Ibid., 25.

140. Box 4, with several iterations of Forbes's preferred autobiography and versions of his biography for various publications, Forbes Papers; see also "Tycoon's Pal," *Time Magazine* (December 2, 1940): 74–76; "B. C. Forbes Dies; Publisher, Was 73," *New York Times*, May 7, 1954, 24.

141. B. C. Forbes to Cornelius J. Westervelt, 10 October 1940, box 2, Forbes Papers; see also Forbes, "Assails Branding of U.S. as a Second-Rate Country," box 7, folder: Memorabilia (Englewood Controversy), Forbes Papers.

142. Forbes, "Assails Branding of U.S. as a Second-Rate Country."

143. Forbes, "Assails Branding of U.S. as a Second-Rate Country."

144. B. C. Forbes, "Assails Teacher's Stand on Our Founding Fathers," *New York Journal and American*, February 15, 1940, box 7, folder: Memorabilia (Englewood Controversy), Forbes Papers.

145. B. C. Forbes, "Discusses Books Criticizing Our Form of Government," *New York Journal and American*, January 10, 1940, box 7, folder: Memorabilia (Englewood Controversy), Forbes Papers.

146. Rugg, *That Men May Understand*, 35.

147. Ibid., 20.

148. Ibid., 24.

149. Ibid.

150. Edward A. Purcell Jr., *The Crisis of Democratic Theory: Scientific Naturalism and the Problem of Value* (Lexington: University Press of Kentucky, 1973).

151. Jones, *Activities of the American Legion*, 68.

152. Rugg, *That Men May Understand*, xi.

153. Ibid., 39.

154. Ibid., xii.

155. Harold Rugg, *The Great Technology: Social Chaos and the Public Mind* (New York: John Day Co., 1933), 172.

156. Ibid., 201.

157. Carbone, *Social and Educational Thought of Harold Rugg*, 63.

158. Boyd Bode, *Progressive Education at the Crossroads* (New York: Newson & Co., 1939), 39.

159. See, for example, John Dewey, *Democracy and Education* (New York: Macmillan, 1916), 100–102.

160. Robert B. Westbrook, *John Dewey and American Democracy* (Ithaca, NY: Cornell University Press, 1991), xv.

161. Richard J. Bernstein, "Community in the Pragmatic Tradition," in Morris Dickstein, ed., *The Revival of Pragmatism: New Essays on Social Thought, Law, and Culture* (Durham, NC: Duke University Press, 1998), 141.

162. Ibid., 147.

163. Ibid., 148.

164. Purcell, *Crisis of Democratic Theory;* Andrew Jewett, *Science, Democracy, and the American University: From the Civil War to the Cold War* (New York: Cambridge University Press, 2012), 6–8.

165. Purcell, *Crisis of Democratic Theory*, 215.

166. Bernstein, "Community in the Pragmatic Tradition," 148.

167. Philip Von Blon, "The Legion Looks at Youth," *American Legion Monthly* (October 1935): 28.

168. Ibid., 29.

169. Ibid.

170. Doherty, "Educators or Propagandists," 53.

171. Ibid.

172. Pencak, *For God and Country*, 240.

173. A. T. Falk to Homer Chaillaux, 22 November 1939, in Jones, *Activities of the American Legion*, 18.

174. "Official Draft of a Memorandum of Industry's Recommendations for the Improvement of American Educational Methods in the Preparing of Students for Citizenship in a Republic," 28 June 1939, private memo from Committee on Educational Cooperation, National Association of Manufacturers (NAM) to Dean William F. Russell, Chairman of the Congress on Education for Democracy, 4, box 847, Robey Textbook Survey, NAM Papers, Hagley Museum and Archive, Wilmington, DE. [NAM Papers]

175. Ibid., 5.

176. Ibid.

177. Rugg, *That Men May Understand*, 79; Rugg also quoted this Hart speech in Rugg's public talks. See William MacDonald, "Dr. Rugg Defends Modern Histories," *New York Times*, February 23, 1941, 47.

178. Hicks, "Ours to Reason Why," 5.

179. Ibid., 55 (emphasis in original).

180. George E. Sokolsky, "Is Your Child Being Taught to Loaf?," *Liberty Magazine* 17 (May 4, 1940): 42.

181. Ibid., 41.

182. Shumaker, "No 'New Order' for Our Schools," 5.

183. Ibid., 7.

184. Ibid., 45.

185. Ibid., 46.

186. Ibid., 45.

187. National Americanism Commission, *Rugg Philosophy Analyzed,* Vol. IV, 4.

188. Ibid.

189. Ibid., 5.

190. "Social Science Textbooks Used in City Schools Part of Plan to Teach Socialism, Says Hart," *Binghamton Press,* December 13, 1939, 3; "Subversive Teaching Checked at Binghamton, NY," New York State Economic Council, broadsheet flyer, box 48, Billy James Hargis Papers (MC 1412), Special Collections, University of Arkansas Libraries, Fayetteville.

191. "School Heads Defend Use of Rugg's Books," *Binghamton Press,* December 14, 1939, 27.

192. Thomas Hutton, "Why Not a Hearing Here?," *Binghamton Press,* Dec. 16, 1939, 6.

193. "PTA Approves One Rugg Book, Knows Nothing about Five Others in Use in Schools," *Binghamton Press,* March 5, 1940, 1.

194. "Kelly Takes Six Rugg Books 'Out of Circulation' to Stop Controversy," *Binghamton Press,* April 4, 1940, 7.

195. Thomas Hutton, "Better So," *Binghamton Press,* April 6, 1940, 6.

196. Thomas Hutton, "This Practically Proves It," *Binghamton Press,* April 8, 1940, 6.

197. "Mrs. Swartwood Wants Bonfire Made of 180 Rugg Textbooks," *Binghamton Press,* April 18, 1940, 3.

198. John Dewey, "Investigating Education," *New York Times,* May 6, 1940, 12.

199. "Book Burnings," *Time* (Sept. 9, 1940): 64-65.

200. Winters, *Harold Rugg and Education for Social Reconstruction,* 149.

201. Forbes, "Assails Subtle Propaganda Fed US Youth in Textbooks," Forbes Papers.

202. "Dr. Dewey's Stand Disputed," *New York Times,* May 9, 1940, 21.

203. Hutton, "Better So," 6.

204. Hicks, "Ours to Reason Why," 50.

205. Ibid., 6.

206. Ibid., 52.

207. Ibid., 50.

208. Ibid.

209. Ibid.

210. Shumaker, "No 'New Order' for Our Schools," 6.

211. Jones, *Activities of the American Legion,* 22; Augustin G. Rudd, in *Garden City* [NY] *News,* March 7, 1940, 14.

212. Rudd to Stephen Chadwick, 6 March 1939, in Jones, *Activities of the American Legion*, 13–14.

213. "The Rugg Social Science Series of Textbooks," minority report, Haworth, New Jersey, School Board, November 13, 1939, in Jones, *Activities of the American Legion*, 28–29.

214. Ibid.

215. A. T. Falk to Homer Chaillaux, 20 December 1939, in Jones, *Activities of the American Legion*, 21.

216. National Americanism Commission, *Rugg Philosophy Analyzed*, Vol. II, 3.

217. Augustin G. Rudd, "Our 'Reconstructed' Educational System," *Nation's Business*, April 1940, clipping in box 45, Billy James Hargis Papers (MC 1412), Special Collections, University of Arkansas Libraries, Fayetteville. [Hargis Papers]

218. Hicks, "Ours to Reason Why," 7.

219. "Subversive Teaching Checked at Binghamton, NY," New York State Economic Council, broadsheet flyer, box 48, Hargis Papers.

220. Hamilton Hicks, Augustin Rudd, and Alfred Falk, eds., *Undermining Our Republic: Do You Know What the Children Are Being Taught in Our Public Schools? You'll Be Surprised* (New York: Guardians of American Education, Inc., 1941), 35.

221. Ibid.

222. Armstrong, "Treason in the Textbooks," 9 (emphasis in original).

223. Alfred T. Falk, *Does Advertising Harm or Benefit Consumers?* (New York: Advertising Federation of America, 1939), 1, box 45, Hargis Papers.

224. Ibid., 9.

225. Rudd, "Our 'Reconstructed' Educational System," *Nation's Business*, April 1940, unpaginated pamphlet, box 45, Hargis Papers.

226. Ibid.

227. George Sokolsky, "Hard-Boiled Babes: Are Your Children That Way? Here's an Arresting Look at One Possible Reason," *Liberty* (March 1940). Reprinted as pamphlet in box 45, Hargis Papers.

228. Ibid.

229. R. Worth Shumaker to Eugene Lathe, 21 February 1941, in Jones, *Activities of the American Legion*, 36.

230. National Americanism Commission, *Philosophy of Dr. Harold O. Rugg on Social, Economic, Political and Educational Problems, The Complete Rugg Philosophy* (Indianapolis, IN: American Legion, 1941), 1.

231. Ibid.

232. Ibid., 3.

233. Armstrong, "Treason in the Textbooks, 71.

234. Edward H. Kenerson to Homer Chaillaux, 28 September 1940, in Jones, *Activities of the American Legion*, 58.

235. Augustin Rudd to Homer Chaillaux, 20 September 1940, in Jones, *Activities of the American Legion*, 61.

236. Ruth G. Myer to Homer Chaillaux, 12 September 1940, in Jones, *Activities of the American Legion*, 66.

237. Jones, *Activities of the American Legion,* 67.

238. Rugg, *That Men May Understand,* 89.

239. Jones, *Activities of the American Legion,* 33.

240. "No Communism in Junior High School Text Books, Register in Survey Finds," *Red Bank* [NJ] *Register,* April 18, 1940. Clipping in box 48, Hargis Papers.

241. Jones, *Activities of the American Legion,* 41.

242. Walter McDonald [Adjutant Rapid City Post 22, Rapid City, SD] to Milo J. Warner [American Legion National Commander], 17 June 1941, in Jones, *Activities of the American Legion,* 39.

243. Walter Goodman, *The Committee: The Extraordinary Career of the House Committee on Un-American Activities* (New York: Farrar, Strauss, & Giroux, 1968), 23.

244. Schrecker, *Many Are the Crimes,* 91.

245. Goodman, *The Committee,* 25.

246. Ibid., 27.

247. Ellen W. Schrecker, *No Ivory Tower: McCarthyism and the Universities* (New York: Oxford University Press, 1986), 76.

248. Quoted in Robert W. Iversen, *The Communists and the Schools* (New York: Harcourt, Brace, and Co., 1959), 180.

249. Michael Paul Rogin, *"Ronald Reagan," The Movie and Other Episodes in Political Demonology* (Berkeley: University of California Press, 1987), xiii.

250. Schrecker, *Many Are the Crimes,* 131–153.

251. Ibid., 141.

252. Frederick Palmer, "The Reds Look to Youth," *American Legion Monthly* (April 1936): 12–13, 50–53.

253. Ibid., 52.

254. Augustin G. Rudd to Stephen F. Chadwick, 18 February 1939, in Jones, *Activities of the American Legion,* 12.

255. Jones, *Activities of the American Legion,* 22; Augustin G. Rudd, in *Garden City* [NY] *News,* March 7, 1940, 14.

256. A. T. Falk to Homer Chaillaux, 22 November 1939, in Jones, *Activities of the American Legion,* 18.

257. Ibid.

258. Forbes to Cornelius J. Westervelt, 7 May 1940, box 2, Forbes Papers.

259. R. Worth Shumaker to Albion Roy King, 6 May 1941, in Jones, *Activities of the American Legion,* 93.

260. Rudd, Hicks, and Falk, eds., *Undermining Our Republic,* 12.

261. Forbes, "Assails Subtle Propaganda Fed US Youth in Textbooks," box 7, Forbes Papers.

262. Hicks, "Ours to Reason Why," 51.

263. Armstrong, "Treason in the Textbooks," 51.

264. Jones, *Activities of the American Legion,* 73.

265. Homer Chaillaux to F. Milo Hettish, 31 March 1942, in Jones, *Activities of the American Legion,* 44–45.

266. National Americanism Commission, *Rugg Philosophy Analyzed,* Vol. I: *Statement of the Philosophy of Dr. Harold O. Rugg on Social, Economic, Political and*

Educational Problems, an Abstract of The Great Technology (Indianapolis, IN: American Legion, 1941), 1.

267. Benjamin Fine, "Un-American Tone Seen in Textbooks on Social Sciences," *New York Times*, February 22, 1941, 1, 6.

268. Ibid., 1.

269. Ibid., 6.

270. W. A. Macdonald, "Publishers Fight Textbook Charges," *New York Times*, February 24, 1941, 1, 10; "Author Replies to Robey," *New York Times*, February 24, 1941, 10; "Educators to Form an Inquiry Board," *New York Times*, February 25, 1941, 19.

271. "NAM Not Backing Textbook Charges," *New York Times*, February 25, 1941, 19.

272. Kim Phillips-Fein, *Invisible Hands: The Making of the Conservative Movement from the New Deal to Reagan* (New York: W. W. Norton, 2009), 13–14.

273. W. D. Fuller to Edmund deS Brunner, 5 March 1941, box 847, Robey Textbook Survey file, NAM Papers.

274. W. D. Fuller, "Open Letter to Teachers and School Administrators," n.d., box 847, NAM Papers.

275. John C. Gebhart to C. E. Harrison Jr., 2 July 1940, box 847, NAM Papers.

276. John C. Gebhart to W. B. Weisenburger, 11 July 1940, memo, box 847, NAM Papers.

277. C. E. Harrison to W. B. Weisenburger, 25 July 1940, box 847, NAM Papers.

278. Manuscript notes from a September 11, 1940 meeting between Robey, Weisenburger, and Harrison, box 847, NAM Papers.

279. "Official Draft of a Memorandum of Industry's Recommendations for the Improvement of American Educational Methods in the Preparing of Students for Citizenship in a Republic," 28 June 1939, private memo from Committee on Educational Cooperation, NAM, to Dean William F. Russell, chairman of the Congress on Education for Democracy, box 847, NAM Papers.

280. Ibid., 1–2.

281. Ibid, 3.

282. Ibid.

283. Ibid.

284. Ibid., 4.

285. Ibid., 5.

286. Charles R. Hook, *What Does Capital Want for Itself and America?* (New York: NAM, 1939), 18, Kheel Center Archives, Cornell University Libraries, Ithaca, NY.

287. Ibid., 16.

288. Ibid., 17.

289. Ibid., 18–19.

290. Henry A. Abt, "Report of Findings—Survey of NAM School Service," January 14–29, 1941, 2, Series III, National Information Committee, box 846, NAM Papers.

291. Ibid., 14.

292. Ibid., 17.

293. Ibid., 15.

294. Macdonald, "Dr. Rugg Defends Modern Histories," 47.

295. "Educators in Row over Rugg Books," 9.

296. "School Board Abandons Nine Textbooks by Rugg," *Philadelphia Inquirer,* March 6, 1941, 25; "Legion May Push Textbook Probe," *Philadelphia Inquirer,* March 8, 1941, 17; "Rugg Textbooks Upheld, Assailed," *Philadelphia Inquirer,* April 7, 1941, 21.

297. Dorn, "Treason in the Textbooks,"477.

298. Zimmerman, *Whose America,* 79.

299. Rugg, *That Men May Understand,* 71.

300. Ibid., xiii.

301. Ibid., 37.

302. Ibid., 293.

303. Ibid., 293.

4. Rich, Republican, and Reactionary

1. Adam B. Golub, "Into the Blackboard Jungle: Educational Debate and Cultural Change in 1950s America" (PhD diss., University of Texas–Austin, 2004), 16–50.

2. T. G. Wood, "Our City," *The Pasadena Independent,* January 25, 1950, 1, 48. [*Independent*]

3. T. G. Wood, "Progressive Education: Mother's Indictment: 'School Has Let Us Down,'" *Independent,* February 17, 1950, 36.

4. T. G. Wood, "Progressive Education Row Stirs New Interest in School Work," *Independent,* February 1, 1950, 1, 24.

5. Mrs. David E. Ireland, "Patrons' Apathy Gets Blame for Public Schools' Failure," *Independent,* February 2, 1949, 2.

6. "HPG," "Our City," *Independent,* January 29, 1950, 1, 31.

7. T. G. Wood, "Our City," *Independent,* January 29, 1950, 31.

8. For instance, conservative activist Nolan Frizzelle told historian Lisa Mc-Girr that his decades-long career began in the Pasadena controversy. See Lisa McGirr, *Suburban Warriors: The Origins of the New American Right* (Princeton, NJ: Princeton University Press, 2001), 75, 111, 117, 265.

9. Matthew D. Lassiter, *The Silent Majority: Suburban Politics in the Sunbelt South* (Princeton, NJ: Princeton University Press, 2006), 4–5.

10. Arthur Zilversmit, *Changing Schools: Progressive Education Theory and Practice, 1930–1960* (Chicago: University of Chicago Press, 1993), 103.

11. National Commission for the Defense of Democracy through Education, *The Pasadena Story: An Analysis of Some Forces and Factors That Injured a Superior School System* (Washington, DC: National Education Association, 1951), 9. [*NEA Report*]

12. *Eighth Report: Senate Investigating Committee on Education: Education in Pasadena* (Pasadena: Senate of the State of California, 1951), 17–18. [*State Senate Report*]

13. From 127,431 in 1940 to 178,800 in 1950, according to Clyde M. Hill and Lloyd N. Morrisett, *Report of a Survey of the Pasadena City Schools: A Cooperative*

Study, 1951–1952 (Pasadena, CA: City Board of Education, 1952), 52. [*Pasadena Survey Report*]

14. Ibid., 18, 22.

15. David Hulburd, *This Happened in Pasadena* (New York: Macmillan, 1951), 13.

16. "School District Retires Last of 1921 Bond Issue," *Pasadena Star News*, August 7, 1948, 7. [*Star News*]

17. "Polio Won't Close Schools," *Star News*, September 14, 1948, 13; "LA Considers School Closing Due to 'Polio,'" *Star News*, September 15, 1948, 4.

18. "Citizenship Held Schools' Goal: Goslin Hits Old-Style Yardsticks," *Star News*, September 13, 1948, 11.

19. Ibid.

20. Ibid.

21. Ibid.

22. "H.G.B.," "Mother Says 'Progressive Education' Step Backward," *Independent*, February 3, 1950, 2, 42.

23. Allen A. Zoll, *Progressive Education Causes Delinquency* (New York: National Council for American Education, n.d.), 87; reprinted in *Eighth Report*, 81–92.

24. Ibid., 88.

25. Ibid.

26. Mary L. Allen, *Education or Indoctrination: A Book for Educators* (Caldwell, ID: Caxton Printers, 1955), 49–50.

27. "Pasadena Schools Reopen with Record Enrollment of 25,074," *Star News*, September 14, 1948, 13.

28. "Editorial: United for Schools," *Star News*, September 28, 1948, 10.

29. "City School Bonds Win by 6 to 1 Majority: Heaviest School Vote in History," *Star News*, October 2, 1948, 1.

30. "Teams Plan Study of School Aims," *Star News*, January 26, 1949, 19; "A Whole School System Works Together under New Plans," *Pasadena School Review* 21 (January 1949): 1, 4.

31. "Teams Plan Study of School Aims," 19.

32. "Schools' Head Tells Women's Council Better Education Demands Money," *Star News*, May 13, 1949, 10.

33. "Big Educator Will Address Pasadenans," *Independent*, December 8, 1949, 12.

34. "Guide to the Eldridge Tracy McSwain Papers," Northwestern University Library, Archival and Manuscript Collections. http://findingaids.library.northwestern.edu/catalog/inu-ead-nua-archon-290 (accessed February 21, 2012)

35. "Big Educator Will Address Pasadenans," 12.

36. John A. Beineke, *And There Were Giants in the Land: The Life of William Heard Kilpatrick* (New York: Peter Lang, 1998), 99–116.

37. John Q. Copeland, "Pasadena Debates Kilpatrick Method," *Los Angeles Times*, May 28, 1950.

38. "A Storm Breaks over Pasadena," n.d., 9, typescript document, National Education Association Records, Gelman Library, George Washington University, Washington, DC. [NEA Records]

39. Ibid., 11.

40. Beineke, *And There Were Giants in the Land*, 225–256.

41. John Dewey, introduction to *William Heard Kilpatrick, Trail Blazer in Education,* by Samuel Tenenbaum (New York: Harper & Bros., 1951), vii.

42. Tenenbaum, *William Heard Kilpatrick*, 185, 283.

43. *State Senate Report*, 31.

44. William Heard Kilpatrick, *Education for a Changing Civilization: Three Lectures Delivered on the Luther Laflin Kellogg Foundation at Rutgers University, 1926* (New York: Macmillan, 1931), 33.

45. William H. Kilpatrick, Boyd H. Bode, John L. Childs, H. Gordon Hullfish, John Dewey, R. B. Raup, and V. T. Thayer, *The Educational Frontier* (New York: Arno Press, 1969), 123; originally published New York: D. Appleton-Century, 1933.

46. Beineke, *And There Were Giants in the Land*, 325.

47. William Heard Kilpatrick and William Van Til, eds., *Intercultural Attitudes in the Making: Parents, Youth Leaders, and Teachers at Work* (New York: Harper & Bros., 1947), 9.

48. Ibid.

49. Ibid., 2.

50. Kilpatrick, *Education for a Changing Civilization*, 50.

51. See, e.g., "A Storm Breaks over Pasadena," 8–11.

52. *State Senate Report*, 32.

53. Kilpatrick, *Education for a Changing Civilization*, 36.

54. Ibid., 38.

55. Kilpatrick et al., *The Educational Frontier*, 126.

56. Ibid.

57. Ibid., 148.

58. Ibid., 148–149.

59. Quoted in Beineke, *And There Were Giants in the Land*, 327.

60. John Q. Copeland, "School Goal Told by Progressives," *Los Angeles Times,* May 29, 1950.

61. T. G. Wood, "Our City," *Independent,* January 25, 1950, 1.

62. Zilversmit, *Changing Schools*, 59.

63. *NEA Report,* 8; John Amherst Sexson, "Report Reveals History of Pasadena City Schools," *Star News,* August 15, 1948, 13.

64. Zilversmit, *Changing Schools*, 60.

65. *45th Annual Report of the Pasadena City Schools, 1928–1929* (Pasadena, CA: City of Pasadena, 1930), 16.

66. *45th Annual Report of the Pasadena City Schools, 1928–1929*, 31.

67. Andrew Hartman, *Education and the Cold War: The Battle for the American School* (New York: Palgrave Macmillan, 2008), 3.

68. Golub, "Into the Blackboard Jungle," 45.

69. Mortimer Smith, *And Madly Teach: A Layman Looks at Public School Education* (Chicago: Regnery, 1949), 22.

70. Ibid., 23.

71. Ibid., 92.

72. Ibid., viii.

73. Bernard Iddings Bell, *Crisis in Education: A Challenge to American Complacency* (New York: McGraw-Hill, 1949).

74. Bernard Iddings Bell, "We Are Indicted for 'Immaturity,'" *New York Times*, July 20, 1947, 8.

75. Ibid., 16.

76. "Dr. Bernard Iddings Bell," *Traveling Culture: Circuit Chautauqua in the Twentieth Century*, promotional brochure, Library of Congress: American Memory. http://sdrc.lib.uiowa.edu/traveling-culture/chau1/pdf/bell/1/brochure.pdf (accessed April 10, 2012)

77. Bell, "We Are Indicted for 'Immaturity,'" 17.

78. Bernard Iddings Bell, "The School Can't Take the Place of the Home," *New York Times*, May 9, 1948, 11.

79. Louise Padelford and Cay Hallberg, "The Case against Progressive Education," *Fortnight* (May 28, 1951): 16; Jane Hood, "A Confidential Report to Mr. Skaife and His Committee" n.d., typescript, NEA Records. Hood, an employee of the Pasadena City School District, acted as an enthusiastic "progressive" informant for Skaife's investigation. She reported that many Pasadena conservatives read and discussed Bell's work.

80. See Allen, *Education or Indoctrination*, 33; Padelford and Hallberg, "The Case against Progressive Education," 16; Catherine Hallberg and Louise Padelford, "The Pasadena Story," n.p., typescript, NEA Records; "A Storm Breaks over Pasadena," NEA Records.

81. Albert Lynd, "Quackery in the Public Schools," *Atlantic Monthly* 185 (1950): 34.

82. Ibid., 33.

83. Ibid., 36.

84. Ibid., 33.

85. Glen Jeansonne, *Women of the Far Right: The Mother's Movement and World War II* (Chicago: University of Chicago Press, 1996), 20.

86. Elizabeth Dilling, *The Red Network: A 'Who's Who' and Handbook of Radicalism for Patriots* (Kenilworth, IL: Author, 1934), 124.

87. Ibid., 198.

88. Ibid., 296.

89. Ibid., 276.

90. Ibid., 273.

91. Ibid., 331.

92. Ibid., 318.

93. Ibid., 258.

94. Ellen Schrecker, *Many Are the Crimes: McCarthyism in America* (Princeton, NJ: Princeton University Press, 1998), xv.

95. Anonymous, "Progressive Education and Its Subversive Influence," June 8, 1948, box 47, folder 56, Billy James Hargis Papers (MC 1412), Special Collections, University of Arkansas Libraries, Fayetteville.

96. Kim E. Nielsen, *Un-American Womanhood: Antiradicalism, Antifeminism, and the First Red Scare* (Columbus: The Ohio State University Press, 2001), 74–76.

97. Amos Fries, "Broadening ('Sophist' or Counterfeit) Education," *Bulletin: Friends of the Public Schools* 3 (April 1941): 4.

98. Gilman H. Stordock to Val W. Ove, n.d., American Legion Wisconsin Papers, Wisconsin Historical Society Archives, Madison, WI.

99. Madeleine P. Scharf, "The Education Finance Act of 1943," *Daughters of the American Revolution Magazine* 77 (October 1943): 637. [*DAR Magazine*]

100. Mrs. Amos A. Fries, "The Educational Work of the Daughters of the American Revolution in the Southern Mountains," 1925, typescript, Daughters of the American Revolution Archives, Washington, DC. [DAR Archives]

101. The fact that Rudd's postmarked copies of the *Friends of the Public Schools* bulletin ended up in Allen Zoll's papers, which ended up in the Billy James Hargis Papers, demonstrates the many connections among activists.

102. Jonathan Zimmerman, *Whose America? Culture Wars in the Public Schools* (Cambridge, MA: Harvard University Press, 2002), 91.

103. Arthur D. Morse, "Who's Trying to Ruin Our Schools?," *McCall's* (September 1951).

104. Zimmerman, *Whose America*, 91–92.

105. John E. Moser, *Right Turn: John T. Flynn and the Transformation of American Liberalism* (New York: New York University Press, 2005), 190.

106. Ibid., 2–4.

107. Ibid., 5.

108. John T. Flynn, *The Road Ahead: America's Creeping Revolution* (New York: Devin-Adair, 1949), 67.

109. Ibid., 60.

110. Ibid., 90.

111. Moser, *Right Turn*, 177.

112. Ibid., 178.

113. Allen, *Education or Indoctrination*, 25.

114. Ellen W. Schrecker, *No Ivory Tower: McCarthyism and the Universities* (New York: Oxford University Press, 1986), 5.

115. Schrecker, *Many Are the Crimes*, 91.

116. Committee on Un-American Activities, US House of Representatives, *100 Things You Should Know about Communism and Education* (Washington, DC: Committee on Un-American Activities, 1948), 5.

117. Ibid., 11.

118. Ibid., 18.

119. Schrecker, *Many Are the Crimes*, 97.

120. David Caute, *The Great Fear: The Anti-Communist Purge under Truman and Eisenhower* (New York: Simon and Schuster, 1978), 425–426.

121. "300 Attend Pro America Convention Banquet Here," *Star News,* February 16, 1949, 19.

122. June Melby Benowitz, *Days of Discontent: American Women and Right-Wing Politics, 1933–1945* (DeKalb: Northern Illinois University Press, 2002), 16.

123. "Ballot Recommendations by Pro-America," *Star News,* October 17, 1948, 9.

124. "Pro America Favors All But One County Issue," *Star News,* October 21, 1948, 27.

125. "Reception to Open Three-Day Pro American Convention Here," *Star News*, February 10, 1949, 7.

126. "Pro America Meets April 6 in San Mateo," *Star News*, March 25, 1949, 10.

127. "Pro America Pays Honor to Mrs. Robert L. Gifford," *Star News*, February 18, 1949, 24.

128. "300 Attend Pro America Convention Banquet Here," *Star News*, February 16, 1949, 19.

129. "Pro America Pays Honor to Mrs. Robert L. Gifford," 24.

130. Hulburd, *This Happened in Pasadena*, 59.

131. "Mrs. Morgan Padelford," *Star News*, June 7, 1947.

132. Padelford and Hallberg, "The Case against Progressive Education," 15.

133. "LHP," "American Education under Fire," *FACTS in Education* 1 (October 1952).

134. Ibid.

135. "Pro America Pays Honor to Mrs. Robert L. Gifford," 24.

136. "Schools Failing in Fundamentals, Says Dr. Benson," *Independent*, June 23, 1950, 1, 42. This college-president George C. S. Benson is not the same conservative college-president George S. Benson described in Bethany Moreton, *To Serve God and Wal-Mart: The Making of Christian Free Enterprise* (Cambridge, MA: Harvard University Press, 2009), 164–168.

137. See Allen, *Education or Indoctrination;* Padelford and Hallberg, "The Case against Progressive Education," 15–18.

138. Hulburd, *This Happened in Pasadena*, 61; *NEA Report*, 14.

139. Hulburd, *This Happened in Pasadena*, 58.

140. *NEA Report*, 21.

141. Padelford and Hallberg, "The Case against Progressive Education," 17.

142. Allen Zoll, *They Want Your Child!* (New York: National Council for American Education, 1949), 3.

143. Zoll, *They Want Your Child*, 5.

144. "Schools' Head Urges Federal Funds Now for Education," *Star News*, February 23, 1949, 19.

145. *State Senate Report*, 35–36.

146. American Patriots Incorporated, *Petition to Congress: Jobs for American Citizens First*, 1939, box 33, folder 2, Billy James Hargis Papers (MC 1412), Special Collections, University of Arkansas Libraries, Fayetteville. [Hargis Papers]

147. Lucille C. Crain to Allen Zoll, 12 June 1948; Zoll to Crain, 14 June 1948; Crain to Zoll, 14 July 1948, box 33, folder 29, Hargis Papers. In this series of letters, Crain and Zoll swapped compliments and traded addresses for Rudd and Fries. Zoll invited Crain to join the advisory board of NCAE. Crain responded that she could only serve in an "unofficial capacity."

148. Campbell Scribner, "The Right Wing and Wisconsin Schools, 1954–1974" (Master's thesis, University of Wisconsin–Madison, 2009), 16–17.

149. See, for instance, Clay Apple Jr. to NCAE, 18 June 1949, box 33, folder 64, Hargis Papers.

150. Elizabeth P. Pittock to NCAE, 28 April 1950, box 33, folder 64, Hargis Papers.

151. Luther O. Griffith to Zoll, 26 March 1951; Griffith to Zoll, 27 August 1952, box 33, folder 64, Hargis Papers.

152. A. Whitford to Zoll, 6 April 1952, box 33, folder 64, Hargis Papers.

153. See typescript memos from Kaub to Zoll, box 49, folder 8, Hargis Papers. Kaub's reviews included the following: "Textbooks Analyzed by Research Department of National Council for American Education and Declared to be Unsuitable as Textbooks"; "Analysis of Textbook on Consumer Cooperatives"; "Analysis of Textbook Which Cannot Be Recommended"; "Analysis of Textbook Available for Indoctrination of Adolescents with New Deal Philosophy"; and "Analysis of Textbook Which Promotes the New Deal–Fair Deal Ideology."

154. Verne Kaub to J. A. Whitlow, 14 February 1951, box 33, folder 64, Hargis Papers.

155. Scribner, "Right Wing and Wisconsin Schools," 17.

156. "'Evil' at Work in Community, Says Morrison," *East Pasadena Herald,* June 8, 1950, box 1 of 3, Clippings, Correspondence, Papers, Letters, 1950–1962, Luverne Lamotte Papers, Pasadena Museum of History; Max Merritt Morrison, "'Ye Shall Know the Truth,'" *Star News,* June 20, 1950, 9; Morrison, "Ye Shall Know the Truth," *Independent,* June 20, 1950, 12.

157. Frederick Woltman, "Zoll, Hate-Monger, Promotes New Racket," *New York World-Telegram,* August 25, 1948, 6.

158. *News Bulletin* No. 5, PEA Committee on Information, June 1, 1950, included as Appendix V, *State Senate Report,* 76–77.

159. Harold Benjamin, "Report on the Enemy," typescript of a talk given at NEA annual meeting, July 3, 1950, in St. Louis, Missouri, NEA Records.

160. "Pasadena 'Polio': It Strikes Entire School Systems," *Point* [a San Diego newsweekly], March 14, 1952, 3–4.

161. Zimmerman, *Whose America,* 92.

162. William F. Buckley to Allen Zoll, 13 April 1951, box 34, folder 66, Hargis Papers.

163. Frank Wells, "To Parents and Taxpayers of Pasadena," *Independent,* June 22, 1950, 18.

164. Hulburd, *This Happened in Pasadena,* 90.

165. *State Senate Report,* 36.

166. Wells, "To Parents and Taxpayers of Pasadena," 18.

167. *State Senate Report,* 35.

168. Wells and Brower only mentioned *Progressive Education* in their testimony, but several copies of Zoll's *They Want Your Child!* remained in "Clippings" file 2, Pasadena Schools, 1950–1959, Pasadena Central Library, Pasadena, CA. Also, critic Ernest Melby claimed both pamphlets were used by the SDC. See Ernest O. Melby, *American Education under Fire: The Story of the 'Phony' Three-R Fight* (New York: Anti-Defamation League of B'nai B'rith, 1951), 14.

169. Adam Laats, "Many Educational Pasts: Conservative Visions and Revisions of the History of American Education," *Teachers College Record* 114:3 (2012): 1–25.

170. Allen Zoll, *Progressive Education Increases Delinquency,* included as Appendix VI, *State Senate Report,* 83.

171. Ibid.

172. Ibid.

173. Ibid.

174. Ibid.

175. Ibid., 85.

176. Ibid.

177. Ibid., 86.

178. Ibid., 88.

179. Ibid., 87.

180. Zoll, *They Want Your Child*, 7.

181. Ibid., 9.

182. Ibid.

183. Ibid., 11.

184. Ibid.

185. See *FACTS in Education* 1:2 (November 1952); *FACTS in Education* 1:3 (December 1952).

186. Allen, *Education or Indoctrination*, 9.

187. Ibid., 28.

188. Ibid., 38–39 [Rugg], 42 [Counts], 47 [Kilpatrick].

189. Ibid., 45.

190. Ibid., 50.

191. Ibid., 49.

192. Ibid., 52.

193. T. G. Wood, "Patrons' Apathy Gets Blame for Public Schools' Failure," *Independent*, February 2, 1949, 2.

194. T. G. Wood, "Mother Says 'Progressive Education' Step Backward," *Independent*, February 3, 1950, 2, 42.

195. "School Teacher Tells Views on Education Row," *Independent*, February 7, 1950, 2, 25.

196. T. G. Wood, "Progressive Education: Mother's Indictment: 'School Has Let Us Down,'" *Independent*, February 17, 1950, 1, 36.

197. Wood, "Mother Says 'Progressive Education' Step Backward," 2, 42.

198. "School Teacher Tells Views on Education Row," 2, 25.

199. "People's Forum on Education," *Independent*, February 23, 1950, 54.

200. Wood, "Patrons' Apathy Gets Blame for Public Schools' Failure," 2, 44.

201. "School Teacher Tells Views on Education Row," 2, 25.

202. Evelyn Tour, "Says Theory May Be Good but It Fails in Practice," *Independent*, February 5, 1950, 4.

203. "Results of Teacher-Sponsored School Survey," September 3, 1950, survey pull-out sheet from *Star News*, commissioned by the PEA, NEA Records.

204. "People's Forum on Education," 54.

205. Wood, "Mother Says 'Progressive Education' Step Backward," 2, 42.

206. Allen, *Education or Indoctrination*, 137.

207. Ibid., 138.

208. Ibid.

209. Zimmerman, *Whose America*, 84–85.

210. Nelson Dilworth, Chris Jespersen, Fred Weybret, Hugh Donnelly, and J. Howard Williams, "Committee Statement," *Third Report: Senate Investigating Committee on Education: Textbooks* (Pasadena: Senate of the State of California, 1948), 11.

211. Ibid.

212. Ibid., 12.

213. Ibid., 14.

214. Ibid., 16.

215. Dilworth et al., "Introduction to Report by Colonel L. S. N. Phillipp," *Third Report,* 27.

216. Louis Samuel Nast Phillipp, "Report by Colonel L. S. N. Phillipp," *Third Report,* 29.

217. Edwin C. Mead, "Excerpts from Testimony of Lt. Col. Edwin C. Mead," *Third Report,* 37.

218. R. E. Combs, "Critical Analysis of 'Building America Series,'" *Third Report,* 47–48.

219. Ibid., 51.

220. Padelford and Hallberg, "The Case against Progressive Education," 17.

221. Ibid. (emphasis in original)

222. Dorothy Higby, "Reader's Editorial," *Independent,* June 2, 1950, 12.

223. Hulburd, *This Happened in Pasadena,* 129.

224. Robert Skaife to Willard Goslin, 26 June 1950, NEA Records.

225. Paul C. Mishler, *Raising Reds: The Young Pioneers, Radical Summer Camps, and Communist Political Culture in the United States* (New York: Columbia University Press, 1999), 132.

226. Ibid., 56.

227. "Polio Won't Close Schools," *Star News,* September 14, 1948, 13; "LA Considers School Closing due to 'Polio,'" *Star News,* September 15, 1948, 4.

228. Bella V. Dodd, *School of Darkness* (New York: Devin-Adair, 1954), 208–209.

229. Mishler, *Raising Reds,* 132.

230. State of New York, *Report of the Joint Legislative Committee on Charitable and Philanthropic Agencies and Organizations, Communist Indoctrination and Training of Children in Summer Camps* (Albany, NY: Williams Press, 1956), 22.

231. Ibid., 29.

232. Mishler, *Raising Reds,* 82.

233. Dilling, *The Red Network,* 249.

234. Elliott Arnold, "Comrades on Vacation," *New York World-Telegram,* August 2, 1937, 17.

235. Schrecker, *Many Are the Crimes,* 65.

236. Grace A. Brosseau, "Keep America American," *DAR Magazine* 62 (February 1928): 114.

237. Christine K. Erickson, "'So Much for Men': Conservative Women and National Defense in the 1920s and 1930s," *American Studies* 45:1 (Spring 2004): 85–102; Elisabeth Ellicott Poe, "Patriotic Women Take Stand for Adequate National Defense," *DAR Magazine* 62 (March 1928): 145–150.

238. "Resolution No. 25, Resolutions Adopted by the Women's Patriotic Conference on National Defense," No. 1: "Women Alert," *Proceedings of the Thirty-Seventh Continental Congress, NSDAR* (Washington, DC: NSDAR, 1928), 614–615, DAR Archives.

239. Elisabeth Ellicott Poe, "Patriotic Women Once More Rally for National Defense," *DAR Magazine* 63 (March 1929): 147.

240. Flora A. (Mrs. William Sherman) Walker, "The Collective Man," *DAR Magazine* 63 (August 1929): 502–504; Flora Walker, "Communists Exclaim 'In United Ranks, Forward!,'" *DAR Magazine* 64 (September 1930): 565–567; Flora Walker, "The Grip of Communism on Youth," *DAR Magazine* 65 (January 1931): 54–55; Edith Irwin Hobart, "The President General's Message," *DAR Magazine* 65 (June 1931): 330–331.

241. John Q. Copeland, "Pasadena Studies Camp Experiment," *Los Angeles Times,* May 27, 1950.

242. Allen, *Education or Indoctrination,* 73.

243. Ibid., 74.

244. Dorothy Higby, "Reader's Editorial," *Independent,* June 2, 1950, 12.

245. "Blast School Officials' Big Politic Setup," *Independent,* June 1, 1950, 3, 22.

246. Neil R. McMillen, *The Citizens' Council: Organized Resistance to the Second Reconstruction, 1954–64* (Urbana: University of Illinois Press, 1971), 17–18, 189–190, 199, 239.

247. Ibid., 16.

248. McMillen, *The Citizens' Council;* Numan V. Bartley, *The Rise of Massive Resistance: Race and Politics in the South during the 1950s* (Baton Rouge: Louisiana State University Press, 1999); Clive Webb, ed., *Massive Resistance: Southern Opposition to the Second Reconstruction* (New York: Oxford University Press, 2005).

249. Lu Spehr, "Propose New Junior High School Boundaries," *Star News,* April 19, 1950, A2, 36.

250. "Board Adopts Controversial Junior High School Boundaries," *Star News,* May 4, 1950, A2, 33.

251. Hill and Morrisett, *Report of a Survey,* 52–53.

252. Ibid., 53.

253. *Ethnic History Research Project, Pasadena, California: Report of Survey Findings,* 1995, 20, 28, Pasadena Museum of History Archives.

254. Charles Wollenberg, *All Deliberate Speed: Segregation and Exclusion in California Schools, 1855–1975* (Berkeley: University of California Press, 1976), 141.

255. *NEA Report,* 11; Golub, "Into the Blackboard Jungle," 73; Wollenberg, *All Deliberate Speed,* 139.

256. Kenneth D. Durr, *Behind the Backlash: White Working-Class Politics in Baltimore, 1940–1980* (Chapel Hill: University of North Carolina Press, 2003), 25; Thomas J. Sugrue, *The Origins of the Urban Crisis: Race and Inequality in Postwar Detroit* (Princeton, NJ: Princeton University Press, 1996), 24–28.

257. "Arroyo Residents Favor La Canada Junior High," *Star News,* April 20, 1950, 36.

258. "Board Adopts Controversial Junior High School Boundaries," A2, 33.

259. "Jr. High Kids Can't Select School Now," *Independent,* May 4, 1950, 2, 40.

260. Ibid.

261. "Board Adopts Controversial Junior High School Boundaries," A2, 33.

262. "Jr. High Kids Can't Select School Now," 40.

263. "Board Adopts Controversial Junior High School Boundaries," A2, 33.

264. Durr, *Behind the Backlash,* 85–86.

265. Arnold R. Hirsch, *Making the Second Ghetto: Race and Housing in Chicago, 1940–1960* (Cambridge: Cambridge University Press, 1983), 35.

266. Sugrue, *Origins of the Urban Crisis,* 233; Hirsch, *Making the Second Ghetto,* 35.

267. Sugrue, *Origins of the Urban Crisis,* 211, 233.

268. Ibid., 41, 73.

269. Durr, *Behind the Backlash,* 100.

270. Ronald P. Formisano, *Boston against Busing: Race, Class, and Ethnicity in the 1960s and 1970s* (Chapel Hill: University of North Carolina Press, 1991), 3.

271. Sugrue, *Origins of the Urban Crisis,* 219.

272. Matthew D. Lassiter, *The Silent Majority: Suburban Politics in the Sunbelt South* (Princeton, NJ: Princeton University Press, 2006), 4–5.

273. *Fact Sheet of General Information concerning the Proposed Tax Levy for the Pasadena Elementary School District,* April 1950, typescript, file 2: Clippings, Pasadena Schools, 1950–1959, Pasadena Central Library, Pasadena, CA.

274. "School Board Rejects Demand to Put Off Election," *Independent,* April 20, 1950, 2, 43.

275. "Crowds Storm Meeting of School Board Here," *Independent,* April 20, 1950, 3.

276. "Pro and Con Discussion on School Tax Continues," *Star News,* May 23, 1950, 1, 2.

277. "Citizens Protest School Tax Boost," *Independent,* May 23, 1950, 3, 20.

278. *State Senate Report,* 12.

279. Ibid., 25.

280. "City School Bonds Win by 6 to 1 Majority: Heaviest School Vote in History," *Star News,* October 2, 1948, 1.

281. "Cuts in School Budget Studied," *Star News,* June 3, 1950, 1, 2; "Nation Eyes Cal Election: Record School 'No' Vote Repudiates Board Stand on Taxes and Curriculum," *Independent,* June 4, 1950, 1, 58.

282. "Committee Appointed to Map Fight against Progressive Education," *Star News,* July 11, 1950, A2, 26.

283. "Request School Loyalty Oaths Here," *Independent,* July 12, 1950, 2, 20; Hulburd, *This Happened in Pasadena,* 106.

284. See, for example, *State Senate Report.*

285. Schrecker, *Many Are the Crimes,* 42.

286. Mrs. Julius Y. Talmadge, *The Eagle's Wings* (Washington, DC: National Society, Daughters of the American Revolution, 1947), 7, DAR Archives.

287. James T. Gallahorn Jr. to Mrs. Julius Y. Talmadge, 6 August 1946; Mrs. Julius Y. Talmadge to James T. Gallahorn Jr., 11 April 1947; Gallahorn to Talmadge, 2 April 1947, DAR Archives.

288. Margaret Gibbs, *The DAR* (New York: Holt, Rinehart and Winston, 1969), 198.

289. Jane Nicholls, "States: Indiana," *DAR Magazine* 84 (January 1950): 35.

290. Gibbs, *The DAR,* 198.

291. Mildred Carter Sherman, "States: District of Columbia," *DAR Magazine* 84 (June 1950): 485.

292. Laura Palmer Stoik, "State Conferences, Iowa," *DAR Magazine* 82 (August 1948): 608.

293. Gibbs, *The DAR,* 159.

294. Katharine G. Reynolds and Frances B. Lucas, "National Defense," *DAR Magazine* 85 (June 1951): 465–468.

295. Florence Whitmore Fuller, "State Activities: California," *DAR Magazine* 85 (September 1951): 725, 745.

296. Wanda Corn, *Grant Wood, the Regionalist Vision* (New Haven, CT: Yale University Press, 1983), 100.

297. See Peggy Anderson, *The Daughters: An Unconventional Look at America's Fan Club—the DAR* (New York: St. Martin's Press, 1974); Gibbs, *The DAR*; Martha Strayer, *The D.A.R.: An Informal History* (Westport, CT: Greenwood Press, 1973); Barbara Truesdell, "God, Home, and Country: Folklore, Patriotism, and the Politics of Culture in the Daughters of the American Revolution" (PhD diss., Indiana University, 1996).

298. "The Silver Jubilee," *DAR Magazine* 47 (December 1915): 354; see also Fanny Harnit, "The Twenty-Fifth Continental Congress," *DAR Magazine* 48 (June 1916): 387.

299. Gibbs, *The DAR,* 118; Francis Ralston Welsh, *Mrs. Carrie Chapman Catt and Her Open Letter to the DAR,* 1927, pamphlet, DAR Archives; Carrie Chapman Catt, "An Open Letter to the DAR," 1927, typescript, DAR Archives.

300. Mary Gray Peck to Grace Brosseau, 2 September 1927; Brosseau to Peck, 8 September 1927; Peck to Brosseau, 25 September 1927, DAR Archives.

301. Gibbs, *The DAR,* 122.

302. Mrs. William Sherman (Flora A.) Walker, "National Defense Committee," *DAR Magazine* 62 (August 1928): 478–481. Note that Walker, like some other DAR leaders, only publicly used her husband's name. Other married leaders, such as Brosseau, preferred to publish under their own names. Most other leaders alternated. They signed their own names to public statements, but listed their married names in official documents.

303. Gibbs, *The DAR,* 160–166. The organizational and ideological scars of this episode can still be seen today. The Frequently Asked Questions section of the current DAR "History" website includes one about the Marian Anderson episode. Today's DAR leadership apparently still feels obliged to assert that it is not a racist or segregationist organization. See http://www.dar.org/natsociety/faq.cfm (accessed March 21, 2012)

304. May Talmadge, "Rebuilding for Security," *DAR Magazine* 80 (July 1946): 348–352.

305. Mrs. John R. Golden, "Work of the Chapters," *DAR Magazine* 63 (August 1929): 544.

306. Lucy Kavaler, "Those Doughty Daughters," *Today's Living, The* [Sarasota, FL] *Herald Tribune Magazine,* April 9, 1961, 4.

307. See, for example, "Twenty-Ninth Continental Congress," *DAR Magazine* 54 (May 1920): 261; "The Thirty-Second Continental Congress of the Daughters of the American Revolution," *DAR Magazine* 57 (May 1923): 275; Mrs. Henry M. Robert Jr., "Department of the Treasurer General—DAR Membership," *DAR Magazine* 70 (February 1936): 140; "Department of the Treasurer General," *DAR Magazine* 85 (April 1951): 162.

308. Elisabeth Ellicott Poe, "Patriotic Women Take Stand for Adequate National Defense," *DAR Magazine* 62 (March 1928): 145–150.

309. "40th Continental Congress, NS, DAR," *DAR Magazine* 65 (May 1931): 261–271.

310. Carol Frank, "DAR Cheers Roosevelt in Defense Talk," *Washington Herald,* April 22, 1938, 1, 4.

311. "40th Continental Congress, NS, DAR," *DAR Magazine* 65 (May 1931): 271.

312. Elisabeth E. Poe, "National War Projects Feature Fifty-Third Continental Congress," *DAR Magazine* 78 (June 1944): 345; "55th Continental Congress Landmark in DAR History," *DAR Magazine* 80 (July 1946); 354–355; Vylla P. Wilson, "The Fifty-Sixth Continental Congress," *DAR Magazine* 81 (July 1947): 328; "The Opening Session of the Fifty-Seventh Continental Congress," *DAR Magazine* 82 (May 1948): 328–329; Dolores Billman Hill, "Opening of the Fifty-Eighth Continental Congress," *DAR Magazine* 83 (May 1949): 390; Dolores Billman Hill, "The Opening of the Fifty-Ninth Continental Congress," *DAR Magazine* 84 (May 1950): 379.

313. J. Edgar Hoover, "Crime Is Challenging You," *DAR Magazine* 80 (May 1946): 235–236; see also J. Edgar Hoover, "Delinquency and the Home," *DAR Magazine* 81 (October 1947): 480–481.

314. Vylla P. Wilson, "The Fifty-Sixth Continental Congress," *DAR Magazine* 81 (July 1947): 328.

315. See, for example, George A. Dondero [US Representative from Michigan], "The Road to Survival Leads to the Right," *DAR Magazine* 81 (November 1947): 530–532; Ralph W. Gwinn [US Representative from New York], "The Implications of Federal Aid to and Control of Education," *DAR Magazine* 81 (December 1947): 581–586; Joseph W. Martin Jr. [Speaker, US House of Representatives], "The DAR Still on Guard," *DAR Magazine* 82 (July 1948): 519–522; Daniel A. Reed [US Representative from New York], "Liberty Is Easier to Retain Than to Regain," *DAR Magazine* 82 (November 1948): 808–809; Karl E. Mundt [US Senator from South Dakota], "America's Major Problem," *DAR Magazine* 83 (January 1949): 4–7; Ralph W. Gwinn, "Socialism—American Variety," *DAR Magazine* 83 (September 1949): 730–734; Alexander Wiley [US Senator from Wisconsin], "The Real Struggle: The Battle of Ideas," *DAR Magazine* 83 (October 1949): 804–807.

316. Karl E. Mundt, "Our American Destiny—1949," *DAR Magazine* 83 (July 1949): 566.

317. Linda K. Kerber, *Women of the Republic: Intellect and Ideology in Revolutionary America* (Chapel Hill: University of North Carolina Press, 1980); Nancy

F. Cott, *The Grounding of Modern Feminism* (New Haven, CT: Yale University Press, 1987); William Chafe, *Women and Equality: Changing Patterns in American Culture* (New York: Oxford University Press, 1977); Robyn Muncy, *Creating a Female Dominion in American Reform, 1890–1935* (New York: Oxford University Press, 1991); Sonya Michel and Robyn Rosen, "The Paradox of Maternalism: Elizabeth Lowell Putnam and the American Welfare State," *Gender & History* 4 (Autumn 1992): 364–386.

318. See David Tyack and Elisabeth Hansot, *Managers of Virtue: Public School Leadership in America, 1820–1980* (New York: Basic Books, 1982); Jackie M. Blount, *Destined to Rule the Schools: Women and the Superintendency, 1873–1995* (Albany: State University of New York Press, 1998); Kate Rousmaniere, *City Teachers: Teaching and School Reform in Historical Perspective* (New York: Teachers College Press, 1997).

319. Glen Jeansonne, *Women of the Far Right: The Mothers' Movement and World War II* (Chicago: University of Chicago Press, 1996); Donald T. Critchlow, *Phyllis Schlafly and Grassroots Conservatism: A Woman's Crusade* (Princeton, NJ: Princeton University Press, 2005); Kim E. Nielsen, *Un-American Womanhood: Antiradicalism, Antifeminism, and the First Red Scare* (Columbus: Ohio State University Press, 2001), 51–52; Francesca Morgan, *Women and Patriotism in Jim Crow America* (Chapel Hill: University of North Carolina Press, 2005); Laura McEnaney, "He-Men and Christian Mothers: The America First Movement and the Gendered Meanings of Patriotism and Isolationism," *Diplomatic History* 18 (Winter 1994): 47–57; Robert Wuthnow and William Lehrman, "Religion: Inhibitor or Facilitator of Political Involvement among Women?," in Louise A. Tilly and Patricia Gurin, eds., *Women, Politics, and Change* (New York: Russell Sage Foundation, 1990); Christine Kimberly Erickson, "Conservative Women and Patriotic Maternalism: The Beginnings of a Gendered Conservative Tradition in the 1920s and 1930s" (PhD diss., Emory University, 1999).

320. Grace L. H. Brosseau, "Annual Message of the President General," *Proceedings of the Thirty-Seventh Continental Congress, DAR* (Washington, DC: DAR, 1928), 13.

321. Edith Scott Magna, "The President General's Message," *DAR Magazine* 68 (February 1934): 72.

322. May E. Talmadge, "The President General's Message," *DAR Magazine* 79 (September 1945): 479.

323. "The 35th Annual Continental Congress of the National Society, DAR," *DAR Magazine* 60 (May 1926): 269; "The 36th Continental Congress, NSDAR," *DAR Magazine* 61 (May 1927): 332; Edith Scott Magna, "Greetings," *DAR Magazine* 66 (May 1932): 262; Florence Hague Becker, "What Is National Defense?," *DAR Magazine* 67 (June 1933): 369; Edith Irwin Hobart, "The President General's Message," *DAR Magazine* 65 (October 1931): 585–596; Mrs. William A. Becker, "Youth," 1936, typescript, DAR Archives; Florence H. Becker, "Report of the President General," *Proceedings of the Forty-Seventh Continental Congress* (Washington, DC: DAR, 1938), 37; Edith Irwin Hobart, "The President General's Message," *DAR Magazine* 65 (March 1931): 140; Helena R. Pouch, "The President General's Message," *DAR Magazine* 75 (November 1941): 3;

Marguerite C. Patton, "The President General's Message," *DAR Magazine* 84 (August 1950): 643.

324. Anne Minor, "The Thirty-Second Continental Congress of the Daughters of the American Revolution," *DAR Magazine* 57 (May 1923): 265.

325. "The Thirty-Seventh Continental Congress of the National Society of the Daughters of the American Revolution," *DAR Magazine* 62 (May 1928): 262.

326. "The 38th Continental Congress, N.S.D.A.R.," *DAR Magazine* 63 (May 1929): 261–271.

327. Edith Irwin Hobart, "The President General's Message," *DAR Magazine* 65 (December 1931): 712–716.

328. Florence Hague Becker, "National Defense Embodying Patriotic Education," *DAR Magazine* 66 (July 1933): 446.

329. Florence Hague Becker, "Pacifism and America," *DAR Magazine* 68 (July 1934): 422–423.

330. Florence Hague Becker, "Editorial," *DAR Magazine* 69 (September 1935): 517.

331. Florence Hague Becker, "Youth," 1936, typescript, DAR Archives.

332. Madeleine P. Scharf, "The Education Finance Act of 1943," *DAR Magazine* 77 (October 1943): 635–637.

333. Lola Lee Bruington, "National Defense Committee," *DAR Magazine* 83 (July 1949): 581–584.

334. Grace L. H. Brosseau, "Annual Message of the President General," *Proceedings of the Thirty-Eighth Continental Congress* (Washington, DC: NSDAR, 1929), 11.

335. Lena A. Hill, "Boudinot Citizenship Club," n.d. [c. 1935–1938], typescript; "Ritual for the Boudinot Citizenship Club," n.d. [c. 1935–1938], typescript, DAR Archives.

336. Grace Ward Calhoun, "The Industrial School for Mountain Girls at Tamassee, S.C.," *DAR Magazine* 57 (January 1923): 31.

337. Mrs. Amos A. Fries, "The Educational Work of the Daughters of the American Revolution in the Southern Mountains," n.d. [1925], typescript, DAR Archives.

338. Frances Tupper Nash, "Tamassee: New York's Contribution and a Look into the Future," *DAR Magazine* 57 (October 1923): 597–601; Sarah Corbin Robert, "Financing Our Endorsed Schools," *DAR Magazine* 62 (December 1928): 745–750; Edith Scott Magna, "Library Work in the Endorsed Schools of the DAR," *DAR Magazine* 64 (April 1930): 214–218.

339. "Thirty-Third Continental Congress of the National Society, Daughters of the American Revolution," *DAR Magazine* 58 (May 1925): 281.

340. Frances Tupper Nash, "Tamassee: New York's Contribution and a Look into the Future," *DAR Magazine* 57 (October 1923): 601.

341. Ibid.

342. Anita Greer, "Be Loyal America? Your Constitution Lives!," May 7, 1942, typescript, DAR Archives.

343. Harriet Simons to "My dear State Chairman," July 1943, DAR Archives.

344. Mrs. Verner Skinner, edited by Mrs. Edward Holloway, New York State Chairman, "Our Approved Schools of the NSDAR," n.d., DAR Archives.

345. "Resolution No. 16, Teachers' Oath," *Proceedings of the Thirty-Eighth Continental Congress* (Washington, DC: NSDAR, 1929), 681–682.

346. Grace L. H. Brosseau, "Annual Message of the President General," *Proceedings of the Thirty-Eighth Continental Congress* (Washington, DC: NSDAR, 1929), 11.

347. Mrs. William A. Becker, *Tapestry Weavers: An Address of Mrs. William A. Becker, President General, National Society, Daughters of the American Revolution at Fall State Conferences, 1935* (n.d.), 6, DAR Archives.

348. N. William Newsom, "Teacher Loyalty Oaths and Related Issues," *Peabody Journal of Education* 32 (November 1954): 174; "Teachers in the Public Schools," *National Education Association Research Bulletin* 27 (December 1949): 146.

349. Howard K. Beale, *Are American Teachers Free? An Analysis of Restraints upon the Freedom of Teaching in American Schools* (New York: Scribner's, 1936), 528.

350. Electa Chase Murphy, "Indiana Teachers Oath of Office Law," *DAR Magazine* 63 (May 1929): 281–282.

351. Vivian Lyon Moore, "Michigan's 'Oath of Allegiance' Bill," *DAR Magazine* 65 (July 1931): 404.

352. Al Ludlow to Robert Skaife, 2 August 1950, NEA Records.

353. "Teachers in the Public Schools," *NEA Research Bulletin* 27 (December 1949): 146.

354. "Impromptu City Teachers' Meet OK's Loyalty Oath," *Independent*, July 13, 1950, 3, 41.

355. "City Teachers Reaffirm Loyalty Oath Pledge," *Independent*, July 13, 1950, 3, 42.

356. George Stewart, *The Year of the Oath: The Fight for Academic Freedom at the University of California* (New York: Doubleday, 1950); Ellen Schrecker, *No Ivory Tower*, 117–123, 126–127.

357. "194 Teachers Indorse [sic] School Administration," *Star-News*, November 8, 1950, A2, 36.

358. "Board to Ban Reading of Teachers' Statements Backing Administration," *Star-News*, November 7, 1950, A2, 16.

359. "Editorial: Opportunity Again Present for Unity within Schools," *Star-News*, November 10, 1950, 8.

360. "Goslin Flies East to Attend Conference with Educators," *Star-News*, November 5, 1950, A2, 22.

361. "Goslin Resignation Asked," *Star-News*, November 10, 1950, 1, 2; "School Board Asks Goslin to Resign," *Independent*, November 10, 1950, 1, 46.

362. "School Board Asks Goslin to Resign," 1, 46.

363. "Goslin Returns, Refuses to Discuss Ouster Action," *Independent*, November 14, 1950, 1, 18.

364. Blair Nixon to Robert Gilchrist, 12 December 1950, NEA Records.

365. "Goslin Willing to Quit Post," *Independent*, November 12, 1950, 1, 50.

366. "Superintendent Goslin 'Talks' to Press about Ouster," *Independent*, November 14, 1950, 3.

367. "Goslin Out! Schools Pay Ex-Chief $23,250," *Independent*, November 22, 1950, 1, 6, 25.

368. Harry E. Tyler, "The New Pasadena Story," *NEA Journal* (November 1959): 14.

369. "A friend" to Donald LaMotte, 10 April 1957, Lu Verne La Motte Collection, Pasadena Museum of History, Pasadena, CA.

370. Wollenberg, *All Deliberate Speed,* 137.

371. Robert W. Iversen, *The Communists and the Schools* (New York: Harcourt, Brace, and Company, 1959), 226; Caute, *Great Fear,* 426.

372. *State Senate Report,* 8.

373. Robert Skaife to Richard Kennan, 21 November 1950, NEA Records; Jane Hood, "A Confidential Report to Mr. Skaife and His Committee" n.d., typescript, NEA Records; "Memo on Dilworth Committee," n.d., typescript, NEA Records.

374. *State Senate Report,* 14.

375. Schrecker, *Many Are the Crimes,* 142.

376. "Records on Goslin Hiring Demanded in State Inquiry," *Star-News,* November 15, 1950, 1, 2.

377. "'Schools' Future Bright,' Goslin Informs Senators," *Star-News,* November 16, 1950, 1, 4–5.

378. "Goslin Lauds City School Setup at Education Probe," *Independent,* November 17, 1950, 1, 3, 50.

379. *NEA Report,* 7.

380. Ibid., 22.

381. Robert Skaife, *Danger! They're After Our Schools* (Washington, DC: National Education Association, 1948), 7.

382. Robert Skaife to Willard Goslin, 26 June 1950; Robert A. Skaife to Richard M. Pearson, 27 March 1952, NEA Records.

383. Skaife, *Danger,* 9.

384. Eugene Caron Blake, *The Issues in Public Education in Pasadena,* May 20, 1951, clippings file, Pasadena Central Library, Pasadena, CA.

385. "Goslin Raps 3 R's Type of Education," *Independent,* September 14, 1950, 3, 46.

386. Helen Becker, Elizabeth Hutchings, Elizabeth Lockridge, Nancy Newton, Elizabeth Purcell, and Elizabeth Wecter, "Two Debates about Education," *NewsCope* 1 (August 10, 1951): 1.

387. Gladwin Hill, "Wide School Study Made in Pasadena," *New York Times,* August 28, 1951, 25.

388. Skaife, *Danger,* 10.

389. Lionel DeSilva to Richard B. Kennan, 22 January 1952; Ted Bass to Kennan, 9 January 1952; Harry A. Fosdick to Kennan, 3 January 1952, NEA Records.

390. "Editorial: The NAACP and Segregated Education," *Crisis* 58 (August–September 1951): 432–433.

391. "Board Casts Split Vote for Gerbner," *Star-News,* November 1, 1950, A2, 22.

392. *State Senate Report,* 21–23.

393. Padelford and Hallberg, "The Case against Progressive Education," 18.

394. "Blast School Officials' Big Politic Setup," *Independent,* June 1, 1950, 3, 22.

395. Lawrence C. Lamb, "Why the 'Battle Royal' in Pasadena," *Vital Speeches of the Day* 17 (August 1, 1951): 625–628.

396. Mary Allen, "Danger," *FACTS in Education* 1 (October 1952).

397. Mary Allen "Alien Influences in Pasadena Schools," *FACTS in Education* 1 (October 1952).

398. Allen, *Education or Indoctrination,* 54.

399. Ibid., 130.

400. Golub, "Into the Blackboard Jungle," 58–66.

401. Hartman, *Education and the Cold War,* 113.

402. "Karl Marx and the American Teacher," *The Social Frontier* II (November 1935): 53–56; "American Education and the Social Struggle," *Science and Society* (Fall 1936); "Biographical Note," Theodore Brameld Papers, University of Vermont Libraries Special Collections. http://cdi.uvm.edu/findingaids/collection/brameld.ead.xml (accessed March 26, 2012)

403. Allen, *Education or Indoctrination,* 91.

404. Padelford and Hallberg, "The Case against Progressive Education," 17.

405. "Citizens Protest School Tax Boost," *Independent,* May 23, 1950, 3, 20.

406. "A Storm Breaks over Pasadena," NEA Records.

407. Padelford and Hallberg, "The Case against Progressive Education," 17.

408. Allen, *Education or Indoctrination,* 91.

5. Save the Children

1. Lynn Withrow, "Dr. Kenneth Underwood: The Man in the Middle," *Charleston Daily Mail,* September 19, 1974, 1D.

2. Kay Michael, "Five Officials Assaulted during Board Meeting," *Charleston Gazette,* December 13, 1974, 1, 10A.

3. Kay Michael, "Underwood, Three on Board Arrested for Textbook Roles," *Charleston Gazette,* November 16, 1974, 1, 2A.

4. Lynn Withrow, "Underwood: 'On a Runaway Locomotive,'" *Charleston Daily Mail,* October 12, 1974, 1.

5. George Hillocks Jr., "Books and Bombs: Ideological Conflict and the Schools: A Case Study of the Kanawha County Book Protest," *The School Review* 86:4 (August 1978): 637.

6. National Education Association, *Inquiry Report: Kanawha County, West Virginia: A Textbook Study in Cultural Conflict* (Washington, DC: National Education Association, 1975), 9. [*NEA Report*]

7. *NEA Report,* 47.

8. See, for example, Carol Mason, *Reading Appalachia from Left to Right: Conservatives and the 1974 Kanawha County Textbook Controversy* (Ithaca, NY: Cornell University Press, 2009), especially Chapter 3; see also Trey Kay, Deborah George, and Stan Bumgardner, "The Great Textbook War," American Radio-Works. http://americanradioworks.publicradio.org/features/textbooks/index.html (accessed January 14, 2013)

9. Karl Priest, *Protester Voices: The 1974 Textbook Tea Party* (Poca, WV: Praying Publishing, 2010).

10. James Moffett, *Storm in the Mountains: A Case Study of Censorship, Conflict, and Consciousness* (Carbondale: Southern Illinois University Press, 1988), 187.

11. Hillocks, "Books and Bombs," 637.

12. David A. Corbin, *Life, Work, and Rebellion in the Coal Fields: The Southern West Virginia Miners 1880–1922* (Urbana: University of Illinois Press, 1981); Lon Savage, *Thunder in the Mountains: The West Virginia Mine War, 1920–21* (Pittsburgh, PA: University of Pittsburgh Press, 1990).

13. School board meeting, April 11, 1974, Audio Recordings of Kanawha County Board of Education Meetings, West Virginia State Archives, Charleston, WV. [Audio Recordings] Special thanks to archivist Dick Fauss who digitized and shared these audio files.

14. Hillocks, "Books and Bombs," 634; Alice Moore, author interview, 15 February 2011.

15. School board meeting, April 11, 1974, Audio Recordings.

16. "Education Methods Destroy Children," *Charleston Daily Mail*, May 8, 1970, 17; Ann Johnston, "Mrs. Moore Dumps Tully," *Charleston Daily Mail*, May 13, 1970, 1.

17. Lynn Withrow, "Underwood: 'On a Runaway Locomotive,'" *Charleston Daily Mail*, October 12, 1974, 1; School board meeting, June 27, 1974, Audio Recordings.

18. Mason, *Reading Appalachia from Left to Right*, 188.

19. Alice Moore, author interview, 15 February 2011.

20. Johnston, "Mrs. Moore Dumps Tully," 1; Moore, author interview, 15 February 2011.

21. Michael Snyder, "Kanawha School Board Is Facing Confidence Vote," *Charleston Gazette*, May 12, 1970, 12.

22. "Candidate Seeking Grade Counseling," *Charleston Daily Mail*, May 4, 1970, 2.

23. Snyder, "Kanawha School Board Is Facing Confidence Vote," 12.

24. Terry Marchal, "Tully Leads Board Race," *Charleston Gazette*, May 11, 1970, 1; Snyder, "Kanawha School Board Is Facing Confidence Vote," 12.

25. Jerry Kessel, "School Testing Draws Anger of School Board Candidate," *Charleston Daily Mail*, May 5, 1970, 12.

26. Kessel, "School Testing Draws Anger of School Board Candidate," 12.

27. "Education Methods Destroy Children," *Charleston Daily Mail*, May 8, 1970, 17.

28. Michael Snyder, "Mrs. Moore Unseats Tully," *Charleston Gazette*, May 13, 1970, 1.

29. Johnston, "Mrs. Moore Dumps Tully," 1.

30. Margaret Calwell, *Speak to the Past: A Memoir Fat with Words* (Parsons, WV: McClain Printing Co., 2000), 174.

31. Ibid., 173.

32. Alice Moore, author interview, 15 February 2011.

33. Rosalie Earle, "Busing in Tyler Mountain Strictly Parents' Wishes," *The Charleston Gazette,* December 18, 1972, 16A.

34. Calwell, *Speak to the Past,* 174.

35. Quoted in Catherine Ann Candor, "A History of the Kanawha County Textbook Controversy, April 1974–April 1975" (EdD diss., Virginia Polytechnic Institute, 1976), 30.

36. Alice Moore, interview on WSAZ, January 19, 1973, miscellaneous DV Tape #4, West Virginia State Archives, Charleston, WV.

37. Alice Moore, interview on WCHS, April 9, 1973, miscellaneous DV Tape #4, West Virginia State Archives, Charleston, WV.

38. Alice Moore, interview on WSAZ, January 19, 1973, miscellaneous DV Tape #4, West Virginia State Archives, Charleston, WV.

39. Alice Moore, author interview, 15 February 2011; "Education Methods Destroy Children," *Charleston Daily Mail,* May 8, 1970, 17.

40. *NEA Report,* 48.

41. James C. Hefley, *Textbooks on Trial* (Wheaton, IL: Victor Books, 1976), 15.

42. Ibid., 14.

43. Mel and Norma Gabler with James C. Hefley, *What Are They Teaching Our Children?* (Wheaton, IL: Victor Books, 1986), 10.

44. Hefley, *Textbooks on Trial,* 17.

45. Ibid., 62.

46. Ibid., 32.

47. Ibid., 26.

48. Ibid., 52.

49. Ibid., 147.

50. Mel and Norma Gabler, *What Are They Teaching Our Children,* 5.

51. Ibid., 18 (emphasis in original).

52. Ibid.

53. Ibid., 19.

54. Ibid., 11.

55. Hefley, *Textbooks on Trial,* 54, 85; Edward B. Jenkinson, *Censors in the Classroom: The Mind Benders* (Carbondale: Southern Illinois University Press, 1979), 116, 118.

56. Hefley, *Textbooks on Trial,* 127.

57. Ibid., 40.

58. Ibid., 44.

59. Ibid., 18.

60. Jenkinson, *Censors in the Classroom,* 87.

61. Hefley, *Textbooks on Trial,* 51, 91.

62. Ibid., 96.

63. Ibid., 139–144.

64. See, e.g., David Hawkins, "We Need to Resume Yea-Saying," *Dallas Morning News,* September 25, 1969.

65. Hefley, *Textbooks on Trial,* 81.

66. Jenkinson, *Censors in the Classroom,* 116–118.

67. Dena Kleiman, "Influential Couple Scrutinize Books for 'Anti-Americanism,'" *New York Times,* July 15, 1981, C1.

68. Joan DelFattore, *What Johnny Shouldn't Read: Textbook Censorship in America* (New Haven, CT: Yale University Press, 1992), 138–139.

69. Hefley, *Textbooks on Trial,* 62.

70. Mel and Norma Gabler, *What Are They Teaching Our Children,* 26; American Humanist Association, "Humanist Manifesto I," *The New Humanist,* 1933. http://americanhumanist.org/humanism/Humanist_Manifesto_I (accessed August 17, 2013)

71. Hefley, *Textbooks on Trial,* 30.

72. Mel and Norma Gabler, *What Are They Teaching Our Children,* 29.

73. Hefley, *Textbooks on Trial,* 31.

74. Mel and Norma Gabler, *What Are They Teaching Our Children,* 30.

75. Ibid., 53.

76. Ibid., 66.

77. Ibid., 68.

78. Ibid., 71.

79. Ibid., 84.

80. Hefley, *Textbooks on Trial,* 23.

81. Ibid., 24.

82. Mel and Norma Gabler, *What Are They Teaching Our Children,* 88.

83. Ibid., 98.

84. Hefley, *Textbooks on Trial,* 86.

85. Ibid.

86. Mel and Norma Gabler, *What Are They Teaching Our Children,* 169.

87. Hefley, *Textbooks on Trial,* 99.

88. Ibid., 26.

89. George Steele, "Text Sentiment Similar," *Charleston Gazette,* October 6, 1974, 1, 15A.

90. Hefley, *Textbooks on Trial,* 167.

91. Ibid., 166.

92. Moffett, *Storm in the Mountains,* 14.

93. Steven H. Kravitz, "250 Attend Book Opposition Rally," *The Charleston Gazette,* June 24, 1974, 12B.

94. School board meeting, June 27, 1974, Audio Recordings; Candor, "A History of the Kanawha County Textbook Controversy," 76.

95. School board meeting, June 27, 1974, Audio Recordings.

96. Ibid.

97. Ibid.

98. Ibid.

99. Ibid.

100. Kay Michael, "Textbook Package Accepted," *The Charleston Gazette,* June 28, 1974, 1, 6A; School board meeting, June 27, 1974, Audio Recordings.

101. "Excerpts Show Materials Drawing CAP Objections," *Charleston Daily Mail,* September 10, 1974, 3B; School board meeting, June 27, 1974, Audio Recordings.

102. "What Is the Kanawha Co. School Text Book Protest All About? Judge for Yourself!," two-sided flyer, Scrapbooks and Other Materials, 1974–1982, SC 2002-053, West Virginia State Archives, Charleston, WV. [Scrapbooks file]

103. "Excerpts Show Materials Drawing CAP Objections," *Charleston Daily Mail*, September 10, 1974, 3B.

104. See, for example, "Stand Up Now . . . Let's Take the Textbooks to Court . . . We Need Your Help!," Scrapbooks file.

105. See copy inserted into "What Is the Kanawha Co. School Text Book Protest All About? Judge for Yourself!," Scrapbooks file.

106. Moffett, *Storm in the Mountains*, 17; Hillocks, "Books and Bombs," 635, 652 fn 1.

107. Sol Gordon, *Facts about Sex for Today's Youth*, rev. ed. (New York: John Day, 1973), 11.

108. Judith Casto, "3 Basic Kanawha Book Objections Evident," *The Herald Advertiser* [Huntington, WV], November 24, 1974, 41, 44.

109. Quoted in Moffett, *Storm in the Mountains*, 70.

110. Moffett, *Storm in the Mountains*, 187.

111. "God is our refuge and strength, a very present help in trouble. Therefore will not we fear, though the earth be removed, and though the mountains be carried into the midst of the sea; Though the waters thereof roar and be troubled, though the mountains shake with the swelling thereof. Selah. There is a river, the streams whereof shall make glad the city of God, the holy place of the tabernacles of the most High. God is in the midst of her; she shall not be moved: God shall help her, and that right early. The heathen raged, the kingdoms were moved: he uttered his voice, the earth melted. The LORD of hosts is with us; the God of Jacob is our refuge. Selah. Come, behold the works of the LORD, what desolations he hath made in the earth. He maketh wars to cease unto the end of the earth; he breaketh the bow, and cutteth the spear in sunder; he burneth the chariot in the fire. Be still, and know that I am God: I will be exalted among the heathen, I will be exalted in the earth. The LORD of hosts is with us; the God of Jacob is our refuge. Selah."

112. A. K. Boyd, "The Point of View: Like in the Bible," *Charleston Daily Mail*, n.d., clipping in Scrapbooks file.

113. "Agonized Parent," "The Point of View: Parents Know Best," *Charleston Daily Mail*, n.d., clipping in Scrapbooks file.

114. L. T. Anderson, "Pulling the Rugg on Principles," box Sc93-3, Scrapbooks file.

115. Candor, "A History of the Kanawha County Textbook Controversy," 65.

116. "Teachers Chapter, Business and Professional People's Alliance for Better Textbooks," MS 2009-025, Scrapbooks file.

117. Kay Michael, "Private Education Subsidies Pushed," *Charleston Gazette*, April 30, 1976, 16A.

118. Francis Schaeffer, *A Christian Manifesto* (Wheaton, IL: Good News Publishing, 1982), 23; Barry Hankins, *Francis Schaeffer and the Shaping of Evangelical America* (Grand Rapids, MI: Eerdmans, 2008), 196–200.

119. Mel and Norma Gabler, *What Are They Teaching Our Children*, 42.

120. Tim LaHaye, *The Battle for the Public Schools* (Old Tappan, NJ: Fleming H. Revell, 1983), 13.

121. Mason, *Reading Appalachia from Left to Right*, 104–113.

122. Kanawha County Textbook Composite video, C74-1492, West Virginia State Archives, Charleston, WV.

123. Moffett, *Storm in the Mountains*, 57.

124. "A Brief Chronology of the West Virginia Textbook Crisis," *Arizona English Bulletin* (February 1975): 204.

125. Onalee McGraw, *Secular Humanism: The Issue Whose Time Has Come* (Washington, DC: Heritage Foundation, 1976), 4.

126. "A Reader," "The Point of View: Try to Remember," *Charleston Daily Mail*, n.d., clipping in Scrapbooks file.

127. "The Point of View: If You Understand, You Don't," *Charleston Daily Mail*, n.d., clipping in Scrapbooks file.

128. "Teachers Chapter, Business and Professional People's Alliance for Better Textbooks," MS 2009-025, Scrapbooks file.

129. Elmer Fike, "Textbook Controversy in Perspective," *Elmer's Tune*, n.d. [fall 1974], 1, West Virginia State Archives, Charleston, WV.

130. Ibid., 2.

131. Quoted in Moffett, *Storm in the Mountains*, 129.

132. "Textbook Protest in W.Va," two-sided flyer from American Opinion Bookstore, Scrapbooks file.

133. "School Board Member Hits Education 'Gap,'" *Charleston Daily Mail*, March 11, 1976, 4A.

134. Moffett, *Storm in the Mountains*, 4.

135. Ibid., 5.

136. Kay Michael, "Schools Get Text Fight Injunction," *The Charleston Gazette*, September 7, 1974, 1, 4A.

137. Yvonne Sciavoni and Richard Haas, "Public Bus Drivers in Boycott," *Charleston Daily Mail*, September 10, 1974, 1.

138. Strat Douthat, "The Controversy—8 Months Later," *Sunday Gazette-Mail* [Charleston, WV], May 11, 1975, 9A, 11A.

139. Kay Michael, "Boycott Takes Its Toll," *The Charleston Gazette*, September 4, 1974, 1.

140. Kay Michael, "Schools Get Text Fight Injunction," *The Charleston Gazette*, September 7, 1974, 1, 4A.

141. Lynn Withrow, "50 Deputies Need Help, Sheriff Says," *Charleston Daily Mail*, September 12, 1974, 1, 4A.

142. Lynn Withrow, "G.W. Students Stage Walkout," *Charleston Daily Mail*, September 12, 1974, n.p., clipping in Scrapbooks file.

143. Kay Michael, "Boycott Takes Its Toll," *The Charleston Gazette*, September 4, 1974, 1.

144. School board meeting, June 13, 1974, Audio Recordings.

145. Lynn Withrow, "Citizens Committee to Review Books," *Charleston Daily Mail*, September 11, 1974, 1; see also Candor, "A History of the Kanawha County Textbook Controversy," 109.

146. Lynn Withrow, "50 Deputies Need Help, Sheriff Says," *Charleston Daily Mail*, September 12, 1974, 1, 4A.

147. "'It's Over,' Says Book Leader," *Charleston Daily Mail*, September 14, 1974, 1.

148. Moffett, *Storm in the Mountains*, 17.

149. Rick Steelhammer, "2nd Boycott of Schools Advocated," *The Charleston Gazette*, October 7, 1974, 1, 10A.

150. Kanawha County Textbook Composite, C74-1473, West Virginia State Archives, Charleston, WV.

151. Quoted in Moffett, *Storm in the Mountains*, 56. This rumor, which Graley credited to Alice Moore, did not have any evidence to support it and did not seem to be widely repeated among protesters.

152. Ibid., 59.

153. Ibid., 57.

154. Ibid., 60.

155. "Rev. Ezra Graley Democrat for Governor," *Gazette-Mail* [Charleston], May 9, 1976.

156. Rev. Avis L. Hill, interview by James Deeter, March 12, 1985, transcript, Oral History of Appalachia Collection No. OH 64-236, Special Collections, Marshall University. Quoted in Mason, *Reading Appalachia from Left to Right*, 171.

157. Quoted in Moffett, *Storm in the Mountains*, 83.

158. Ibid., 84.

159. Moffett, *Storm in the Mountains*, 71.

160. Ibid., 73.

161. Elmer Fike, "The Textbook Dispute Updated," *Textbook Controversy Essays* (Nitro, WV: Author, 1976). Excerpt in Moffett, *Storm in the Mountains*, 73–74.

162. "The Business and Professional People's Alliance for Better Textbooks" [Advertisement], *Charleston Daily Mail*, October 11, 1974, n.p., clipping in Scrapbooks file.

163. Rick Steelhammer, "2nd Boycott of Schools Advocated," *The Charleston Gazette*, October 7, 1974, 1, 10A.

164. Kay Michael and Thomas A. Knight, "Rev. Graley Gets 60-Day Term, $1,500 Fine in Contempt Case," *The Charleston Gazette*, October 9, 1974, 1–2.

165. Ibid.

166. Lynn Withrow, "School Attendance Shows Biggest Dip," *Charleston Daily Mail*, October 21, 1974, 1; Lynn Withrow, "School Attendance Lowest since Sept. 3," *Charleston Daily Mail*, October 26, 1974, 1.

167. Albert Anson Jr., "Anson Explains Textbook Stand," *Charleston Daily Mail*, October 11, 1974, n.p., clipping in Scrapbooks file.

168. Lynn Withrow, "Underwood Plans to Resign Post," *Charleston Daily Mail*, October 11, 1974, 1.

169. "School Officials' Arrests Thwarted," *Charleston Daily Mail*, November 13, 1974, 1; Kay Michael, "Underwood, Three on Board Arrested for Textbook Roles," *Charleston Gazette*, November 16, 1974, 1, 2A.

170. See, for example, Otis K. Rice, *The Hatfields and the McCoys* (Lexington: The University Press of Kentucky, 1982); Charles L. Sonnichsen, *I'll Die Before I'll Run: The Story of the Great Feuds of Texas* (Lincoln: University of Nebraska Press, 1988).

171. Lynn Withrow, "Dr. Kenneth Underwood: The Man in the Middle," *Charleston Daily Mail*, September 19, 1974, 1D.

172. "'Vigilantes' Urge Book Action," *Charleston Gazette*, September 20, 1974, n.p., clipping in Scrapbooks file.

173. See, for example, Robert Shogan, *The Battle of Blair Mountain: The Story of America's Largest Labor Uprising* (New York: Basic Books, 2004); Lon Savage, *Thunder in the Mountains: The West Virginia Mine War, 1920–21* (Pittsburgh, PA: University of Pittsburgh Press, 1990).

174. Charles Ferguson, "Beaten Man Wanted to Work," *Charleston Daily Mail*, September 13, 1974, n.p., clipping in Scrapbooks file.

175. Bob Adams and Keith Walters, "Man Surrenders to Deputies in Shooting, Claims He Fired to Frighten Off Pickets," *Charleston Daily Mail*, September 13, 1974.

176. Hefley, *Textbooks on Trial*, 175.

177. Kay Michael and Thomas A. Knight, "Rev. Graley Gets 60-Day Term, $1,500 Fine in Contempt Case," *The Charleston Gazette*, October 9, 1974, 1–2; Charles Ferguson, "Rev. Graley, Rev. Hill, 10 Others Freed," *Charleston Daily Mail*, October 18, 1974, 1.

178. Kay Michael and Thomas A. Knight, "Rev. Graley Gets 60-Day Term, $1,500 Fine in Contempt Case," *The Charleston Gazette*, October 9, 1974, 1–2.

179. Scott Widemeyer, "Horan, Stevens Get 3-Year Jail Terms," *Charleston Daily Mail*, May 19, 1975, 1.

180. "Horan Released on $50,000 Bail in Bomb Charge," *Charleston Daily Mail*, January 18, 1975, 1.

181. Scott Widemeyer, "Horan, Stevens Get 3-Year Jail Terms," *Charleston Daily Mail*, May 19, 1975, 1.

182. Moffett, *Storm in the Mountains*, 73; Priest, *Protester Voices*, 309. Both Elmer Fike and Avis Hill used the term "railroaded" to describe the judge's treatment of Horan.

183. "Board Office Blasted," *Charleston Daily Mail*, September 16, 1974, 1.

184. Bob Adams and Lynn Withrow, "Dynamite, Firebombs Rock Schools," *Charleston Daily Mail*, October 9, 1974, 1, 10A.

185. Lynn Withrow, "Dynamite Blast Damages School," *Charleston Daily Mail*, October 22, 1974, 1.

186. Bob Adams and Robert Kelly, "School Violence Continues," *Charleston Daily Mail*, October 11, 1974, 1.

187. "Bomb Threats," *Charleston Daily Mail*, n.d., clipping in Scrapbooks file.

188. Sam Hindman, "School Employee Ignores Rumor, Survives Blast," *Charleston Daily Mail*, October 31, 1974, 1.

189. Bob Adams, "Textbook Protest Violence Mounting," *Charleston Daily Mail*, November 12, 1974, 1.

190. Bob Adams, "Sniper Shots Hit Cruiser," *Charleston Daily Mail,* November 13, 1974, 1.

191. Yvonne Schiavoni, "Books Being Returned to Schools as Parent-Permission Slips Go Out," *Charleston Daily Mail,* November 20, 1974, 1C.

192. Bob Adams and Lynn Withrow, "Dynamite Blast, Roving Picketing Mark Book Action," *Charleston Daily Mail,* December 2, 1974, 1.

193. "Du Pont Protesters Break Ranks, Leave," *Charleston Daily Mail,* November 15, 1974, 1B; Bob Adams and Lynn Withrow, "Dynamite Blast, Roving Picketing Mark Book Action," *Charleston Daily Mail,* December 2, 1974, 1.

194. "'Vigilantes' Urge Book Action," *Charleston Gazette,* September 20, 1974, n.p.

195. Glenn C. Roberts, *A Message to All True Sons of Appalachia* (Reedy, WV: The Liberty Bell, 1974).

196. "Horan Released on $50,000 Bail in Bomb Charge," *Charleston Daily Mail,* January 18, 1975, 1.

197. "A Brief Chronology of the West Virginia Textbook Crisis," *Arizona English Bulletin* (February 1975): 206.

198. Priest, *Protester Voices,* 285.

199. Kay Michael, "Boycott Takes Its Toll," *The Charleston Gazette,* September 4, 1974, 1.

200. Bob Adams, "Textbook Picket Activity Limited to Tongue Lashing," *Charleston Daily Mail,* n.d., clipping in Scrapbooks file.

201. "Bomb Threats," *Charleston Daily Mail,* n.d., clipping in Scrapbooks file.

202. *NEA Report,* 47.

203. Moffett, *Storm in the Mountains,* 40.

204. Joel A. Carpenter, *Revive Us Again: The Reawakening of American Fundamentalism* (New York: Oxford University Press, 1997), 44–45, 150–151.

205. Kay Michael, "Rev. McIntire Protest Speaker," *Charleston Gazette,* November 29, 1974, 5B.

206. George W. Shannon, "Pro-Integration Textbooks Opposed," *The Citizen* (February 1975): 10.

207. For Rafferty's influence among publishers, see Gordon R. Hjalmarson to Patrick Murphy, 10 March 1975, West Virginia State Archives, Charleston, WV. Ephemeral materials from Rafferty's US Senate bid remain in box 49, folder 38, Billy James Hargis Papers (MC 1412), Special Collections, University of Arkansas Libraries, Fayetteville.

208. Lynn Withrow and Charles Ferguson, "Rafferty Hits Publishers," *Charleston Daily Mail,* January 14, 1975, 1.

209. A. A. Baker, *The Successful Christian School: Foundational Principles for Starting and Operating a Successful Christian School* (Pensacola, FL: A Beka Book Publications, 1979). Appendix E lists Rafferty titles among "Some Books That Will Help You" (start your own Christian school).

210. Kanawha County Textbook Composite video, West Virginia State Archives, Charleston, WV.

211. Walter Fremont, "Straight Talk on Traditional Education," *Balance* 2 (May 1982): 1.

212. "Education Methods Destroy Children," *Charleston Daily Mail*, May 8, 1970, 17; Max Rafferty, *What They Are Doing to Your Children* (New York: New American Library, 1964), 43, 90–95.

213. Alice Moore, author interview, 15 February 2011.

214. Rafferty, *What They Are Doing to Your Children*, 90.

215. Max Rafferty, *Max Rafferty on Education* (New York: Devin-Adair, 1968), 76.

216. Rafferty, *What They Are Doing to Your Children*, 94.

217. Ibid., 41.

218. Rafferty, *Max Rafferty on Education*, 158.

219. Rafferty, *What They Are Doing to Your Children*, 84.

220. Ibid., 18–19.

221. Max Rafferty, *Suffer, Little Children* (New York: Signet, 1963), vii.

222. Ibid.

223. Rafferty, *Max Rafferty on Education*, 149.

224. Ibid., 150.

225. Ibid., 151.

226. Ibid.

227. Ibid., 246.

228. Rafferty, *What They Are Doing to Your Children*, 21.

229. Ibid., 65.

230. Max Rafferty, "Speech to the California Small School Districts Association Convention," Sacramento, March 8, 1965, 3, typescript, box 48, Billy James Hargis Papers (MC 1412), Special Collections, University of Arkansas Libraries, Fayetteville.

231. Rafferty, *What They Are Doing to Your Children*, 63.

232. Michael W. Apple, *Educating the "Right"Way: Markets, Standards, God, and Inequality*, 2nd ed. (New York: Routledge, 2006), 31.

233. Rafferty, *Suffer, Little Children*, 26.

234. Rafferty, *Max Rafferty on Education*, 32; Rafferty, *What They Are Doing to Your Children*, 25.

235. Rafferty, *What They Are Doing to Your Children*, 162, Rafferty, *Max Rafferty on Education*, 54.

236. Rafferty, *What They Are Doing to Your Children*, 29.

237. Rafferty, *Max Rafferty on Education*, 54.

238. Rafferty, *What They Are Doing to Your Children*, 73.

239. Rafferty, *Max Rafferty on Education*, 63.

240. Rafferty, *What They Are Doing to Your Children*, 43.

241. Rafferty, *Suffer, Little Children*, 30.

242. Sam Hindman, "School Employee Ignores Rumor, Survives Blast," *Charleston Daily Mail*, October 31, 1974, 1.

243. Judith Casto, "3 Basic Kanawha Book Objections Evident," *The Herald Advertiser* [Huntington, WV], November 24, 1974, 41, 44.

244. Lynn Withrow, "Board Returns All Books to Schools," *Charleston Daily Mail*, November 8, 1974, 1; Yvonne Schiavoni, "Books Being Returned to Schools as Parent-Permission Slips Go Out," *Charleston Daily Mail*, November 20, 1974, 1C.

245. Yvonne Schiavoni, "Most Say Nay in Upper Kanawha," *Charleston Daily Mail*, November 21, 1974, 1B.

246. "Du Pont Protesters Break Ranks, Leave," *Charleston Daily Mail*, November 15, 1974, 1B.

247. Hefley, *Textbooks on Trial*, 171.

248. Moffett, *Storm in the Mountains*, 23.

249. "School Board in West Virginia Sets Rules on New Textbooks," *New York Times*, November 24, 1974, 20.

250. Kay Michael, "Five Officials Assaulted during Board Meeting," *Charleston Gazette*, December 13, 1974, 1, 10A.

251. Kanawha County Textbook Composite, WCHS Miscellaneous 1974, West Virginia State Archives, Charleston, WV.

252. "KKK Wizard Slated for Saturday Rally," *Charleston Daily Mail*, January 17, 1975, n.p., clipping in Scrapbooks file.

253. Richard Grimes, "NAACP Charges Klan Uses Texts for Own Gain," *Charleston Daily Mail*, January 20, 1975, 1.

254. "5 Klan Members Protest at School Board Office, *Charleston Daily Mail*, September 17, 1975, 10A.

255. Mason, *Reading Appalachia from Left to Right*, 61–69; "Wizard Hits Rival KKK Organization," *Charleston Daily Mail*, April 9, 1975, n.p.; "'Framed' Klansman Contends," *Charleston Daily Mail*, April 15, 1975, n.p.; Bob Kittle, "Klansmen Launch Campaign against School Busing, Texts," *Charleston Daily Mail*, August 15, 1975, 1B.

256. Sara Diamond, *Roads to Dominion: Right-Wing Movements and Political Power in the United States* (New York: Guilford Press, 1995), 152.

257. David M. Chalmers, *Hooded Americanism: The History of the Ku Klux Klan* (Durham, NC: Duke University Press, 1981), 399.

258. Kanawha County Textbook Composite, WCHS Miscellaneous 1974, West Virginia State Archives, Charleston, WV.

259. Ronald English, interview by James Deeter, March 12, 1985, Oral History of Appalachia Collection No. OH 64-238, Special Collections, Marshall University. Cited in Mason, *Reading Appalachia from Left to Right*, 48.

260. Kay et al., "The Great Textbook War."

261. School board meeting, June 27, 1974, Audio Recordings.

262. *NEA Report*, 46.

263. Kay Michael, "Blacks Unify, Criticize Handling of Text Clash," *Charleston Gazette*, March 14, 1975, 1.

264. Kay et al., "The Great Textbook War"; see also Candor, "A History of the Kanawha County Textbook Controversy," 156.

265. Moffett, *Storm in the Mountains*, 97.

266. "Text Groups Cool to Klan," *Charleston Daily Mail*, January 3, 1975, n.p., clipping in Scrapbooks file.

267. Ibid.

268. Kay Michael and Thomas A. Knight, "Rev. Graley Gets 60-Day Term, $1,500 Fine in Contempt Case," *The Charleston Gazette*, October 9, 1974, 1–2.

269. Priest, *Protester Voices*, 9–10.

270. Ibid., 295.

271. Kanawha County Textbook Composite, C74-1564, West Virginia State Archives, Charleston, WV.

272. Alice Moore, author interview, 15 February 2011; Priest, *Protester Voices*, 17, 155, 203.

273. School board meeting, June 27, 1974, Audio Recordings.

274. Elmer Fike, "Textbook Controversy in Perspective," *Elmer's Tune*, n.d. [fall 1974], West Virginia State Archives, Charleston, WV.

275. Rafferty, *What They Are Doing to Your Children*, 217.

276. Rafferty to John W. Holmdahl, 23 August 1963, Department of Education, F3752:840, California State Archives, Sacramento, CA. Cited in Joseph Moreau, *Schoolbook Nation: Conflicts over American History Textbooks from the Civil War to the Present* (Ann Arbor: University of Michigan Press, 2003), 294.

277. "Board of Education Scene of Cross Burning," *Charleston Daily Mail*, September 16, 1975, 1B.

278. Bob Kittle, "Klansmen Launch Campaign against School Busing, Texts," *Charleston Daily Mail*, August 15, 1975, 1B.

279. Scott Widemeyer, "Horan, Stevens Get 3-Year Jail Terms," *Charleston Daily Mail*, May 19, 1975, 1.

280. Moffett, *Storm in the Mountains*, 73; Priest, *Protester Voices*, 309.

281. Lynn Withrow, "Educators Pick S.C. Elementary as Basic School," *Charleston Daily Mail*, April 10, 1975, n.p., clipping in Scrapbooks file.

282. "School Boards Setting Up '3-Rs' Schools," *WVEA School Journal*, December 15, 1974, n.p., clipping in Scrapbooks file; "N.C. School Impresses Local Board," *Charleston Daily Mail*, January 16, 1975, n.p., clipping in Scrapbooks file; Gene I. Maeroff, "The Return to Fundamentals in the Nation's Schools," *New York Times*, December 6, 1975, 58; Iver Peterson, "The Newest Innovation: Back to Basics," *New York Times*, January 15, 1975, 91.

283. Lynn Withrow, "Traditional School Use Causes County Education Board Members Skepticism," *Charleston Daily Mail*, June 4, 1975, 1B.

284. "West Virginians: Let's Continue to Protect Human Life," *Charleston Gazette*, May 7, 1976, 12B.

285. Alice Moore, "Moore for Board of Education," *Twin City Shopping Guide*, May 5, 1976, 18.

286. Lynn Withrow, "Return to Educational Basics Urged," *Charleston Daily Mail*, May 1, 1976, 6A.

287. Lynn Withrow, "Alice Moore Sees Win as Confidence Vote," *Charleston Daily Mail*, May 12, 1976, C1.

288. Ben Brodinsky, "Back to the Basics: The Movement and Its Meaning," *Phi Delta Kappan* 58:7 (March 1977): 522–527; Gene I. Maeroff, "The Return to Fundamentals in the Nation's Schools," *New York Times*, December 6, 1975, 58.

289. Vernon Smith, "The Back-to-Basics Movement: A Firmer Stand for English Teachers," *English Education* 9:4 (Summer 1978): 195.

290. Margaret T. Morgan and Norman Robinson, "The 'Back to the Basics' Movement in Education," *Canadian Journal of Education* 1:2 (1976): 7.

291. Andrew Hartman, *Education and the Cold War: The Battle for the American School* (New York: Palgrave Macmillan, 2008), 123–130.

292. Iver Peterson, "The Newest Innovation: Back to Basics," *New York Times*, January 15, 1975, 91.

293. Gene I. Maeroff, "The Return to Fundamentals in the Nation's Schools," *New York Times*, December 6, 1975, 58.

294. Brodinsky, "Back to the Basics," 522.

295. "Board of Education," *Charleston Gazette-Mail*, May 2, 1976, 10G.

296. See, for example, Mason, *Reading Appalachia from Left to Right*, especially Chapter 3. Mason argued that Alice Moore "helped shape a discursive strategy that distinguished the New Right from the Old Right" (91). See also Priest, *Protester Voices*, and Kay et al., "The Great Textbook War." Connie Marshner and Larry Pratt of the Heritage Foundation told journalist Trey Kay they considered the Kanawha County controversy to be the beginning of the modern conservative movement.

297. Donald E. Abelson, *Do Think Tanks Matter? Assessing the Impact of Public Policy Institutes* (Montreal: McGill University Press, 2002), 24.

298. Ibid., 39.

299. Kay et al., "The Great Textbook War."

300. Rick Steelhammer, "2nd Boycott of Schools Advocated," *The Charleston Gazette*, October 7, 1974, 1, 10A; Kay Michael, "Rev. McIntire Protest Speaker," *Charleston Gazette*, November 29, 1974, 5B.

301. Abelson, *Do Think Tanks Matter?*, 40.

302. Connaught Coyne Marshner, *Blackboard Tyranny* (New Rochelle, NY: Arlington House Publishers, 1978), 166, 231–237.

303. See Catherine A. Lugg, *For God and Country: Conservatism and American School Policy* (New York: Peter Lang, 1996).

304. "A Brief Chronology of the West Virginia Textbook Crisis," *Arizona English Bulletin* (February 1975): 201–211.

305. See Adam Laats, "Inside Out: Christian Day Schools and the Transformation of Conservative Protestant Educational Activism, 1962–1990," in Debra Meyers and Burke Miller (eds.), *Inequity in Education: A Historical Perspective* (Lanham, MD: Lexington Books, Rowman and Littlefield Press, 2009), 183–209.

306. Priest, *Protester Voices*, 264.

307. Kanawha County Textbook Composite, C74-1439, C74-1442, West Virginia State Archives, Charleston, WV.

308. Lynn Withrow, "Christian Schools Ready Classrooms," *Charleston Daily Mail*, August 21, 1975, n.p., clipping in Scrapbooks file.

309. Rosalie Earle, "Woes Spawn School," *Charleston Gazette*, November 15, 1974, 5A.

310. Charles Ferguson, "3 Campbells Creek Churches Establish Christian School," *Charleston Daily Mail*, November 14, 1974, n.p., clipping in Scrapbooks file.

311. Strat Douthat, "The Controversy—8 Months Later," *Sunday Gazette-Mail*, May 11, 1975, 9A, 11A.

312. Kay Michael, "Private Education Subsidies Pushed," *Charleston Gazette*, April 30, 1976, 16A.

313. "Donna" to "Barbara," 17 September 1974, Scrapbooks file.

314. "Teaching Chaos Hit; Principal to Resign," *Charleston Gazette,* December 13, 1974, 12A.

315. Kay et al., "The Great Textbook War."

316. Margaret Calwell, *Speak to the Past: A Memoir Fat with Words* (Parsons, WV: McClain Printing Co., 2000), 174.

317. Lynn Withrow, "School Officials Asking Court to Oust 20 Women Protesters," *Charleston Daily Mail,* August 29, 1975; Lynn Withrow, "Women Protesters Removed by Police," *Charleston Daily Mail,* August 30, 1975, 1.

318. Marti Vogel, "Parents Block Buses," *Charleston Daily Mail,* March 5, 1976, 1C.

319. Kay et al., "The Great Textbook War."

320. Karl Priest, author interview, 10 February 2011, Charleston, WV.

321. Kay Michael, "Mrs. Moore Aiming at Science Texts," *Charleston Gazette,* March 3, 1977.

322. Jack McCarthy, "Moore Fights Sex Education," *Charleston Gazette,* October 30, 1982.

323. See, for example, Edwin Barber, "Birth of a Textbook: Much Labor and Risk," *New York Times,* March 23, 1975, 198. Barber cites similar "less noticed" conflicts in Texas, Maryland, Virginia, New Jersey, and Minnesota.

Conclusion

1. David Tyack and Larry Cuban, *Tinkering toward Utopia: A Century of Public School Reform* (Cambridge, MA: Harvard University Press, 1995), 88.

2. Michael W. Apple, *Educating the "Right" Way: Markets, Standards, God, and Inequality,* 2nd ed. (New York: Routledge, 2006), 8.

3. Mark A. Chancey, *Reading Writing & Religion II: Texas Public School Bible Courses in 2011–2012* (Austin: Texas Freedom Network, 2013).

4. Gina Bellafante, "An Issue Divides School, Congressman Takes a Side," *New York Times,* June 19, 2012, A22.

5. Joan DelFattore, *The Fourth R: Conflicts over Religion in America's Public Schools* (New Haven, CT: Yale University Press, 2004), 299–314.

6. See Tyack and Cuban, *Tinkering toward Utopia.*

7. Chester E. Finn Jr. and Theodor Rebarber, "The Changing Politics of Education Reform," in Finn and Rebarber, eds., *Education Reform in the Nineties* (New York: Macmillan, 1992), 191.

8. Economic Policy Institute, "Obama Education Policies: A Lot like Bush Policies," n.d. http://www.epi.org/publication/obamas_education_policies/ (accessed March 27, 2013)

9. Bill Frezza, "Governor Walker's Victory Spells Doom for Public Sector Unions," *Forbes,* June 5, 2012. http://www.forbes.com/sites/billfrezza/2012/06/05/governor-walkers-victory-spells-doom-for-public-sector-unions (accessed April 4, 2013)

10. Peter Applebome, "Governor Christie vs. the Teachers: Nastiness in New Jersey," *New York Times,* April 25, 2010, A17.

11. Diane Ravitch, "Holding Education Hostage," *New York Review of Books Blog,* February 1, 2013. http://www.nybooks.com/blogs/nyrblog/2013/feb/01/holding-education-hostage (accessed May 14, 2013)

12. "Education Activist Michelle Rhee," *Tavis Smiley Show,* PBS, March 6, 2013. http://www.pbs.org/wnet/tavissmiley/interviews/michelle-rhee (accessed March 27, 2013)

13. Harold Ordway Rugg, *That Men May Understand: An American in the Long Armistice* (New York: Doubleday, 1941), 293.

14. Frederick M. Hess and Michael J. Petrilli, "Wrong Turn on School Reform," *Policy Review* (February & March 2009): 57–58.

15. Ibid., 59.

16. "Communism," *Americanism Handbook* (Indianapolis, IN: American Legion, 1930), 9.

17. Mel and Norma Gabler with James C. Hefley, *What Are They Teaching Our Children?* (Wheaton, IL: Victor Books, 1986), 31–32.

Acknowledgments

This book would not have been possible without the help of a generous postdoctoral fellowship from the Spencer Foundation and the National Academy of Education. Binghamton University's Graduate School of Education and Institute for Advanced Studies in the Humanities also provided necessary funding for travel and writing, as well as priceless collegial homes.

As with any history book, this one has been made possible only with the help of a small army of librarians and archivists. First mention must go to Howard Trace of the American Legion Archives in Indianapolis, who offered to stay late on a Friday evening to give me more time with the collection. Also of inestimable help have been Dick Fauss and Debra Basham of the West Virginia State Archives in Charleston. Their work digitizing the recordings of school board meetings has made those records infinitely more accessible. Thanks, too, to Cynthia Van Ness of the Buffalo and Erie County History Society Archives; Chloe Raub of the George Washington University Libraries, home of the National Education Association papers; Lucas Clawson at the Hagley Museum and Library, home of the National Association of Manufacturers papers; Rebecca Baird at the National Society of the Daughters of the American Revolution; Dan McLaughlin of the Pasadena Central Library; Anuja Navare of the Pasadena Museum of History; and Geoffery Stark of the University of Arkansas–Fayetteville Libraries Special Collections. For extra help with images and illustrations, thanks to Trey Kay, Stan Bumgardner, Ronald Evans, Stephen M. Charter of Bowling Green State University's Center for Archival Collections, and Superintendent Jon R. Gundry and Manager Diane Orona of Pasadena Unified School District. I also appreciate the time and generosity of Karl Priest and Alice Moore, who both shared their memories and continuing interest in the subject.

The manuscript also benefited enormously from the critical input of readers and colleagues. Jon Zimmerman read the manuscript in its entirety and offered insights that helped me reimagine the book in fundamental ways. Thanks, too, to those who generously agreed to read sections, including Natalia Mehlman Petrzela, Cam Scribner, Eric Pullin, Dave Bernstein,

Ruben Flores, Jeffrey Moran, Andrew Hartman, Michael Clapper, Carol Mason, and the anonymous readers from Harvard University Press. Their feedback helped me see the book with new eyes.

As this book worked its way from idea to manuscript, I was lucky to get help and advice from a number of astute friends and mentors, including Bill Reese, Maris Vinovskis, Milton Gaither, and Shawn Lay. Thanks to all, though all errors of fact or interpretation are mine alone.

Along the way, I've also been helped by uniquely qualified graduate assistants, including Justin Nevin and Karen Poland. Karen's research assistance and feedback on my chapter drafts proved invaluable.

Particular thanks to the folks at Harvard University Press, especially Elizabeth Knoll for her interest in the idea and for her tireless willingness to talk about the manuscript and answer my questions.

Finally, I must thank my family, friends, and colleagues for putting up with and even encouraging my endless talk about schools, conservatives, and history.

Index